PROMOTING PHYSICAL ACTIVITY & HEALTH IN THE CLASSROOM

ROBERT PANGRAZI
Arizona State University,
Emeritus

AARON BEIGHLE
University of Kentucky

DEB PANGRAZI
Mesa Public Schools

Benjamin Cummings

San Francisco   Boston   New York   Cape Town   Hong Kong   London   Madrid
Mexico City   Montreal   Munich   Paris   Singapore
Sydney   Tokyo   Toronto

Acquisitions Editor: Sandra Lindelof
Project Editor: Susan Scharf
Development Manager: Barbara Yien
Development Editor: Laura Bonazzoli
Editorial Assistant: Jacob Evans
Managing Editor: Deborah Cogan
Manufacturing and Production Supervisor: Dorothy Cox
Production Service/Compositor: Progressive Publishing Alternatives
Design Manager: Marilyn Perry
Interior and Cover Designer: Derek Bacchus
Marketing Manager: Neena Bali
Director, Image Resource Center: Melinda Patelli
Image Rights and Permissions Manager: Zina Arabia

Cover Photo Credit: Getty Images

Library of Congress Cataloging-in-Publication Data

Pangrazi, Robert P.
  Promoting physical activity & health in the classroom / Robert Pangrazi, Aaron Beighle,
Deb Pangrazi.
       p. cm.
  Includes bibliographical references and index.
  ISBN-13: 978-0-321-54762-0 (alk. paper)
  ISBN-10: 0-321-54762-4 (alk. paper)
  1. Physical education for children—United States. 2. Physical fitness for children—
United States. 3. Health education (Elementary)—United States. I. Beighle, Aaron, 1972–
II. Panagrazi, Deb. III. Title. IV. Title: Promoting physical activity and health in the classroom.

GV443. P3444 2008
372.86—dc22   2008032709

                                  ISBN 0-321-59605-6
                                  ISBN 978-0-321-59605-5

Benjamin Cummings
is an imprint of

1 2 3 4 5 6 7 8 9 10—**QWV**—13 12 11 10 09 08
www.aw-bc.com

Brief Contents

Text

1 **Improving the Health of America's Children** 2

2 **Understanding Children's Needs and Readiness for Physical Activity** 30

3 **Teaching Physical Activities Safely and Effectively** 56

4 **Improving the Effectiveness of Instruction and Feedback** 90

5 **Management and Discipline in an Activity Setting** 122

6 **Teaching Children with Special Needs** 162

7 **Integrating Physical Activity and Academics** 186

8 **Increasing Students' Activity Levels** 210

9 **Helping Students Develop Physical Fitness** 246

10 **Improving Students' Nutrition** 284

11 **Teaching Sun Safety** 310

12 **Promoting Children's Health Beyond the School Day** 330

Activity Card Content Areas

- **Implementing the Instructional Activities (Grades K–6)**
- **Classroom-Based Activities (Grades K–2, 3–6)**
- **Large Area Activities (Grades K–2, 3–6)**
- **Basic Skills (Grades K–2)**
- **Sports on the Playground (Grades 3–6)**
- **Multicultural Activities (Grades K–6)**
- **Nutrition and Sun Safety Activities (Grades K–6)**
- **Health and Fitness Activities (Grades K–6)**

Contents

About the Authors   xi

Preface   xii

Special Features of This Text   xiv

Text Overview and Organization   xvii

Acknowledgments   xx

1

Improving the Health of America's Children   2

The Need for Active and Healthy Schools   4

The Number of Overweight Children Is Increasing   4

Childhood Overweight Predicts Adult Obesity   5

Physical Activity Improves Children's Health   6

Physical Activity Can Improve Academic Performance   6

Active Children Become Active Adults   6

America's Wellness Mandate: The WIC Reauthorization Act   7

The Active and Healthy School Environment   8

Quality Physical Education   8

Physical Activity Breaks   9

Nutrition and Healthful Eating Activities   10

Sun Safety Instruction   11

Before- and After-School Programs   12

Classroom Teacher Involvement   13

Parental Involvement   13

Community Involvement   15

Incorporating Physical Activity into Your Classroom   17

Content Standards for Physical Education   19

Standard 1   20

Standard 2   21

Standard 3   21

Standard 4   22

Standard 5   23

Standard 6   23

2

Understanding Children's Needs and Readiness for Physical Activity   30

Understanding the Needs of Children   32

The Need for Movement   32

The Need for Success and Approval   32

The Need for Peer Acceptance and Tolerance   32

The Need to Cooperate and Compete   32

The Need for Physical Competency   33

The Need for Adventure and Novelty   33

The Need for Creative Satisfaction   33

The Need for Rhythmic Expression   33

The Need to Know   33

Understanding the Characteristics of Children   34

Growth Patterns   34

Strength and Endurance   40

Maturation   41

Capacity for Aerobic Activity   42

Ability to Endure Heat Stress   45

Understanding Children's Skill Development   47

Sequence of Skill Development   48

Stages of Skill Development   48

Teaching Physical Activities Safely and Effectively   56

Preparing the Space for Physical Activity   58

Predetermine Your Instructional Space Needs   58

Plan for the Appropriate Amount and Type of Equipment   59

Distribute Equipment Effectively   60

Modify Equipment as Appropriate   60

Promoting a Safe Environment   61

Write Down, Communicate, and Practice Safety Rules   61

Properly Supervise Activities   61

Provide Adequate and Appropriate Instruction   63

Avoid Using Physical Activity for Punishment   65

Designing Effective Practice Sessions   66

Manage the Level of Arousal   66

Focus Practice on Process   67

Encourage Mental Practice   67

Decide on Whole or Part Practice   67

Consider the Length and Distribution of Practice Sessions   68

Use Random Practice Techniques   69

Offer Variable Practice Experiences   69

Fostering the Development of Sport Skills   70

Integrate Simple Mechanical Principles   71

Throwing   74

Catching   77

Kicking   78

Striking   80

Helping Children Participate in Sports and Games   82

Avoid Early Specialization   82

Avoid Labeling Students   83

Avoid Early Pressure to Excel   83

Improving the Effectiveness of Instruction and Feedback   90

Characteristics of an Effective Learning Environment   92

Improving the Effectiveness of Your Instruction 93

Design Measurable Student Outcomes 93

Determine the Students' Skill Level 94

Use an Anticipatory Set 95

Make Skill Instruction Meaningful 96

Use Instructional Cues 97

Demonstrate Skills 98

Check for Understanding 99

Offer Guided Practice 100

Monitor Class Performance 100

Bring Closure 101

Improving the Effectiveness of Your Feedback 102

Use the Appropriate Type of Feedback 102

Make Feedback Statements Specific, Focused, and Concise 104

Offer Feedback Immediately, but Allow Time for Improvement 105

Distribute Feedback Evenly 106

Use Nonverbal Feedback 106

Considering Your Students' Personal Needs 107

Teach for Diversity 107

Avoid Gender Stereotyping 110

Allow Students to Participate in Decision Making 112

Personalize Instruction 113

Communicating with Empathy and Understanding 114

Be an Effective Speaker 114

Be an Effective Listener 116

Management and Discipline in an Activity Setting 122

Use Proper Teaching Behaviors 124

Develop an Assertive Communication Style 125

Create a Personal Behavior Plan 127

Be a Leader, Not a Friend 128

Communicate High Standards 128

Try to Understand Why Students Misbehave 128

Avoid Giving Feedback That May Cause Backlash 129

Define Class Procedures, Rules, and Consequences 130

Step 1: Determine Class Management Routines 130

Step 2: Determine Rules for the School Year 131

Step 3: Define Consequences When Rules Are Not Followed 132

Step 4: Share Your Rules with Parents, Teachers, and Administrators 132

Step 5: Have the Class Practice Rules Systematically 132

Incorporate Efficient Management Skills 133

Deliver Instruction Efficiently 133

Start and Stop a Class Consistently 134

Move Students into Groups and
Formations Quickly   135

Use Equipment Effectively   137

**Teach and Increase Acceptable
Student Behavior   137**

Teach, Post, and Reinforce Levels of
Responsibility   138

Employ Strategies for Increasing
Responsible Behavior   140

Prompt Acceptable Behavior   141

Reinforce Acceptable
Behavior   142

Shape Acceptable Behavior   144

**Decrease Unacceptable Student
Behavior   145**

Deliver Corrective Feedback
Respectfully   145

Apply Consequences   147

Use Criticism Sparingly   150

Make Punishment a Last Resort   151

**Establish Procedures for Resolving
Conflict   152**

Use Teacher-Directed Conflict
Resolution   153

Encourage Peer-Directed
Mediation   154

**Teaching Children with Special
Needs   162**

Legislative Requirements   164

Federal Legislation   164

Least Restrictive Environment   165

Mainstreaming for Physical
Activity   166

Screening and Assessment   167

Due Process Procedures   167

The Impact of Diversity on
Assessment   168

**Developing an Individualized
Education Program   169**

Content of the IEP   169

Formulating and Implementing the
IEP   171

**A Systematic Approach to Effective
Mainstreaming for Physical
Activity   172**

Determine What Support Is
Necessary   173

Learn About the Child   173

Teach Tolerance to All Students   173

Modify Your Instruction   174

Modify Activities for Student
Success   175

Integrate Students with Special
Needs into the Activity Session   180

**Integrating Physical Activity and
Academics   186**

Why Integrate?   188

Types of Integration   189

**Academic Integration
Activities   192**

Math   192

Language Arts   196

Science   200

Social Studies   202

8

Increasing Students' Activity Levels 210

Understanding Physical Activity 212

Levels of Physical Activity 212

The Benefits of Moderate to Vigorous Physical Activity 213

Recommendations for Children's Physical Activity 214

NASPE Activity Guidelines for Elementary School Children 214

The Physical Activity Pyramid 216

Structuring the Playground to Increase Physical Activity 220

Make an Activity-Friendly Playground 220

Supervise the Playground Actively 223

Monitoring Physical Activity: The Case for Pedometers 226

Help Students Set Realistic Goals 227

Teach Students About Pedometer Placement and Accuracy 228

Using Pedometers in a Class Setting 230

Suggested Pedometer Activities 231

Promoting Walking: The Real Lifetime Activity 233

Benefits of Walking 233

Walking and Weight Management 233

Recommendations for Walking 235

Implementing a School Walking Program 236

Suggested Walking Activities 237

9

Helping Students Develop Physical Fitness 246

Types of Physical Fitness 248

Health-Related Physical Fitness 249

Skill-Related Physical Fitness 250

Common Questions About Children's Fitness 252

How Effective Is Fitness Training for Children? 252

What Factors Influence Children's Fitness? 252

Are Fitness Awards Effective? 254

Promoting a Positive Attitude Toward Fitness 255

Be a Role Model 255

Expose Students to a Variety of Fitness Activities 255

Personalize Fitness Activities 255

Challenge Children Appropriately 256

Start Easy and Progress Slowly 256

Encourage Activity of Low to Moderate Intensity 256

Give Students Positive Feedback About Their Efforts 256

Avoid Harmful Practices and Exercises 257

Implementing Fitness Routines 258

Fitness Activities for Children in Kindergarten Through Second Grade 259

Arm-Shoulder Girdle Strength Challenges 260

Abdominal Strength Challenges 262

Trunk Development Challenges 263

Leg Development and Cardiovascular
Endurance Challenges 263

**Fitness Activities for Children in
Third Through Sixth Grade 265**

Flexibility Exercises 266

Arm-Shoulder Girdle Exercises 267

Abdominal Exercises 268

Leg and Agility Exercises 270

Trunk-Twisting and Bending
Exercises 272

Examples of Fitness Routines 273

Fitness Games 277

Improving Students' Nutrition 284

**Schoolwide Strategies for
Improving Students' Nutrition 286**

Form a School Health Committee 287

Conduct Some Initial Research 288

Develop an Action Plan 288

Establish Policies Promoting Healthful
Nutrition 289

Reflect, Evaluate, and Progress 294

**Classroom Strategies for Improving
Students' Nutrition 294**

Gather Data About Students' Eating
Behaviors 295

Teach the Basics of Good
Nutrition 296

Teach Age-Appropriate Weight
Management 298

Reinforce Students in Making
Healthful Food Choices 298

Involve Parents 298

Teaching Sun Safety 310

**Understanding Ultraviolet
Radiation 312**

Factors Affecting UV Exposure 312

The UV Index 313

Benefits of Exposure to UV
Radiation 314

Risks of Exposure to UV
Radiation 315

Effects of Sunscreens on UV
Exposure 318

**Implementing a Sun-Safety
Program 320**

Schoolwide Initiatives 320

Sun-Safety Behaviors for
Students 321

Sun-Safety Teaching Tools 323

**Promoting Children's Health
Beyond the School Day 330**

Health-Promoting Homework 332

Benefits of Health-Promoting
Homework 334

Guidelines for Assigning Health-
Promoting Homework 334

After-School Programs 335

Benefits and Challenges of After-School Programs 335

Assuring a Quality After-School Program 336

Selecting an After-School Program 337

Developing an After-School Program 339

Family and Community Involvement 340

Include Education for Families in Children's Health Initiatives 340

Help Families Increase Their Activity Level 341

Promote Family Pedometer Activities 341

Community-Based Efforts to Promote Children's Health 344

Appendix A: Sample Lesson Plans (K–2, 3–4, 5–6) 350

Appendix B: Activity Cards Quick Reference Guide 356

Appendix C: Definitions of Academic Concepts 365

Appendix D: National Association for Sport & Physical Activity (NASPE) Standards 369

Glossary 370

Index 373

Activity Card Content Areas

Implementing the Instructional Activities (Grades K–6) 11 cards

Classroom-Based Activities (Grades K–2, 3–6) 68 cards

Large Area Activities (Grades K–2, 3–6) 46 cards

Basic Skills (Grades K–2) 36 cards

Sports on the Playground (Grades 3–6) 37 cards

Multicultural Activities (Grades K–6) 28 cards

Nutrition and Sun Safety Activities (Grades K–6) 18 cards

Health and Fitness Activities (Grades K–6) 24 cards

About the Authors

Aaron

Aaron Beighle, Ph.D., is a university instructor in Physical Education and Physical Activity for Youth courses. In addition to numerous scholarly articles and academic materials, including chapter contributions to a number of widely used texts including *Dynamic Physical Education for Elementary School Children* (15th ed., 14th ed.), he co-authored *Pedometer Power* (2nd ed., 2007, Human Kinetics), and *Physical Activity for Children: A Statement of Guidelines for Children Ages 5–12* (2nd ed., 2004, NASPE). His areas of research include physical activity promotion, specifically examining school-based physical activity programs, and the use of pedometers to encourage activity in young people. He is currently Assistant Professor at the University of Kentucky, Lexington, in the Department of Kinesiology and Health Promotion.

Bob

Deb

Robert Pangrazi, Ph.D., taught for 31 years at Arizona State University, Tempe, in the Department of Exercise Science and Physical Education, and is now Professor Emeritus. An American Alliance for Health, Physical Education, Recreation and Dance (AAHPERD) Honor Fellow and a Fellow in the Academy of Kinesiology and Physical Education, he was honored by the National Association for Sport & Physical Education (NASPE) with the Margie Hanson Distinguished Service Award. He is a best-selling author of numerous books and texts, including multiple editions of *Dynamic Physical Education for Elementary School Children* (currently in revision for the 16th edition, Pearson Benjamin Cummings), and *Dynamic Physical Education for Secondary School Children*, 6th edition, with Paul W. Darst (Pearson Benjamin Cummings). He co-edited *Toward a Better Understanding of Physical Fitness and Activity: Selected Topics*, for the President's Council on Physical Fitness and Sports, with Chuck Corbin. In addition to numerous other books and texts, he has written many journal articles and scholarly papers for publication, and he tours and lectures on a national level frequently.

Deb Pangrazi, M.S., has been an elementary physical education specialist for 34 years. She was selected as the Arizona Elementary Physical Education Teacher of the Year in 1996 and represented seven southwestern states as the AAHPERD/NASPE Southwest District Elementary Physical Education Teacher of the Year in 1997. She twice received the Governor's Council Awards for Outstanding Leadership; in 1994 for designing an exemplary elementary physical education program at Kerr Elementary School, and again in 2004. She is currently the director of Mesa Public Schools' Elementary School Physical Education Program, a nationally recognized program providing P.E. instruction to 44,000 children in grades K–6 and employing over 90 elementary physical education specialists across 57 schools. The model program is one of the largest in the nation, and was the 2004 Arizona School Boards Association's First Place winner of the Golden Bell Award.

Preface

The Purpose and Goals of This Text

Classroom teachers are among the hardest working professionals in our culture. They are required to prepare lessons across a wide variety of academic areas each and every school day. They often spend more time with their students than do many parents, and as such, are frequently frontline responders for many of the complex problems that children bring with them to school. In recent years, the added stress of high-stakes testing has further complicated the scope of their responsibilities, ramping up the pressure and ongoing challenges as they strive to shape and prepare the young lives in their classrooms.

In addition to the pedagogical challenges facing teachers, America today is also increasingly concerned about the inactivity and weight problems that affect a growing number of young people, and for good reason: the health of school-age children has suffered significantly in recent years from a host of factors contributing to higher obesity rates and lower fitness levels, including sedentary lifestyle habits; the proliferation of junk foods and high-calorie, low-nutrition snacks; everyday stress in family life; and decreased funding for school programs dedicated to physical activity and fitness. These confluent trends, along with increased interest in assuring that children receive adequate physical activity and health instruction in their elementary school years have resulted, in many cases, in classroom teachers being called on to prepare and teach their own physical education units with minimal training, preparation, equipment, and institutional support.

But don't despair just yet. Many classroom teachers faced with these new duties are beginning to discover that—when expectations are realistic and school administrators are supportive—this demand to integrate physical activity into daily teaching duties can become an unexpected boon, as they discover new ways to enhance their in-class learning environment through teaching students the joys of an active life and good health.

My career started as an elementary school classroom teacher, and I have always had warm regard and deep empathy for the special people who dedicate themselves to teaching. The challenge of this book was to develop an approach that works for teachers where they are, with what they have in hand: one that is realistic and practical, with concrete guidelines for implementing physical activities in a classroom setting, while providing the basic groundwork for the theoretical underpinnings that accompany them.

My initial writing efforts focused on developing physical education lesson plans for classroom teachers. However, it became increasingly clear that there are many constraints preventing classroom teachers from teaching activity lessons that are of comparable quality to those offered by a physical education specialist. Examples of some of the personal and environmental barriers to constructing specialist-level activity plans include the following:

- Classroom attire—you can't teach vigorous physical education in narrow heels, suits, or everyday working clothes.
- Equipment—Where does a classroom teacher get equipment for a P.E. lesson? What if

there isn't enough equipment to go around? Who maintains it?

- Facilities and scheduling—When does a teacher get access to the gym? What if the weather is inclement? What types of activities can be taught in limited spaces?
- Lack of knowledge—Most activity programs for classroom teachers are developed by physical educators who are experts in implementation. Classroom teachers often have little experience in this arena, which can make them uncomfortable delivering the material; and if the instructor's discomfort gets picked up on by students, it can become a negative experience for everyone involved.
- Academic expectations—Classroom teachers are trained in academic preparation. They know their success or failure as an instructor is based on the academic success of students, not their physical training or abilities.

There has been some controversy and debate in recent years about whether classroom-level instructors without formal P.E. training can or should teach activity modules and take primary responsibility for students' physical development. The assumption that a classroom teacher with only one or two semesters of preparation can teach quality physical education has been met with skepticism by some college- and university-affiliated physical education professionals. And indeed, research has shown that physical education curricula taught by classroom teachers is usually not on par with that of field specialists.

However, classroom teachers can offer students much in the way of an enhanced appreciation for and understanding of the need for physical strength, agility, fun, and participation. They are able to regularly provide students with activity experiences that foster positive attitudes and help students develop skills and appropriate play behaviors—with minimal formal training. In fact, if classroom teachers never taught or reinforced the lessons of physical activity and health, many students would likely never learn to appreciate them. The further reality is that teachers are being increasingly called on everyday to cover physical activity requirements, ready or not: this book offers them a way to do that—responsibly, effectively, and knowledgeably.

Hence, this text is not intended for physical education specialists who will be required to implement a complete P.E. program. (My book, *Dynamic Physical Education for Elementary School Children* [16th ed.] and its accompanying *Lesson Plan* guide, offer a complete orientation to a comprehensive, formal physical education curriculum.) Rather, this text presents an approach that classroom teachers can use to help make their students active and healthier. Parents, teachers, administrators, and other stakeholders in children's development are encouraged to work together to develop a total school environment that offers positive health experiences for all students. Schools need to be "active and healthy" in addition to being academic. Without good health and an active lifestyle to support students' developing bodies, movement needs, and often, their social skills development, classroom learning can be compromised. A healthy mind best resides in a healthy body. The goal of this book is to help teachers keep health and physical activity in front of students on a regular basis, and to assist schools in conveying the message, "We value physical academic performance *and* health, and our school makes time for both."

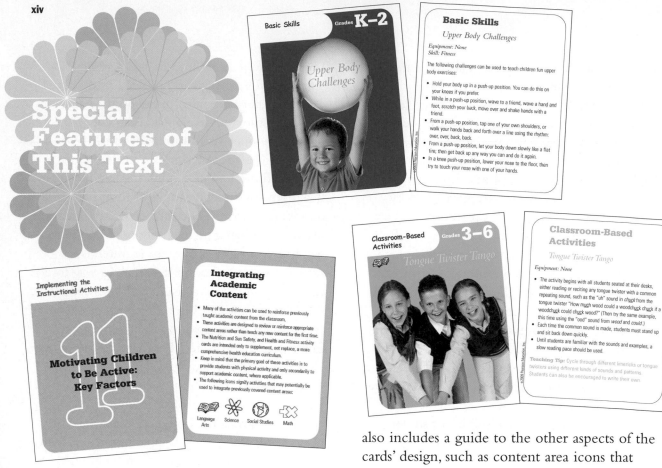

Special Features of This Text

Activity Cards

The Activity Cards accompanying this text effectively constitute a second part to the book with the goal that, taken together, the text and cards provide a truly full resource for classroom instructors who will be teaching activity lessons. The card contents pans seven instructional areas—Implementing the Activities, Classroom-Based Activities, Large Area Activities, Basic Skills, Sports on the Playground, Multicultural Activities, Nutrition and Sun Safety Activities, and Health and Fitness Activities.

The Implementation section stands apart from the other cards in both design and purpose. It contains information on 11 cards that will orient new users and provide instruction in basic activity management techniques, such as suggestions for how to group students effectively, or reinforce the social skills needed to smoothly implement the games. The section

also includes a guide to the other aspects of the cards' design, such as content area icons that appear on many of the cards, tips for success, and key factors for motivating children. We encourage teachers to begin with these cards and familiarize yourself with them before commencing into the activities.

Many of the activity cards include quick-reference icons for identifying classroom content tie-ins (where applicable) for subject matter in the key areas of math, social studies, science, and language arts. Chapter 7 is devoted to the topic of content integration into activities, and we wanted to make it as easy as possible for teachers to identify integration areas as they sort through the cards. Additionally, two appendices are included specifically as card reference resources: Appendix B is a Quick Reference Guide identifying all the cards by title, instructional area, equipment needs, emphasized skill areas, and academic content tie-ins. Appendix C is a detailed listing of the definitions of academic concepts, delineating the rationale for integrating certain activities and their academic "counterpart" areas.

All cards are image- and color-coded by content area, allowing for easy sorting, access, and storage. Certainly, some preparation will be required by teachers as you implement the activities, and we recommend reading through the activities in advance to familiarize yourself with their equipments needs, skill levels, organization and protocols; but the expectation is that can be done efficiently, flexibly, and with a minimum of advance planning in most cases.

Language used in the cards is direct and concise, and they are loosely grouped into developmentally appropriate areas by grade level. These grade level designations are not hard-and-fast; rather, they are suggested content groupings that can serve as general guidelines for instructors. Almost any activity may be applied to groups of older children. However, younger students may have difficulty with the degree of complexity or the motor skills required in the activities for Grades 3–6, while older children may become quickly bored by the rudiments of the Basic Skills units designed for the younger child. Use your judgment and knowledge of the capacities of your individual classes in selecting activities, but by all means, experiment and be open to trying any that you as a teacher feel would work well.

Equipment needs have been kept to a minimum, though you will find variation among the activities. While many require no equipment of any kind, others utilize materials that are either readily accessible to most teachers—at low- or no-cost—or that may become integrated into the activity itself (such as preparing signs that will be used in an upcoming activity).

You will also find a range of skill designations on most of the cards. These broadly indicate areas of physical emphasis included in individual activities, covering a range of skills addressed in more detail in the text, including

fitness skills, locomotor and non-locomotor skills, and animal movement skills, among others. They are, again, included as a way for instructors to further sort, focus, and personalize their implementation. Numerous cards also include brief Teaching Tips—additional quick reference points that anticipate possible hurdles or suggest ideas for enhancement.

Packaged conveniently in a separate box accompanying the text, and designed to be portable and sortable, the Activity Cards are intended to provide teachers with a wide range of resources that enable you to quickly adapt activities to your individual needs. They come out of the box in sheets of four-to-a-page with perforations, and when disassembled fit neatly as separate cards in a standard 4×5 inch index card holder.

Classroom Challenge and Back to Class

These paired features provide new teachers without extensive classroom teaching experience with realistic scenarios that they might encounter, referencing each chapter's specific content. The Classroom Challenge is a case study presented at the opening of each chapter, highlighting potential situations that teachers might encounter as they implement the content. They are followed up several times within each chapter by Back to Class, which revisits the original challenge in light of new material covered, and is intended to integrate the content and stimulate different ways of viewing the problem and arriving at solutions. Taken together, they encourage course takers to consider different ways the concepts in the text might arise in an elementary school setting. Suggested answers to all Back to Class prompts are posted on the Companion Website.

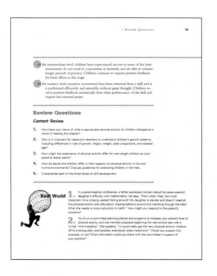

Real World

This end-of-chapter feature provides another way into interpreting the content through a "real world" lens by prompting more specific, deeper, and more varied responses from course takers via questions that track the content and suggest additional scenarios. In this respect, it complements and expands on the applied aspects of the Classroom Challenge with new situations and an emphasis on "reality."

What About You?

This self-reflection feature at the back of each chapter uses probing questions to stimulate further engagement with the content on a more personal level. Designed to encourage productive reflection and self-awareness in teachers who may be dealing with the material for the first time, it may also be useful to more experienced practitioners who might benefit from new introspective exercises.

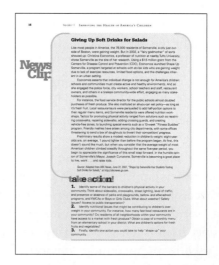

News Clip and Take Action!

These features, included in all chapters, presents current, relevant news stories from varied media sources and connect them with content covered in the text in a way that illuminates how easily even simple pedagogical concepts can become complicated when they're implemented in a real school environment. The News Clip is followed by the complementary feature Take Action! which uses the news item as a springboard for students to incorporate into their coursework or to enhance their own understanding of the material.

Videos

Videos used widely in related Pangrazi texts have been updated and digitized, with additional new segments that update the content and connect it specifically with the material in this text. They offer full-screen views in a user-friendly format available both on the Instructor Resource DVD and the Companion Website. Video content for this text includes a detailed segment on *Managing Activities in the Classroom*, plus 10 sample activity lessons drawn directly from the Activity Cards demonstrating implementation.

Additional videos include *Pedometers and Physical Activity*, a new video on using pedome-

ters in a physical education setting; *Active and Healthy Schools*, another new segment focusing on steps to create a total school environment supporting healthy eating and physical activity; *Quality P.E. in the Four-Part Lesson Format*, displaying complete lessons, geared to Developmental Level I and II students, that model successful teaching techniques; and *Planning a Quality Lesson*, outlining how to plan effective and enjoyable lessons for elementary school students.

Companion Website (www.aw-bc.com/pangrazi)

The interactive Companion Website, designed to serve the needs and interests of both course instructors and students, includes Chapter Guides, Chapter Quiz Questions in multiple formats, updated and expanded videos, Review Questions, suggested Back to Class answers, Flashcards, Glossary, Web Links, and editable PDFs of the Sample Lesson Plans contained in Appendix A of this text.

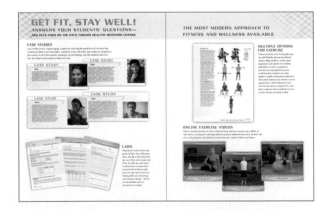

Text Overview and Organization

Instructors who prepare classroom teachers need core content for lecturing and monitoring

student performance. The main body of this text, which can be characterized as Teaching Students to be Active and Healthy, covers important concepts and knowledge areas that teachers need to know when instructing students in activities and health behaviors. The text is augmented by a second and complementary section, which is the Activity Cards containing a wide variety of instructional activities addressing fitness, physical skill development, and classroom- and playground-based games and learning activities.

Chapter 1 offers an overview of—and an argument for—the need for active and healthy school environments. It helps classroom teachers understand what is specifically meant by an "active and healthy school," and the role they play in furthering their own school's progress toward that goal.

Chapter 2 broadly reviews key aspects of children's physical, emotional, and psychological development; their needs and responses; and how instructors can ensure that young students have every opportunity to learn skills and develop their potential capabilities.

Chapter 3 deals with important issues in using equipment and helping young people learn activity skills in a safe and welcoming environment, including how to teach physical skills and understand the development of sport skills. Many teachers also understandably worry about how much activity children can tolerate, so a section is included on how to ensure that exercising children is kept within safe limits.

Chapter 4 addresses ways to improve the effectiveness of instruction, including learning the characteristics of what comprises a high-quality lesson. Planning for successful class presentations requires a specific sequence of steps that are covered in detail, in addition to addressing how to provide effective student feedback and knowing how the personal needs of students may affect instruction.

Chapter 5 examines discipline and management in an activity setting in detail, incorporating guidelines developed from the authors' many combined years of implementing activities with elementary-age schoolchildren. It is clear that in order for classroom teachers to teach physical activities, they must be able to manage children effectively. If, as is likely, physical activities excite a class of young people and make it difficult to return to academic work, many teachers might be reluctant to initiate future activities. For the sake of clarity, the treatment of management and discipline issues are separated: management is defined here as moving and organizing students effectively, while discipline refers to what is used when student behavior is disruptive and needs correction and redirection.

Chapter 6 discusses how to effectively integrate students with special needs into the classroom setting, including ways to adapt activities to ensure successful and enjoyable experiences for all students. Developing Individualized Education Programs (IEPs), teaching tolerance, and working with parents are among some of the key issues covered here.

Chapter 7 concerns the need to integrate physical activity and academics into complementary parts of an educational "whole," and how such integration can enhance learning. We have addressed a range of integration activities across four key academic disciplines—math, science, social studies, and language arts—by adapting numerous sample activity cards in a way that delineates the integration of these four core areas in an activity context.

Chapters 8 and 9 cover the important, separate-but-related topics of increasing and promoting activity levels in a school setting, and developing health-related fitness in young students. Content includes detailed ways to create an active playground environment, and how to teach fitness activities and implement physical routines.

Chapters 10 through 12 complete the content by addressing critical areas that are part of the school day for every student and classroom teacher, namely, nutrition and eating habits, sun safety skills, and promoting activity outside the school setting. Taken as a whole, the chapters in this text offer classroom instructors the information and concepts needed to help their students develop active and healthy lifestyles, and to use the skills they learn in school to maintain health and fitness throughout their lives.

Additional Features

Design and Layout

Even a cursory look through this book's pages reveals the engaging interior design and easy accessibility that characterizes both the look and also the pedagogical intent of the text. By designing and organizing the text in a way that invites readers in and gives them tools, references, and resources that are both practical and accessible, our aim is to educate, stimulate, and even inspire readers as they encounter this material.

Learning Objectives

Key Learning Objectives appear at the start of each chapter, providing students and instructors a clear picture of the material that will be covered.

Key Terms

Key Terms are highlighted in green boldface type throughout each chapter, indicating their inclusion in the glossary at the end of the text.

Chapter Summary and Review Questions

Each chapter ends with an overview of key material and targeted review questions that enable course takers to test their learning and review the main content points.

Supplements

This textbook is accompanied by a supplements package that includes print, digital, and online resources to support both instructors and students, providing an integrated set of learning and instructional tools.

Instructor Resource Manual and Test Bank

The combined Instructor Resource Manual and Test Bank is a comprehensive resource available to all adopting instructors. The Instructor Resource Manual includes chapter overviews, learning objectives, and outlines, in addition to discussion questions, suggested student activities, lab activities, media resources, additional readings, and web links. The Test Bank includes multiple choice and true/false format questions, and is available in computerized form as part of the cross-platform DVD, which allows instructors to create tests, edit questions, and add their own material to the existing Test Bank. Both sets of materials were developed by Dr. Heather Erwin, University of Kentucky, Lexington.

Instructor Resource DVD

This cross-platform DVD for course instructors includes the Computerized Test Bank in addition to PowerPoint™ Lecture Outline slides, Word files for the Instructor Resource Manual and Test Bank, all art and tables contained in the text, and updated and expanded activity videos.

Acknowledgments

Effective textbooks are the result of cohesive teamwork between the authors, the publisher, reviewers, and many others. Aaron, Deb, and I appreciate the teamwork demonstrated in the development of this text. We are indebted to the Applied Sciences editorial team at Pearson Benjamin Cummings for their important contributions. Sandy Lindelof, Senior Acquisitions Editor, provided ongoing support and encouragement. Her leadership and early vision were critical in giving proper direction to this text. Susan Scharf, Project Editor, guided the journey of this book with efficiency and thoughtfulness. She has a unique combination of focus and creativity that helped give it some *pizzazz*.

Early in the conception of this text, Sandy brought together and headed a team that was instrumental in developing the key ideas that became integrated into it and which included, from Benjamin Cummings, Claire Alexander, Neena Bali, Becky Ruden, and Laura Bonazzoli—in addition to academic colleagues Dorothy Lambdin, University of Texas, Austin; Colleen Poole, Cabrini College; Matt Lucas, Longwood College; Johnny Newsome, Morehead State University; and Carri Rogers, University of Louisville.

The design and production team—in particular, Production Supervisor Dorothy Cox and Design Supervisor Derek Bacchus—also played a key role in helping this book reach its fullest potential through their commitment and innovative approach to the design, layout, artwork, and materials. And special recognition must go to Laura Bonazzoli, who developmentally edited the text and contributed so much to this material. As a result of her many insightful organizational ideas, features development, and her writing acumen, I consider her a "silent author" on this project. To these and many other individuals at or affiliated with Pearson Benjamin Cummings who go unnamed, please accept a hearty thank you.

Finally, a sincere note of thanks goes to the following academic reviewers who provided valuable and thoughtful feedback mid-stream on the development of both the text and Activity Cards: Nancy Speed, University of Southern Mississippi; Erin Hall, California State University, Stanislaus; Melissa Parks, Louisiana State University, Alexandria; Wendy Zwissler, University of LaVerne; Elaine Brown, Baptist Bible College; Mark Urtel, Indiana University/Purdue University; Christine Heusser, California State University, Fullerton; Lurelia Hardy, Augusta State University; Susan Eastham, California State University, Stanislaus; Shaunna McGhie, Utah Valley State University; Douglas Callahan, Winona State University; Joel Bloom, University of Houston; Colleen Poole, Cabrini College; Patricia Kneiffner, University of Louisville; Carri Rogers, University of Louisville; Freeta Jones, University of Central Oklahoma; Johnny Newsome, Morehead State University; and Matt Lucas, Longwood University.

PROMOTING PHYSICAL ACTIVITY & HEALTH IN THE CLASSROOM

1

Improving the Health of America's Children

Learning Objectives

After reading this chapter, you will be able to . . .

○ Use current research data to defend the need for active and healthy schools.

○ Identify several recommendations of the Child Nutrition and WIC Reauthorization Act.

○ Define physical education and explain how a quality physical education program can contribute to a child's overall development.

○ Identify the eight elements of an active and healthy school environment.

○ Explain to administrators, parents, and other community members the benefits that an active and healthy school environment offers children.

○ Describe the role of the classroom teacher in increasing children's physical activity.

○ List the six major standards for a quality physical education program.

Classroom Challenge

Crystal Lopez is back in her elementary physical education methods course after assisting in the local public schools. When Professor Erwin opens class by asking what students observed during their in-service assignments, Crystal airs her concerns. "Back when I was in elementary school, a few kids were pudgy, but now a lot of kids seem seriously overweight. In the school where I was placed, the lunch menu included a few nutritious foods, but mostly offered things like hot dogs and pizza . . . and guess which foods the kids chose? In addition, the kids had P.E. only once a week for 30 minutes, but when you took away the time to explain the activity and manage the equipment, they only actually moved their bodies for about 20 minutes. Otherwise, all they got was a 15-minute morning recess, mainly spent sitting around, and a 30-minute lunch break. Often, I'd see them just get a game going and then the bell would ring. I also noticed that most kids got rides home even if they only lived a few blocks away." Crystal sighs. "Did anyone else see these problems at their schools, or is it just me? It sure does seem like there are a lot more overweight kids than there used to be."

Professor Erwin challenges the class to consider the issues Crystal has raised. "Is Crystal right in thinking there's an increase in overweight kids? If she is, what can classroom teachers do about it? Is it the school's responsibility to watch kids' weight? Shouldn't parents take the blame? Or food producers? Or the people who design our drive-everywhere communities?"

The declining health of America's children (and adults) is a subject of national concern. As we'll see shortly, research data consistently show that the number of overweight American children is rapidly increasing while their level of physical activity is decreasing. But as our case study points out, many factors have been involved in creating and maintaining this trend. This chapter begins with some of the main factors affecting obesity rates among school children.

- More meals are being eaten out. Restaurant portions, especially in fast-food establishments, have increased enormously in the last two decades, and calorie intake has increased accordingly. Even the portion sizes of supermarket foods, such as bagels, muffins, and soft drinks, have increased. For example, 20 years ago, an average blueberry muffin weighed about 1.5 ounces and provided 210 calories. Today, that muffin averages 5 ounces and 500 calories!

- In more and more families, both parents must work to make ends meet. Thus, many children come home from school to an empty house. Parents are concerned about letting their children play alone outdoors, even in typically safe neighborhoods.

- At the same time, the number of options for children's sedentary activities has exploded, with a proliferation of Internet websites for kids, hand-held video games, and children's software. In addition, prior to the advent of cable television, children's programs were shown for only a few hours of a broadcast day; now, children's cable TV stations broadcast cartoons and other kids' programs all day. And while they're passively watching their favorite program, children are bombarded with ads for high-fat, high-sugar foods.

- Because of the design of many suburban and rural communities, it is not possible to walk to and from schools, parks, shops, and friends' homes. Attending a soccer match means mom or dad must drive the child to the field.

- Schools may be safe places for children to play, but partly in response to federal legislation mandating increases in students' academic performance, many schools have dropped physical education classes and reduced recess and other free time. While this increases the time available for teaching math, reading, and other academic subjects, it eliminates what for many kids is their only opportunity for sustained physical activity.

Although many of these factors are societal, there's no reason for discouragement. Ample evidence suggests that classroom teachers can improve the activity level and health of school children by making rather small changes in their instructional methods and personal behavior. As classroom teachers, you need not be experts in physical education. Rather, you can work within your strengths and limitations to promote physical activity in the classroom. This book will show you how.

The Need for Active and Healthy Schools

Research data supporting the need to improve the health of America's children are overwhelming. Only a few studies can be mentioned here, but they provide convincing evidence that we must change how our youth are educated.

The Number of Overweight Children Is Increasing

The percentage of children age 6 to 11 who are overweight has more than tripled in the past 30 years (U.S. Department of Health and Human Services

[USDHHS], 2002). A recent study suggested that the prevalence of overweight in children is more strongly related to a decrease in energy expenditure than to an increase in energy intake (Jebb and Moore, 1999). In other words, this study shows that weight problems are not caused so much by eating more as they are by being less active.

The school environment discourages physical activity. Students are asked to move slowly, sit still, and walk everywhere they go, which results in a decrease in energy expenditure. In addition, many schools are trying to reduce the free time students have for physical activity. In contrast, by assuring in-class activity breaks, traditional recess time, and lunchtime activity, some schools are helping students accumulate about half of their total daily requirement for physical activity. This contribution to their daily energy expenditure is particularly important for students who are inactive at home.

Unfortunately, too many children fall into this group. A 2003 national survey of children, sponsored by the Kaiser Family Foundation, showed that 8- to 14-year-olds watched an average of 3 hours and 16 minutes of television a day. However, when videos, DVDs, computers, and video games are added to the TV time, the total is more than 6 hours a day (Roberts, Foehr, and Rideout, 2005). Another study (Anderson et al., 1998) showed that children who watched 4 or more hours of television per day had significantly greater body mass index (BMI) compared to children watching fewer than 2 hours per day.

America's health goals for the year 2010 (USDHHS, 2000) include reducing children's inactivity and increasing their daily participation in moderate to vigorous physical activity. Many of the goals directly target schools or programs that can take place within the school setting.

Back to Class

Was Crystal right that the number of overweight children in America is increasing? What is the precise statistic? What difference can classroom teachers make in tackling a problem with so many factors?

Childhood Overweight Predicts Adult Obesity

Overweight children grow into overweight—or obese—adults. Studies (Guo et al., 1994; Must et al., 1992) show that adolescent overweight is a good predictor of adult obesity. A study by Whitaker et al. (1997) showed that the risk of childhood obesity persisting into adulthood is much higher among adolescents than younger children: the risk increases from 20 percent at 4 years of age to 80 percent by adolescence (Guo and Chumlea, 1999).

These data suggest that we should do all we can to reduce overweight among children during the elementary school years, before the problem becomes difficult to rectify. Classroom teachers can play a vital role in encouraging active behavior, but an organized approach focused on specific outcomes is essential. We describe the components of such an approach later in this chapter.

Physical Activity Improves Children's Health

Physical activity provides immediate and long-term health benefits for children (Bar-Or, 1995). For overweight children, increased physical activity results in a reduction in the percentage of body fat. Additionally, increased activity improves both blood pressure and blood lipid profiles for high health-risk children. Evidence also shows that weight-bearing activities performed during the school years can help increase children's bone mineral density (Bailey et al., 1996). This in turn can help prevent osteoporosis in later life.

Physical Activity Can Improve Academic Performance

An argument often heard is that spending time on physical education or activity breaks lowers the academic performance of students because they have less time to study and learn. On the contrary, studies have shown that students who spent time in physical education classes did equally well or better in academic classes than students who did not. Two studies that looked at this issue were the Three Rivers Study (Trudeau et al., 1998) and a SPARK-related (Sports, Play, and Active Recreation for Kids) program study (Sallis et al., 1999). In both cases, students received the health benefits of physical activity without any negative impact on their academic performance.

On the other hand, we also need to examine carefully the hypothesis that adding more time for academics results in improved achievement scores. There is little data to support this belief. All we really know is that increasing time for academics typically results in decreased physical activity for children.

Active Children Become Active Adults

Active children are more likely to become active adults. Telama et al. (1997) looked at retrospective and longitudinal tracking studies and concluded that the results "indicate that physical activity and sport participation in childhood and adolescence offer a significant prediction for physical activity in adulthood." The relationship is low but does offer evidence that activity during youth has an impact on adult activity levels. Another study (Raitakari et al., 1994) suggested that being an inactive youth tracks into adulthood. In that study, the probability of an inactive 12-year-old remaining sedentary at age 18 years was 51–63 percent for girls and 54–61 percent for boys. This indicates that parents, schools, and communities that fail to promote physical activity will produce not only inactive children, but also inactive adults.

The evidence is clear and convincing: Children are not getting enough physical activity, and their health is suffering. School administrators and teachers must help implement programs that teach youngsters how to live an active and healthy lifestyle.

America's Wellness Mandate: The WIC Reauthorization Act

To address the issue of increasing overweight among children (and adults), the Child Nutrition and WIC (Women, Infants and Children) Reauthorization Act of 2004 was passed into law. In part, the law states that by the beginning of the 2006 school year, all school districts with a federally funded school meals program (the majority of public schools) must establish a wellness policy for schools under the local educational agency that, at a minimum, "includes goals for nutrition education, physical activity and other school-based activities that are designed to promote student wellness in a manner that the local educational agency determines is appropriate."

The act highlights the importance of developing solutions that increase the physical activity of children, provide nutrition education, and ultimately foster healthful eating and activity habits that last a lifetime. The act recommends that schools implement some of the following actions in an effort to meet the wellness policy plan:

- Make recess and lunchtime active settings for all students.
- Offer regularly scheduled activity breaks in the classroom. These breaks last 3–5 minutes and give students a respite from long periods of sitting.
- Design school walking programs that are buddy based or small group based.
- Develop activity contracts for students (teaching students to monitor their daily activity patterns).
- Facilitate programs for parents; sharing information with parents through newsletters and school-based programs.
- Place point of decision prompts in schools to encourage healthful eating, physical activity, and other health-promoting behaviors.
- Encourage students to participate in after-school activities.
- Maintain and strengthen nutritional service programs.

The act attempts to address childhood health issues while maintaining local control for states and schools. This local control implies that the federal government will not dictate to local school districts specifically what their wellness policy must contain. Since each school district has the latitude to develop its own policy, local personnel, including classroom teachers, are typically made responsible for developing a wellness plan. Unfortunately, the act does not provide funding for the recommended programs. Indeed, the only clout that the government has to encourage schools to change is to withhold funding for school lunches. Presenting schools with such unfunded mandates often results in schools failing to take the recommended actions. Regardless of clout, laws work well only when school personnel at the local level support them.

Some school districts assume that because they have a physical education specialist on the faculty they have met the Child Nutrition and WIC Reauthorization Act mandate. However, a physical education specialist is not enough:

wellness needs to permeate the entire school environment. Classroom teachers and staff members need to be involved in creating and implementing policies and programs that improve the activity levels and overall health of children. These new measures need to involve parents and members of the wider community. In short, to fully meet the goals of the act, we must work together to create active and healthy school environments.

> ### Back to Class
>
> Professor Erwin challenged his class to think of ways that classroom teachers could help address the growing number of overweight children in the United States. Which steps of the Child Nutrition and WIC Reauthorization Act (bulleted on the previous page) might a classroom teacher be able to take on independently?

The Active and Healthy School Environment

Almost everyone would agree that a school is a place for learning. Ask children what they are learning in school and they will mention academic subjects such as math, social studies, reading, and writing. Few will say they are learning how to live an active lifestyle, eat a nourishing diet, and take care of their bodies. That is because children learn what their schools value. As we have seen, in a typical American school, there is little evidence that an active and healthy lifestyle is valued. To turn this around, the overall environment of schools and their communities must change. The following are components found in an active and healthy school (AHS) environment.

Quality Physical Education

A quality physical education program serves as the foundation for developing an AHS environment. Before we explore why it is so fundamental, let's make sure we understand what physical education is.

The term *physical education* means many things to many people. Academic professionals often describe it as essential subject matter dedicated to learning in the psychomotor domain and committed to developing lifetime physical activity patterns. Laypeople often mistakenly equate it with athletics or competitive sports. Others think of it as recess or free-time play. In contrast, we define **physical education** as that part of the educational program that contributes, primarily through movement experiences, to the total growth and development of all children.

To put it another way, physical education is education through movement. It is an instructional program that addresses all learning domains: psychomotor, cognitive, and affective. No other area of the curriculum is designed to help children learn motor and lifetime activity skills. This makes physical education a necessary component of the total school curriculum.

Although physical education programs often support students' acquisition of academic learning, they should always emphasize the acquisition of physical skills. Many children, especially low-income children, have little opportunity to learn physical skills in their communities. From soccer clubs to Little League baseball teams, many community activities accept only those children who have already acquired a certain level of skill. A school-based physical education class may thus be the only place that offers children the opportunity to learn new skills. It can also increase children's acquisition of social skills, such as cooperation, teamwork, and taking responsibility. In short, a strong physical education program helps all youngsters succeed.

Although children benefit greatly when physical education is offered, it's just one component of an AHS environment. Regardless of whether a physical education specialist is employed in your school, by addressing the remaining components discussed next, you and other staff members can successfully create positive health-related experiences that will make a difference in students' quality of life.

Physical Activity Breaks

Active and healthy schools schedule time for activity in three basic formats: morning and afternoon breaks, activity time at lunch, and classroom mini-breaks offered throughout the school day. Let's look at each of these separately.

Morning and Afternoon Activity Breaks

Students should be provided with at least two 15-minute breaks per day to satisfy their need for physical activity. One study found that girls averaged almost 1,200 steps and boys 1,400 steps during a 15-minute activity break. In just 15 minutes, children can accumulate more than 10 percent of their recommended daily physical activity of 11,000 to 13,000 steps (President's Council on Physical Fitness and Sports, 2007).

Incidentally, it is time to change the terminology for such breaks from recess to activity break. The term *recess* implies that such time is a "recess from learning" and has no educational purpose. To the contrary, an activity break offers students a chance to socialize, to learn how to cooperate and compete, and to enjoy an active lifestyle. Even more importantly, such physical activity breaks promote children's growth and development. For example, students on the playground often run as fast as possible for about 30 seconds until fatigued and then stop and discuss the situation until rested. A study by Bailey et al. (1995) suggests that this intermittent form of physical activity releases growth hormone and helps to stimulate optimal growth and development. As a classroom teacher, it makes sense for you and your students to value the short, but important, activity break.

Lunchtime

Lunchtime offers an excellent opportunity for physical activity. Tudor-Locke and colleagues (2006) found that during a 40-minute lunch break, boys averaged 2,521 steps and girls 1,913 steps each day (nearly 20 percent of their recommended daily activity). This study clearly indicates that children use lunchtime to be active.

Nutritionists recommend that students be active first and then eat lunch so that they don't feel pressured to eat quickly to gain more time for play. There is some evidence, for instance, that there is less wasted food when children are active before eating. However, this proposal is somewhat controversial because, while increasing the time students have to eat, it cuts down the time they have to play. A number of experts question whether eating more food and being less active is a desirable goal for many students.

Classroom Mini-Breaks

Classroom mini-breaks allow students to accumulate physical activity in short bouts throughout the day. For example, the activities in the Classroom-Based section of the Activity Cards accompanying this book typically last 3–5 minutes and do not require leaving the classroom. For these reasons, they may be offered frequently (as often as three times per day).

When young people are expected to sit still for longer than 50–60 minutes at a time, they become restless. Pellegrini, Huberty, and Jones (1995) found that offering activity breaks every hour decreased behavioral problems with inattentive students. Other research has shown that participating in activity breaks, along with journaling about one's activity from the previous day, increases the daily physical activity levels of children, particularly girls (Ernst and Pangrazi, 1999; Pangrazi et al., 2003).

Mini-breaks provide students with physical activity, yet disrupt classroom lesson time only minimally. With practice, students become efficient in the routine of participating in an activity and then resuming class work following the break. Just as with other routines, establishing and practicing procedures for implementing the activities at the beginning of the school year minimize disruption.

Nutrition and Healthful Eating Activities

Active and healthy school personnel know that to stay healthy, youngsters must have access to an adequate amount and variety of nutritious food (Anspaugh and

Ezell, 2008). We also know that healthy students perform better academically (Hanson et al., 2005). For students participating in school breakfast and lunch programs, two of their presumably three daily meals are provided by the school. For these reasons, it's essential that the meals schools offer are nutritionally balanced, offering low-fat sources of high-quality protein, complex carbohydrates, and all essential vitamins and minerals. In addition, schools should provide students with age- appropriate nutrition education so that they learn how to make healthful food choices. Classroom teachers can also devise methods for sharing nutrition information with students' families. Nutrition for school children is discussed in more detail in Chapter 10.

Sun Safety Instruction

Because children (and adults) are more active when outdoors, one of the best ways to increase children's level of physical activity is to increase the amount of time they spend participating in outdoor activities. However, with this strategy comes an increased risk of sunburn and other forms of skin damage caused by the sun. In the United States, one in five people will develop skin cancer. Children are of particular concern because an estimated 80 percent of a person's sun exposure occurs before age 18, and overexposure in childhood puts individuals at an increased risk of skin cancer throughout life (Stern, Weinstein, and Baker, 1986). Also, experiencing even one blistering sunburn during childhood significantly increases the risk of developing skin cancer later in life (American Academy of Pediatrics, 1999). Despite these ominous data, parents and schools continue to send students outdoors without teaching them the fundamentals of sun safety.

Arizona was the first state in the United States to mandate a course for teachers related to sun safety, and active and healthy schools in other states now offer sun safety instruction as well. Key recommendations include the following:

- Encourage or require children to wear long-sleeve tops, long pants, hats with full brims (not baseball caps), and sunglasses (to reduce the risk of early cataracts) when playing outside.
- Encourage or require children to wear sunscreen. For low-income families, the cost of sunscreen can be a barrier: thus, many schools buy it in gallon jugs for all children to use before going outside. This strategy requires collaboration with the school nurse in case of allergies.
- Schedule activity breaks before or after the peak sun hours of 10:00 a.m. to 2:00 p.m.

- Include in the curriculum classroom lessons discussing the importance of sun safety, risks of sun exposure, and strategies for maximizing sun safety.
- Send newsletters home notifying parents of the sun safety measures taken at school and encouraging them to take similar precautions at home.

Another issue related to sun safety is the need for adequate shade. It is obvious that children are going to be exposed to the sun; however, they should also have access to a well-shaded area where they can continue their play sheltered from the sun. Unfortunately, many playgrounds lack even a single shaded area suitable for children's activities. On such playgrounds, sun shades provide an effective option, particularly over play equipment. Shade structures over a teaching slab can provide protection for teachers and students during outdoor physical education classes.

The United States Environmental Protection Agency (EPA) sponsors the Sunwise School Program, which is designed for educators. Sunwise is a comprehensive program that includes lesson plans, brochures and letters for parents, and workbooks for students. Included in the materials are a number of active games that can be played to teach concepts about sun safety and how to become a Sunwise school. Sun safety is discussed in more detail in Chapter 11.

Before- and After-School Programs

Because of the sedentary nature of the school day, it is no surprise that students perform most of their physical activity outside of school hours (Morgan, Pangrazi, and Beighle, 2003). In many AHS environments, the YMCA, Boys and Girls Club, or local recreation department uses the school property for after-school programs. These programs are usually activity based, with students playing informal games or team sports in the gymnasium, on the playground, or in a grassy space. Many after-school programs also teach about nutrition.

Before-school hours also offer an opportunity for students to be active. At many schools, parents drop students off early in an effort to get to work on time. Without before-school programs, these students are left to just sit and wait outside the school building. Opening the school grounds and offering activities for students who arrive before school can increase students' daily energy expenditure while increasing their personal safety, promoting team building, and offering friendship.

Implementing effective extracurricular activities often requires teachers and administrators to overcome barriers. The most common barrier is cost; however, with the recent national engagement in the problem of childhood obesity, government funding for programs that offer physical activity and nutrition education is often available. Other funding sources include school fund-raisers, private businesses, PTAs, community charitable organizations, and external grant sources. Most districts have resources that assist teachers who are seeking grants.

Another barrier is transportation. Often the success of a program, particularly an after-school program, is strongly influenced by the availability of transportation for students (Jago and Baranowski, 2004). For example, attendance in after-school programs may be limited because students who are bused to school have to leave immediately after school. Also, if parents feel that additional transportation is a burden, they may not allow their child to participate in a program. Ideas for eliminating this barrier vary from school to school. Some districts provide later buses for students participating in district-sponsored after-school activities. Others facilitate ride sharing among families or find other solutions that work for their communities.

Classroom Teacher Involvement

Active teachers increase the chances of students becoming active. In a study by Ernst and Pangrazi (1999), it was found that students, particularly girls, were more active when their classroom teacher participated in some of the activities. It wasn't necessary for teachers to instruct students to be active—their participation alone increased the activity levels of students. This study shows the power of teachers modeling desired student behavior.

Not surprisingly, then, encouraging faculty to improve their own health through school-based activities is another key component of an AHS environment. As just mentioned, students see teachers as role models, and the impact that their behaviors can make on students is significant. If they see their teacher eating nutritious foods, they are more likely to choose nutritious foods. If they see faculty and staff participating in walking clubs, after-school aerobics, or friendly "steps" competitions, they pick up the message that physical activity is important for everyone.

In fact, this last idea of a "steps" competition provides an excellent example of how a few teachers working together can increase physical activity levels throughout the entire school. It all begins when a few classroom teachers start wearing pedometers and comparing their step totals. This piques the curiosity of other teachers, staff members, and students. Youngsters are usually quite curious about pedometers and want to try them out. This can prompt a fund-raising campaign to purchase pedometers for schoolwide use: Some companies sell pedometers at a discounted price for schools to resell for profit. Selling pedometers is a much more healthful way to generate funds than selling candies, cookies, and other high-calorie, low-quality foods. Profits can then be used to purchase class sets of pedometers, further reinforcing the importance of physical activity every day. Soon kids are encouraging their parents and siblings to track their steps with pedometers, and the game spreads into the community. Below, we'll discuss other aspects of the classroom teacher's role in creating AHS environments.

Parental Involvement

Parents (or legal guardians) are the most significant adults in children's lives, so it's not surprising that they have a substantial impact on their children's attitude toward activity and their actual physical activity level (Welk, Wood, and Morss, 2003). Thus, programs that involve parents and encourage them to be active with their children can be effective in promoting physical activity not just for children, but also for an entire family. The following are some activities that have worked in AHS environments to increase parental involvement.

Activity Calendars

Family members can be encouraged to participate in all the activities listed on an activity calendar (**Figure 1.1**). Students within a classroom can design the activity calendar each month. They can choose activities they think are good for their health and enjoyed by other students and parents. If desired, the names of families that accomplish a stipulated percentage of the goals each month for the year could be posted on the "Moving Family Wall of Fame" in a prominent place in the school, such as the cafeteria or multipurpose room.

Physical Activity and Health Fairs

Physical activity and health fairs are excellent ways to involve parents and others interested in the school. Public and private health and fitness organizations are usually willing to participate in and donate funding for the fair because health fairs give them access to future clients. Examples of possible donors are local hospitals, health insurance providers, pharmacies, medical supply companies, fitness clubs, sporting goods companies, YMCAs, and Boys and Girls Clubs. A health fair should offer a variety of activities that appeal to adults and children. For parents, the focus of the health fair should be on providing feedback on health and lifestyle, that is, blood

February

Sunday	Monday	Tuesday	Wednesday	Thursday	Friday	Saturday
1 *Active families stay healthy*	2	3 Play football with a friend	4	5 Play basketball for 10 minutes	6	7
8	9 Make a snowman	10 How many times can you jump rope without stopping?	11	12 Create a dance and practice it for 20 minutes	13 NO SCHOOL! BE ACTIVE ALL DAY!	14 Be kind to your heart . . . be active. ♥
15 *Children should be active at least 60 minutes per day*	16 Teach someone your favorite stretch	17 Teach a family member a PE game	18 Do extra chores as a favor to your parents	19 Jump rope for a total of 10 minutes	20 Invent a new exercise	21 Shovel snow
22	23 Do your favorite fitness challenge	24 Play a new game at recess	25	26	27 Start a game of tag in your neighborhood	28

If you want to do an activity other than the one on the calendar, GREAT! Write the new activity on your calendar. Mrs. Panko may even put your activity on the calendar as an activity next month.

How many minutes of activity should you do a day? _____

What types of activities are cardiovascular activities? _____

Name three lifetime activities. _____ _____ _____

What is a locomotor skill? _____

Figure 1.1 An activity calendar is a fun and creative way to involve the whole family in promoting physical activity every day.

pressure, weight, BMI, diet, smoking cessation, etc. Additionally, a fair is a good venue for signing up parents who are willing to help supervise activity days and other activity field trips.

Activity Days

Activity days are school days set aside to celebrate physical activity and the joy of moving. Typically, several stations are organized, and classes move from station to station participating in the activities. Stations can offer activities that are taught during physical education or novel activities that are simply safe and enjoyable. Parents are recruited to serve as planning committee members and to help produce and supervise the event. Upper-level elementary and older students can also serve on the committee to plan and set up the event as well as supervise the stations.

Charity Events

Charity events offer an opportunity for families to be active together. Events can vary from a walk/run race, a walk-a-thon, chores for change, or even a physical activity festival where all proceeds go to a charity. The charity can be an outside organization, a local family, or support for school or physical education programs. As with any event, extensive planning and coordination are necessary. Collaborating with the school's PTA organization or other school-based organizations may help distribute the planning duties.

Back to Class

Crystal reported that in the school where she'd been assigned some parents were contributing to the problem of increased weight and decreased activity in their children. How could classroom teachers involve parents in becoming part of the solution?

Community Involvement

As discussed in the accompanying News Clip, increasing the physical activity and health of our children requires the participation of the entire "village." Every community has people who can help. Business leaders can contribute their experience in planning events and fund-raising; people working in public offices and social services can tap into their networks with various community organizations; attorneys can give legal advice; healthcare workers can offer their services teaching or staffing health fairs; and media experts can help publicize, photograph, and report on events.

Organizations can help by donating monies or supplies. If they cannot donate, they may have a program that encourages their employees to volunteer in the

News Clip

Giving Up Soft Drinks for Salads

Like most people in America, the 78,000 residents of Somerville, a city just outside of Boston, were gaining weight. But in 2002, a "fairy godmother" of sorts showed up: Christina Economos, a professor of nutrition at nearby Tufts University, chose Somerville as the site of her research. Using a $1.5 million grant from the Centers for Disease Control and Prevention (CDC), Economos launched Shape Up Somerville, a program targeted at schools with at-risk kids who are gaining weight due to lack of exercise resources, limited food options, and the challenges inherent in an urban setting.

Economos asserts that individual change is not enough for America's children: schools and communities must create active and healthy environments. And so she engaged the police force, city workers, school teachers and staff, restaurant owners, and others in a tireless community-wide effort, engaging as many stakeholders as possible.

For instance, the food service director for the public schools almost doubled purchases of fresh produce. She also instituted an all-you-can eat policy—as long as it's fresh fruit. Local restauranteurs were persuaded to add half-portion options to their regular menu items, and Somerville residents were offered nutrition workshops. Tactics for promoting physical activity ranged from solutions such as repainting crosswalks, repairing sidewalks, adding crossing guards, and creating vehicle-free zones, to launching special events such as a 10-week "Fitness Buddies" program. Friendly rivalries have arisen among city departments, with some offices threatening to send a box of doughnuts to thwart their competitors' progress.

Preliminary results show a modest reduction in children's weight: eight-year-olds are, on average, 1 pound lighter than before the program began. At first, this doesn't sound like much, but when you consider that the average weight of most American children climbed steadily throughout the same five-year period, you begin to appreciate the significance of this small step forward. In the humble opinion of Somerville's Mayor, Joseph Curtatone, Somerville is becoming a great place to live, work . . . and raise kids.

Source: Adapted from ABC News, June 22, 2007, "Shape Up Somerville Has Students Trading Soft Drinks for Salads," at http://abcnews.go.com.

take action!

1. Identify some of the barriers to children's physical activity in your community. Think about sidewalks, crosswalks, street lighting, level of traffic, and presence or absence of parks and playgrounds, before- and after-school programs, and YMCAs or Boys or Girls Clubs. What about weather? Safety issues? Access to public transportation?

2. Identify nutritional issues that might be contributing to children's overweight in your community. For instance, how many fast-food restaurants are in your community? Do residents of all neighborhoods within your community have access to a market with fresh produce? Obtain a copy of a monthly menu from an elementary school in your district. What are children's options for fresh fruits and vegetables?

3. Finally, identify one action you could take to help "shape up" your community.

community. The following are examples of groups with resources and expertise in developing and leading activities that support and augment school programs. By partnering with such groups, teachers and schools increase their opportunity to help students.

YMCAs, Recreation Centers, and Boys and Girls Clubs. These organizations are dedicated to increasing physical activity among young people. In addition, they all are involved in before-school, after-school, and even during-school programs. Many offer expertise and training for classroom teachers in promoting physical activity and health. Many will also want to bid on running after-school programs for youth. The more administrators and teachers can work with these organizations, the more students will benefit.

County Health Agencies. Many county health departments and extension agents are already involved with health-related programs in the schools. This involvement makes them excellent resources and potential collaboration partners in promoting AHS environments. For example, the state of Arizona sponsored and supported a statewide activity program for children (Pangrazi et al., 2003). As part of this program, county health agents provided training and activities that classroom teachers taught their students. The program significantly increased the physical activity levels of students.

Businesses. Most businesses within a school district have a vested interest in contributing to the lives of youth in their community. Banks, hospitals, HMOs, local gyms and weight-loss centers, sports clubs, bike shops, sporting goods stores, and "whole foods" markets are often willing to offer support. Such businesses may be willing to partner with schools to develop programs, to donate funds directly, or to fund the purchase of physical education equipment in exchange for authorization to post their company's banner in the gym or have their logo on team T-shirts or newsletters.

Incorporating Physical Activity into Your Classroom

At the elementary school level, no individual spends more time influencing children than the classroom teacher. This book describes a wide variety of simple games that you can offer within your classroom to engage children in physical activity and healthy eating behaviors. When you offer these mini-breaks throughout your school day, you demonstrate clearly to students that you value physical activity. By keeping activity and health in front of your students on a regular basis, you communicate to students: "We value physical health and academic performance and our school takes time for both."

Although mini-breaks are by definition brief, lasting from 3 to 5 minutes, they're not ineffective. As noted earlier in this chapter, research has shown that classroom mini-breaks increase children's daily physical activity levels while reducing inattention. All activity is good activity, even if students are moving only their upper bodies, are moving slowly or awkwardly, or are moving in fits and starts. Try to avoid comparing your classroom activities with those of the PE specialist or anyone else. Trust that your activities are beneficial. What is most important is that your students enjoy the experience and feel positive about participating. Too often students who excel in physical activity because of their genetic gifts are continually praised, while we ignore students who are less capable but are working hard and doing their best. Make it a goal to convey to your students that you value all activity, regardless of how it is performed. In fact, most activities that people do for a lifetime are low-intensity, noncompetitive, and valued by those who do them. A feeling of competence and a demonstrated ability to perform some type of activity help ensure that children will continue to be active into adulthood.

Another commonly overlooked benefit of offering classroom physical activity breaks is that they can be used to foster students' development of relational skills. Children must learn to cooperate, maintain their composure, compete fairly, and accept the decisions of others. Playing together in different physical activities is probably the best laboratory for learning these skills. Thus, you can use classroom physical activity to help your students master one of the most important lessons in life—how to get along with others.

An additional benefit of incorporating classroom activities into your school day is the opportunity these brief sessions provide for you to see your students in a new way. Many teachers form opinions about their students' personalities and abilities solely according to what they have seen them do in the academic sphere. Suddenly, when the same students participate in physical activity, new aspects of their characters emerge. Students who rarely participate during an academic lesson may be more vocal and confident during physical activity. At the same time, some academically confident students may hesitate to join in the game. Thus, incorporating physical activity provides you with a unique opportunity for both seeing and educating the whole child.

Admittedly, teaching children physical activity is very different from teaching an academic subject. Managing students effectively is absolutely essential to the success of the lesson, but the management techniques that work during academic lessons don't always succeed during classroom physical activity. One of the reasons many teachers avoid promoting classroom activity is that they fear their students will get out of control and that it will take too much time to settle them down again. That's unfortunate, because just as there are effective management techniques to use for academic lessons, there are effective techniques for managing physical activities. We discuss these in detail in Chapter 5.

Classroom teachers have many responsibilities, and physical activity can easily be perceived as just one more burden. But it doesn't have to be this way: using the techniques described throughout this book, you may discover that physical activity can be a joy to teach. In fact, you may find that it becomes your own and your students' favorite part of the day, bringing happiness and laughter into the classroom. Consider the following scenario:

It is the middle of the afternoon at Jefferson School, and Ms. Massoney's fifth-grade class is tired and listless. She doesn't want to release the students for recess because, by the time they

go out and return, she'll have lost a half hour of instruction time. Besides, they had recess an hour ago, and it is tough to justify another break. Instead, Ms. Massoney pulls out one of her physical activity cards and plays a quick game of Balloon Volleyball. Students stand alongside their desks and hit the balloon back and forth past the middle of the room. No net is needed because students have agreed to where the dividing line is delineated. The goal is to volley the balloon back and forth until a player hits it twice in a row or the balloon touches some inanimate object. At that time, a point is scored for the other team. During the game, Ms. Massoney notices that Bashir, a small, shy boy whose family recently emigrated from Afghanistan, is doing very well for his team. She smiles, glad that he has had a chance to shine today. After playing for 5 minutes, the students put away the balloon and go back to work with more enthusiasm and energy than they had earlier. Little instructional time is lost, and Ms. Massoney and her students feel refreshed and ready to refocus on academics.

Content Standards for Physical Education

Whether in academics or physical education, a key to effective teaching is to follow content standards. By definition, **content standards** identify the outcomes of a model educational program, that is, what knowledge students should possess and how they should demonstrate that knowledge when they exit a developmental level. Content standards also determine the framework of the program, that is, the focus and direction of instruction, assessment, and accountability. The establishment of content standards can make a significant contribution to the overall goal of education and socialization: the development of a well-rounded individual capable of contributing to a democratic society.

Six content standards for physical education have been identified by an association of professional physical educators, the National Association for Sport and Physical Education (NASPE, 2004a). These NASPE standards provide the basis for describing a physically educated person and form the foundation for most physical education programs. We discuss them here because by identifying what a physical education program should accomplish, the standards can guide you in contributing to these outcomes in your classroom.

Standard 1: Demonstrates competency in motor skills and movement patterns needed to perform a variety of physical activities.

The elementary school years are an excellent time to teach motor skills because children have the time and predisposition to learn. As a classroom teacher, you can expose students to as many different physical activities as possible so that they can learn about their personal abilities and challenge themselves to acquire new skills. The skills children need to learn are basic to a wide range of activities they'll perform throughout life, including sports, recreation, career, and health maintenance. These skills are discussed next.

Fundamental Motor Skills

Fundamental motor skills are requisite for children to function fully. They are divided into three categories: locomotor, non-locomotor, and manipulative skills.

- *Locomotor* skills are used to move the body from one place to another or to project the body upward, as in jumping and hopping. These skills also include walking, running, skipping, leaping, sliding, and galloping.
- *Non-locomotor* skills are performed in place and include bending and stretching, pushing and pulling, balancing, rolling, curling, twisting, turning, and bouncing.
- *Manipulative* skills are developed through handling some type of object. Most of these skills involve the hands and feet, but other parts of the body may also be used. Manipulative skills form the basis of many game and sport skills. Propulsion (throwing, striking, striking with an implement, kicking) and reception (catching) of objects are important skills. Rebounding or redirecting an object in flight (such as a balloon) is another useful manipulative skill. Continuous control of an object, such as a wand or a hoop, is also a manipulative activity.

Specialized Motor Skills

Specialized motor skills are used in various sports, apparatus activities, tumbling, dance, and specific games. They are grouped into five areas: body management, rhythmic movement, gymnastic, game, and sport skills.

- *Body management* skills bring together a number of physical traits, including agility, balance, flexibility, and coordination. In addition, youngsters need to develop an understanding of how to control their bodies while on large apparatus, such as balance beams, benches, and jumping boxes.
- *Rhythmic movement* involves motion with a regular and predictable pattern. The ability to move rhythmically is basic to skill performance in all areas. A rhythmic program that includes dance, rope jumping, and rhythmic gymnastics offers a variety of activities to help attain this objective. Instruction capitalizes on locomotor skills that children already possess, such as walking, running, hopping, and jumping.
- *Gymnastic* activities develop body management skills without the need for equipment and apparatus. Flexibility, agility, balance, strength, and body control are outcomes that are enhanced through participation in gymnastic activities. Basic gymnastic skills such as body rolling, balance skills, inverted balances, and tumbling skills are learned in a safe and progressive manner.
- *Games* are laboratories where children can apply learned motor skills in a meaningful way. Many games develop large-muscle groups and enhance the ability to run, dodge, start, and stop under control while sharing space with others. Through games, children experience success and accomplishment. Social objectives addressed through games are the

development of interpersonal skills, acceptance of rule parameters, and a better understanding of oneself in a competitive and cooperative situation.

Sport skills are learned in a context of application. Students learn the appropriate set of basic skills and then practice them doing different drills. After the skills have been learned and practiced, they are applied in lead-up activities, simplified versions of a sport in which the number of skills youngsters have to use to be successful is reduced.

Standard 2: Demonstrates understanding of movement concepts, principles, and tactics as they apply to the learning and performance of physical activities.

This standard addresses the need for understanding the basic concepts behind what, where, and how the body can move. It also identifies the need for children to understand the tactics involved in many different types of physical activities. Again, this standard emphasizes the importance of children experiencing the diversity of human movement. Allied to this experience is learning the mechanics of skill performance, such as stability, force, leverage, and other factors related to efficient movement.

Standard 3: Participates regularly in physical activity.

Active children mature into active adults (Raitakari et al., 1994), and standard 3 is concerned with children's regular participation in a wide range of physical activities. Specifically, children should learn how to monitor their activity levels, how to plan meaningful activity programs, and how to make informed decisions about physical activity. Youngsters also need to learn where they can participate within their community and how to join clubs, YMCAs, and sport programs.

Several factors influence students' likelihood of remaining active as adults. First, they must derive pleasure from their physical activity. Not incidentally, enjoyment increases when a child has achieved an adequate level of proficiency in a favored activity. Second, social and environmental influences also affect lifetime activity patterns. These factors include having family and peer role models, receiving encouragement from significant others, and having opportunities to participate in activities with others. Third, children need time and opportunities to develop the practice of being active. This includes adequate programs and facilities, adequate equipment and supplies, and safe outdoor environments near home and at school. It also includes adequate school opportunities such as activity breaks, lunchtime activity, classroom mini-breaks, physical education, intramural games, recreational programs, and sports.

A NASPE publication authored by Corbin and Pangrazi, *Physical Activity for Children: A Statement of Guidelines* (2004b), identifies reasons why youngsters need daily physical activity and how much they need (a minimum of 60 minutes per day). The publication discusses the physical activity pyramid and importance of participating in different types of physical activity, including lifestyle activity, active aerobics, active sports and recreation, flexibility, and muscle fitness exercises. The document offers support and direction for teachers who need to offer justification to administrators for increasing the amount of daily physical activity for students.

Standard 4: Achieves and maintains a health-enhancing level of physical fitness.

Physical fitness is a set of attributes that people have or achieve relating to their ability to perform physical activity (USDHHS, 1996). Instruction for elementary school children should concentrate on the process of developing fitness rather than being concerned about the product (how many repetitions, how fast, or how far). Giving students an opportunity to offer input about their fitness program and make personal activity choices prepares them for a lifetime of activity. When students accept personal responsibility for participating in regular activity, fitness is an authentic learning experience that can last a lifetime. Meeting this standard means helping students develop positive attitudes that carry over into adulthood. What is gained if students develop high physical fitness levels in the elementary school years but leave school with a strong dislike of physical activity?

Meeting this standard also implies students will leave elementary school understanding the basic facts of fitness. Such concepts as the FIT principle (frequency, intensity, and time) can be taught in short question-and-answer episodes. Because each individual has unique needs, and because programs must be developed according to these needs, an understanding of genetic diversity among people (such as differences

in cardiorespiratory endurance and motor coordination) is requisite for helping students understand their physical capabilities. But it is not enough for elementary students to learn the facts of fitness; they must have participatory experience. Knowledge is important, but many people who know the facts of fitness do not stay active because they have not learned the habit of regular activity. The best way to learn how to maintain personal fitness is to experience it.

Standard 5: Exhibits responsible personal and social behavior that respects self and others in physical activity.

Responsible behavior includes participation, cooperation, competition, and tolerance, in short, behaving in a manner that doesn't negatively affect others. Children internalize responsible behavior when adults model it themselves and when adults reinforce their expectations for it on a regular basis. Classroom physical activities offer an excellent opportunity for teaching responsible behavior because every child's behavior is visible to everyone else. If youngsters in a competitive game act in an irresponsible fashion, they offer you a "teachable moment" to point out their unacceptable behavior and to help them learn how to win and lose graciously, as well as how to assume responsibility for their performances.

Cooperation precedes the development of competition, which makes it an especially important behavior to teach in elementary physical education. The nature of competitive games demands cooperation, fair play, and sportsmanship, and when these attributes are not present, the joy of participation is lost. Cooperative games teach children that all teammates are needed to reach group goals.

Many diversity and gender issues arise in activity settings, and insightful and caring instruction can destroy negative stereotypes. Learning about the similarities and differences among cultures, genders, and people of different abilities is an important outcome of physical activity. When children see you responding to all students in a caring fashion, they learn to respect others. For those children who face discrimination, the lesson that they belong, that they are loved and respected, and that their successes outweigh their failures can help them develop a positive self-concept.

Back to Class

After the Balloon Volleyball activity in the scenario on page 19, a child who was on the losing team snickers to Bashir that his team "wouldn't have won the game if they'd been using a *real* volleyball." How could Ms. Massoney use this opportunity to model Standard 5?

Standard 6: Values physical activity for health, enjoyment, challenge, self-expression, and/or social interaction.

The value of being active is rarely taught in schools. In fact, many teachers fight an ongoing battle to get their students to sit still. This is a mistake: children want to move, and you can capitalize on this natural inclination by incorporating physical activity into academic lessons. See the Activity Cards accompanying this book for ideas. By encouraging movement throughout their school day, you can help instill in students the value of physical activity.

To value physical activity, students also need knowledge. Students cannot make choices that support their wellness if they don't understand the consequences of their decisions. Simple principles relating physical activity to weight control and stress management, as well as lessons on substance abuse and sun safety, can be woven into daily instruction so children have an opportunity to learn about healthful lifestyles. But again, meeting this standard does not have to turn lessons into sedentary fact-learning experiences. Instead, integrate your instruction into activity and skill-development sessions.

As you can see, the six NASPE standards focus on physical activity and motor skill development, but also promote cognitive development, interpersonal skills, and assimilation of positive values. These are skills that last a lifetime, and incorporating them into your school day is essential. There is no greater goal for teachers than to send students into the world with a trained mind, a healthy body, and a generous character.

Chapter Summary

The Need for Active and Healthy Schools

- The percentage of youth who are overweight has more than tripled in the past 30 years. This increase in overweight is thought to be attributable more to decreased energy expenditure than increased energy intake, although both factors play a role.

- Overweight in childhood, and especially in adolescence, increases the risk of adult obesity.

- Physical activity improves children's health. For overweight children, increased physical activity reduces the percentage of body fat and improves both blood pressure and blood lipid profiles. For all children, increased weight-bearing physical activity improves bone mineral density.

- Physical activity can improve academic performance. On average, students who spend time in physical education classes do equally well or better in academic classes than students who do not.

- Active children tend to become active adults, whereas inactivity in childhood is a predictor of inactivity in adulthood.

America's Wellness Mandate: The WIC Reauthorization Act

● The Child Nutrition and WIC (Women, Infants and Children) Reauthorization Act of 2004 actually took effect in 2006. It mandates that schools receiving federal "school lunch program" funds establish a wellness policy that includes goals for nutrition education, physical activity, and other school-based activities designed to promote student wellness. It does not provide funding for implementation.

● Recommended initiatives include making lunch and recess break times for physical activity, offering regularly scheduled activity breaks, establishing walking programs, making activity contracts with children, and involving parents and after-school programs in goals for increased physical activity.

The Active and Healthy School Environment

● The eight components of an active and healthy school (AHS) environment are as follows: physical education, physical activity breaks, nutrition and healthful eating activities, sun safety instruction, before- and after-school programs, classroom teacher involvement, parental involvement, and community involvement.

● Physical education is that part of the educational program that contributes, primarily through movement experiences, to the total growth and development of all children. It addresses all learning domains: psychomotor, cognitive, and affective.

● Active and healthy schools schedule time for physical activity in three basic formats: morning and afternoon breaks, activity time at lunch, and classroom mini-breaks offered throughout the school day.

● Active and healthy schools provide breakfasts and lunches containing a nutritionally balanced variety of high-quality foods. They also provide nutrition education so that students learn how to make healthful food choices and share nutrition information with their families.

● Sun safety is another important component of active and healthy schools, and should include instruction for teachers, students, and parents. Children should wear protective clothing, sunglasses, and sunscreen and avoid outdoor activity between 10:00 a.m. and 2:00 p.m., except in shaded areas.

● In many AHS environments, the YMCA, Boys and Girls Club, or local recreation department uses the school property for after-school programs. Some schools open early to provide activities for children who are dropped off early. Barriers to before- and after-school programs include cost and transportation.

Students see teachers as role models; thus, encouraging faculty to improve their health through school-based activities is another key component of an AHS environment.

Parental involvement can increase the level of physical activity for an entire family. Some common school-sponsored programs involving parents include activity calendars, physical activity and health fairs, activity days, and charity events.

Community involvement can greatly increase the scope and effectiveness of efforts to increase children's activity levels and health. Organizations that commonly support such efforts include YMCAs, Boys and Girls Clubs, recreation centers, and county public health agencies.

Incorporating Physical Activity into Your Classroom

When you allow time for playing simple games in the classroom, you demonstrate to students that you value physical activity. Classroom physical activities not only benefit children's health, but also help them learn how to get along with others. In addition, watching students engage in physical activity can give you new insights into their personalities and abilities.

One challenge of offering regularly scheduled classroom physical activities is managing the children's behavior. This is discussed in Chapter 5.

Content Standards for Physical Education

Content standards identify the content of a model educational program; that is, what knowledge students should possess and how they should demonstrate that knowledge when they exit a developmental level. Standards also determine the framework of the program, that is, the focus and direction of instruction, assessment, and accountability.

Six content standards for physical education have been identified by the National Association for Sport and Physical Education (NASPE, 2004a). They provide the basis for describing a physically educated person and form the foundation for most physical education programs.

By identifying what a physical education program should accomplish, the NASPE standards can guide you in contributing to these outcomes in your classroom.

Review Questions

Content Review

1. Defend or refute the statement that childhood overweight predicts adult obesity. Cite evidence for your answer.

2. Explain the role of classroom teachers in implementing some of the recommendations of the Child Nutrition and WIC Reauthorization Act of 2004.

3. List and describe the eight components of an active and healthy school environment.

4. Identify the recommended duration and frequency of classroom mini-breaks, and list at least three benefits of these breaks to students and teachers.

5. Propose four ways to get parents involved in increasing students' level of physical activity.

Real World

1. In the faculty lunchroom, you overhear a colleague saying that he doesn't have time for classroom physical activity because he is too busy trying to improve his students' academic performance. How might you respond?

2. At a planning meeting, you raise the issue of the increasing number of overweight children in your community and propose that your school implement an after-school physical activity program. Before you've finished speaking, a more senior teacher interrupts you. "We've looked into that before," she says, "but it would cost too much. We just don't have the resources." How might you respond?

What About You?

Earlier in this chapter, we noted that active teachers increase the chances of students becoming active. In a study by Ernst and Pangrazi (1999), it was found that students were more active when their classroom teacher participated in some of the activities. This study shows the power of teachers' modeling desired student behavior. Reflect on the level of daily physical activity you model for your students. Below, list two or more ways you could demonstrate to your students that you value physical activity.

_____

_____

_____

References and Suggested Readings

American Academy of Pediatrics. (1999). Ultraviolet light: A hazard to children. *Pediatrics*, 104: 328–333.

Anderson, R.E., Crespo, C.J., Bartlett, S.J., Cheskin, L.J., and Pratt, M. (1998). Relationship of physical activity and television watching with body weight and level of fatness among children: Results from the Third National Health and Nutrition Examination Survey. *Journal of the American Medical Association*, 279, 938–942.

Anspaugh, D.J. and Ezell, G. (2008). *Teaching today's health* (8th ed.). San Francisco, CA: Pearson Benjamin Cummings.

Bailey, D.A., Faulkner, R.A., and McKay, H.A. (1996). Growth, physical activity, and bone mineral acquisition. *Exercise and Sport Science Reviews*, 24, 233–266.

Bailey, R.C., Olson, J., Pepper, S.L., Porszaz, J., Barstow, T.J., and Cooper, D.M. (1995). The level and tempo of children's physical activities: An observational study. *Medicine and Science in Sport and Exercise*, 27(7), 1033–1041.

Bar-Or, O. (1995). Health benefits of physical activity during childhood and adolescence. *Physical Activity and Fitness Research Digest*, 2(4), 1–6.

Ernst, M.P. and Pangrazi, R.P. (1999). Effects of a physical activity program on children's activity levels and attraction to physical activity. *Pediatric Exercise Science*, 11, 393–405.

Guo, S.S., and Chumlea, W.C. (1999). Tracking of body mass index in children in relation to over-weight in adulthood. *American Journal of Clinical Nutrition*, 70, 145S–148S.

Guo, S. S., Roche, A. F., Chumlea, W.C., Gardner, J. D., and Siervogel, R.M. (1994). The predictive value of childhood body mass index values for overweight at age 35 y. *American Journal of Clinical Nutrition*, 59, 810–819.

Hanson, T.L., Muller, C., Austion, G., and Lee-Bayha, J. (2005). Research findings about the relationship between student health and academic achievement. In California Department of Education's Getting Results: Developing Safe and Healthy Kids Update 5. Sacramento, CA: CDE Press.

Jago, R. and Baranowski, T. (2004). Non-curricular approaches for increasing physical activity in youth: A review. *Preventive Medicine*, 39(1), 157–163.

Jebb, S.A. and Moore, M.S. (1999). Contribution of a sedentary lifestyle and inactivity to the eti-ology of overweight and obesity: Current evidence and research issues. *Medicine and Science in Sports and Exercise*, 31, S534–S541.

Morgan, C.F., Pangrazi, R.P., and Beighle, A. (2003). Using pedometers to promote physical activity in physical education. *Journal of Physical Education Recreation and Dance*, 74(7), 33–38.

Must, A., Jacques, P.F., Dallal, G.E., Bajema, C.J., and Dietz, W.H. (1992). Long-term morbidity and mortality of overweight adolescents: A follow-up of the Harvard Growth Study of 1922 to 1935. *New England Journal of Medicine*, 327, 1350–1355.

National Association for Sport and Physical Education. (2004a). *Moving into the future: National standards for physical education* (2nd ed.). Reston, VA: Author.

National Association for Sport and Physical Education. (2004b). *Physical activity for children: A statement of guidelines* (2nd ed.). Reston, VA: Author.

Pangrazi, R.P., Beighle, A., Vehige, T., and Vack, C. (2003). Evaluating the effectiveness of the State of Arizona's Promoting Lifestyle Activity for Youth program. *Journal of School Health*, 73(8), 317–321.

Pellegrini, A.D., Huberty, P.D., and Jones, I. (1995). The effects of recess timing on children's playground and classroom behaviors. *American Educational Research Journal*, 32(4), 845–864.

President's Council on Physical Fitness and Sports. (2007). *The president's challenge handbook*. Washington, DC: President's Council on Physical Fitness and Sports.

Raitakari, O.T., Porkka, K.V.K., Taimela, S., Telama, R., Rasanen, L., and Viikari, J.S.A. (1994). Effects of persistent physical activity and inactivity on coronary risk factors in children and young adults. *American Journal of Epidemiology*, 140, 195–205.

Roberts, D.F., Foehr, U.G., and Rideout, V. (2005). *Generation M: Media in the lives of 8–18 year olds*. Palo Alto, CA: Kaiser Family Foundation.

Sallis, J.F., McKenzie, T.L., Kolody, B., Lewis, M., Marshall, S., and Rosengard, P. (1999). Effects of health-related physical education on academic achievement: Project SPARK. *Research Quarterly for Exercise and Sport,* 70, 127–134.

Stern, R.S., Weinstein, M.C., and Baker, S.G. (1986). Risk reduction for nonmelanoma skin cancer with childhood sunscreen use. *Archives of Dermatology*, 122: 537–545.

Telama, R., Yang, X., Laakso, L., and Viikari, J. (1997). Physical activity in childhood and adolescence as predictors of physical activity in young adulthood. *American Journal of Preventative Medicine*, 13, 317–323.

Trudeau, F., Laurencelle, L., Tremblay, J., Rajic, M., and Shephard, R.J. (1998). A long-term follow-up of participants in the Trois-Rivieres semi-longitudinal study of growth and development. *Pediatric Exercise Science*, 10, 366–377.

Tudor-Locke, C., Lee, S.M., Morgan, C.F., Beighle, A., and Pangrazi, R.P. (2006). Children's pedometer-determined physical activity patterns during the segmented school day. *Medicine and Science in Sports and Exercise*, 38(10), 1732–1738.

U.S. Department of Health and Human Services. (1996). *Physical activity and health: A report of the Surgeon General*. Atlanta, GA: Centers for Disease Control and Prevention, National Center for Chronic Disease Prevention and Health Promotion.

U.S. Department of Health and Human Services. (2000). *Healthy people 2010: National health promotion and disease objectives*. Washington, DC: U.S. Government Printing Office.

U.S. Department of Health and Human Services. (2002). *Prevalence of overweight among children and adolescents: United States, 1999*. Center for Disease Control and Prevention, National Center for Health Statistics.

Welk, G.J., Wood, K., and Morss, G. (2003). Parental influences on physical activity in children: An exploration of the potential mechanisms. *Pediatric Exercise Science*, 15(1), 19–33.

Whitaker, R.C., Wright, J.A., Pepe, M.S., Seidel, K.D., and Dietz, W.H. (1997). Predicting obesity in young adulthood from childhood and parental obesity. *New England Journal of Medicine*, 337, 869–873.

Web Resources

Child Nutrition and WIC Reauthorization Act of 2004:
www.fns.usda.gov/TN/Healthy/108-265.pdf
Food Research and Action Center/Highlights of WIC Reauthorization Act:
www.frac.org/html/federal_food_programs/cnreauthro/cnrc_highlights.htm
National Heart Lung and Blood Institute:
www.nhlbi.nih.gov
Sunwise School Program:
www.epa.gov/sunwise

2 Understanding Children's Needs and Readiness for Physical Activity

Learning Objectives

After reading this chapter, you will be able to . . .

- Identify several needs of children that can be met through classroom physical activity.
- Provide a rationale for adapting your method of teaching physical activity to accommodate a child's stage of growth.
- Explain why boys and girls are similar in strength and endurance prior to adolescence.
- Describe the relationship between maturation and physical performance.
- Discuss children's capacity for aerobic activity, including distance running.
- Explain how excess weight affects children's physical performance.
- Describe the effect of high environmental heat and humidity on children's activity and health.
- Provide a rationale for adapting your method of teaching physical activity to accommodate a child's level of skill development.

Classroom Challenge

It's a hot and humid September afternoon, and Mr. Kohl's fourth-grade class is getting the fidgets. He decides to take them outside for a mini-break. Since they'll be discussing the American Revolution when they return to class, he divides the kids into Redcoats and Minutemen and improvises a running game in which the Redcoats have to run the entire periphery of the field, dodging the Minutemen, while trying to make their way to a "safe" post. If they are tagged, they have to start over. He plans to let the kids play for 15 minutes, but 5 minutes into the game, one of the Redcoats, Jason, throws himself onto the grass. Jason is the heaviest student in Mr. Kohl's class, and he is panting and sweaty. Mr. Kohl approaches him and asks why he has stopped participating. "I need a break!" Jason answers. "It's too hot, and I'm no good at running games!"

Mr. Kohl speaks without thinking. "The other kids don't seem to be bothered by the heat! And you need the exercise more than they do! I'll give you 30 seconds, and then I want you back in the game!"

Jason frowns and crosses his arms over his chest. After 30 seconds, he gets up and walks slowly back to the field. He then leans against the safe post for the remainder of the game.

To promote physical activity effectively, you need a clear understanding of children—their needs and urges, their characteristics, and how they develop skills. Without such understanding, you risk presenting activities that are not physically or developmentally appropriate or that do not appeal to children. Sometimes classroom teachers avoid teaching physical activity because they lack this understanding. In short, they feel incompetent. But imagine if you chose not to teach your students fractions for the same reason! Obviously, a better strategy is to develop the requisite competence. Because physical activity is essential to children's health, you must learn how to teach it in a way that engages students and accommodates their needs, characteristics, and level of skill. This chapter should help you do just that.

Understanding the Needs of Children

A **need** is defined here as a drive to do or accomplish something. Needs are similar among children of all ages and are not affected by developmental maturity. However, children's needs can be influenced by their genetics, environment, or social contacts, including parents, peers, and teachers. The following discussion will help you gain a general understanding of children's shared needs.

The Need for Movement

Children have an insatiable appetite for moving, performing, and being active. They run for the sheer joy of running. They want to touch, pick up, move, and handle objects; to try things for themselves; and to experience learning by using their active bodies. In short, in contrast to most adults, children are kinesthetic learners: activity is the means by which they learn. In the classroom, physical activity not only offers an outlet for children to satisfy their need for movement, but it actually facilitates their overall learning.

The Need for Success and Approval

Children like to achieve and to have their achievements recognized. They wilt under criticism and disapproval, whereas encouragement and friendly support promotes growth and development. Failure can lead to frustration, lack of interest, and inefficient learning. Successes should far outweigh failures, and students should achieve a measure of success during each session of physical activity. It's important that you structure classroom physical activities in a way that ensures that all of your students can achieve an adequate level of success.

The Need for Peer Acceptance and Tolerance

Children want others to accept, respect, and like them. By teaching peer acceptance and tolerance in the classroom, you help students develop respect for others in other domains as well. Learning to work with others who may be different from themselves, feeling accepted as a contributing team member, and sharing accomplishments with friends are important outcomes of student participation in physical activity.

The Need to Cooperate and Compete

Children want to work and play with other children. They find satisfaction in being an integral part of a group, and often experience sadness when they are rejected. Cooperation is the foundation of competition, and it needs to be taught early in the primary grades so that students can enjoy competitive experiences as they mature. Constructive competition is not possible among children who do not cooperate. On the other hand, children who do learn to cooperate often discover that the joy of being part of a group far outlasts the fleeting satisfaction of beating someone in a one-on-one competition.

The Need for Physical Competency

Both boys and girls are eager to gain competence in physical activities. Youngsters who are overweight, have a chronic illness, or have any type of disability often suffer from feelings of humiliation. When you offer physical activities that give all students an opportunity to feel good about being active, you help a group of students become a group of friends.

Developing a sense of **perceived competence** ("I can") is often even more important than developing actual competence. Students who *believe* they are capable will participate more fully in an activity and are able to derive satisfaction from participation in itself. Students who perceive that they are not "good at it" will avoid activities and feel a diminished sense of self-worth.

The Need for Adventure and Novelty

The need for adventure and novelty motivates children to participate in exciting or unusual activities and teaching methodologies. When youngsters ask, "What are we going to do today?" they are expressing this need. Introduce a variety of classroom activities to keep your students motivated and looking forward to the next movement experience.

The Need for Creative Satisfaction

Children like to try different ways of doing things, experiment with a variety of materials, change aspects of their environment, and devise new strategies for accomplishing goals. By finding different ways to express themselves physically, they satisfy this need for creativity. Similarly, when you present games and activities in a fluid rather than a rigid manner—for instance by encouraging students to experiment with changing the rules and creating new versions of activities to suit their needs— you help satisfy their creativity needs.

The Need for Rhythmic Expression

Children have an innate need for rhythmic expression. Music teachers often offer students the opportunity to experience rhythmic activities, but classroom teachers can meet this need as well with physical activities that incorporate marching, drumming, stomping, and clapping to rhythm. Jump rope and other movement games with rhymes also offer children the chance to hear and feel rhythm. Many sports also incorporate effective and beautiful movements that are rhythmic in nature.

The Need to Know

Young people are naturally curious. They are interested not only in what they are doing but also in why they are doing it. When you take a moment to share with your class the reasons why you are offering a particular activity, including the contribution it makes to their physical development, you motivate them to participate.

(Back to Class)

Now that you have a better understanding of children's needs related to physical activity, think back to the chapter-opening scenario. When Mr. Kohl asked Jason why he had stopped playing, what was Jason's reply? What do his words reveal about his unmet needs? Did Mr. Kohl miss an opportunity to foster perceived competence? If so, what might he have said to help meet Jason's needs and kindle enthusiasm for physical activity?

Understanding the Characteristics of Children

The needs of children represent broad traits that are typical of most children regardless of age, gender, or race. In contrast, **characteristics** are age- and maturity-specific attributes that influence children's learning. Table 2.1 lists physical, cognitive, and social characteristics of children grouped by grade level. It also identifies the implications of these characteristics for teachers, providing information that should help you select appropriate activities for your students.

Growth Patterns

Growth patterns are generally controlled by a child's genetic makeup. Although unhealthy parents or poor nutrition can negatively affect growth and development, this section examines typical maturation differences common to the majority of youngsters.

Rate of Growth

All children follow the same general growth pattern, with growth occurring at different rates in different periods throughout children's developmental years. Within this general pattern, however, each child's timing is unique. Some children are tall and appear physically mature for their chronological age, whereas others mature more slowly. Only when the deviation from the norm is excessive should teachers and parents become concerned. When assessing a child's growth pattern, it is useful to consult a velocity curve, which reveals the rate of average growth of children on a year-to-year basis (Figure 2.1).

As you can see, children go through a rapid period of growth from birth to age five. From age six to the onset of adolescence, growth velocity slows. This makes the elementary school years an ideal time to learn motor skills. A general rule regarding motor learning is that when skeletal growth is rapid, the ability to acquire new skills decreases. Thus, if children fail to acquire motor skills during the

Table 2.1 Characteristics of Children and Implications for Teachers

Kindergarten Through Second Grade

Characteristics	Implications for Teachers
Physical Development	
Noisy, active, egocentric, imitative, and want attention	Offer active games and dramatic story plays where students have individual roles.
Fine motor skills not developed	Avoid games that require throwing, catching, and kicking small or fast-moving objects.
Enjoy rhythms	Use music that encourages moving rhythmically in small and large groups.
Tire and recover quickly	Offer 20–30 seconds of activity followed by the same amount of rest to keep students on task.
Cognitive Development	
Short attention spans	Change activities often; avoid playing the same activities day after day.
Desire to understand movement and games	In short, concise terms, explain why movements and games are played and how to perform well.
Need to understand teamwork	Explain how all players like to participate and be part of a team.
Approaching peak of creativity	Allow students to modify activities; encourage imagery and make believe.
Need to know simple rules of activities	Teach activities with one or two rules; reinforce following rules.
Social Development	
Little gender difference in play interests	Offer the same activities for both boys and girls.
Most students have strong self-concepts and think they can perform any challenge.	Use this as a stepping stone to build positive self-concepts; reinforce performances; avoid embarrassing them; allow time for sharing performances.
Like pleasing the teacher	Teacher approval is powerful, i.e., "I like the way John is freezing." Reinforcement of performance is important.
Want to be the center of attention	Simple games offer many opportunities for teaching students that they can't all be the center of attention; teach sharing the spotlight.

(continued)

Table 2.1: continued

Third Through Sixth Grade

Characteristics	Implications for Teachers
Physical Development	
Increasing interest in sports with age	Give students opportunities to talk about sports and sports heroes; assist them in learning how to play sports and be a part of a team.
Hand-eye coordination is developing	Offer many tossing and catching activities; use different objects to develop tracking skills.
Reaction time is slow in grades 3 and 4	Use objects that are soft and don't travel too fast to avoid developing the fear of getting hurt.
Individual skill and maturity differences among students increase with age	Accept a wide range of performance; avoid letting some students dominate activities.
Girls begin growth spurt in grades 5 and 6	Encourage girls to develop pride in their ability; help boys understand that girls are more mature at this age and may excel physically.
Cognitive Development	
Less egocentric and more interested in group play	Offer small-group activities and the opportunity to work with other students.
Need to understand rules of games	Following the rules becomes important; teach the penalties for not following rules.
Older students become interested in learning and applying game strategy	Games that require thinking and working out strategies should be taught.
Interested in how the body functions	Offer basic information about training, the respiratory system, checking heart rate, and factors that influence performance.
Attention span increases with age	Provide opportunities for students to be more self-directed in their learning; when motivated, students will practice skills on their own.

elementary school years, it will be difficult for them to do so later on, when their growth accelerates again.

Height and Weight

During the pre-adolescent school years, boys are generally taller and heavier than girls. However, girls generally reach their adolescent growth spurt first, and typically

Table 2.1: continued

Third Through Sixth Grade

Characteristics	Implications for Teachers
Social Development	
Want to perform well and be admired for skill level	Athletic ability is a strong indicator of popularity among youth; help less-athletic children experience success and acceptance.
Losing becomes more difficult with age	Children need to learn to be gracious in losing and winning; discuss and practice proper behavior in both situations.
Cliques and peer groups become important	To ensure all students are included in activities, offer activities in which all students play important roles or positions, or share roles and positions with students taking turns; discuss the importance of inclusion.
Little interest in the opposite sex in the intermediate grades	Avoid forcing students into difficult situations with the opposite sex; they can accept all partners without having to hold hands; change partners often.

grow taller and heavier than boys during the fifth- and sixth-grade years. Boys quickly catch up, however, and on average surpass girls in height, size, and strength by approximately age 14. You can observe this pattern in the growth charts shown in **Figures 2.2** and **2.3**, which are based on a large national sample of children. These charts offer stature and weight percentiles for children aged 2 through 20. They reveal marked differences among children in the U.S. population. In addition, they serve as excellent reference points for discussing concerns about a student's growth pattern with parents.

Body Proportions

Figure 2.4 illustrates how body proportions change with growth. The head makes up one-fourth of the child's total length at birth and about one-sixth at age six. In addition, the trunk is longer in relation to the legs throughout early childhood. Young children continue to have big heads and short legs relative to their height through about the second grade.

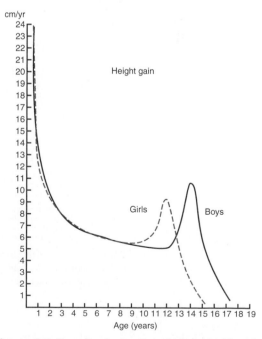

Figure 2.1 Growth velocity curve for height. *Adapted from Tanner, J.M., Whitehouse, R.H., and Takaishi, M. (1966). Archives of Diseases in Childhood, 41, 466.*

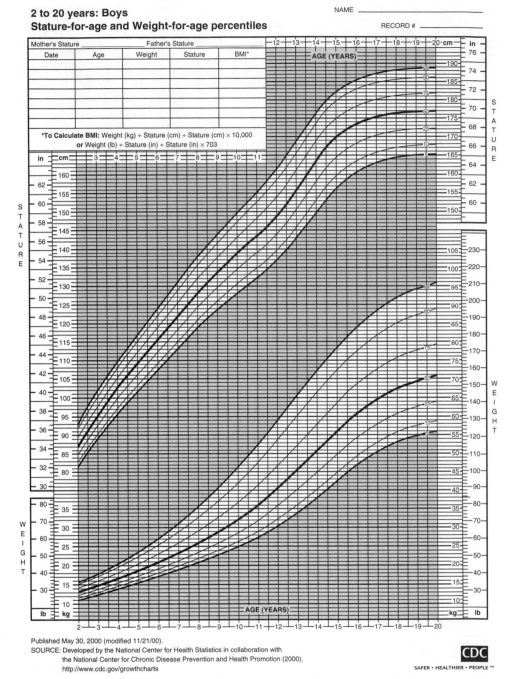

Figure 2.2 Growth chart for boys 2 to 20 years. Boys' stature-for-age and weight-for-age percentiles, 2000. *Courtesy of the National Center for Health Statistics in collaboration with the National Center for Chronic Disease Prevention and Health Promotion (2000).*

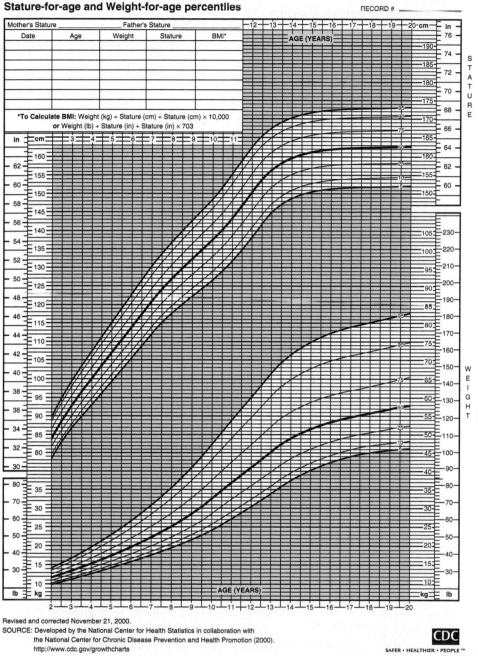

Figure 2.3 Growth chart for girls 2 to 20 years. Girls' stature-for-age and weight-for-age percentiles, 2000. *Courtesy of the National Center for Health Statistics in collaboration with the National Center for Chronic Disease Prevention and Health Promotion (2000).*

Because kindergarten through grade two students have short legs in relation to their upper body and heads, they have a high center of gravity and are "top-heavy." This helps explain why kindergarten students often fall over and have limited success when trying to perform activities such as push ups or sit ups. Thus, primary grade teachers need to understand how their students' normal growth and development can limit success in certain physical activities at certain times.

The ratio of leg length (standing height) to trunk length (sitting height) gradually evens out during the upper elementary grade years. This growth gradually lowers the center of gravity and gives children increased stability and balance. From the onset of puberty, the trunk grows rapidly, contributing more than leg growth to the increased height seen during the adolescent growth spurt for both boys and girls.

Strength and Endurance

Strength is a characteristic that greatly influences children's performance in physical activity. A study by Rarick and Dobbins (1975) identified and weighted factors that contribute to children's motor performance. The factor identified as most important was strength or power in relation to body size. High relative strength helped predict which students were most capable of performing motor skills.

In the elementary school years, muscular strength increases linearly with chronological age (Beunen, 1989). In other words, as children grow older they become stronger. Pre-adolescent children show few strength differences between the sexes. Boys and girls generally perform similarly in strength activities such as push ups and sit ups. Many teachers accept lower performances from girls even though they are capable of strength activities equal to those of boys. Expectations should be similar for elementary school boys and girls.

Strength differences do occur among children of widely differing weight and height, regardless of gender. Differences in weight and height should be taken into consideration when pairing children for competitive activities such as races, games that require physical contact, and games that require strength. Problems occur when a student is paired with someone who is considerably taller, heavier, or more mature and therefore stronger. As a classroom teacher, when you match students, for safety reasons remember that weight and stature are much more important factors than gender.

The Rarick and Dobbins study also found that the fourth most important factor in predicting children's performance of motor skills was the amount of body fat in relation to body size. Not surprisingly, the relationship was negative; that is, excessive body fat detracts from motor performance by reducing a child's strength relative to his or her body size. Overweight children may be stronger than normal-weight children in absolute terms, but they are less strong when strength is adjusted for body weight. This lack of relative strength makes it more difficult to perform a strength-related task (e.g., push up or curl up) compared to normal-weight children. Thus, you will probably need to modify certain activities to keep your overweight students "turned on" to physical activity. If you don't, and your overweight students frequently experience failure in performing physical activities, they may go on to choose a sedentary lifestyle. Have different expectations for individual children

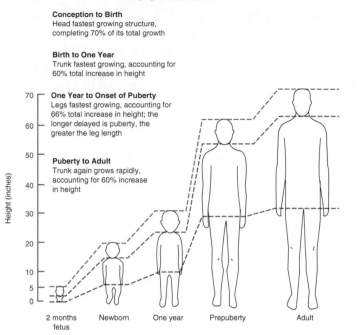

Figure 2.4 Changing body proportions from conception to adulthood. *Adapted from Whipple, D. (1966). Dynamics of development: Euthenic pediatrics (p. 122). New York: McGraw Hill.*

rather than giving an entire class the same physical challenge. For information on strength training and children, visit the American College of Sports Medicine (ACSM) website (see Web Resources), and type "youth strength training" in the search bar.

Maturation

Teachers have long recognized differences in emotional maturity among students of similar ages. Differences in physical maturity have been less widely recognized, yet they're important for teachers to understand because they greatly influence children's performance in physical activities. A method used in research studies to determine physical maturity is to compare chronological age with **skeletal age**. Ossification (hardening) of the bones occurs in the center of the bone shaft and at the ends of the long bones (growth plates). The level of ossification that a child has reached can be identified by X-rays of the wrist bones. When the images are then compared against a set of standardized X-rays, this comparison reveals a child's skeletal age (Gruelich and Pyle, 1959; Roche, Chumlea, and Thissen, 1988). Children whose chronological age is behind their skeletal age are said to be late (or slow) maturers. Children whose skeletal age is ahead of their chronological age are considered early (fast) maturers.

Studies examining skeletal age (Gruelich and Pyle, 1959; Krahenbuhl and Pangrazi, 1983) consistently show that a five- to six-year variation in maturity exists among youngsters in a typical classroom. For example, third graders (8-year-olds) will range in skeletal age from 5 to 11 years. It would not be appropriate to ask a 5-year-old kindergarten child to perform tasks that 11-year-olds are expected to accomplish. The message here is that even though students in a classroom may be around the same age, there are large individual differences in physical maturity. Teachers need to monitor and adjust program activities to allow students to progress at a rate suitable to their level of physical maturity.

Early-maturing children of both sexes are generally heavier and taller for their age than average- or late-maturing children. They have larger amounts of muscle and bone tissue, and also tend to carry a greater percentage of their body weight as fat tissue. The motor performance of boys is related to skeletal maturity because more-mature boys usually perform better than less-mature boys on motor tasks (Clarke, 1971). For girls, however, motor performance is less related to physiological maturity. Among girls, a study by Malina (1978) showed that late maturation is commonly associated with exceptional motor performance.

Admittedly, the job of teaching would be easier if all students could learn at the same rate. However, since students do not mature at the same rate and may not be at comparable levels of readiness to learn, it is best to help them progress at their individual rates.

Capacity for Aerobic Activity

Aerobic activity is sustained movement performed at a pace for which the body can supply adequate oxygen to meet the demands of the activity. When performing aerobic activity, we typically experience increases in heart rate and respiration. Aerobic activity can be of high, moderate, or low intensity.

Children's Capacity for High-Intensity Aerobic Activity

Adults typically want to exercise as quickly as possible so they can get on with their work and other interests. Thus, they tend to choose exercise that is high intensity, burning the greatest number of calories in the shortest period of time. Children's preferences are exactly opposite: they usually prefer low-intensity activity and high volume. For example, many children enjoy long sessions of backyard exploration, swinging, or riding a bike on level terrain.

Although most children also enjoy short bursts of high-intensity activity, such as dashing away from an opponent in a game of tag, they fatigue quickly. This makes it difficult for them to sustain high-intensity activity, such as when running a mile. On the other hand, children recover rapidly, so you can successfully plan longer sessions of high-intensity activity if you intersperse the bouts of activity with opportunities to rest. You can also have children pause periodically during aerobic activities for periods of restful stretching and strength-development. In short, aerobic activities for children should be presented in a manner that maintains their motivation and love of movement, while taking into account their natural activity cycles.

Some people are concerned that children may actually be harmed physiologically by high-intensity activity. There was concern at one time that the large blood vessels do not grow in proportion to other body parts. This, it was theorized, placed a child's heart and the circulatory system under stress during strenuous exercise. However, research over many years has established that fatigue causes healthy children to stop exercising long before any danger occurs (Shephard, 1984).

Physically training elementary school children with vigorous exercise does not appear to improve their performance of aerobic activity. A study by Payne and Morrow (1993) analyzed 28 studies dealing with the impact of exercise on aerobic performance in children. The results showed training caused little, if any, increase in aerobic power in pre-pubescent children. On the other hand, pushing children to perform high-intensity exercise may instill in them a dislike for all forms of physical activity. Thus, whether or not your students are physiologically capable of exercising strenuously, it's wise to avoid forcing them to do so. Provide children with varied opportunities to be active and praise them for their participation and efforts.

Overweight Children's Capacity for Aerobic Activity

Being overweight reduces children's ability to perform physical tasks (Bar-Or, 1983). Overweight children must expend more energy compared to normal-weight youngsters to accomplish the same task, and they perform at a higher percentage of their aerobic capacity. This gives overweight children less reserve capacity and causes them to perceive activities as requiring more effort, which indeed they do (Bar-Or and Ward, 1989).

Despite these differences, some classroom teachers require their entire class to participate in the same aerobic activity. Most commonly, teachers instruct their students to run a certain distance. When their increased exertion causes overweight students to perceive the task as too demanding, these teachers perceive that "overweight kids don't like to run." Indeed, many overweight children don't like to run because they cannot keep up with their peers. Thus, their needs for both peer acceptance and physical competency go unmet. Furthermore, running may not even be a physically appropriate activity for them because it can place too much stress on their joints. For all these reasons, it is inappropriate and counterproductive to require overweight children to run—or to perform other types of aerobic activities—to the same standards as normal-weight children.

To avoid this problem, rather than basing your performance expectations on distance, speed, or number of repetitions, base them on *time*. A principle to keep in mind is that the intensity of the activity is secondary to the amount of time a student is involved in it. In weight control, for example, long bouts of moderate activity are more effective than short bouts of intense exercise. Allow students to adjust the intensity of a physical activity to fit their individual needs. They know better than anyone else what they are capable of performing. When you base your expectations on time, you will not fault overweight runners for covering less distance than lean runners during a stipulated time period, or for performing fewer repetitions of an assigned exercise. Instead, you will reward all children for doing their best.

Concerns Related to Distance Running

Even for children of normal weight, the advisability of distance running is the subject of debate. The American Academy of Pediatrics Executive Committee (1991) has identified a number of concerns centered on distance running, including potential long-term adverse effects that may not be seen for many years after a running

program has started. Two main areas of concern are psychological consequences and physical consequences.

Psychological problems can result when adults set unrealistic goals for distance running by children. A child who participates in distance running primarily for adult approval may tire of it after a time and quit, or may push on unadvisedly while chafing under the pressure. In either case, psychological damage may be done and the child discouraged, either immediately or in the long run, from participating in future activity. Elementary school children should be given opportunities to run for the sheer joy of it, without fear of adult assessment. Children's sense of accomplishment, satisfaction, and appreciation—by parents, teachers, and peers—simply for participating will foster their involvement in running and other physical activities throughout childhood and in later life.

For school-age children, participation in distance running training and competition also poses physical dangers. A position taken by the International Athletics Association Federation (IAAF) Medical Committee (1983) states, "The danger certainly exists that with over-intensive training, separation of the growth plates may occur in the pelvic region, the knee, or the ankle. While this could heal with rest, nevertheless definitive information is lacking whether in years to come harmful effects may result." In view of this concern, it is the opinion of the committee that training and competition for long-distance track and road-running events should not be encouraged in young children. It is suggested that up to the age of 12, children not run more than 800 meters (one-half mile) in competition.

Concerns Related to Fitness Testing

We need to help children and families incorporate physical activity into their lifestyles. Health goals for the nation for the year 2010 are primarily stated in terms of activity objectives rather than fitness objectives (USDHHS, 2000). These goals emphasize reducing inactivity and increasing **moderate to vigorous physical activity (MVPA).** Unfortunately, rather than promoting MVPA, many schools have focused on testing children for physical fitness. This can be counterproductive for two reasons. First, when fitness test results become more important than participation in regular activity, children learn the importance of short-term goals (doing well on the test) rather than long-term lifestyle changes (daily activity). Second, when fitness testing anoints only a few athletically gifted children and fails the majority, students' needs for competency and success are not met and their motivation to be physically active decreases. In contrast, programs that increase the activity patterns of all students provide opportunities for recognizing children for their willingness to participate rather than their achievement, and promote long-term health.

Many schools test their students' fitness by having them run a mile. Unfortunately, the mile run test has probably done more to turn students off to lifetime physical activity than any other single practice. Concerns about using the mile run as a fitness test include lack of physical preparedness and the psychological stress it causes some children.

Running a mile safely requires at least a minimal level of cardiovascular conditioning. Yet teachers often test children at the start of the school year, after a summer during which children may not have had adequate physical activity to prepare them to participate safely in the activity. In addition, in many parts of the country, the start of the school year is hot and humid, increasing the stress placed on the cardiovascular system during the run. If the mile run must be used to test fitness, the recommendation is to test only at the end of the school year after youngsters have had an opportunity to become more conditioned. If this is not possible, the test should be delayed at least four to six weeks to allow time for students to get conditioned. Rowland (1990) recommends starting with a one-eighth mile run/walk and gradually building to a mile run/walk over a four-week period.

Psychological stress results when teachers require children to run an entire mile before their level of performance is assessed. Too often, this policy creates a humiliating event in which overweight children and those with asthma or other physical limitations finish last and have to stay on the track much longer.

A better alternative is to completely avoid using the mile run as a test. A new aerobic test called the PACER has been designed for administration indoors. The PACER is part of a Fitnessgram/Activitygram that is available from Human Kinetics (Cooper Institute, 2007). This test involves running back and forth between two lines 20 meters apart within a certain time limit. Students who are less able can stop when they reach their limit, while children with more athletic capacity are able to run for longer periods of time. For more information on fitness testing, visit the President's Challenge website, listed in the Web Resources section at the end of this chapter.

Ability to Endure Heat Stress

Use care when exercising children in warm climates. As discussed in the accompanying News Clip, some school districts cancel recess when the temperature rises. Although hot days do not necessarily mean that exercise must stop, certain measures should be used to avoid heat-related illness. Children are not "little adults," and they do not adapt to extremes of temperature as effectively as adults do for the following reasons (Bar-Or, 1983; American Academy of Pediatrics, 2000):

- Children have higher surface area-to-mass ratios than do adults. This allows a greater amount of heat to transfer between the environment and the body.
- When walking or running, children produce more body heat per unit of mass than do adults. Because they are not as efficient at executing movement patterns, children generate more metabolic heat than do adults performing a similar task.
- Sweating capacity is not as great in children as it is in adults, so children have a reduced ability to cool their bodies.
- The ability to convey heat via blood from the body core to the skin is reduced in children because of their lower cardiac output at a given oxygen uptake.
- Children appear to adjust to heat up to two times more slowly than adults.

These physiological differences put children at a distinct disadvantage compared with adults when exercising in an environment where the ambient air temperature is higher than skin temperature. Also, children do not instinctively drink enough liquids to replenish fluids lost during exercise, increasing their risk for dehydration.

The American Academy of Pediatrics (2000) offers the following guidelines for exercising children in hot climates:

● The intensity of activities that last 30 minutes or more should be reduced whenever relative humidity and air temperature are above critical levels. **Table 2.2** shows the relationship between humidity and air temperature, and when activity should be moderated.

Too Hot for Recess?

When temperatures in Greenville, South Carolina, broke the 100-degree mark for the first few days of the 2007 school year, the school district canceled recess for all K–2 children. Citing the fact that the intense heat is dangerous for children because they don't process heat the same way that adults do, Teri Mitchell, a representative for Safe Kids Upstate, an advocacy group for children's safety, added that the American Academy of Pediatrics urges young children to take about 30–45 minutes to get used to the heat before beginning any intensive activity and to drink plenty of fluids. She noted that in some cases children who go to the emergency room for heat illness have become dehydrated before they actually start their activities.

This assertion is supported by research conducted by Douglas Casa, director of athletic training education at the University of Connecticut. Casa visited youth soccer camps and found that two-thirds of the children were dehydrated before they even began playing and that most did not drink enough throughout games to replace the fluids they were losing. Fortunately, he also found that teaching the kids about proper hydration was all it took to get them to drink more.

Source: Adapted from "Upstate Burns through Heat Records with 102-Degree Day," *The Greenville News,* August 22, 2007, at http://greenvilleonline.com/apps/pbcs.dll/article?AID=/20070822/NEWS01/708220378/1004.

take action!

1. Find out whether or not your local school district has a policy in place for altering children's activity when the temperatures rise. If so, what actions are taken, and how high does the temperature have to go before prompting a change in the school-day routine? Presuming the schools in your district are air-conditioned, can you recommend a more healthful alternative to canceling recess entirely?

2. Most healthcare associations recommend drinking at least eight to ten 8-ounce glasses of fluid daily, and more if you are physically active, especially in hot weather. How much fluid do you drink each day? Is your urine typically clear to pale yellow, indicating adequate hydration, or dark yellow to brown, indicating dehydration? If necessary, write up a plan for increasing your fluid intake gradually over the next two weeks.

3. Are children in your local school district chronically dehydrated like the children in the Casa study? List the actions you could take to find an answer to this question.

At the beginning of a strenuous exercise program or after traveling to a warmer climate, the intensity and duration of exercise should be restrained initially and then gradually increased over a period of 10–14 days to acclimate to the heat.

Children should be hydrated 20–30 minutes before strenuous activity. During the activity, drinking cool tap water periodically (e.g., 150 ml, about ¼ cup, every 30 minutes for a child weighing 90 lb) should be implemented. If youngsters are adequately hydrated before going out for recess or to a physical education class, it probably is not necessary to drink until the end of the exercise period unless the session is unusually long or conditions are unusually severe.

Clothing should be lightweight and limited to one layer of absorbent material to facilitate evaporation of sweat and to expose as much skin to the air as possible.

Table 2.2 **Weather Guide**	
When the humidity and air temperature exceed these levels, intense activity should be curtailed.	
Humidity Level (%)	Air Temperature (°F)
40	90
50	85
60	80
70	75
80	70
90	65
100	60

The committee identifies children with the following conditions as being at a potentially high risk for heat stress: obesity, febrile (feverish) state, cystic fibrosis, gastrointestinal infection, diabetes insipidus, diabetes mellitus, chronic heart failure, caloric malnutrition, anorexia nervosa, sweating insufficiency syndrome, and mental retardation.

Back to Class

In our chapter-opening scenario, Jason took himself out of the game of Redcoats and Minutemen. Identify two characteristics of all children that Mr. Kohl does not appear to have considered in assigning this game. Now identify at least one reason that the game was even more challenging for Jason.

Understanding Children's Skill Development

The learning and development of motor skills varies among individual children of similar chronological age. However, the *sequence* of skill development in youngsters and the *stages* of learning through which they progress are similar.

Sequence of Skill Development

Three development patterns typify the sequence of skill development in elementary school children:

1. Development, in general, proceeds from head to foot (cephalocaudal); that is, coordination and management of body parts develop in the upper body before the lower. For example, children develop throwing skills before kicking competency.
2. Development occurs from inside to outside (proximodistal). Children control their arms before they control their hands. They reach for objects before they can grasp them.
3. Development proceeds from general to specific. Large motor movements are learned before fine motor coordination and refined movement patterns. As children learn motor skills, non-productive movement is gradually eliminated. When learners begin to eliminate wasteful and tense movements and are able to concentrate on repeatedly producing a smooth and consistent performance, motor learning is occurring.

Stages of Skill Development

Children also acquire skills in a natural progression of stages even though they do not all learn each skill at the same rate. Encouraging youngsters to progress at a rate that is best suited for their stage helps to foster their self-esteem and keeps them motivated. This premise forms the basis for teaching developmentally appropriate activities.

In general, children in kindergarten through second grade should be offered activities that are minimally difficult and that are performed either individually or with a partner, to increase the children's chances of success. Examples are tossing and catching, striking a stationary object, and playing games that incorporate fundamental **locomotor movements** (movements where the body travels through space). The number of performance techniques these young children have to concentrate on while performing a skill should be minimized so that they can focus on a single point.

As youngsters mature and progress into grades three and four, they can handle more challenging tasks. Many activities are performed within small groups at this stage. Environmental factors such as different speeds of objects, different sizes of objects, and games requiring locomotor movements and specialized skills (throwing, catching, and so on) are introduced at this level.

In grades five and six, students use skills in a greater variety of sport and game situations. Simple skills previously learned are sequenced into more complex motor patterns. Cognitive decisions about when to use a skill and how to incorporate strategy into the game are integrated into children's learning experiences at this level.

It is common to identify three stages through which children progress in their development of motor skills. Different terms are used, but researchers refer to a beginning or introductory level, a semiskilled or intermediate level, and a mastery or advanced level. Although these stages are not exact, they do offer insight about how children learn and how you should teach them. At the same time, there will always be exceptions. Expect to vary your instruction frequently to meet the developmental needs of individual students. (*Note:* In Chapter 3, we discuss children's acquisition of four specific sport-related skills: throwing, catching, kicking, and striking.)

Introductory Level

Students at the introductory level may have no perception of how to perform a skill. This may be their first exposure to the skill, and they will need time and practice to develop the basic skill pattern. Usually, the initial performance is a rough approximation of the skill, and children find it difficult to refine their movements at this stage. Frustration often sets in because the success rate is low. Physical and mental fatigue show up quickly and students often quit as soon as they tire. By modifying the task at regular intervals, you can help students stay focused. As a general rule, when a number of students go off task, it is time to change the task or to refocus students by discussing the skill for 10–20 seconds. Short and frequent breaks help keep young students on task.

Incidentally, children are no different from adults in their frustration over learning new skills. People of all ages respond the same way if they perceive they are failing to learn a skill that is novel and difficult. An example is the response of adults learning juggling skills. Many adults find juggling difficult to master. In the attempt, they quickly become frustrated and go off task by talking to others, laughing, teasing others, or asking to go to a different challenge.

The following are some key points to remember when working with students who are at the introductory stage for a new skill:

- Teach one point at a time. Few people can concentrate on two focus points at once. For example, if you are teaching catching skills, talk only about keeping their eyes on the ball. Later, you can focus on other aspects of the skill.
- Some skills can be broken into smaller parts. This sometimes makes it easier for learners at this level to find success. For example, if a student can perform a step and a hop, then you are ready to teach skipping by asking them to take a step followed by a hop.
- Ensure rapid success by using equipment that makes performing the skill easier. An example would be using balloons instead of playground balls with kindergarten students. Because a balloon moves more slowly than a playground ball, it is much easier to track and catch.
- Every student should have a piece of equipment so that each can perform the maximum number of repetitions. Beginners are excited to learn, and standing around waiting for a turn or a piece of equipment can be frustrating and demoralizing.
- Talk about how to perform the skill (process) rather than the outcome of the skill (product). Again, if teaching catching, it shouldn't matter whether students catch or drop the ball. What is important is the process of keeping their eyes on the ball (if that is the point of emphasis).
- Be positive and reinforce students' efforts. As students improve, their success rate increases and they require less reinforcement.

Intermediate Level

As students gain greater exposure to skills and have the opportunity for repetition and refinement, their success rate increases. Their ability to practice for longer periods of time (still relatively short) allows them to show rapid improvement. Continued emphasis on the process of performing the skill correctly is still important, but the

outcome becomes more important at this stage. Concentration is still required to perform the skill correctly, but intermediate-level performers have incorporated some of the basic components and no longer think about them.

Instilling a feeling of success in students is still important at this stage of development because students are not sure they are capable of performing these skills. If they fail too often, they may feel that they are incapable of the skill being taught, and will avoid the activity in the future. Some learning theorists feel that children develop their perceptions of competency by the age of eight. If they perceive they are competent at a skill, they will continue. If not, they will avoid it when the choice is theirs to make. Reinforcement and feedback is therefore still critical at this stage because youngsters will begin to compare their skill level to those of their peers. Points to remember at this level include the following:

- Keep feedback short and to the point. Excessive feedback only frustrates students. After delivering feedback, walk away and let students experiment with your suggestions. Don't hover to see if they are doing it correctly because that increases the pressure on them to perform well.
- Students at this level start to vary in ability. These differences indicate the need for modifying tasks and increasing challenges on an individual basis. Large group instruction will leave some students bored or frustrated at this stage.
- Avoid excessive competition since it lowers performance at this level. Children will be more concerned about winning than performing the skill correctly. Use cooperative skills where students work together as a way to focus on helping others in the group succeed.
- Teach students to critique their own performance. Ask questions such as, "If the ball is always going in that direction, what do you need to do to get it to the target?"

Mastery Level

Few students will reach mastery in elementary school, but some may approach it. When a skill is mastered, it can be performed without much thought. Excessive movements have been removed from the performance, and the skill performance is efficient and smooth in nature. The mastered skill is performed correctly and repeatedly in similar fashion. Achieving mastery level does not mean the outcome is successful every time the student performs that skill. For example, basketball players never make all the shots they take regardless of their skill level. However, how they perform the skill (technique) is the same time after time.

Back to Class

After school had ended for the day, Mr. Kohl was tidying the classroom when Jason's teacher from the previous year walked by. When he shared with her the incident with Jason in the game of Redcoats and Minutemen, she sighed. "Jason gets teased a lot by the other kids because of his weight. One time last year, another boy got really nasty in a competitive game when he thought that Jason wasn't playing well and was causing his team to lose. From what you said happened today, I'd guess that Jason has decided he just isn't athletic, but if so, that's really a shame. I've seen some kids like him grow into their weight and succeed in football and other sports in adolescence. That'll never happen with Jason if he's afraid to try." In the future, what strategies might Mr. Kohl adopt with Jason to help him overcome his fear of being teased and change his perception that he is not athletic?

Another factor to consider at this stage is related to game strategy. Often, teachers and coaches want to introduce strategy too early in skill development stages. If students at the intermediate level start thinking about the game, their performance will taper off because they are not concentrating on developing the skill. However, students who reach the mastery level are able to think about game strategy and still perform the skill correctly.

To help students at the mastery level, implement the following:

- Students at this level can focus on the outcome of the skill performance. Therefore, with a skilled performer it is appropriate to reinforce the outcome.
- Since students at the mastery level receive feedback inherently from their own successful skill attempts, less feedback from you is required.
- Maximize the number of practice repetitions.
- Understand that the variation in students' ability increases as they mature. It soon becomes apparent who the more-skilled and less-skilled youngsters are in a given skill area. Sensitive teaching requires working one on one with students and giving as much individual feedback as possible.
- Students at this level like to use their skills in game applications. Avoid excessive emphasis on winning, but allow students to use their skills to implement game strategy.

Chapter Summary

Understanding the Needs of Children

- We define a need as a drive to do or accomplish something. Needs are similar among children of all ages and are not affected by developmental maturity.

- To help children incorporate physical activity into their lifestyle, you must understand children's needs for movement, success and approval, peer acceptance and tolerance, and cooperation and competition. Children also have a need to perceive themselves as competent.

- Children have an innate need for adventure and novelty, creative satisfaction, rhythmic expression, and understanding of why they are asked to perform a task.

Understanding the Characteristics of Children

- Characteristics are age- and maturity-specific physical, cognitive, and social attributes that influence children's learning. When offering physical activities, avoid expecting all children to perform at the same level despite varying characteristics.

- Children exhibit the same general growth pattern; however, their growth rate and timing may differ.

- Strength is the primary factor influencing children's ability to perform physical skills. Excess body fat reduces performance by reducing relative strength.

- Children's skeletal age, which measures individual level of ossification as compared to national standards, may vary widely from their chronological age.

- Children prefer low-intensity activities of longer duration. High-intensity activities should be brief or interrupted with plenty of opportunities for rest breaks. Overweight children have a reduced capacity for aerobic activity.

- Compared with adults, children have a reduced ability to tolerate heat stress and are at increased risk for dehydration.

Understanding Children's Skill Development

- The progression of children's skill development has three characteristics: it is cephalocaudal, proximodistal, and proceeds from general to specific.

- At the introductory level, children may have no previous exposure to a skill. They progress slowly, requiring repeated practice, and may experience frustration and physical and mental fatigue. Lots of positive feedback and frequent rest breaks are important at this level.

At the intermediate level, children have experienced success at some of the basic movements, do not need to concentrate as intensely, and are able to tolerate longer periods of practice. Children continue to require positive feedback for their efforts at this stage.

At the mastery level, excessive movements have been removed from a skill and it is performed efficiently and smoothly without great thought. Children receive positive feedback intrinsically from their performance of the skill and require less external praise.

Review Questions

Content Review

1. How have your views of what is appropriate physical activity for children changed as a result of reading this chapter?

2. Why is it important for classroom teachers to understand children's growth patterns, including differences in rate of growth, height, weight, body proportions, and skeletal age?

3. How might the experience of physical activity differ for overweight children as compared to leaner peers?

4. How do adults and children differ in their capacity for physical activity in hot and humid environments? Discuss guidelines for exercising children in the heat.

5. Characterize each of the three levels of skill development.

Real World

1. In a parent-teacher conference, a father expresses concern about his seven-year-old daughter's difficulty with mathematics. He says, "From what I hear, too much classroom time is being wasted fooling around! My daughter is slender and doesn't need all this physical activity she talks about, tossing balloons around and marching through the halls! What she needs is more instruction in math!" How might you respond to this parent's concerns?

2. You're on a committee planning policies and programs to increase your school's level of physical activity, and one member proposes beginning the next school year with a 2-mile "mini-marathon." She explains, "It would really get the new physical activity initiative off to a strong start, and besides, everybody loves marathons!" Would you support this proposal, or not? What information could you share with the committee in support of your position?

What About You?

Earlier in this chapter, we discussed children's need to perceive themselves as being competent in assigned tasks. Reflect on your own level of perceived competence in some physical activities. For example, how do you feel about your ability to throw, catch, serve, or dribble a ball; clap, march, or dance in time to a beat; perform a somersault, pass a swim test, climb a rock wall, or run a mile? Below, jot down some thoughts about what might have contributed to your perceived competence in a skill you feel particularly good about. Do you remember receiving encouragement that helped you develop this skill? Now write about what might have contributed to your feelings about a skill for which you have a low level of perceived competence. What memories arise related to this skill?

I have a high level of perceived competence in _____

because _____.

I have a low level of perceived competence in _____

because _____.

Finally, how does your own level of perceived competence affect your confidence in offering your students physical activity? _____

_____

References and Suggested Readings

American Academy of Pediatrics. (2000). Climatic heat stress and the exercising child and adolescent. *Pediatrics*, 106(1), 158–159. (Reaffirmed September 1, 2007.)

Athletic Footwear Association. (1990). *American youth and sports participation.* North Palm Beach, FL: Athletic Footwear Association.

Bar-Or, O. (1983). *Pediatric sports medicine for the practitioner.* New York: Springer-Verlag.

Bar-Or, O., and Ward, D.S. (1989). Rating of perceived exertion in children. In O. Bar-Or (ed.), *Advances in pediatric sport sciences. Vol. 3.* Champaign, IL: Human Kinetics.

Beunen, G. (1989). Biological age in pediatric exercise research. In O. Bar-Or (ed.), *Advances in pediatric sport sciences. Vol. 3.* Champaign, IL: Human Kinetics.

Clarke, H.H. (1968). Characteristics of the young athlete: A longitudal look. *Kinesiology Review*, 3, 33–42.

Clarke, H.H. (1971). *Physical motor tests in the Medford boys' growth study.* Englewood Cliffs, NJ: Prentice-Hall.

Cooper Institute. (2007). *Fitnessgram/Activitygram test administration manual* (4th ed.). Champaign, IL: Human Kinetics.

Gruelich, W., and Pyle, S. (1959). *Radiographic atlas of skeletal development of the hand and wrist* (2nd ed.). Stanford, CA: Stanford University Press.

Hale, C. (1956). Physiological maturity of Little League baseball players. *Research Quarterly*, 27, 276–284.

Harter, S. (1978). Effectance motivation revisited. *Child Development*, 21, 34–64.

International Athletics Association Federation. (1983). Not kid's stuff. *Sports Medicine Bulletin*, 18(1), 11.

Krahenbuhl, G.S., and Pangrazi, R.P. (1983). Characteristics associated with running performance in young boys. *Medicine and Science in Sports*, 15(6), 486–490.

Malina, R.M. (1978). Physical growth and maturity characteristics of young athletes. In R.A. Magill, M.H. Ash, and F.L. Smoll (eds.), *Children and youth in sport: A contemporary anthology*. Champaign, IL: Human Kinetics.

Payne, V.G., and Morrow, Jr., J.R. (1993). Exercise and VO^2max in children: A meta-analysis. *Research Quarterly for Exercise and Sport*, 64(3), 305–313.

Petersen, G. (1967). *Atlas for somatotyping children*. The Netherlands: Royal Vangorcum Ltd.

Petlichkoff, L.M. (1992). Youth sport participation and withdrawal: Is it simply a matter of fun? *Pediatric Exercise Science*, 4(2), 105–110.

Rarick, L.G. (ed.). (1973). *Physical activity, Human growth and activity*. New York: Academic.

Rarick, L.G., and Dobbins, D.A. (1975). Basic components in the motor performances of children six to nine years of age. *Medicine and Science in Sports*, 7(2), 105–110.

Roche, A.F., Chumlea, W.C., and Thissen, D. (1988). *Assessing the skeletal maturity of the hand-wrist: FELS method*. Springfield, IL: Thomas.

Rowland, T.W. (1990). *Exercise and children's health*. Champaign, IL: Human Kinetics.

Sheldon, W.H., Dupertuis, C.W., & McDermott, E. (1954). *Atlas of men: A guide for somatotyping the adult male at all ages*. New York: Harper & Row.

Shephard, R.J. (1984). Physical activity and child health. *Sports Medicine*, 1, 205–233.

Thomas, J.R., & Tennant, L.K. (1978). Effects of rewards on changes in children's motivation for an athletic task. In F.L. Smoll & R.E. Smith (Eds.), *Psychological perspectives in youth sports*. New York: Hemisphere.

U.S. Department of Health and Human Services. (2000). *Healthy people 2010: National health promotion and disease objectives*. Washington, DC: U.S. Government Printing Office.

Whitehead, J.R., & Corbin, C.B. (1991). Effects of fitness test type, teacher, and gender on exercise intrinsic motivation and physical self-worth. *Journal of School Health*, 61, 11–16.

Web Resources

American Academy of Pediatricians:
www.aap.org
American College of Sports Medicine:
www.acsm.org
The Cooper Institute:
www.cooperinst.org
International Athletics Association Federation:
www.iaaf.org
The President's Challenge:
www.presidentschallenge.org

3

Teaching Physical Activities Safely and Effectively

Learning Objectives

After reading this chapter, you will be able to . . .

- Delineate the space you need for safe and effective physical activity with groups of varying size.
- Determine the amount and type of equipment you need for a physical activity and teach students how to secure and take care of it.
- Properly supervise students to ensure a safe environment.
- Identify when it is best to reinforce the process of skill performance and when it is best to reinforce the product of skill performance.
- Identify the types of skills that are best taught by the "whole" method and the types best taught by the "parts" method.
- Compare and contrast random and blocked practice.
- Apply basic mechanical principles such as stability and force to increase the effectiveness of children's skill performance.
- Help students learn sport skills, such as throwing and catching, that are appropriate to their developmental levels.
- Identify three behaviors to avoid when actively helping children participate in sports and games.

Classroom Challenge

Mr. Lonkowski and Mrs. Li are having breakfast while attending the second day of a student learning conference. Both teachers have more than 10 years of teaching experience at various elementary grade levels. They teach at schools in the same district and are friends. Over coffee, Mr. Lonkowski asks, "What did you think of the presentation yesterday on physical activity in the classroom?"

Mrs. Li replies, "Well, I already knew that physical activity in the classroom can improve kids' health, but I'd never heard that it might be able to improve their attention and behavior, too. It makes sense, though. I've always thought that some students just need to get up and wiggle every once in a while. But with all the curriculum pressures we face, it's not practical. I just can't afford the time for physical activity when they could be learning."

Mr. Lonkowski nods. "I know what you mean. But I started to think it might be worth it when the speaker mentioned those studies that suggest activity breaks could actually facilitate learning."

"I hate to be a naysayer," Mrs. Li sighs, "but I'm not convinced I could handle it, either in the classroom or outside. In the classroom it would be so chaotic. I'm only trained to manage students when they're sitting in rows, pods, or centers, not when they're up and moving around. How do I keep them from bumping into one another? It sort of scares me! And outside? How can I get them out and back into the classroom efficiently? And while they're out there, how do I keep them under control? As you can tell, the whole idea makes me a little nervous—no—*very* nervous! I think it could be good for the kids, but I just don't know how to do it!"

When teachers like Mrs. Li feel "nervous" about classroom physical activity, they typically find reasons why they "just can't afford the time." But there's no need for anxiety: with adequate preparation, you'll find that offering physical activity is neither a complicated nor a difficult task. Factors such as space, equipment, and safety are important considerations, and this chapter covers them all. You'll also learn key instructional strategies, including how to design effective

practice sessions, how to integrate mechanical principles such as stability and force into activity sessions, and how to foster children's acquisition of developmentally appropriate sport skills such as catching and kicking.

When you consistently take the actions recommended in this chapter, your confidence will increase, and both you and your students will be more likely to enjoy physical activity. Success fosters further success: when teachers have positive experiences with activity breaks, they continue to offer them. What's more, teachers bring their own creativity to the process, designing activity sessions that are even more effective and engaging for their mix of students.

Preparing the Space for Physical Activity

For effective and engaging physical activity sessions, you'll need to prepare the space. Whether using a classroom, gymnasium, or outdoor playground, you'll need to clearly delineate an activity area and use equipment effectively and efficiently.

Predetermine Your Instructional Space Needs

How large a space will you need for a given activity? To answer this question, consider the skills you'll be having your students practice as well as your own ability to manage the class. A common error is to take a class to the playground area, tell students the tasks they are to accomplish, and then instruct them to "spread out and practice." The students expand into an area so large it becomes difficult to communicate with and manage the class. In smaller areas, it's easier for you to control your class because you and your students can see and hear one another better. As students become more responsive and self-disciplined, you'll need to issue verbal instructions less frequently, so you will be able to enlarge the size of the activity area.

A related factor affecting the size of the practice area is the amount of instruction your students need. When they are learning a skill and need constant feedback and redirection, it is important that your students stay near you. In such cases, you should delineate a relatively small space. Another alternative is to establish two areas: a smaller area where students can move in close for instruction and a larger area where they can spread out for practice.

Regardless of the size of the space, you can quickly delineate a rectangular practice area by setting a cone at each of four corners. These cones mark the perimeter of the rectangle and make it easy for students to see the size of the instructional space. Chalk lines, evenly spaced equipment, or natural boundaries can

also serve as perimeter lines. Another benefit of marking the area with cones is that other students on the playground can be taught to stay out of the instructional area when it is being used.

To maximize student participation, consider dividing the available space into several smaller areas. For example, let's say you offer your 20 students a chance to play volleyball, but only 10 students can play on one available court. You should consider dividing the area into two courts to give all of your students a chance to play. A related consideration when partitioning space is safety: keep the spaces far enough apart that the two groups of players and equipment stay separated. If the partitioned playing areas are too close together, players from one area might run, kick, or fall into the other players, or their equipment might enter the other area. For certain sports, partitioning areas is impractical. For example, a softball setting is unsafe if a player on one field can hit a ball into another play area.

Plan for the Appropriate Amount and Type of Equipment

Before beginning the lesson, determine exactly how much equipment is available. Only after finding this out should you make a firm decision about what activity to offer and how to present it. For example, if there are only 16 paddles and balls available for your class of 30, you'll have to plan for some type of sharing or station work. Also, be sure that the equipment you're planning to use is in working condition. It is embarrassing and frustrating to roll out a cart of playground balls only to find that half of them are not inflated!

How much equipment is enough? For individual-use equipment such as racquets, bats, and balls, there should be one piece of equipment for each student (**Figure 3.1**). If you're planning a group-oriented activity, there should be enough equipment to ensure waiting lines of no more than four students. When you have a lot of equipment available, in most cases it's smart to go ahead and use it. For example, imagine that an instructor is teaching throwing skills and has a box of a dozen balls available. Nevertheless, the instructor decides to divide the class into two long lines and use just two balls. Most of the equipment remains on the sidelines, leaving the majority of students with nothing to do but wait for a turn. Make sure that students don't spend more time waiting in line than they do practicing skills. Give each student the opportunity to practice individually (each with a ball) against the wall or in pairs, with two partners sharing a ball.

Figure 3.1 All students should have a piece of equipment.

If equipment at your school is limited, it will be necessary for you to adapt. However, you have a responsibility to your students to explain to your principal or other administrator that physical activity sessions are much more effective when adequate equipment is available. Speak with parent-teacher groups about conducting fundraisers to purchase necessary equipment. Just as math teachers are not expected to teach math without a book for each student, you shouldn't be expected to promote physical activity without adequate equipment. When you settle for less, you end up with less.

Figure 3.2 Children enjoy helping move equipment, such as the balls and hoops in this cart, into the play area.

What are temporary alternatives when equipment is lacking? One solution is to divide students into small groups so that each group has enough equipment. For example, in a softball unit, one group of students practice fielding, others work on hitting, while a third group of students is pitching, and so on. Another approach is to divide the class in half and assign the two groups unrelated activities. For example, if there's a shortage of paddles and balls, while half of the class is involved in racquet skill practice, the other half may be playing a game that requires different equipment, such as "Pirate's Loot," or no equipment at all, such as "Red Light, Green Light." (See the Large Area Activity Cards.) That said, this mixed approach is less educationally sound and increases your responsibilities as you must manage and instruct two groups. Another approach is to use peer coaching and review: while one student practices an activity, one or more peers offer feedback and evaluation. The peers share equipment and take turns being involved in practice and evaluation.

Distribute Equipment Effectively

Smooth and speedy distribution of equipment reduces the time children spend on a task unrelated to their learning and is a key component of an effective activity session. Usually, the most effective method for distributing individual equipment is to place it around the perimeter of the area. This requires some setup time prior to the lesson but makes it easy for students to get their equipment without confusion.

When you don't have time to ready the equipment before an activity, have your students help (Figure 3.2). Children enjoy sharing duties such as pushing out the ball cart and distributing the balls, and at the end of the session each child should be responsible for putting his or her equipment away. Such help can make physical activity sessions both more productive and more fun for everybody. Take a little time to teach your students how you like equipment placed and put away and then give them the responsibility to carry out the tasks. Don't forget to praise them for a job well done.

Modify Equipment as Appropriate

If modifying the equipment improves the quality of learning, go ahead and do so. For example, if your students are learning to play basketball, you may lower the height of the basket to emphasize correct shooting form rather than have students wildly throwing the ball at the basket at the standard height. Or if early elementary children are learning to throw and catch, try using inflatable beach balls. Indeed, you should always feel free to modify equipment and apparatus to best suit the needs of your learners. There is nothing sacred about a 10-foot basket or a regulation-size ball.

Promoting a Safe Environment

Because they require students to move, all physical activities involve a certain degree of risk. But when you promote a safe environment, physical activities of all types offer your students important opportunities to take calculated risks and overcome their personal fears. When students feel adequate safety precautions are in place, they are less hesitant to learn new activities that involve some risk. Again, although you're not responsible for guaranteeing all children's safety at every moment, you are responsible for promoting a safe environment. But how do you do it?

Write Down, Communicate, and Practice Safety Rules

If a student is injured because of your poor preparation, you will feel and probably be held responsible. Before offering a physical activity, think about what aspects of the environment or the activity might result in student injury. Write down clear and firm rules dictating safe and sensible behavior. Communicate the rules to your students in developmentally appropriate language, and offer them adequate opportunities to practice those rules.

For example, if students are using equipment such as batons, racquets, or baseball bats, they need to be told to carry them vertically, close to their body, so as to avoid hitting other students, and they should all have an opportunity to practice proper carrying. If they are participating in a game in the classroom, they need instruction and practice in how to move safely in a confined space. Write out safety procedures such as taking turns, moving under control, and following directions, then communicate them clearly, and allow students multiple opportunities to practice them.

When you need to modify your rules, rewrite them and make sure you communicate the revisions to your students. There is no substitute for documentation if the need to defend policies and approaches arises.

Make sure that you also write down and communicate to children the consequences of breaking a rule (such as having to apologize out loud and go to the end of the line for pushing ahead of a classmate, etc.) and that you follow through with the consequences if a rule is broken. Behavior management is the subject of Chapter 5.

Properly Supervise Activities

Supervision is necessary during recess, before and after school, during the lunch break, and during other activities when instruction is not offered (such as when students are playing a basketball game during a class break). The person in charge should know the school's plan for supervision as well as the emergency care procedures to follow in case of an accident. Supervision is a positive act that requires being actively involved and moving throughout the play area. For more information on safety during recess, check out the News Clip.

When offering structured activities in any setting, you must always remain with your students. Just as you would spot students who are performing challenging

Supervision + Recess = Injury Prevention

Children love recess, and it's important to their overall wellness to get some fresh air and sunshine and engage in unstructured play. Unfortunately, the elementary school playground is too often the site of injury. According to *Risks to Students in Schools*, published by the U.S. Office of Technology Assessment, unintentional playground injuries are the leading cause of all injuries for elementary school children. Why? The National Program for Playground Safety (NPPS) suggests that one of the most crucial elements in playground safety is supervision. It is estimated that nearly 40 percent of all playground-related injuries each year are attributed to inadequate supervision. NPPS conducted a survey that found that the average ratio of supervisors to students on the playground was 1 to 50. This far exceeds its recommendation that playground supervision be equal to the indoor teacher-to-student classroom ratio.

So what can be done? Propose actions to increase playground safety such as establishing a pool of trained volunteers (parents, grandparents, etc.) who are willing to commit to supervising recess. Volunteers should be trained in safety procedures and playground rules, as well as in supervisory procedures. Supervisors should perform a daily check of equipment (Is it broken, dented, or otherwise unsafe? Is the surfacing beneath it at the proper depth?) and should ensure that no trash is strewn about the area. They should also learn how to file a report of hazards in the area so that repairs may be done.

In addition, teachers should routinely instruct children in playground safety and appropriate playing behavior. Children should have opportunities to drill safety rules periodically throughout the school year. All children should be able to state the consequences of unsafe play and know how to identify playground hazards and report them to supervisors.

Source: Adapted from "Supervision + Recess = Injury Prevention," available at www.pta.org/archive_article_details_ 1117833728250.html.

take action!

1.   Next time you're on an elementary school playground, take a look around. Is all of the equipment in good repair? Do you notice equipment with jagged edges, missing bolts, splintering wood, or metal or plastic surfaces that are burning hot in the sun? Are playground rules and regulations posted in a prominent place? If not, find out whether rules are communicated to children in their classrooms.

2.   During recess, what is the supervisor-to-student ratio? (How many supervisors monitor how many children?) Does this ratio approximate the teacher-to-student ratio in the classrooms?

3.   If necessary, report your findings to the school principal or administration. Cite the research and recommendations of the NPPS and propose actions the school can take to improve playground safety.

gymnastic activities, you should remain physically present with students who are marching, running, jumping, or kicking, whether or not they are using equipment. Incidentally, equipment and apparatus should not go unsupervised at any time when they are accessible to students. When teaching, arrange the class in the space so that all students are in view. This implies supervising from the perimeter of the area. If you are standing in the center of the class, there will be many students out of view, and you won't be able to supervise the class safely and effectively. Do not agree to supervise an activity if you do not feel qualified to anticipate the activity's possible hazards. If this situation arises, send a written memo to the department head or principal stating your lack of qualification to supervise and your inability to ensure a safe environment. Maintain a copy for your files.

Merriman (1993) offers five recommendations to ensure that adequate supervision occurs:

1. The supervisor must be in the immediate vicinity (within sight and hearing of the students).
2. If required to leave, the supervisor must have an adequate replacement before departing. Adequate replacements do not include paraprofessionals, student teachers, custodial help, or untrained teachers.
3. Supervision procedures must be preplanned and incorporated into daily lessons.
4. Supervision procedures should include what to observe and listen for, where to stand for the most effective view, and what to do if a problem arises.
5. Supervision requires that age, maturity, and skill ability of participants always be considered, as well as the inherent risk of the activity.

Provide Adequate and Appropriate Instruction

When teaching a physical activity, you have a duty to protect students from unreasonable physical or mental harm, including any acts or omissions that might cause such harm. As an educated and experienced professional, you are expected to be able to foresee situations that could be harmful.

One of your primary concerns should be to ensure that all students have received adequate instruction before participating and will continue to receive adequate instruction as necessary during the activity. Adequate instruction includes teaching children how to perform activities and use equipment properly and teaching necessary safety precautions.

Instructions must be correct, developmentally appropriate, and include proper technique. The risk involved in an activity must be communicated to the learner.

The age and maturity levels of students play an important role both in the selection of activities and in the content and method of your instruction. For older students, posting the proper sequence of skills and lead-up activities helps ensure that these instructions have been presented properly. Younger students require step-by-step spoken instructions that are easy to comprehend. In particular, they need firm restrictions to ensure their safety. This is because some young students lack appropriate fear and may have little concern about performing an activity safely.

Thus, it is essential that you give youngsters adequate instruction and supervision. If you do so, and a child continues to choose to be reckless, remove him or her from the activity.

Careful planning is a necessity for effective and safe instruction, yet classroom teachers are often limited in the amount of time they have to plan physical education lessons. This text offers more than 260 safe and developmentally appropriate activities (see Activity Cards) that don't require excessive planning time. If, however, you are expected to teach a complete lesson plan, it will be helpful to review lesson planning. Several sample lesson plans are provided in Appendix A of this book. Written curriculum guides also promote safe instruction because they offer a tested approach that withstands scrutiny and examination by other teachers and administrators. A curriculum guide specifically for K–6 teachers (e.g., Pangrazi, 2007) should include comprehensive lesson plans that are developmentally appropriate for different grade levels. All the lesson plans in a thorough curriculum guide should include proper sequence and progression of skills. Teachers are on defensible ground if they can show that the activities taught are based on presentations designed by seasoned field experts.

Proper instruction demands that students not be forced to participate. If a youngster is required to perform an activity unwillingly, you may be open to a lawsuit. In a lawsuit dealing with stunts and tumbling (Appenzeller, 2003), the court held the teacher liable when a student claimed that she was not given adequate instruction before she was forced to try a stunt that required her to roll over two peers. Tread the line carefully between helpful encouragement and forcing students to try activities they fear.

In summary, incorporating the following points will help ensure safe instruction:

- Scrutinize activities you feel uncomfortable teaching to ensure that all safety procedures have been implemented. If in doubt, discuss the activities with experienced teachers and administrators.
- Make sure activities are within the developmental limits of your students. Often, experts in physical education assign appropriate developmental levels to different activities. The activities accompanying this text are grouped into two major developmental levels by grade.
- Preplan how you will arrange or distribute equipment for instruction. In most cases, it is best to let students secure a piece of equipment individually, assuming they can do so safely.
- Make sure activities included in the instructional process are appropriate for the equipment and space being used for instruction. For example, if a soccer game is brought indoors because of inclement weather, it may not be a safe and appropriate activity.
- Make it clear to students that the choice to participate belongs to them. When they are afraid or perceive they can't perform the activity, allow them to opt out.
- If a student claims injury or brings a note from parents asking that their child not participate in physical activity, honor the request. If you question the validity or need for the excuse, ask the school nurse to intervene. The school nurse is qualified to make judgments related to health and

participation in activity settings. If the excuses continue over a long period of time, the principal or nurse should schedule a conference with the parents to rectify the situation.

Learn what you should do if you have an injury in your class. All schools should have a written emergency care plan, and it should be posted in all classrooms. This plan is usually approved by healthcare professionals and should be followed to the letter if an injury occurs.

Avoid Using Physical Activity for Punishment

Some teachers believe that students may be disciplined for misbehavior safely and effectively by forcing them to run laps or perform another physical activity. But before deciding to use physical activity as a form of punishment, you should examine its consequences carefully. For example, consider the consequences of making students perform physical activity when they misbehave in the classroom. This policy may prompt not only the child who misbehaves but all of the children in the class who witness the incident to associate physical activity with punishment. This is unacceptable: we want children to associate physical activity with feelings of happiness, accomplishment, and self-esteem, not with feelings of misbehavior and shame.

Back to Class

Mrs. Li is back in the classroom the week after the student learning conference. Her third-graders are reciting a Halloween poem they have memorized when she notices two girls off-task, whispering together, and several boys "wiggling" in their seats. Deciding to try a few minutes of classroom physical activity, she abruptly shouts, "Students! Stand beside your desks!" The children give one another startled looks as they jump to their feet. "Now!" Mrs. Li shouts, "March in time with me!" She begins to march from the front to the back of the classroom, continuing to recite the poem as she weaves between the groups of desks. Some children move to follow her, others start to march in random directions, while still others stand in place, darting uncertain glances at their classmates. Pandemonium breaks out when two boys march straight into each other and one is knocked to the floor. "Ow!" he cries, "I think my arm is broken!"

Look back at what you have read thus far in this chapter. Can you identify at least two actions that Mrs. Li could have taken to improve the outcome of this physical activity session?

Physical punishment that has the potential to cause permanent or long-lasting damage is also indefensible. For example, the practice of having students run laps when they have misbehaved has gone unchallenged for years in some schools. What if a student with asthma, epilepsy, or congenital heart disease is forced to run and becomes ill? What if you were to force a healthy student to run and he fell and twisted his ankle? How would you explain his injury to his parents? Could you defend yourself if his parents took you to court? Clearly, the wisdom, safety, and legality of using physical activity for punishment are untenable.

Designing Effective Practice Sessions

Practice is a key part of learning motor skills. But it is not enough to give your students ample time to practice; they must practice correctly, with emphasis on technique, if they are to master motor skills. This section explains how to design practice sessions that optimize motor skill learning.

Manage the Level of Arousal

Arousal as we use the term here refers to a level of excitement produced by stress (Schmidt and Wrisberg, 2008). It is closely related to motivation. The level of arousal can have a positive or negative impact on children's motor performance. The key to proper arousal is finding the amount that is "just right." Too little, and a youngster is uninterested in learning. Too much arousal increases children's stress and anxiety, resulting in decreased motor performance. The more complex a skill, the more likely it is that arousal may disrupt learning. On the other hand, if a skill is simple and already learned, such as skipping or running, a greater amount of arousal may be tolerated without causing a reduction in skill performance. Optimally, youngsters should be guided to a level at which they are excited and confident about participating.

Competition affects the arousal level of children. We see this when the pressure and stress of a high-stakes game lowers players' performance levels. Even experienced athletes may become too aroused when the stakes are high, making more errors in championship games, for example, than in regular season games. With children, when competition is introduced too soon, in the early stages of skill learning, stress and anxiety reduce their ability to learn new skills. In contrast, when introduced after a skill has been *over-learned* (performed easily with little concentration and thought), competition may improve the level of performance. Since most elementary school youngsters have not over-learned skills, you should usually avoid competitive situations, especially when teaching new or unlearned skills.

For example, assume the objective is to practice basketball dribbling. Youngsters are placed in squads and asked to run a relay requiring that they dribble to the opposite end of the gym and return. The first squad finished will be declared the winner. As a result, instead of concentrating on dribbling form, students focus on winning the relay. They are over-aroused and determined to run as quickly as possible. Because dribbling skills are not yet over-learned, the quality of performance is poor (the balls fly out of control and some children fail to dribble at all) and the teacher is dismayed by the result.

Focus Practice on Process

Earlier we suggested that for elementary school children you provide feedback that emphasizes process. The same is true for practice sessions: we suggest that you focus on process. In process-based practice, the teacher encourages students to learn the skill correctly without concern for the outcome. In contrast, with product-based practice, the teacher asks students to do the best they can and then reinforces those who reach the desired outcome. This method is less successful for motor skill development because students who think their teacher is interested in the product are less likely to concentrate on proper technique. Emphasis on the outcome also decreases a student's willingness to take risks and to learn alternative ways of performing a skill. Excessive pressure to perform without mistakes may also stifle a student's willingness to try (especially if the child lacks confidence to begin with).

To encourage your students to focus on learning skills correctly, emphasize technique and encourage experimentation. If it is necessary to evaluate a skill outcome, tell students why the outcome is important and say, "We will practice doing our best today."

Encourage Mental Practice

Mental practice involves practicing a motor skill in a quiet, relaxed environment by thinking about the skill and its related sounds, colors, and other sensations. Students visualize themselves performing the activity successfully and at regular speed. Images of failure should be avoided (Schmidt and Wrisberg, 2008). Mental practice stimulates children to think about and review the skill they are attempting to learn.

Some experience or familiarity with the motor task is required before the performer can derive value from mental practice. This implies that it is probably not effective for early elementary school children because they have learned few skills. Also, notice that mental practice should be used in combination with regular practice, not in place of it.

To encourage mental practice, explain the concept to your class. Then, before asking the students to perform a skill, prompt them to mentally review the skill's critical factors and sequence. Ask them if there are any aspects of which they're uncertain. If so, provide the appropriate instruction. If not, have them move into physical practice.

Decide on Whole or Part Practice

Skills may be taught by either the whole method or the part method. With the **whole method,** the instructor presents the entire skill or activity in one "dose." With the **part method,** the instructor breaks down a skill into a series of parts that the students practice and then helps the students combine the parts into the whole skill. For example, in a rhythmic activity, each section of a dance would be taught, and then the children would work on putting the whole dance together. Or a gymnastics routine might be broken into component parts and put back together for the performance.

Whether to use the whole or part method depends on the complexity and organization of the skills to be learned. **Complexity** refers to the number of serial skills or components there are in a task. **Organization** defines how the components

are related to each other. High organization means the parts of the skill are closely related to each other, making separation difficult. Here are some examples.

- Complex and highly organized: throwing, which is difficult to practice without going through the complete motion. Use the whole method.
- Complex but not highly organized: folk dancing, in which footwork and arm movements may be rehearsed separately. Generally, if the skills are high in complexity but low in organization, they may be taught in parts. Bear in mind, though, that even when students have mastered the skill components separately, they still have to practice until they have organized and sequenced the skills properly. Practice time should be allowed for sequencing.
- Simple skills: marching, clapping, etc. When complexity is low, you can usually feel confident using the whole method.

A final consideration is the duration of the skill. Too often, complex skills of short duration (performed at high speed)—such as throwing, striking, or kicking—are broken into parts and slowed down in an attempt to make them easier for youngsters to learn. Although well-intended, these efforts are counterproductive: little is learned, and students become frustrated. If you have students slow down their kicking, for example, in order to master each component, they will not be able to develop proper pattern and timing. Instead, complex skills need to be practiced at maximum speed. An effective method of teaching complex skills of short duration is to arrange the learning environment so students may throw, strike, or kick as hard as possible. Encourage hard throws against the wall, for example, or kicking for distance to ensure skill development. Incidentally, in order to progress in their acquisition of short-duration skills such as throwing, children need to begin with individual practice before moving to partnered activities, such as throwing and catching, or team activities.

Consider the Length and Distribution of Practice Sessions

For young children, short practice sessions are usually best for promoting efficient learning. This is because young children more quickly experience physical and mental fatigue (boredom) and require frequent rest breaks. The challenge is to offer as many repetitions as possible within short practice sessions. To maintain children's motivation, use a variety of approaches, challenges, and activities that target the same skill. For example, offering a wide variety of beanbag, beach ball, and balloon activities helps maintain motivation but still focuses on tossing and catching skills.

Another way to determine the appropriate length of practice sessions is to examine the tasks being practiced. If a skill causes physical fatigue, demands intense concentration, or has the potential to become tedious, practice sessions should be short and frequent, with adequate rest between intervals. Stop practice when youngsters become bored or tired, and play a game until they regain their enthusiasm to learn.

Here is an example: You decide to teach juggling skills to your third-grade class. Juggling demands intense concentration in the early stages of learning, and students may quickly become frustrated. Soon they start chatting with others, horsing around, and complaining to you about the activity. Such behavior occurs because they are frustrated and mentally fatigued.

In the initial stages of skill learning, brief practice sessions that are held frequently over several weeks are more effective than longer sessions crowded into a short time span. These enable you to teach a short unit, offer ample sessions for practice, and allow for sufficient review. Later, when students' skill performance improves and their motivation increases, practice sessions may be lengthened.

Use Random Practice Techniques

Two methods for organizing the practice of skills are blocked practice and random practice. In **blocked practice**, all the trials of one skill component are completed before moving on to the next component. Blocked practice is effective during the early stages of skill practice because the children are practicing the same skill in the same setting over and over. As a result, they find themselves rapidly improving and are motivated by their early success to continue practicing. However, there is a downside to blocked practice in that it makes learners believe they are more skilled than they actually are. When the skill is applied in a natural setting, performance levels go down, and some youngsters end up feeling discouraged.

To illustrate, assume partners have been practicing throwing and catching skills with each other. They are a few yards apart and are throwing and catching in a stationary position, which promotes a high success rate. Later, they participate in a softball game. The result is a number of errors and mistakes because the children are now moving quickly, balls are hit in all directions, and throws have to be made on the move.

The other method is **random practice**, in which the order of multiple task presentations is mixed, with no task practiced exactly the same way twice in succession. Goode and Magill (1986) showed that random practice was the most effective approach to use for mastering motor skills. Blocked practice gives the best results during the acquisition phase of skill learning and is a good choice for beginners. But after students have learned basic skill techniques, random practice sessions result in a much higher level of retention.

One reason that random practice promotes better retention is that this method requires children to mentally generate solutions. When the same task is practiced over and over, youngsters become bored and don't think about how to perform the task. Because the same motor pattern is practiced repeatedly, little effort or thinking is required to accomplish the task. In contrast, students using random practice have to perform a different pattern each time to be successful. Thus, they have to consciously think about each task performance and recreate a solution. In addition, youngsters become bored when asked to do the same task over and over, and by engaging their minds, random practice helps minimize this negative side effect.

Offer Variable Practice Experiences

Motor tasks are usually grouped into classes of movement. For example, throwing a ball in a sport may be performed in many different ways: the ball can travel at different speeds, different trajectories, and varying distances. But even though throwing tasks are all different, the variations have fundamental similarities because they are all characterized by the same **class of movements**. Movements in a class usually involve the same body parts and have similar rhythm, but they may be performed with many variations. These differences create the need for variable practice in a variable setting.

Practice sessions should include a variety of skills in a movement class in a variety of situations in which the skill is performed. If the skill to be learned involves one fixed way of performing it (a "closed" skill), such as placekicking a football or striking a ball off a batting tee, variability is much less important. However, most skills are "open," and responses are somewhat unpredictable, making variability in practice preferred (catching or batting a ball moving at different speeds and approaching from different angles). Motor skills should be practiced under a variety of conditions so students can respond to a variety of novel situations.

Back to Class

Mr. Lonkowski returns from the student learning conference excited about offering his second-grade class opportunities for physical activity. His first day back, he talks to the children about the benefits of staying active throughout the day and explains that he will be offering more opportunities for classroom physical activity than in the previous weeks. He then goes over some ground rules, which he posts in both words and pictures on the front wall of the classroom. He asks the students to read the rules aloud together, and then they take turns practicing them. Mr. Lonkowski then has the children push their desks to the sides of the room and describes the rules of a game called "One Behind" (see the Classroom-Based Activity Cards). He leads the children in the game for about 10 minutes, then has them push their desks back into place and take their seats. The children settle down, and Mr. Lonkowski begins a math lesson.

Identify at least three actions that Mr. Lonkowski took that contributed to the success of his classroom activity.

Fostering the Development of Sport Skills

Basic sport skills involve using some type of implement and the hands, feet, or other body parts. These skills develop and require hand-eye and foot-eye coordination as well as dexterity. Basic sport skills include throwing, catching, kicking, and striking, among others.

Helping students develop sport skills requires that you understand the principles of children's growth and development that were covered in Chapter 2. If necessary, review these principles before continuing here. With that foundation, teaching sport skills should not be difficult, because once children learn the basic performance techniques, they can apply them to all skills regardless of their age and physical development. For example, throwing skills are practiced throughout the school years, and even professional basketball players continue to practice shooting baskets throughout their career. In short, learning sport skills involves the two Rs of physical development: repetition and refinement. Here, we explore some actions that you may take to help students acquire sport skills.

Integrate Simple Mechanical Principles

Many of us have experienced the frustration of trying to change the way we perform a sport skill after we have learned it incorrectly. To avoid fostering this frustration in your students, teach them the proper way to perform a skill from the start so they won't have to unlearn it later. Your teaching of basic skills will be more effective if you include a few simple mechanical principles related to technique and performance. Stability, force, leverage, motion, and direction are basic concepts that are best learned when they accompany a skill being taught. A discussion of each is provided in the following sections.

Stability

Stability reflects overall body balance and equilibrium when performing sport skills. A stable base of support is necessary when one applies force to a projectile (throwing or striking) or absorbs force (catching). For many such movements, the feet should be at least hip-width apart, and the torso should be balanced vertically over the thighs. Instability (such as leaning forward) is useful in some activities, such as when a rapid start in a sprint is desired. Introduce the following concepts to your students:

- The wider the base of support, the greater the stability. Teach children to widen their base of support in the direction of the force being applied or absorbed. For example, children facing each other practicing throwing and catching should have one foot in front of the torso and one foot behind, rather than their feet spread horizontally.
- The body's center of gravity, which in an erect body is in the low torso, must be moved lower or closer to the base of support when stopping quickly or applying/absorbing force (as in pushing/pulling). Teach children to lower their center of gravity by bending at the hips and knees.
- For increased stability and balance, the center of gravity should be kept over the base of support (that is, within the boundaries of the base). In other words, the torso should form a straight or gently curved vertical line with the hips. When children greatly flex their torso forward or hyperextend backward, their center of gravity passes outside the boundaries of their base of support, and their balance is less stable. For most activities, instruct children to keep the head up and eliminate excessive body lean. The ready position (**Figure 3.3**) is an example of a stable position used in many sport activities.

Figure 3.3 Ready position.

- Teach children to use their "free" or non-weight-bearing limbs as counterbalances to aid stability. Have them experiment by pretending they are walking a balance beam or railroad track. Explain that this principle is also the reason an acrobat uses a long pole while walking a tightrope.

Force

Force is a measure of the push or pull that one object or body applies to another. Force is necessary to move objects of various types and sizes. The larger and heavier the object to be moved, the greater the amount of force required to cause the movement and the greater the involvement of large muscle groups. **Torque** is the twisting or turning effect that force produces when it acts eccentrically (away from the center) with respect to a body's axis of rotation. We'll discuss torque with specific sport skills shortly. Concepts to convey to children include the following:

- When resisting or applying maximum force, the bones on either side of the major joints involved should form a right angle to each other. For example, when you push with both arms against a wall, you can generate the greatest force when your forearm and upper arm form a right angle.

- To generate greater force, body parts should be activated in a smooth, sequenced, and coordinated manner. For example, when throwing, the hips and trunk are rotated first and followed in sequence by the upper arm, lower arm, hand, and fingers.

- More force is generated when more muscles are used. Muscles are capable of generating higher levels of force when the contraction speed is slow. For example, lifting a very heavy object rapidly is impossible.

- Force should be absorbed over a large surface area and over as long a period of time as possible. For example, a child rolling after a fall is absorbing force over a large surface area. The roll absorbs the force with the hands and the large surface area of the body. Another illustration is when a player reaches to catch a ball and then absorbs the momentum by bringing the ball to the body ("giving"). The force of the ball is absorbed over a longer period of time because of the reach with the hands. Reaching and giving in this way makes it much easier to catch fast-moving objects.

- The follow-through in striking and throwing activities is necessary to ensure maximum application of force and gradual reduction of momentum, for example, the continued swing of the baseball bat after striking the ball.

Leverage and Motion

A **lever** is a bar or other rigid structure that can rotate about a fixed point to overcome a resistance (weight of object) when force is applied. Levers offer a mechanical advantage so that less effort is needed to accomplish tasks. The long bones of the body (the upper arm, forearm, thigh, and lower leg) act as levers, transferring force into motion. That is, after a bone has applied or absorbed force, motion occurs. Levers serve one of two functions: (a) They allow resistance greater than the applied force to be overcome, or (b) they serve to increase the distance or the speed at which resistance can be moved. The following are characteristics of levers and the effects they have on movement:

- The three types of levers in the body are first-, second-, and third-class levers (**Figure 3.4**). Most of the body's levers are third-class; they have the point of force (produced by the muscles) between the fulcrum (the joint) and the point of resistance (produced by the weight of the object to be moved). A child swinging a racquet or kicking a soccer ball is using third-class levers.

- Most of the levers in the body are used to gain a mechanical advantage for speed, not to accomplish heavy tasks. For example, a tossing motion is used to throw a small, light object at a fast speed. It would be impossible to use the same motion for lifting a heavy object.

- A longer force arm (distance from joint to point of force application) allows greater resistance to be overcome (**Figure 3.5**). This concept is useful when manipulating an external lever. For example, to pry open a paint can, force is applied to the screwdriver away from the rim rather than near the paint can. This allows the screwdriver to act as a longer lever.

- A longer resistance arm (distance from joint to point of resistance) allows generation of greater speed (**Figure 3.6**). Racquets and bats act as extensions of the arm, giving players a longer resistance arm for applying greater speed to the object they project. The longer the racquet or bat, the greater the speed it can generate, but the more difficult it is to control its rotation. This is why young baseball players are encouraged to "choke up" (move their hands up) on the bat; this makes the bat shorter and easier to handle. Even though the lever is shortened, bat velocity (at point of contact with the ball) is not reduced much. The important benefit of choking up is that it improves the hitter's performance because it increases his or her opportunity to make contact with the ball (which reinforces the hitter).

Motion and Direction

The majority of sport skills are associated with propelling an object. The following concepts of motion and direction are basic to throwing, striking, and kicking skills:

- The angle of release determines how far an object will travel. Theoretically, the optimum angle of release is 45 degrees. When teaching youngsters to throw for distance, encourage them to release the ball so it travels as close to 45 degrees as possible on the way to its apex. Have students experiment with the angle of release so they see what a difference it makes in determining how far the ball travels.

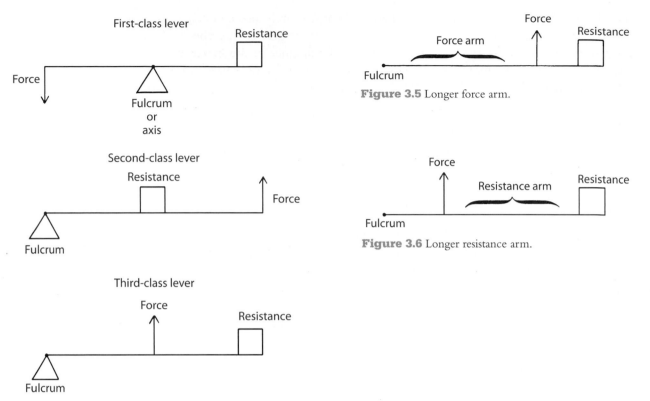

Figure 3.5 Longer force arm.

Figure 3.6 Longer resistance arm.

Figure 3.4 Types of levers.

A ball rebounds from the floor or from the racket at the same angle at which it is hit. However, various factors, such as rotation applied to the ball, the type of ball, and the surface contacted by the ball, can modify the rebound angle.

In most throwing situations, the propelled object should be released at a point tangent to the target. During throwing, for example, the arm travels in an arc, and the ball must be released when the hand is in line with the target.

Throwing

For specific skills such as throwing, catching, kicking, and striking, general stages of development have been identified, from initial stages through mature patterns of performance. Knowing these stages makes it easier to have reasonable expectations for children. For example, it is unreasonable for children to exhibit mature throwing form before the age of eight or nine. Catching is even more difficult to master, and most children are unable to show mature form before the age of 10.

As mentioned earlier, these rather complex skills should be practiced at near-normal speed so that children learn the proper rhythm. Thus, it's important to use the proper type of equipment and allow enough space for children to practice the skills with maximum force. Balloons, beanbags, and yarn balls are excellent for practicing throwing skills with young children.

In throwing, an object is accelerated using movement of the arm and the total coordination of the body to generate maximum force. Young children often go through two preliminary tossing stages before they reach the early stages of throwing.

The first toss is a two-handed underhand throw that involves little foot movement. A large ball, such as a beach ball, is best for teaching this type of throw, which begins with the ball held in front of the body at waist level. The toss is completed using the arms only. Youngsters often have difficulty maintaining balance when encouraged to throw the ball for distance.

The second preliminary toss is a one-handed underhand throw. In this toss, which resembles pitching a softball, body torque is generated and weight shifted from the rear to the front foot. This toss requires a smaller object such as a beanbag, fleece ball, or small sponge ball. It is reasonable to expect children around the age of two to be capable of these tosses.

Teach proper form before concentrating on accuracy. Velocity, not accuracy, is the primary goal when trying to develop mature patterns because it will help youngsters learn the sequence and rhythm of the skill. Throwing for accuracy should only be practiced after proper form has been acquired.

The following analysis of throwing considers overhand throwing only.

Stage One

Stage-one throwing is generally observed between the ages of two and three years. This stage is basically restricted to arm movement from the rear toward the front of the body. The feet remain stationary and positioned at shoulder width, with little or no trunk rotation occurring (**Figure 3.7**). Most of the force for the throw originates from flexing the hip, moving the shoulder forward, and extending the elbow.

Stage Two

The second stage of development usually occurs between the ages of three and five years. Some rotary motion is developed in an attempt to increase the amount of force. This stage is characterized by a lateral fling of the arm, with rotation occurring in the trunk. Some children will step in the direction of the throw, although many keep their feet stationary. This throwing style sometimes looks like a discus throw or a fling rather than a softball throw.

Stage Three

Typically, stage-three throwing form is found among children around the ages of five to six years. The starting position is similar to that of stages one and two in that the body is facing the target area, the feet are parallel, and the body is erect. In this stage, however, a step is made toward the target with the foot that is on the same side of the body as the throwing arm. This prevents rotation of the body but allows shifting of the body weight forward as the step occurs. The arm action is nearer to the overhand style of throwing than is the fling of stage two, and there is an increase in hip flexion. Unfortunately, the throwing pattern of many students never matures beyond this stage.

Figure 3.7 Throwing form, stage one.

Figure 3.8 Throwing pattern, stage four.

Stage Four

Stage four is a mature form of throwing (similar to the form displayed by athletes), allowing the youngster to generate greater force on the object being thrown. The thrower uses the rule of **opposition** in this stage, taking a step in the direction of the throw with the leg opposing the throwing arm. In other words, when throwing with the right arm, a step is taken toward the target with the left foot. This develops maximum torque because the trunk is able to rotate. The starting position is with the non-throwing side of the body facing the target. This contrasts with stage three, where the thrower faces the target throughout the throw.

Beginning with the weight on the back leg, the movement sequence is as follows: (1) step toward the target, (2) rotate the upper body, and (3) throw with the arm (Figure 3.8). A common cue is "step, turn, and throw." The elbow should lead the way in the arm movement, followed by forearm extension and a final snapping of the wrist. This pattern must be practiced over and over to develop total body coordination. Through a combination of sound instruction and practice, the majority of youngsters are able to develop a mature pattern of throwing by age eight or nine years.

Points to Stress

Here are some points to stress with your students:

- Stand with the non-throwing side of the body facing the target. The throwing arm side of the body should be away from the target.
- Step toward the target with the foot opposite the throwing hand.
- Rotate the hips as the throwing arm moves forward.
- Bend the arm at the elbow. The elbow should lead the forward movement of the arm.
- Keep the weight on the rear foot (away from the target) during early phases of the throw. Just prior to the forward motion of the arm, shift the weight from the rear foot to the forward foot (nearer the target).

Teaching Tips for Throwing

- Offer a variety of objects to throw so that youngsters understand how varying the weight and diameter can regulate throwing distance and speed.

When youngsters are learning to throw, they should throw for distance and velocity. Throwing for accuracy discourages the proper development of a mature throwing form. Encourage youngsters to throw as hard as possible. Stress distance and velocity before introducing accuracy.

It is usually ineffective for partners to work on throwing and catching at the same time. If learning to throw is the objective, youngsters should throw with velocity. This will make their throws inaccurate. As a result, it would be difficult for a partner to catch the throw. Throwing should be practiced against a wall (velocity) or on a large field (distance).

Use rubber spots or circles drawn on the floor to teach youngsters proper foot movement (stepping forward).

Beanbags and yarn balls are excellent for developing throwing velocity since they do not rebound throughout the play area.

Catching

Catching uses the hands (or feet in soccer) to stop and control a moving object. Catching is more difficult to learn than throwing because the object must be tracked and the body moved into the path of the object simultaneously. Another common reason that catching is difficult to master is that youngsters fear getting hurt by the ball. Yet, as with throwing, it's important to encourage children to practice with maximum force. Balloons, fleece balls, and beach balls move slowly, make tracking easier, and do not hurt if they hit a child.

Stage One

In stage-one catching, children hold their arms in front of the body, with elbows extended and palms up, until the ball makes contact. To catch the ball, the arms are bent in a right angle at the elbows. The catch is actually more of a trapping movement, since the arms press the ball against the chest. Children often turn their heads away or close their eyes because of the fear response. Start by using a slow-moving object such as a balloon or lightweight ball to help students track the object. This will encourage and train them to keep their eyes on the object in motion rather than on the person throwing it.

Stage Two

In stage two, much of the same behavior from stage one is repeated. Rather than waiting for the ball to make contact with their arms, however, children in this stage make an anticipatory reaching movement with their hands and cradle the ball.

Stage Three

As students mature, they enter stage three, in which they prepare to catch by lifting their arms and bending them slightly. The chest is used as a backstop for the ball. During this stage, children make contact with the hands first and then guide the object to the chest (**Figure 3.9**). This is common among students in grades K–2.

Figure 3.9 Catching form, stage three.

Stage Four

The mature and final stage of catching occurs at approximately age nine and is characterized by catching with the hands. Encourage catching with the hands by decreasing the size of the ball to be caught. Teach giving with the arms (absorbing force) while catching. Giving is characterized by reaching for the ball and absorbing the force into the body as the ball contacts the hands. Teach children to give with their legs as well, by bending at the hips and knees.

Points to Stress

Here are some points to stress with your students:

- Maintain eye contact with the ball.
- Reach for the ball and absorb its force by bringing the hands into the body. This giving makes catching easier by reducing the chance that the object will bounce out of the hands.
- Place the feet in a stride position rather than a straddle position. A fast-moving object will cause a loss of balance if feet are in the straddle position.
- Place the body in line with the object. Don't reach to the side of the body to make the catch.

Teaching Tips for Catching

- Remove the fear factor by using objects that will not hurt the youngster. It is a normal reaction to dodge an object when one feels it will cause harm. The use of foam balls, yarn balls, beach balls, paper balls, and balloons helps children learn to keep their eyes on the ball.
- Use smaller balls as youngsters improve their catching skills. Larger objects move more slowly and are easier to track visually than are smaller projectiles.
- Prepare youngsters for a catch by asking them to focus on the ball while it is in the thrower's hand. Use a verbal cue such as "look (focus), ready (for the throw), catch (toss the ball)." It is common for youngsters to look into the thrower's eyes rather than at the ball.
- Balls and background colors should strongly contrast to facilitate visibility.
- If the ball is lofted as it is tossed to a young child, it gives the youngster more opportunity for successful tracking. Beach balls move slowly throughout a high trajectory, giving children time to focus and move into the path of the oncoming object.
- Bounce objects off the floor so that youngsters learn to judge the rebound angle of a projectile.

Kicking

Kicking is a striking action executed with the feet. There are different types of kicking. *Punting* (in which the ball is dropped from the hands and kicked before it touches the ground) and *placekicking* (kicking the ball in a stationary position on the ground) are two of the most common. A third type is *soccer kicking*, which is probably the most difficult of all kicking skills because the ball is moving before the kick is executed.

Stage One

In stage one, the body is stationary and the kicking foot is flexed in preparation for the kick. The kicking motion is carried out with a straight leg and with little or no flexing at the knee. There is minimal movement of the arms and trunk and concentration is on the ball. This method is common among two- to four-year-olds.

Stage Two

In the second stage of kicking, the striking foot is lifted backward by flexing at the knee. Usually, the child displays opposition of the limbs. When the kicking leg moves forward, so does the opposite arm. In stage two, the kicking leg moves farther forward in the follow-through motion compared to stage one. Kindergarten through second-grade youngsters enjoy this stage of kicking.

Stage Three

Movement toward the object to be kicked is added in stage three. There is an increase in the distance the leg is moved, coupled with a movement of the upper body to counterbalance the leg movement.

Stage Four

Mature kicking involves a preparatory extension at the hip to increase the range of motion. The student runs to the ball and makes a small leap to get the kicking foot in position. As the kicking foot is carried forward, the trunk leans backward, and the child takes a small step forward on the support foot to regain balance (Figure 3.10).

Points to Stress

Stress the following points with your students:

- Step forward with the non-kicking leg. Stand behind and slightly to the side of the ball. Eyes should be kept on the ball (head down) throughout the kick.
- Practice kicking with both feet.
- Move the leg backward in preparation for the kick. Beginners often fail to move the leg backward, making it difficult for them to generate kicking force.
- Move arms in opposition to the legs during the kick.

Figure 3.10 Kicking a soccer ball, stage four.

Teaching Tips for Kicking

- Use objects that don't hurt youngsters. For example, regulation soccer balls hurt young children's feet because they are heavy and have hard covers. Foam balls and beach balls are excellent substitutes to use for kicking practice.
- When teaching kicking skills, focus on velocity and distance rather than accuracy. If youngsters are asked to kick accurately, they will poke at the ball rather than develop a full kicking style.
- Kicking is similar to throwing in that each youngster should have a ball to kick. Beach balls (for primary grades) and foam balls are excellent because they do not travel a long distance and the youngster can kick and retrieve the ball quickly.
- Stationary balls are easier to kick than moving balls, so use a stationary ball when teaching beginners to kick.
- After the child has developed kick velocity and distance, focus on altering the force of the kick. Many youngsters learn to kick only with velocity; activities such as soccer demand both soft "touch" kicks and kicks of maximum velocity.
- Teach various types of kicks: the toe kick, instep kick, and the side-of-the-foot kick.

Striking

Striking occurs when an object is hit with an implement. The most common forms of striking are hitting a softball with a bat, using a racquet for striking in tennis and racquetball, and striking a ball with the hand as in volleyball.

Stage One

The feet are stationary and the trunk faces the direction of the tossed ball (or a ball on a tee). The elbows are fully flexed, and force is generated by extending the flexed joints in a downward plane. Little body force is generated because there is no trunk rotation and the motion developed is back to front. The total body does not play a role in generation of forces; rather, force comes from the arms and wrists.

Stage Two

In stage two, the upper body begins to generate force. The trunk is turned to the side in anticipation of the ball. The weight shifts from the rear foot to the forward foot prior to contacting the ball. The trunk and hips are rotated into the ball as the swing takes place. The elbows are less flexed, and force is generated by extending the flexed joints. Trunk rotation and forward movement are in an oblique plane.

Stage Three

There are only three stages of striking. When youngsters are capable of mature striking, they stand sideways to the path of the oncoming object. The weight is shifted to the rear foot and the hips are rotated. This is followed by a shift of weight toward the ball as it approaches the hitter. Striking occurs with the arms extended in a long arc. The swing ends with weight on the forward foot. Mature striking is characterized by a swing through the full range of motion and a sequential transfer of weight from the rear to the front of the body.

Back to Class

Mr. Lonkowski's first session of physical activity went so well that today he decides to try something more ambitious. He moves his 20 students outside onto the playground and has them stand in two lines facing each other, about 12 feet apart. He has brought a softball from home and gives it to the student at the front of the first line. He instructs the student as follows: "I want you to throw the ball across to Tim. When you throw, step toward Tim with your opposite foot. Rotate your hips as you move your arm forward. And don't forget to bend your arm at the elbow. Oh, and keep your weight on your backward foot!"

He then turns to Tim, who is the leader of the second line. "Tim, I want you to catch the ball. Keep your eye on the ball, and just bring it right into your body. Keep one foot forward, and try to keep yourself right in the path of the ball. Don't catch it from the side!"

He then instructs the group: "Practice throwing and catching the ball five times each, then pass the ball to the next person in line and move to the back of the line."

Given what you've learned in this chapter, how do you predict that Mr. Lonkowski's session of physical activity might turn out today? What, if anything, did Mr. Lonkowski do wrong?

Points to Stress

Stress the following points with your students:

Track the ball visually as soon as possible, and keep tracking it until it is hit. Even though it is impossible to see the racquet hit the ball, it is an excellent teaching hint and encourages tracking the object as long as possible.

Grip the bat with the hands together. If batting right-handed, the left hand should be on the bottom (near the small end of the bat).

Keep the elbows away from the body. Emphasis should be placed on making a large swing with the elbows extended as the ball hits the object.

Swing the bat in a horizontal (parallel to the ground) plane. Beginners have a tendency to strike downward in a chopping motion.

Teaching Tips for Striking

Encourage beginners to strike with maximum force and bat velocity.

Have children practice hitting stationary objects before progressing to moving objects. Batting tees and balls suspended on a string are useful for beginners.

- Use slow-moving objects such as balloons and beach balls in the early stages of striking practice. This helps the child track the moving projectile.
- As skill in striking increases, the size of the projectile and bat (or racquet) may be decreased.
- Ensure that there is contrast between the ball and the background to enhance visual perception.
- Use rubber footprints to help children learn to stride (step) into the ball.

Helping Children Participate in Sports and Games

Sports and related games are offered in most school settings, and children who want to participate often ask classroom teachers for help. You don't have to be an outstanding athlete to help: an understanding of the basic principles of growth and development explored in Chapter 2 will provide a good foundation, as will the preceding discussion of specific sport skills. You can also check out the advice on youth sports from the National Alliance for Youth Sports website (see Web Resources). In addition, if you find yourself actively assisting students in sports and games, strive to avoid the following three behaviors: assigning children to a particular role or position, labeling children, and pressuring children to excel beyond their developmental readiness.

Avoid Early Specialization

All children need opportunities to develop their skills and experience success. Unfortunately, the question of whether a child will be a pitcher or a right fielder, play in the line, or be a quarterback, is often dictated by the child's skeletal maturity. When teachers and coaches assign playing positions according to a child's physical appearance, they fail to offer all participants an opportunity to realize their potential.

This was demonstrated in a classic study by Hale (1956) involving a Little League World Series. All players were 11 years old, with the wide range in skeletal age normally found in most groups of U.S. children. Among these children, the skeletally mature were found to be playing in the skilled positions in the series. The most mature were pitchers and catchers, and the least mature played right field. The skeletally mature children thus received more opportunity for skill practice through their many opportunities to throw and catch in games and practice. In contrast, the children who were less mature and were forced to play right field received limited throwing and catching opportunities and probably would not have the chance to close the skill gap and develop adequate skill competency.

Youngsters should have the opportunity to play all positions in sports and games rather than specialize in one role. In addition, they should receive similar amounts of practice time and should have positive reinforcement for participation, regardless of their current skill level. Children like to participate in activities that offer positive experiences; they will become discouraged if they receive little encouragement and praise while they are struggling to learn new skills and positions. With a classroom of students, mandate that they rotate positions often.

Avoid Labeling Students

In Chapter 2, we said that the willingness to participate in activities is driven by how children *feel* about their ability, in other words, by their level of perceived competence. Perceived competence becomes more specific as students mature. Younger primary grade students often approach new tasks feeling that they are competent at everything they try. However, as they become older (by about the third or fourth grade), they start to realize that other students may be better in some areas. If these maturing students are not given the chance to succeed in physical activity, they may develop a feeling of incompetence. Sometimes called *learned helplessness* (Harter, 1978), this feeling can eventually prompt students to avoid all types of physical activity.

One of the ways to avoid fostering learned helplessness is to avoid labeling some children as athletically gifted and others as not gifted at a young age. Early labeling creates a self-fulfilling prophecy, where students identified as gifted receive more feedback and are expected to reach higher levels of performance. Students identified as less able receive less feedback and expectations remain low.

Moreover, when we identify children as outstanding athletes at an early age, we're usually wrong! A classic study by Clarke (1968) was designed to determine whether it was possible to identify outstanding athletes by viewing their performance in the elementary school years. Surprisingly, the athletes identified as outstanding in elementary school were seldom outstanding in junior high school, and predictions based on elementary school performance were correct only 25 percent of the time. So rather than discouraging children who seem less capable, we should treat all children as if they have the potential to become successful. One of the purposes of activity in the elementary school years is to help all students develop physical skills within the range of their given abilities.

Avoid Early Pressure to Excel

Many parents, teachers, and coaches push children to compete in sports at an early age. But there is no evidence to support the idea that starting a child in a sport at a young age increases the child's success. When they are eight or nine years old, such early starters may seem more athletically gifted compared to children who started later because they have been practicing the related skills for years. In most cases, however, genetically gifted children quickly catch up and surpass "early superstars" in one to three years. As Shephard (1984) states, "Any advantage that is gained from very prolonged training probably lies in the area of skill perfection rather than in a fuller realization of physical potential."

In addition, there is justified concern that pushing children into documented programs increases the possibility of burnout at an early age. A *documented program* is one that offers extrinsic rewards such as trophies, published league standings, ribbons, and excessive parental involvement (keeping score, giving rewards, etc.). Evidence shows that excessive extrinsic rewards may actually decrease intrinsic motivation, particularly in children age seven years and older. Researchers found that younger children (age five) perceived rewards as a bonus that added to the joy of performing a throwing motor task (Thomas and Tennant, 1978; Whitehead and Corbin, 1991). However, this effect decreased with age, and by age nine, the reward was seen as a bribe and thus undermined intrinsic motivation. Thus, we need to encourage young children to participate in physical activity simply for the sheer enjoyment and excitement involved in moving and interacting with peers.

There is also concern about "elitist" programs that start "cutting" less-gifted players at an early age. Research suggests that many such children would continue to participate if given the opportunity (Petlichkoff, 1992). Thus, it is difficult to justify this approach, especially at the elementary school level. All children should be given the opportunity to participate if they choose to do so.

If starting youngsters early creates early burnout, why do parents feel pressured to force their children into a sport program? One reason is that they compare their children to other children. Parents see other children participating and practicing sport skills in an organized setting. They worry their child will be unable to "catch up" if they do not get them involved in a similar program at the same age. Parents need to know that there is no evidence to support this fear. Teachers can help parents identify programs that minimize pressure and focus on skill development and fun, allowing all youngsters to participate regardless of ability. Children consider having fun and improving their skills to be more important than winning (Athletic Footwear Association, 1990).

Back to Class

At a faculty party just before the beginning of the winter break, Mr. Lonkowski corners Mrs. Li. "So," he asks, "have you had any success at increasing your students' physical activity?"

Mrs. Li laughs. "I'm getting the hang of it! At first I made some pretty silly mistakes, but then I came to realize that physical activity requires preparation, just like anything else we do in the classroom. Once I taught the kids some ground rules, they started to relax and get into it. What about you?"

"I guess I was a little too enthusiastic at first," Mr. Lonkowski confesses. I tried to do too much too quickly, and the kids got overwhelmed. Now I remind myself to take it easy. Most kids just need to move. They're not going to be competitive athletes. Except for this one little girl in my class! She's got the makings of an Olympic gymnast! Now I know she's only seven, but you should see her somersault, or jackknife, or stand on her head! I told her parents they've just got to get her into serious training!"

Do you think Mr. Lonkowski is still "a little too enthusiastic"? Why or why not? What behaviors discussed in this chapter should he avoid in his interactions with this little girl and her parents?

Chapter Summary

Preparing the Space for Physical Activity

- To determine how much space you need for a session of physical activity, consider the skills your students will be practicing and the amount of instruction they need from you. Use cones to delineate the area, and if you have too many students for a single activity, consider dividing the space into two or more smaller-sized activity areas.

- Before beginning the lesson, make sure you have enough equipment and that it is in working order. For individual-use skills such as throwing, you should have one ball per student.

- Position equipment effectively, such as around the perimeter of the playing area, and have students assist with equipment and apparatus setup and storage.

Promoting a Safe Environment

- To promote safe physical activity sessions, write down, communicate, and practice safety rules.

- Make sure that all physical activity sessions are appropriately supervised, and stay at the periphery of the activity so that you can see all children at all times.

- Offer children step-by-step instructions in how to perform the activity, use any related equipment, and follow safety procedures. Make sure that both activities and instructions are developmentally appropriate, and never force children to participate in an activity.

- Avoid using physical activity, such as running laps, for punishment.

Designing Effective Practice Sessions

- To teach motor skills effectively, manage students' level of arousal; for example, postpone competition until students have over-learned skills. In addition, in the early learning stages, focus on process, not product, and encourage mental practice as appropriate.

- For effective practice sessions, you need to determine whether a skill is simple or complex, as well as whether organization is low or high. Select whole or part practice accordingly.

- In the early stages of learning motor skills, many short practice sessions spaced out over a long period of time are more effective than a few long practice sessions in a short period of time.

After students have mastered basic skill components, use random practice techniques and offer variable practice experiences.

Fostering the Development of Sport Skills

Share with students some basic principles of body mechanics, such as stability, force, leverage, motion, and direction, to help them master sport skills.

Children should practice throwing for accuracy only after they have acquired the proper throwing form. Have children work independently, throwing as hard as possible, while they are developing the skill.

Catching is more difficult to learn than throwing because the object must be tracked and the body moved into the path of the object simultaneously. Also, children typically fear getting hurt by the ball. Balloons, fleece balls, and beach balls are easier for children to track visually and much less likely to cause injury.

When teaching kicking skills, focus on velocity and distance rather than accuracy. If youngsters are asked to kick accurately, they will not develop a full kicking style. When children are learning kicking, use a beach ball or foam ball, as these are soft, do not travel far, and can be retrieved quickly.

Have children practice hitting stationary objects before progressing to moving objects. Batting tees and balls suspended on a string are useful for beginners. Then have children progress to slow-moving objects such as balloons and beach balls, which are easier for them to track visually.

Helping Children Participate in Sports and Games

Sports and related games are offered in most school settings, and you can help children who participate to succeed without being an outstanding athlete yourself, if you understand children's intrinsic needs, characteristics, and stages of skill development.

If you actively assist students in sports and games, strive to avoid the following three behaviors: assigning children to a particular role or position, labeling children, and pressuring children to excel beyond their developmental readiness.

Review Questions

Content Review

1. In addition to identifying and communicating safety rules to children, what step should you take to ensure that students fully understand these rules?

2. Categorize each of the following scenarios as blocked practice or random practice, and explain the reasons for your choice: (a) First-graders stand with their toes at a

line, a beach ball in front of their feet. They are instructed to kick the ball as hard as they can against the far wall. Each student practices this repeatedly for five minutes. (b) A group of middle school students plays a game of soccer.

3. Imagine that you are teaching 21 fourth-graders a set of simple dance movements to perform to a recording of a three-minute popular song. Jot down some notes to yourself regarding your instructional space needs, safety rules, choice of whole or part practice, the length and distribution of your practice sessions, and the appropriateness of random practice techniques.

4. Classify each of the following activities in terms of complexity and organization, then state whether you would use whole or part practice for each: (a) skipping (which is a series of step-hops done with alternate feet, with the arms swinging to shoulder height in opposition to the feet); (b) jumping rope; (c) performing a forward roll (which begins from a squat with hands and feet on the ground); (d) dribbling a ball.

5. Explain how the principle of stability relates to mastery of the following sport skills: (a) throwing, (b) catching, (c) kicking.

Real World

1. You are student teaching in an elementary school and have been asked to supervise the lunchtime recess. It is a cold and rainy day, and the children are spending their recess in the gymnasium. You see a group of about 20 children in one corner playing tag, another group of about the same size is at the basketball hoop, and a third group at the far end of the gym is organizing what appears to be a game of kick ball or soccer. You are the only teacher in the gym. What, if any, concerns are raised by this scenario, and what should you do?

2. You are chatting with a teacher who is close to retirement age. Over coffee, she talks about the "old days," when corporal punishment in the classroom was acceptable. "I had very few discipline problems then," she says, "because the kids knew I meant business! It's much more difficult to control my class nowadays." She goes on to describe an incident that occurred earlier that day: as punishment for stealing and eating another student's morning snack, she had a child perform 50 jumping jacks at the front of the classroom. She sighs, "I'm not sure this kind of thing is very effective, though. Many of the children just laughed. Nobody laughed when I used to get out my paddle!" What potential consequences of this teacher's new method of punishment might you point out to her?

References and Suggested Readings

Appenzeller, H. (1993). *Managing sports and risk management strategies*. Durham, NC: Carolina Academic Press.

Appenzeller, H. (ed.). (1998). *Risk management in sport: Issues and strategies*. Durham, NC: Carolina Academic Press.

Appenzeller, H. (2003). *Managing sports and risk management strategies* (2nd ed.). Durham, NC: Carolina Academic Press.

Athletic Footwear Association. (1990). *American youth and sports participation*. North Palm Beach, FL: Athletic Footwear Association.

Baley, J.A., and Matthews, D.L. (1988). *Law and liability in athletics, physical education, and recreation*. Boston: Allyn & Bacon.

What About You?

Think of a motor skill that you have found challenging to master. It needn't be related to sports: what about playing piano, ballroom dancing, sailing a boat, or learning to chop firewood? As you think about this motor skill, journal your responses to the following questions:

Did your teacher seem to focus more on the process or on the outcome? _____

Were you ever advised to use mental practice techniques? _____

When you were initially acquiring this skill, did you mostly use whole practice or part practice? _____

_____

Did you ever engage in random practice sessions? _____

If so, what form did these take? _____

Finally, how will you apply the lessons from this learning experience in your work with children?

_____

_____

_____

Clarke, H.H. (1968). Characteristics of the young athlete: A longitudinal look. *Kinesiology Review,* 3, 33–42.

Dougherty, N.J. (ed.). (2002). *Principles of safety in physical education and sport* (3rd ed.). Reston, VA: AAHPERD.

Dougherty, N.J., Golberger, A.S., and Carpenter, A.S. (2002). *Sport, physical activity, and the law.* Champaign, IL: Sagamore Publishing.

Gabbard, C. (2004). *Lifelong motor development* (4th ed.). San Francisco: Pearson Benjamin Cummings.

Gallahue, D.L., and Donnelly, F.C. (2003). *Developmental physical education for all children* (4th ed.). Champaign, IL: Human Kinetics Publishers.

Goode, S., and Magill, R.A. (1986). The contextual interference effects in learning three badminton serves. *Research Quarterly for Exercise and Sport,* 57, 308–314.

Hale, C. (1956). Physiological maturity of Little League baseball players. *Research Quarterly,* 27, 276–284.

Hart, J.E., and Ritson, R.J. (2002). *Liability and safety in physical education and sport: A practitioner's guide to the legal aspects of teaching and coaching in elementary and secondary schools* (2nd ed.). Reston, VA: AAHPERD.

Harter, S. (1978). Effectance motivation revisited. *Child Development, 21,* 34–64.

Merriman, J. (1993). Supervision in sport and physical activity. *Journal of Physical Education, Recreation, and Dance, 64*(2), 20–23.

Pangrazi, R.P. (2007). *Dynamic physical education curriculum guide: Lesson plans for implementation* (15th ed.). San Francisco: Pearson Benjamin Cummings.

Petlichkoff, L.M. (1992). Youth sport participation and withdrawal: Is it simply a matter of fun? *Pediatric Exercise Science, 4*(2), 105–110.

Rink, J.E. (2006). *Teaching physical education for learning* (5th ed.). Boston: WCB/McGraw-Hill.

Schmidt, R.A., and Wrisberg, C. (2008). *Motor learning and performance* (4th ed.). Champaign, IL: Human Kinetics Publishers.

Shephard, R.J. (1984). Physical activity and child health. *Sports Medicine, 1,* 205–233.

Siedentop, D., and Tannehill, D. (2000). *Developing teaching skills in physical education* (4th ed.). Mountain View, CA: Mayfield Publishing Co.

Thomas, J.R., and Tennant, L.K. (1978). Effects of rewards on changes in children's motivation for an athletic task. In F.L. Smoll and R.E. Smith (eds.), *Psychological perspectives in youth sports.* New York: Hemisphere.

U.S. Consumer Product Safety Commission. (1994). *Handbook for public playground safety.* Washington, DC: U.S. Government Printing Office.

Whitehead, J.R., and Corbin, C.B. (1991). Effects of fitness test type, teacher, and gender on exercise intrinsic motivation and physical self-worth. *Journal of School Health, 61,* 11–16.

Web Resources

Consumer Product Safety Commission/Playground Safety Publications:
www.cpsc.gov/CPSCPUB/PUBS/playpubs.html
The Master Teacher:
www.masterteacher.com
National Alliance for Youth Sports:
www.nays.org
National Program for Playground Safety:
www.uni.edu/playground
National School Safety and Security Services:
www.schoolsecurity.org
PE Central:
www.pecentral.org
PE Links 4U:
www.pelinks4u.org
PE4life:
www.pe4life.org
PlayWorld Systems/PlayDesigns Products:
www.playworldsystems.com

4

Improving the Effectiveness of Instruction and Feedback

Learning Objectives

After reading this chapter, you will be able to . . .

- Identify the characteristics of an effective learning environment.
- Design measurable student outcomes related to physical activities.
- Explain how a student's skill entry-level influences his or her success or failure.
- Deliver instruction to students in a manner that facilitates learning.
- Use instructional cues that help students focus on performance techniques.
- Develop a number of methods for checking that students understand your instruction.
- Identify the characteristics of meaningful and effective feedback.
- Implement instruction that is sensitive to diversity and gender issues.
- Help students learn how to make responsible decisions.
- Communicate effectively by showing empathy and understanding to all students.

Classroom Challenge

It's a sunny autumn day, and Miss Pimentel has planned a session of rope jumping as a mid-morning activity break for her first-grade students. As they march onto the playground, she divides them into groups of three and hands each group a jump rope. Then she instructs them to decide which child in the group is going to jump first and which two children are going to hold the rope. When two children in each group are holding each end of the rope, she calls out, "Ready? Start jumping!"

Miss Pimentel sits on top of a picnic table at the edge of the playground and observes. In one of the groups, a student is jumping quite ably while her two partners cooperate in swinging the rope in a steady rhythm. "Good job!" Miss Pimentel calls out to the group.

A second group is not doing as well: Alec, who is jumping, keeps stepping on the rope. One of the rope turners, Lizzie, says, "Here, switch with me," and hands him the rope. Alec takes it with a scowl. Miss Pimentel hears him say, "Go ahead! Jumping rope is for girls and sissies anyway!"

Miss Pimentel is about to chastise Alec when the jumper from a third group runs up to her with tears in her eyes. It's Maya, the smallest girl in the class, and Miss Pimentel notices a red welt rising on her spindly leg. "I hate jumping rope!" Maya cries, as she collapses on the grass. "I'm never gonna play this game again!"

In Chapter 3, we discussed practical considerations for teaching physical activity: delineating a space, using equipment, implementing safety rules, and designing appropriate skill practice sessions. In this chapter, we look at the interpersonal aspects of effective teaching: improving the effectiveness of your instruction and feedback, considering students' personal needs, and communicating with empathy and understanding. With this information, we hope you'll be able to avoid the experience Miss Pimentel's class had and instead create an effective learning environment.

Characteristics of an Effective Learning Environment

Before we can discuss how to create an effective learning environment, you need to be able to recognize its characteristics. For example, high rates of student-engaged time and positive attitudes toward the subject matter are considered part of an effective learning environment. Evidence from teacher-effectiveness research (Brophy and Good, 1986; Evertson, 1989; Siedentop and Tannehill, 2000) indicates that regardless of the teacher's instructional style, an educational environment is most effective when the following elements are present.

- *Students are engaged in appropriate learning activities for a large percentage of class time.* Effective teachers use class time wisely. They plan appropriate learning activities for the subject matter. Students need time to learn; effective teachers ensure that students use class time to receive information and practice skills. Developmental learning activities are matched to students' abilities and contribute to overall class objectives.

- *Students spend a limited amount of time waiting in line or in other unproductive behaviors.* In an effective learning environment for physical activity, students spend a high percentage of time practicing, drilling, and playing. Students learn by practicing the activity, not by waiting in line for an opportunity to do so.

- *Teachers spend a limited amount of class time managing students and transitioning from one activity to another.* Effective teachers are efficient managers of students. Time-saving measures are planned and implemented efficiently, and instructional procedures are tightly organized with little wasted time. Students make the transition from one learning activity to another smoothly and without wasting time. For example, students spend little time moving from classroom to playing field, and equipment is accessible and in working order.

- *Students receive clear objectives and meaningful feedback.* Students need to know what they are expected to learn. Make sure instructional activities are clearly tied to the class objectives and that students spend most of their time focusing on them. Give students positive and corrective feedback (discussed shortly) often.

- *Student progress is monitored regularly, and students are held accountable for learning.* Students are expected to make progress toward achieving class objectives. Teach students how to assess and record their progress. Tell them exactly what is expected of them and how the expectations are tied to the accountability system.

- *Teachers have high but realistic expectations for student achievement.* Structure learning activities that challenge students. Activities must not be too easy or too difficult. Students need both success and challenge from learning activities, and a balance of both is a key to quality teaching. Expect students to learn, and hold them accountable for their progress.

- *The learning atmosphere is success oriented, with a positive, caring climate.* Teachers and students need to feel positive about working and learning in the physical activity environment. Teachers who promote appropriate social and organizational behavior foster a supportive atmosphere, which encourages learning and positive student attitudes toward school.

Teachers show enthusiasm in their teaching and are actively involved in the instructional process. Students need an enthusiastic model—someone who incorporates physical activity into his or her lifestyle. Active involvement means active supervision, enthusiasm, and high interaction rates with students. These characteristics enhance learning regardless of the teaching style used; they are important for ensuring student achievement and positive attitudes.

Back to Class

Which of the elements above were missing from Miss Pimentel's physical activity session?

Improving the Effectiveness of Your Instruction

Learning occurs when a well-planned curriculum is presented in a sound instructional manner. The curriculum is a critical component of the educational process; however, when even a superior curriculum is poorly taught, student progress is limited. This section discusses the steps that you should take to ensure efficient and effective instruction in physical activity.

Design Measurable Student Outcomes

Stated educational outcome goals give a lesson direction and meaning. Outcomes that are stated clearly tell learners what they are expected to accomplish and learn. Effective learning outcomes are characterized as follows.

First, outcomes must define observable behavior. Teachers and students must know when an outcome is achieved. If an objective does not define observable behavior, neither student nor teacher knows if it has been reached. For example, could you observe whether or not "students will be able to understand how to skip"? Certainly not, yet you could observe "students will be able to skip around the periphery of the court." Accomplishment in physical activities is easier to evaluate than in other areas because physical activities are overt and easy to observe.

Second, objectives must identify clearly and specifically the content to be learned. Teachers and students are comfortable when both understand what is expected of them. Problems arise when students have to guess what the teacher wants them to learn. Students have a right to know what is expected and what they need to accomplish. Achieving stated outcomes ensures that learning has occurred and that students know more than they did prior to beginning the lesson. If outcomes are ambiguous or nonexistent, students have no way of knowing if they have improved or learned anything.

Outcomes for physical activity are easy to write. For example, if you are playing a game in your classroom, such as "Rock, Paper, and Scissors," it is easy to see if students have learned who wins and who loses. Thus, an outcome might be "all students will be able to instantly identify who has won the match in a game of 'Rock, Paper, and Scissors.'" Certainly, it is not necessary to write a large number of outcomes for classroom activities. Activity component objectives may be written in a short and concise style. The following are examples of outcomes written for students:

- Using a long jump rope, partners will be able to turn the rope 15 consecutive times.
- Using a balloon, students will be able to keep the ball in the air by striking it six consecutive times.
- Students will be able to explain the rules of classroom volleyball.
- Students will be able to state three benefits of regular physical activity.

Back to Class

Write at least one outcome statement that Miss Pimentel might have communicated to her class.

Determine the Students' Skill Level

Selecting the appropriate level of difficulty for skill instruction is challenging because a class of students presents a wide variety of abilities and maturation levels. Instruction should begin with an activity that most students can accomplish easily. In other words, begin at **entry level**, which is a rough estimation of the skill level for the majority of students in the class. This promotes a positive feeling among students and allows them to build upon their success.

Most students are not motivated by failure. Many adults feel students will want to try harder than ever when they fail; however, early failure causes most students to dislike and even avoid an activity. Thus, beginning at entry level is critical.

One way to determine the entry level of the class is to move through a progression of activities (ranging from easy to more difficult) until several students find it difficult to be successful. This method accomplishes two things: it offers a review of skills (review makes students feel successful), and it gives you an estimate of the students' ability levels. Another approach is to let students determine an entry level that they feel is best suited for them. For example, when playing classroom football, ask students how many like the game. Most students who are competent will say they like it, but if their experience has been negative, they will not want to participate. Students pick activities they feel competent in performing. Instruction and learning occur when students are able to find an entry level that is appropriate for them.

Use an Anticipatory Set

The **anticipatory set** is an activity designed to focus students' attention on an up-coming learning task. In any lesson, the opening instructional sequence is one of the most difficult parts of the lesson. Students are tentative about beginning a new game or activity and need to be focused and prepared to move into the "learning mode." They need to understand the benefit of the new activity—that is, what's in it for them.

For example, a common type of anticipatory set informs students of what the desired outcome for the lesson will be. Tell students what they are going to learn and why it is important. Few people care about learning if the outcome is not stated or is thought to be unimportant. The more convinced students are about the importance of learning something, the more motivated they are to participate.

Anticipatory sets are most effective when they tie into students' past learning experiences. For example, in a rope-jumping lesson, you might ask students if they have had trouble with this skill in the past and invite them to say why. In response to their feedback, your instructional focus might include directing students to watch the turner's hand, jump where the rope hits the ground, or reduce the height of their jumps.

You may also use an anticipatory set to reveal the skill level of students in the class. For example, you might ask students, "What are three things we have to remember when tossing and catching beanbags?" Their answers will reveal whether they know the basic tenets of catching skills. Identifying what students know is necessary for designing an effective lesson.

Other examples of anticipatory sets are the following:

- "What is agility?" Name some activities that require a lot of agility. Which students in class seem to display agility? Allow time for discussion. Then introduce an activity such as a game of tag, and explain how agility is more important than speed in this instance.
- "I was watching many of you play basketball at recess. It seemed as though you had a lot of trouble making baskets. What could we do to increase your success?" After the discussion, say, "I am going to teach you a couple of techniques that will improve your shooting skills."
- "Try juggling the two scarves you've just picked out. I will come around and observe how you are doing." You observe for a few minutes and note a great deal of frustration. This is a common way to use the anticipatory set; it establishes the need for instruction in how to juggle the scarves.

It is not always necessary to use an anticipatory set, but there should be a reason for omitting it. If students already know the necessary information, there is little value in taking time for it. On the other hand, when beginning a new activity, an anticipatory set is effective.

Make Skill Instruction Meaningful

Instruction is the cornerstone of learning because it is how information is transmitted to students. Meaningful skill instruction includes:

the definition of the skill,
the elements or parts of the skill, and
information about when, why, and how the skill should be used.

The following are suggestions for giving effective and meaningful instructions:

Limit instruction to one or two key points. It is difficult for anyone to remember a series of instructions. Giving the students too much information related to skill performance leaves them baffled and frustrated. When given a series of points, most learners remember the first and the last points. Strong emphasis on one or two key points makes it easier for students to focus their concentration.

Refrain from lengthy skill descriptions. When instructions last longer than 30 to 60 seconds, students become listless because they can't comprehend and remember all of the information. Develop a pattern of giving short, concise instructions followed by applied practice. Short practice sessions offer an opportunity to refocus on key points of a skill several times.

Present information in a basic, easy-to-understand form. If a class or student does not understand the presentation, you—not your students—have failed. Check for understanding (discussed further in the next section) to see if students comprehend the material.

Separate management and instructional episodes. Consider the following instructions during the presentation of a new game: "In this game, we will move into groups of five. Each group will get a ball and form a small circle. On the command, 'Go!' the game will start. Here is how you play the game." A lengthy discussion of game rules and conduct follows. Because the instructions are long, students forget what they were asked to do earlier. Or, they think about whom they want in their group rather than the game rules. Instead, move the class into game formation (management) and then discuss the activity to be learned (instruction). This serves two purposes: it reduces the length of the episode and makes it easier to conceptualize how the game is played.

Back to Class

Of the previous suggestions for giving effective instruction, which did Miss Pimentel use?

Use Instructional Cues

Instructional cues are keywords that quickly and efficiently communicate proper technique and performance of skills and movement tasks. Children require a clear understanding of key skill points because motor learning and cognitive understanding of the skill are developed simultaneously. Teaching activities without instructional cues may result in ineffective learning if students do not clearly understand proper technique and the key points of performance. When using instructional cues, consider the following points:

Develop Precise Cues

Make cues short, descriptive phrases that call attention to key points of a skill technique—for example, "Look, ready, catch!" Cues must be precise and accurate because they are concise reminders of how to perform the skill. Cues should guide learners and enhance the quality of learning. Cues make it easier for learners to remember a sequence of new motor patterns. Study an activity and design cues that focus student learning on correct skill technique.

All teachers occasionally have to teach activities that they know little about. To develop cues in areas where you lack expertise, refer to textbooks and media aids. For example, *Teaching Cues for Basic Sport Skills for Elementary and Middle School Students* (Fronske and Wilson, 2002) offers teaching cues for a wide variety of physical activities. Other teachers who have strengths in different activities are good sources of information.

Use Short, Action-Oriented Cues

Effective cues should be short and to the point. To avoid confusing and overwhelming the learner, choose a small number of cues to present during each lesson. Design cues that are short, that contain keywords, and that encourage the learner to focus on one part of a skill. For example, if a student is learning to throw, offer a cue such as "Begin with your throwing arm farthest from the target." This cue reminds the student not to face the target, which precludes trunk rotation in later phases of the throw. Other examples of throwing cues are as follows:

"Step toward the target."
"Keep your eye on the target."
"Shift your weight from the rear to the front foot."

To be effective, your cues should communicate the skill as a whole. Have all the critical points been covered? For most skills, performance can be broken down into three parts: preparation, action, and recovery. Focus on one phase of a skill at a time, as most beginners can best concentrate on only one thing at a time.

In addition, use action-oriented words. These words are especially effective with young children, particularly if the words have an exciting sound; for example, "*Pop up* at the end of the forward roll," "*Twist* the body during the throw," or "*Explode* off the starting line." In other situations, let your voice influence the effectiveness of the cue. For example, if a skill is to be done smoothly and softly, speak in a soft tone and ask students to "let the movement *floooooow*" or to "move *smooooothly* across the balance beam." The most effective cues combine voice inflections, body language, and action words to signal the desired behavior.

Integrate Cues

Integrating cues means combining multiple parts of a skill so that learners focus on the skill as a whole. Integrated cues build on the initial cues used during the presentation of a skill and assume that students understand the concepts introduced in the earlier phases of instruction. Examples of integrated cues are "step, rotate, and throw" or, "run, jump, and forward roll."

The first integrated cue ("step, rotate, and throw") reminds students to sequence parts of the skill. The second ("run, jump, and forward roll") helps young children remember a sequence of movements. Integrated cues help learners to remember proper sequencing of skills and to form mental images of the performance.

Demonstrate Skills

A quick and effective way to present a physical activity is to demonstrate it. You may do this yourself, use visual aids such as a DVD, or ask students to demonstrate it. Regardless of how it is presented, in the early stages of learning it is important that the demonstration be clear and unambiguous, accentuating critical points of performance.

Children love to see their teacher demonstrate skills (**Figure 4.1**). When you do so, verbalize key points so students know what to focus on. When possible, slow down the demonstration and present it step-by-step. Through reading, study, and analysis of movement, you'll be able to develop an understanding of how to present most activities. That said, even skilled teachers need to devise an alternative plan for activities they are not able to perform. If you are unable to perform an activity, know what key points of the activity should be emphasized.

Visual aids, such as a DVD or videotape, can enhance your instruction. Many skills may be recorded and played back in slow motion. The replay may be stopped at critical moments so students can imitate a position or technique shown. For example, in a throwing unit, freeze the video at a point that illustrates the position of the arm. Have students imitate moving the arm into proper position based on the stop-action pose.

If you can't demonstrate a skill and don't have a visual aid, find a student who can help. Be sure students are able to correctly demonstrate the desired skill so they will not be embarrassed in front of the class. Usually, it is possible to find a capable student simply by asking the class if anyone is willing to demonstrate the desired skill. Another alternative is to identify a student who is correctly performing the skill

Figure 4.1 Effective teachers demonstrate skill techniques.

during a practice session and ask if he or she would be willing to demonstrate. Most students will not volunteer to demonstrate unless they feel able.

Student demonstration adds original ideas into the lesson (**Figure 4.2**). It also helps build self-esteem in a youngster who successfully demonstrates a skill. If you are unsure about students' abilities to demonstrate, ask them to try the activity while all other students are engaged. If they are successful, have them demonstrate it. If not, let them know you will call on them at another time. At opportune times, stop the class and let children volunteer to show what they have done. Comment on satisfactory demonstrations. If a demonstration is unsatisfactory, go on to another child without reprimand, saying only, "Thank you, Janet. Let's see what Carl can do." Or, redirect the class to continue practicing. Ensure that all students who want to be selected are given an opportunity to demonstrate at one time or another.

Whether you are demonstrating a skill yourself, using a video, or having a student demonstrate, you should integrate instructional cues with the demonstration. The following are two examples:

- Students are in partners spread out about 20 yards apart; one partner has a football. "When kicking the football, take a short step with your kicking foot, a long step with the other foot, and kick (*demonstrate*). Again, short step, long step, kick (*teaching cue*)."

- "Listen to the first verse of this schottische music. I'll do the part of the schottische step we just learned, starting with the second verse (*demonstrate*). Ready, step, step, step, hop (*teaching cue*). When I hit the tambourine, begin doing the step."

Check for Understanding

Students may display an expression that says they understand something even when they do not. Thus, you need a reliable way of checking to see if they understand what you've taught them. A common (but poor) method is to ask periodically, "Does everybody understand?" Although the teacher appears to be checking for understanding, this is seldom the case. Often, the teacher does not even wait for a response. But even when given time to answer, students rarely do. It takes a brave and confident student to admit to a lack of understanding in front of the entire class. Therefore, it is important to find a quick and easy way to check for understanding without causing student embarrassment. The following are suggestions:

- *Use hand signals.* Direct students to signal their understanding by using signals. Examples might be "Thumbs up if you

Figure 4.2 Use a student to demonstrate a skill.

understand," or "If you think this demonstration is correct, put your left hand in the air," or "Raise the number of fingers to signal which student you think did a correct forward roll." If the signals are given quickly and without comment, students will signal quickly and privately without embarrassment. Having students signal with heads down and eyes closed may be useful if the situation is touchy or embarrassing.

Ask questions that may be answered as a group response. Some students may mouth an answer even though they do not know the correct response. Estimate the number of students who understand by the intensity of the group response. A strong response by the class indicates that the majority of youngsters understand.

Prepare the entire class to respond to a skill check rather than a specific student. For example, say, "Be ready to demonstrate the grapevine step." This encourages all members of the class to focus on the activity, knowing they may be called on to demonstrate. Even though it does not ensure that everyone understands, it increases the possibility that students will think about the skill check.

Use peer-checking methods. Have students pair up and evaluate each other's performance using a checklist you have designed. Repeat evaluations using different students to help ensure the validity of the scoring.

Use tests and written feedback to monitor cognitive concepts. For example, use written tests to see if students can diagram and explain the options of an offense or a defense. Asking students to list safety precautions for an activity ensures student understanding. Use some restraint when administering written tests—too many written assessments will take too much time away from skill practice. Use these instruments when the information cannot be gathered efficiently with other methods.

Offer Guided Practice

As you know, correct practice develops correct skill patterns, whereas incorrect practice ingrains mistakes. Thus, in the early stages of skill development, your guidance is critical. You should offer guided practice sessions as quickly as possible after teaching students a new skill. Allow students to get a feel for the skill as a whole before having them work on parts of it. The opportunity to perform the whole skill before practicing smaller components enables them to see how the parts fit together.

Once they have an initial feel for the skill, help your students move through each step correctly. Present small amounts of information, one component at a time, helping students build new skills on previous learning. Monitor class performance and offer meaningful feedback, as discussed shortly. Finally, make sure that all students have the same opportunity for practice. If anyone has to receive less practice, make sure it's the student who can already perform the skill successfully.

Monitor Class Performance

Monitoring class performance ensures that students stay on task and practice activities correctly. To monitor the class effectively, stand in a position that allows you to make eye contact with all students. Students generally stay on task when they know someone is watching them.

A false assumption held by many teachers is that they must always stand in the same area when monitoring students or giving instructions and feedback. The assumption is that students pay attention only when the teacher is on or near this "instructional spot." Not only is this incorrect, but it sometimes allows negative behavior. There are always students who enjoy being near the instructor and those who like to be as far away as possible. Students who choose to exhibit deviant or off-task behaviors usually move away. If you always instruct from the same place, less-compliant students will learn to move to a position that is difficult for you to observe. Try to be unpredictable when positioning yourself. By moving around, you'll be able to observe and give an equal amount of feedback and attention to all students. Deliver instruction from the perimeter of the area, and vary your location regularly.

Another reason for varying your location is to allow you to observe students from the most effective vantage point and to move into position to better observe important aspects of your students' practice. For example, if you were observing kicking, you could see more of the student's form if you were standing to the side of the student rather than behind him or her. When observing, avoid staying too long with a single group of students because the rest of the class will begin to move off task. Give a student one or two focus points and then move to another student.

Because movement increases your instructional effectiveness, it should be a part of your lesson plan. To facilitate coverage, divide the instructional area into four imaginary quadrants and make an attempt to move into the far corner of each a certain number of times during the lesson. Try to give instructions and reinforcement from all four quadrants of the area. Some teachers are surprised to find that they stand in the same area and rarely move to a new quadrant. If you are uncertain of how much you are moving, ask a student to watch you and record the number of times you enter a new quadrant during an instructional session.

Bring Closure

Closure is a time to review learning that has taken place during the lesson. Closure helps increase retention because students review what they have learned. Focus closure discussions on what has been learned rather than on merely naming activities practiced. Closure is not simply a recall of activities that were completed but rather a discussion of the application of skills and knowledge learned through practice.

Closure provides an opportunity to show how movement patterns in different skills are similar. Often, students do not realize that a movement pattern they are currently practicing is similar to one learned earlier. Discussing what was learned focuses students on what they should be learning through practice. Use closure as a time to remind students to tell their parents and others what they have learned. How many times do parents ask, "What did you learn at school today?" only to hear the reply, "Nothing"? The following prompts are ways to initiate closure discussions:

"Describe two or three main points about skill performance to your partner."

"Demonstrate the proper skill when I (or a partner) give you a verbal cue."

"Show me an activity that requires you to use the skill you've just learned."

"Describe and demonstrate one important part about the new skill you learned in today's lesson."

An additional note about closure is in order here. Often, teachers line up students at the end of the lesson to return to the classroom. Teachers then conduct closure, asking a number of questions. Unfortunately, when students stand close to each in a line, they have a greater opportunity to disrupt the class by talking and bothering others than when they are spread out. So, leave your class spaced throughout the instructional area while you conduct closure. When it is time for students to line up, they can do it quickly and start moving immediately. This reduces the opportunity for disruptive behavior.

Back to Class

Comment on Miss Pimentel's effectiveness in demonstrating the skills involved in jumping rope, in checking for understanding, in offering guided practice, and in monitoring her students' performance.

Improving the Effectiveness of Your Feedback

Delivering student feedback is an important part of instruction. Used properly, feedback enhances a student's self-concept, improves the focus of performance, increases the rate of on-task behavior, and improves student understanding. Consider the following points in order to enhance the quality of your instructional feedback.

Use the Appropriate Type of Feedback

Feedback is important in the skill-teaching process because it affects what is to be learned, what should be avoided, and how the student's performance of the skill might be modified. There are various types of feedback, some of which are more effective than others.

Negative, Corrective, and Positive

Negative feedback is feedback that focuses on negative aspects of a student's performance. Outright negative feedback (such as "That was a lousy throw") should always be avoided. Instead, offer **corrective feedback**; that is, feedback given with the intention of correcting or solving a problem (such as "Remember to keep your arms up as you dismount"). Most feedback delivered by teachers is corrective and focuses on improving student performance.

Some corrective feedback is expected by students; however, when it is the only feedback offered, it can promote an ineffective learning environment in which students worry about making errors for fear the instructor will embarrass or belittle them. In addition, overuse of corrective feedback makes youngsters believe that no matter what they do correctly, they will never be recognized for their efforts. Sometimes corrective feedback is directed to a youngster in such a way that other students hear it. Corrective feedback that "ripples" across the class can be debilitating for youngsters. Instead, direct corrective feedback quietly to an individual so only you and the student can hear it. This method avoids resentment that might build from being humiliated in front of peers.

Try to make most of your feedback **positive feedback**; that is, praise a student for an aspect performed correctly. Remember that a supportive learning environment makes it easier for students to accept a challenge and to risk error or failure. Positive feedback also makes it easier for you to feel good about your students because it focuses on their strengths. This is not to suggest that corrective feedback should never be used; Siedentop and Tannehill (2000) suggest that a four-to-one ratio of positive-to-corrective feedback is desirable. If your past physical education and/or athletic experiences have been those in which most feedback was corrective, you may teach in a similar fashion, using little positive feedback. Most teachers need to consciously increase positive feedback and decrease negative feedback given to students.

Intrinsic and Extrinsic

Feedback can also be classified as intrinsic or extrinsic. **Intrinsic feedback** is internal, inherent to the performance of the skill, and is derived through the senses, such as vision, hearing, smell, touch, and proprioception. For example, when a child on a balance beam feels herself swaying, she is experiencing intrinsic feedback.

Extrinsic feedback is external and comes from an outside source, such as a teacher, a videotape, a stopwatch, and so on. Extrinsic skill feedback that is encouraging (or constructive) should be given frequently and delivered publicly so all students benefit. Next, we discuss two types of extrinsic feedback.

Knowledge of Results   **Knowledge of results** is extrinsic feedback given after a skill has been performed and is focused on the outcome or product. For example, tell players when they have succeeded or failed at a task by saying, "You tossed it over the net! Good for you!" or "You hit the net that time. Try it again." As such, knowledge of results is an external variable most often controlled by the teacher to stimulate effective skill performance.

Knowledge of results is critical in the early stages of learning motor skills because it provides information about an incorrect or unsuccessful performance. Learners need feedback about performance errors so they can adjust the practice trials that follow. This type of feedback need not be negative but rather a statement of fact that tells the student whether the skill performance resulted in a successful outcome. After students start to master a skill, they can analyze their own performance and develop a personal system of internal feedback rather than depend on knowledge of results.

Knowledge of Performance   **Knowledge of performance** is similar to knowledge of results in that it is verbal, extrinsic in nature, and occurs after the performance. However, whereas knowledge of results focuses on the outcome (*product*) of a skill performance, knowledge of performance relates to the quality of the skill performance (the *process* of how it was performed). For example, a teacher might say, "That's the way to step toward the target—with your left foot."

Knowledge of performance may increase a youngster's level of motivation because it provides feedback about improvement. Many youngsters become frustrated because they find it difficult to tell whether or not they are improving at a skill. When an instructor mentions something performed correctly, this feedback provides a lift and helps children rededicate themselves to continued practice. Knowledge of performance is thus a strong positive reinforcer, motivating students to repeat the same pattern and ultimately to improve their performance.

Although neither type of feedback is more appropriate than the other, with young children it is best to focus on knowledge of performance because they are learning new skills and need feedback about their technique. Knowledge of results, which only reflects the outcome, doesn't consider whether the process was technically correct. A youngster who manages to throw a ball into a basket might believe that she performed the skill correctly even though her execution was technically poor. The goal with elementary school students is to teach skills correctly, so you should avoid emphasizing the outcome. In contrast, when students reach the high school years, emphasis shifts to product rather than process because the skills are well learned.

Make Feedback Statements Specific, Focused, and Concise

It is easy to develop habitual patterns of interaction. For example, statements such as "Nice job," "Way to hustle," "Much better," "Right on," and "Great move" are often used repetitiously. When used habitually, students often tune out and fail to feel the positive nature of these comments. These general comments also contain little specific information or value content and thus allow misinterpretation. Imagine, for example, that after a student performs a forward roll, you say, "Nice job!" You were pleased with the performance because the student's head was tucked. However, the student thought you were pleased because his legs were bent. Non-specific feedback easily results in reinforcing an incorrect behavior. Instead, make your feedback specific to the skill component your students are practicing. Examples of feedback with specific content are as follows:

"That's the way to tuck your head on the forward roll."
"Wow! Everybody was dribbling the ball with their heads up."
"I'm impressed with the way you kept your arms straight!"

Adding *value content* to feedback also improves student performance (**Figure 4.3**). The value content of a feedback statement tells students *why* it is important to perform a skill in a certain manner. When students understand why their performance was positive, they can build on the reinforced behavior. Examples of positive feedback with value content are as follows:

- "Good throw! When you look at your target, you are much more accurate."
- "Excellent catch! You bent your elbows, which created a soft home for the ball."
- "That's the way to stop! When you bend your knees, you always stop under control."

Focus feedback on the desired refinement of a task. For example, if you want students to "give" with their hands while catching a ball thrown by a partner, avoid giving feedback about the quality of the throw. If catching is the focus, feedback should be on catching, as in "Rachel is reaching out and giving with her hands when she catches the ball."

Finally, keep your feedback concise. Concentrate on one key point to avoid confusing the youngster. Imagine a young student whose teacher tells him, "On your next throw, you should step with your left foot, not your right, then rotate your trunk. Lead with your elbow, and don't forget to snap your wrist!" Such excessive feedback would confuse anyone trying to learn a new skill.

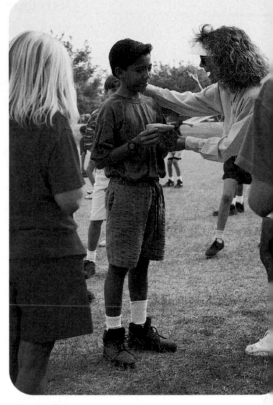

Figure 4.3 When feedback includes value content, the student learns why a particular aspect of his or her performance is correct.

Offer Feedback Immediately, but Allow Time for Improvement

Offer feedback to students as soon as possible after a skill is performed. Also, allow students an opportunity to practice immediately after the feedback in order to apply the information given. Little is gained if students are told how to improve but are not given a chance to practice before leaving class. Few, if any, students remember points given in previous classes. If the end of class is approaching, it is probably best to limit feedback to aspects that can be practiced immediately. Write down points of emphasis that you want to teach during the next class meeting.

After offering feedback, allow time for the student to internalize your comments. Often, teachers give corrective feedback and in the next breath ask the student to "try it again." Many students become tense when you tell them how to do something and then watch to see if they do it exactly as instructed. They are highly likely to make the same mistake because they have not had time to think about the feedback. Students will be more willing to try new ways of performing if they are allowed time to practice without close observation. So, observe carefully, offer the feedback, move on to another student, and recheck the original student's progress later. This method gives the child a chance to relax, internalize the feedback, and modify future practice attempts.

Distribute Feedback Evenly

Often feedback is group oriented; that is, it is delivered to the entire class. This is an expedient method of giving feedback, but it also allows the most room for misinterpretation. Some students may not understand the feedback, and others may not listen because it does not seem relevant.

Instead, try distributing feedback evenly to all students by moving systematically from student to student, assuming there are no major discipline problems. This approach fosters contact with students a number of times during the lesson. In addition, it keeps students on task because they know the teacher is moving and "eyeballing" everybody regularly. If skills are complex and refinement is a goal, it may be better to take more time with individual students. This involves watching a student long enough to offer specific and information-loaded feedback. The result is high-quality feedback to fewer students.

It is not necessary to have students observe each other as they accomplish the desired outcome. Observing other students is effective only if the performer is capable of showing the skill correctly. If this approach is used exclusively, less-skilled (or shy) performers will never have an opportunity to receive class feedback. Instead, tell the class how well a student is doing and move on, saying, for example, "Mike always keeps his head up when dribbling." Note that younger students are willing to be praised in front of other students; however, some older students dislike being singled out. In this case, give your positive feedback quietly to the individual.

Use Nonverbal Feedback

Nonverbal behavior is another way to deliver feedback. Most students can interpret nonverbal feedback easily, and many perceive it to be more meaningful than words. Teachers may use many types of nonverbal feedback to encourage a class or show approval: a smile, a thumbs-up, high fives, shaking hands, and so on. Nonverbal behaviors that communicate displeasure may be effective when students go off task. These behaviors include hands on the hips, finger to the lips, frowning, and staring. In addition, use nonverbal feedback to increase the validity and strength of your verbal communication.

When using nonverbal feedback, find out how different cultures interpret different types of gestures. For example, Hmong and Laotian children may be touched on the head only by parents and close relatives. A teacher who pats that child on the head for approval is interfering with the child's spiritual upbringing. The "okay" sign, touching thumb and forefinger together, is an indication of approval in the United States. However, in several Asian cultures it symbolizes a zero, indicating the child is not performing properly. In many South American countries, the "okay" sign carries a derogatory sexual connotation. Take these possibilities into consideration and, when possible, ask for advice before using nonverbal gestures with children from families who may have cultural roots outside of the mainstream.

Beginning teachers often have a difficult time coordinating their feelings and words with body language. They may be pleased with student performance, yet they carry themselves in a less-than-pleased manner (with a frown on the face and hands on the hips, for example). They may want to be assertive, but take a submissive stance. For instance, when undesirable behavior occurs, an unsure teacher might place his hands in his pockets, stand in a slouched position, and back away from the class. These nonverbal behaviors signal anything but assertiveness and send students a mixed message.

To make nonverbal feedback more convincing, practice it in front of a mirror and attempt to display different emotions. Another way to practice is to display a variety of behaviors to someone who does not know you well. If this person can identify the emotions and see them as convincing, you are an effective nonverbal communicator. Videotape and digital recorders are also effective tools for self-analysis. Analyze how you look when under stress, when disciplining a student, when praising, and so on. It may be possible that you exhibit distracting or unassertive nonverbal behaviors such as playing with the whistle, slumping, putting your hands in your pockets, or shuffling your feet. Just as verbal feedback must be practiced and critiqued, so must nonverbal behavior.

Back to Class

During the short time that her students were engaged in the rope-jumping activity, Miss Pimentel had only one opportunity to offer feedback. Look back at the scenario to find it, and comment on the effectiveness of that feedback.

Considering Your Students' Personal Needs

If teaching only involved presenting physical activities to students, it would be a rather simple endeavor. The uniqueness of each student in a large class is a factor that makes teaching complex and challenging. This section focuses on ways to make instruction meaningful and personal. Teachers who are able to make each student feel important will strongly impact the lives of their students. Respecting the diversity of your students and helping them to make responsible decisions are just some of the ways a teacher makes a lesson feel as if it were specifically designed for each student.

Teach for Diversity

Multicultural education allows all students to reach their potential regardless of the diversity among learners. Four major variables of diversity influence how teachers and students think and learn: race/ethnicity, gender, social class, and ability. Multicultural education creates an educational environment in which students from a variety of backgrounds and experience come together to experience educational equality (Manning and Baruth, 2004). It assumes that children come from different backgrounds and helps them make sense of their everyday lives. It emphasizes the contributions of various groups that make up our country and focuses on how to learn rather than on what to learn.

Teaching in the United States and Canada requires a pluralistic mind-set and the ability to communicate across cultures. It is the responsibility of educators to teach children to live in harmony and to prosper in this diverse and changing world. It is important that students celebrate their own culture while learning to integrate into the diversity of the world. For most students, classroom interaction between teachers and students is the major part of multicultural education they will receive.

There are a number of things you can do to teach and value diversity.

- Help students learn about the similarities and differences among cultures.
- Encourage students to understand that people from similar cultures share common values, customs, and beliefs.
- Make children aware of acts of discrimination, and teach them ways to deal with inequity and prejudice.
- Help youngsters develop pride in their family's culture.
- Teach youngsters ways to communicate effectively with people regardless of race/ethnicity, gender, sexual orientation, socioeconomic bracket, and ability.
- Instill respect for all people regardless of race/ethnicity, gender, sexual orientation, socioeconomic bracket, and ability.

Teachers' expectations of their students strongly influence their students' performance. Teachers who hold high expectations for all students, including those in an ethnic minority, promote their students' success. Unfortunately, research indicates that teachers tend to have lower expectations for ethnic minority youth (Vasquez, 1988). These low expectations are revealed in interpersonal interactions and in students' access to opportunities for enrichment and personal growth. At-risk youth need a rich curriculum that allows no room for failure and provides the necessary support for success.

Teaching for diversity implies respecting differences not only between groups, but also within a group. When you are teaching children of different cultures, your focus should be on understanding not only the culture but also the individuals. Thus, while it is important to gather information about cultures that are different from your own, it's counterproductive to learn about a culture—or any other type of group—only to stereotype its members as "all the same." Fuller (2001) offers a number of questions to consider when working with children of different ethnic groups:

- *What is their history?* Certainly, few teachers can become experts in the history of all the cultures of the students they teach. However, they can recognize and be familiar with major events and themes, or important names, within the cultures.
- *What are their important cultural values?* Different cultures interact with and discipline children in different ways. Ask parents how they work with their children and what values are particularly important in their households.

Who are influential individuals in their group? Students will often identify with local individuals who are held in high esteem in their community. When you know the role models your students admire, you'll gain insight into their values and culture.

What are their major religious beliefs? Some students are members of communities whose religious values drive many of their beliefs. Consider the possibility that the values of some children may be driven by their religious orientation.

What are their key political beliefs? Important political issues are often discussed at home. By making an effort to learn about these issues, teachers show they are interested in how their students live within their community

What political, religious, and social days do they observe and celebrate? Students will discuss these important days and expect teachers to understand why they celebrate them. Talking about these events with students creates goodwill and shows students that their culture is valued.

Focus on cooperative learning. This offers students the opportunity to work together toward common goals and to feel positive about the different contributions of each member of the group. Respect for diversity may also be increased through discussion sessions. The greater the number of students from different backgrounds who participate, the better will be the chance for different points of view to emerge. When students are involved in discussions, they are usually highly engaged in the learning process. Helping students to learn about each other in this way helps to foster an effective and supportive learning environment.

Some teaching tips that can help increase instructional effectiveness for students from diverse cultural and ethnic backgrounds follow.

At the start of the school year (and at regular intervals thereafter), speak about the importance of encouraging and respecting diversity.

When offering group activities, insist that groups diversify.

Be aware of how you speak about different groups of students. Do you refer to all students alike? Do you address boys and girls differently? Develop a consistent style for addressing all students regardless of their differences.

Encourage all students to participate in discussions. Avoid allowing some students from certain groups to dominate interaction. Use a random method of picking students so that all have an equal chance of contributing.

Treat all students with respect, and expect students to treat each other with dignity. Intervene if a student or group of students is dominating.

When a difficult situation arises over an issue with undertones of diversity, take a time-out and ask students to evaluate their thoughts and ideas. Allow all parties time to collect their thoughts and plan a response.

Make sure evaluations and grades are written in gender-neutral or gender-inclusive terms.

Encourage students to work with different partners every day. Students need to get to know other students in order to appreciate their differences.

- Invite to class guest speakers who represent diversity in gender, race, and ethnicity, even if they are not speaking about multicultural or diversity issues.
- When students make comments that are sexist or racist, ask them to restate their ideas in a way that is not offensive to others. Teach students that it is all right to express one's opinion but not to do so in an inflammatory manner.
- Use rotating leaders when using groups. Give all students the opportunity to learn leadership skills.

Avoid Gender Stereotyping

Although discrimination based on gender has been illegal in U.S. education for more than 35 years, research shows that teachers still treat boys and girls differently. (See the accompanying News Clip for a discussion of discrimination against girls in athletics.) For example, teachers pay more attention to boys and call on them more often than they call on girls. They tend to give boys more encouragement as well, praising them for achievement more often than they do girls, and tolerate aggression in them more than they do in girls. However, boys are reprimanded more than girls, and teachers use more physical means of disciplining boys. Also, disruptive talking is tolerated more in girls than in boys (Grossman and Grossman, 1994).

The expectations a teacher has for boys and girls strongly influence how they interact with them. For example, teachers expect boys to be more rambunctious and less able academically. As a result, teachers pay closer attention to boys, and when boys do well, they are more likely to get positive attention. Girls, on the other hand, are expected to be more reserved and to do well academically, so they tend to be overlooked when they are doing "what they are supposed to do." When girls misbehave, teachers see this as an aberration and respond more negatively to the female than they might to the male. This is a common, yet unacceptable, pitfall for teachers. It takes a concerted effort to overcome these biases.

Some teachers believe that girls aren't able to perform athletically at a level similar to boys, even though research shows otherwise. Particularly in elementary school, differences in strength, endurance, and physical skills are minimal. An effective physical activity environment helps all youngsters find success. Use the following teaching behaviors to minimize stereotyping by gender.

- Reinforce the performance of all students regardless of gender.
- Provide activities that are developmentally appropriate, and allow all students to find success.
- Design programs that ensure success in coeducational experiences. Boys and girls may challenge each other to achieve higher levels of performance if the atmosphere is positive.
- Don't use and don't accept students' stereotypical comments, such as, "You throw like a girl."
- Include activities in the curriculum that cut across typical gender stereotypes such as "dancing is for girls," or "football is for boys."

Despite Public Support for Title IX, Discrimination Against Female Athletics Remains Widespread

Title IX of the Education Amendments of 1972 protects American students from discrimination based on gender in educational programs or activities receiving federal assistance, including physical education, athletics, and recreation. In recognition of the 35th anniversary of Title IX, the National Women's Law Center released the results of a national poll showing overwhelming support for Title IX and its principles. Unfortunately, the outcome of their five-year investigation into Title IX-based complaints also shows that discrimination against girls and women in athletics remains widespread.

The investigation examined 416 complaints filed between 2002 and 2006. Its analysis revealed that girls and women still receive fewer opportunities to participate in athletics than do men, and when given the opportunity to be on a team, they are often treated worse than their male counterparts. Here are some of the report's specific findings.

- Complaints challenging discrimination against female athletes were filed 11 times more frequently than complaints challenging discrimination against males.
- Complaints by female athletes were far less likely to be regarded as having enough merit to force schools to change their athletics programs than complaints by male athletes.
- Coaches reported fearing retaliation if they protested unequal treatment of female students.
- In K–12 education, the most common athletics complaint was unequal treatment of female athletes, including poorer facilities, less-favorable game schedules, lower compensation for girls' coaches, and unequal access to school-sponsored transportation to games compared with boys' teams.

Source: Adapted from National Women's Law Center, June 19, 2007, at: www.nwlc.org/details.cfm?id=3063&section=newsroom.

take action!

1. Log on to the National Women's Law Center's new website (see Web Resources), which is designed to enable the public to evaluate and hold schools accountable for compliance with Title IX. Sign their Fair Play Now pledge or take their Get Girls in the Game survey.

2. Volunteer to coach a girl's hockey team, soccer team, or any other team activity. If opportunities don't currently exist in your community, form a team yourself! For information on how to go about it, visit the National Women's Law Center website listed at the end of this chapter.

3. Contact the Women's Sports Foundation (see Web Resources) and request a copy of "Playing Fair," a document that explains Title IX rules and regulations to help athletes, coaches, teachers, parents, and others better analyze their school's athletics opportunities. Make copies available to others at your school.

- Arrange activities so the more aggressive and skilled students do not dominate the class. Little is learned if students are taught to be submissive or to downplay their abilities.
- Arrange practice sessions so that all students receive equal time to practice and opportunity to participate. Practice sessions should not give more practice opportunities to the skilled while the unskilled stand aside and observe.
- Expect all boys and girls to perform equally well. Teacher expectations communicate much about a student's ability level. Students view themselves through the eyes of their teacher.

Back to Class

In our opening scenario, a first-grader named Alec is frustrated about his inability to jump rope and states that the activity "is for girls and sissies anyway." If you heard a comment like this from one of your students, how might you respond?

Allow Students to Participate in Decision Making

Considering students' personal needs also means including them—to the extent possible—in the decision-making process. Part of the decision-making process requires considering the consequences that are tied to decisions and the impact those consequences have on others. Enhance your students' cognitive development by allowing them to make decisions related to their learning. Have them choose from a variety of alternatives regarding the content of the lesson, how you will implement the lesson, and how assessments of techniques and progress will take place. When students are allowed to make decisions at a young age, incorrect decisions result in much less serious consequences than those made when students are older, offering an opportunity for youngsters to learn how to make decisions in a safe environment. If students are always told how to behave when they are young, they may not know how to make more serious decisions about their behavior that will impact their future as they age. The following are strategies that help youngsters learn to make decisions:

- *Limit the number of choices.* This strategy retains ultimate control for the teacher but gives students a chance to decide, in part, how the outcome is reached. Use this technique when learners have had little opportunity in the past to make decisions. If you have a new class and know little about the students, limit their choices. For example, permit students the choice of practicing either throwing or catching beanbags. The desired outcome is that students practice both skills, but they can decide which to practice first.
- *Let students modify activities.* Giving students the option to modify activities according to their ability reduces the pressure on them, but it also makes

your job easier because you won't have to make exceptions or listen to "it is too hard to do" or "I'm bored." Modification also allows learners to apply their creativity to a task. Among the many ways to modify activities, some examples are

- Use a slower-moving, softer ball rather than a handball.
- Invite the children to create their own movement variations (**Figure 4.4**).
- Lower the basket in a basketball unit.
- Decrease the length of a distance run or the height of hurdles.

Offer open-ended tasks. This approach offers wide latitude for making decisions about the content of the lesson. You decide the educational outcome, and students determine the means to reach it. This problem-solving approach has no predetermined answers. Students apply principles they have learned previously and transfer them to new situations. Ultimately, the problem is solved through a movement response guided by cognitive involvement. For example, instruct the students to do the following:

- "Develop a game that requires four passes before a shot on goal."
- "Plan a floor exercise routine that contains a forward roll, a backward roll, and a cartwheel."
- "Design a rope-jumping routine that involves a long rope, four people, and two pieces of manipulative equipment."

Personalize Instruction

Even though most instruction is conducted in a group, it is obvious that the ability levels of students vary widely. As students mature, the range of ability increases as many students begin to participate in extracurricular pursuits such as Little League baseball, karate, and other activities. This range of experience requires that tasks be modified so that all students find success. The following are some ways to personalize instruction to accommodate ability differences among youngsters.

Modify the conditions. Modify tasks and activities to help all children experience success. For example, if students are learning to catch, utilize some of the following modifications: move partners closer together, provide a slower-moving object such as a beach ball or a balloon, increase the size of the target, change the size of boundaries or goal areas, allow students to toss and catch individually, or increase the size of the striking implement. An optimum ratio of minimum error and maximum success is a goal. When students find little success, they will exhibit off-task behavior in an attempt to draw attention away from their sub-par performance. Such behavior indicates that the error rate is too high and learning is stymied.

Use self-competition. As surprising as it sounds, if the success rate is too high, students become bored. With upper-grade students, encourage personal goal setting. For example, ask youngsters to see if they can beat their personal best performance. Offer challenges by asking students to accomplish higher levels of performance by using a faster-moving object, increasing the distance to the goal, or decreasing its size. Students respond best to challenges that are personal and slightly above their current skill level. Avoid holding all students to a single standard of performance.

Figure 4.4 Foster decision-making skills by allowing your students to create their own movement variations.

Offer students a choice of tasks. All students do not have to work on the same tasks simultaneously. If a variety of tasks are offered, students will usually select one they feel they can accomplish. This starts the activity off on a positive note. Offer a number of tasks of varying complexity so that students can find personal challenges.

Communicating with Empathy and Understanding

The elements of communication include a sender, a message, a medium, and a receiver. As a teacher, you most often take the role of sender, and your message is usually spoken. However, in this section we'll discuss body language as well as the importance of effective listening.

Be an Effective Speaker

If children are to learn, you must speak to them in a manner that encourages them to listen. This begins with proper body positioning. Assume a physical pose that expresses interest and attention. Kneel at times so that youngsters do not always have to look up. Looking down on a student puts you in a dominant role. There are times when the teacher needs to be dominant; however, in most cases equality ensures greater sincerity and caring. Make sure that your facial and verbal cues reinforce your interest and concern.

Use some of the following suggestions to help you establish a positive bond with students and create a learning environment of trust.

Speak about the behavior of students, not their personal character. The following is an example of speaking about a student's behavior: "Talking when another student is talking is unacceptable behavior. Please wait your turn." Such feedback identifies behavior that can be improved upon and avoids diminishing the self-worth of the student. This approach helps students feel you are helping rather than belittling them. In contrast, saying, "Why do you always have to act silly?" reflects on the child's character and undermines his or her self-esteem. Such comments are also non-specific, making it difficult to determine what behavior you are reprimanding. Focus on specific misbehavior and state the type of behavior that should be displayed.

Offer corrective feedback privately. Imagine that a teacher criticized you in front of a class. How would you feel? As suggested earlier, when giving corrective feedback that might be embarrassing to the student, do so privately and allow the student to practice without scrutiny.

Communicate about problems when they occur. Some teachers who are unhappy with a student because of a previous incident may offer unkind or sarcastic feedback about that student's performance. This is destructive. It is much more effective to respond to the initial incident as soon as possible after it has occurred. Wait until you have cooled down, and then calmly and quietly communicate how you feel (even though it may be negative). Make sure your comments are respectful, constructive, directed at the behavior and not at the student, and communicate caring.

Accentuate the positive. When teaching key instructional points of a skill, accent positive performance points rather than incorrect actions. For example, stress that children "land lightly," rather than saying, "Don't land so hard." An easy way to emphasize key points positively is to include value content. For instance, say, "Do this because it will help you . . . ." If there are several different and acceptable ways to perform movement patterns, be explicit with your comments.

Optimize speech patterns. Excessive reliance on certain words and phrases—*okay, all right,* and *good job*—are unappealing to children. Acquire a broad vocabulary of effective phrases that indicate approval. A list used by many teachers identifies 100 ways to say "good job." Also, avoid repeating the irritating phrase, *and uh.* Recognize that there are times when a period of silence is effective; it allows students time to internalize and digest the information.

Respect student responses. Avoid humiliating a child who gives a wrong answer. Instead, try responding in any of the following ways: Pass over inappropriate answers by directing attention to more appropriate responses. Suggest that the student has offered a good answer, but that "my question was not correctly asked." Ask the student to "save that answer" and then go back to him when the answer is correct for another question. When injecting your personal opinion into the question-and-answer process, label it as such and avoid overemphasizing its worth in comparison to student opinion.

Ask students how they feel. Discover how students feel by asking them. If you ask, however, you must be ready to accept the feedback. Try not to show

shock, surprise, or offense if children comment negatively when you ask for candid opinions about an activity or about your teaching. Instead, thank the child for the feedback and promise to think it over. When opinions are honest, some are bound to be negative.

Be an Effective Listener

Teachers are trained to impart knowledge to students, and they have practiced effective speaking for years; however, many teachers receive no training in effective listening. This fact may contribute to the reputation of teachers as people who speak but do not listen. If you want to avoid this reputation, and want to create an effective learning environment for your students, bear in mind the old adage, "You were given two ears and one mouth so you could listen twice as much as you speak."

Each of the following behaviors promotes effective listening.

Be an active listener. Active listeners convince the speaker they are interested in the message being conveyed. Much of this is done through nonverbal behavior such as eye contact, nodding the head in agreement, facial expressions, and moving toward the speaker.

Listen to the child's hidden message. Young children often find it difficult to clearly express their feelings. The words expressed may not signal what the child is actually feeling. For example, a child may say, "I hate activity." Most children do not hate all activity, and most likely something more immediate (such as fear of being hit by the jump rope or a recent experience of being teased) is the problem. Try acknowledging their feelings with a response such as, "You sound angry (upset, sad, blue); are you having a problem you want to discuss?" This helps students realize their feelings are important and gives them an opportunity to clarify their concerns. It prevents the teacher from internalizing students' anger (or frustration) and responding in an emotionally charged manner, such as, "I don't want to hear that; now get back on task!"

Paraphrase the message. Paraphrasing is restating in your own words what was said to you, including your interpretation of the other person's feelings. For example, you might respond, "Do I hear you saying you are bored with tag?" If the paraphrasing is correct, it makes the student feel validated and understood. If the interpretation is incorrect, the student has an opportunity to restate his or her concern.

Let students know you value what they have to say. Teachers who listen to students learn about students' feelings. If you are a good listener, what you hear will not always be positive. For example, students may state honestly which activities they enjoy and which they do not. They may express how they felt when they were criticized. If you don't take them personally, messages such as these can open the door to effective communication.

Back to Class

If you were Miss Pimentel, how would you respond to Maya's declaration that she hates jumping rope and will never participate in this activity again?

Finally, communicate to students that you expect them to value listening too. Let them know that interrupting you or other students is unacceptable behavior and that the appropriate behavior is to wait one's turn. In short, when you foster respect for the words of others, you promote an atmosphere in which students are likely to develop positive attitudes toward learning.

Chapter Summary

Characteristics of an Effective Learning Environment

- An effective learning environment is one in which the following elements are present: students are engaged in appropriate learning activities, little time is wasted waiting in line or transitioning from one activity to another, students are given clear objectives and meaningful feedback, student progress is monitored, teachers have high but realistic expectations, the learning atmosphere is positive and caring, and teachers show enthusiasm and are actively involved in the instructional process.

Improving the Effectiveness of Your Instruction

- Effective outcomes define observable behavior and clearly and specifically identify the content to be learned.

- Instruction should begin at entry level, which is defined as a rough estimation of the skill level for the majority of students in the class. This promotes a positive feeling among students and builds upon their success.

- Use an anticipatory set to focus students on an upcoming learning task. For example, tell them what the outcome of the activity will be or tie it to past learning experiences.

- Effective instructions are limited to one or two key points, do not last longer than about 60 seconds, are easy to understand, and include either management or instructional content, but not both.

- Instructional cues are keywords that quickly and efficiently communicate proper technique and performance of skills and movement tasks. Make cues precise, short, and action oriented.

- A quick and effective way to present a physical activity is to demonstrate it. Do this yourself, use visual aids such as a DVD, or ask students to demonstrate the activity.

- To check for understanding without causing student embarrassment, use hand signals, ask questions that can be answered by a group response, check understanding by directing a query to the entire class, use peer-checking methods, or use tests or other written feedback.

- In the early stages of skill development, your guidance is critical. You should offer guided practice sessions as quickly as possible after teaching students a new skill.

- When monitoring class performance, move around so that you'll be able to observe and give an equal amount of feedback and attention to all students. Deliver instruction from the perimeter of the area, and vary your location regularly.

- Closure is not simply a recall of activities that were completed, rather it is a discussion of the application of skills and knowledge learned through practice. Use closure to help students retain their learning.

Improving the Effectiveness of Your Feedback

- Effective feedback enhances a student's self-concept, improves the focus of performance, increases the rate of on-task behavior, and improves student understanding.

- Avoid giving negative feedback. Instead, offer some corrective feedback when appropriate, but make most of your feedback positive.

- Intrinsic feedback comes from within the student. Extrinsic feedback is external. Knowledge of results focuses on the outcome or product, whereas knowledge of performance focuses on the process. The latter is more appropriate during the early stages of skill development.

- Make feedback statements specific, avoiding generic phrases such as *nice job*. Also, include value content so that students understand why a performance was correct, and focus on the desired refinement of the task. Finally, keep feedback concise, focusing on one point at a time.

- Offer feedback to students as soon as possible after performing a task and then allow an opportunity for immediate practice so that students internalize the feedback and apply it.

Distribute feedback evenly to all students by moving systematically from student to student.

Nonverbal communication increases the validity and strength of verbal communication. Use nonverbal feedback to encourage the class, show approval, or communicate displeasure.

Considering Your Students' Personal Needs

Teach appreciation for diversity by fostering respect for differences. When working with children of different groups, find out their history, cultural values, religious and political beliefs, and whom they hold in esteem. What special days do they celebrate?

Focus on cooperative learning. This offers students the opportunity to work together toward common goals and to feel positive about the different contributions of each member of the group. Respect for diversity may also be increased through discussion sessions.

Avoid gender stereotyping and foster an environment that helps all youngsters find success. Some teachers believe that girls aren't able to perform athletically at a level similar to boys, even though research shows otherwise. Particularly in elementary school, gender differences in strength, endurance, and physical skills are minimal.

Enhance your students' cognitive development by allowing them to participate in decision making. For example, let them make decisions about choice of lesson content, how you'll implement the lesson, and assessment of techniques and progress by choosing from a limited number of appropriate alternatives. Give students opportunities to modify activities or offer open-ended tasks. When students are allowed to make decisions at a young age, incorrect decisions result in much less serious consequences and offer an opportunity to learn.

Try to personalize instruction to accommodate the youngsters' different abilities. For example, modify the task, offer students a choice of tasks, and encourage self-competition.

Communicating with Empathy and Understanding

Assume a physical pose that expresses interest and attention when speaking to a child. Speak about the behavior, not about the child's character. Offer corrective feedback privately and immediately, and accentuate the positive. Ask for students' opinions. Respect students' responses, and if they do not respond, discover how they feel by asking them.

Be an active listener. Listen to the child's hidden message, paraphrase the message, and let students know you value what they have to say.

Review Questions

Content Review

1. List two measurable outcome statements that describe observable behavior and clearly identify the specific content to be learned.

2. Imagine that you are teaching a kindergarten child how to tie a bow. In developmentally appropriate language, define the skill, list the elements or component parts that make up the skill, and provide information about when, why, and how the skill is used.

3. Develop five meaningful instructional feedback statements other than those used in this chapter. Identify why each of the statements is meaningful.

4. Identify at least two ways you could allow your students to participate in decision making in a session of physical activity focusing on throwing and catching.

5. Provide two examples of how to speak about a student's behavior rather than the student's personal character.

Real World

1. You are introducing a group of kindergarten students to the skill of balancing. The outcome for today's lesson is that the children will be able to walk heel-to-toe on a straight line painted on the gym floor without moving off the line. Using developmentally appropriate language, give an example of an anticipatory set that you could use with these children.

2. You are supervising lunchtime recess with another teacher when you notice a fifth-grade boy pushing a third-grade boy away from the basketball hoop. "Basketball is an American game," says the older boy. "No foreigners allowed!" You recognize the younger boy as Rajiv, whose family emigrated from India two years ago. As you approach the two students, you hear the other teacher call out to the older boy, "Mark, cut it out!" Then you see her move toward another group. What would you say to each of the two boys? Would this incident prompt you to take any other actions? If so, what might you do?

References and Suggested Readings

Banks, J.A. (2003). *Teaching strategies for ethnic studies.* 7th ed. Boston: Allyn & Bacon.

Bennett, C.L. (2003). *Comprehensive multicultural education: Theory and practice.* 5th ed. Boston: Allyn & Bacon.

Brophy, J., and Good, T. (1986). Teacher behavior and student achievement. In M. Wittrock (ed.), *Handbook of research on teaching.* New York: Macmillan.

Evertson, C. (1989). Classroom organization and management. In M. Reynolds (ed.), *Knowledge base for the beginning teacher.* Washington, D.C.: American Association of Colleges for Teacher Education.

Fronske, H., and Wilson, R. (2002). *Teaching cues for basic sport skills for elementary and middle school students.* San Francisco: Benjamin Cummings.

What About You?

Think back to physical education classes you had in elementary or middle school. Which of the characteristics of an effective learning environment were present? Which were not?

Fuller, M.L. (2001). Multicultural concerns and classroom management. In C.A. Grant and M.L. Gomez (eds.), *Campus and classroom: Making schooling multicultural.* Upper Saddle River, NJ: Prentice Hall.

Gordon, A., & Browne, K.W. (1996). *Guiding young children in a diverse society.* Boston: Allyn & Bacon.

Grossman, H., and Grossman, S.H. (1994). *Gender issues in education.* Boston: Allyn & Bacon.

Koppelman, K., and Goodhart, L. (2005). *Understanding human differences: Multicultural education for a diverse America.* Boston: Allyn & Bacon.

Manning, M.L., and Baruth, L.G. (2004). *Multicultural education of children and adolescents* (4th ed.). Boston: Allyn & Bacon.

Pang, V.O. (2005). *Multicultural education: A caring-centered, reflective approach* (2nd ed.). Boston: McGraw-Hill.

Siedentop, D., and Tannehill, D. (2000). *Developing teaching skills in physical education* (4th ed.). Mountain View, CA: Mayfield Publishing Co.

Vasquez, J. (1988). Contests of learning for minority children. *Educational Forum,* 52(3), 243–253.

Web Resources

Center for Rural Studies, University of Vermont, Education Services:
www.crs.uvm.edu/education
Exploring Nonverbal Communication:
www.nonverbal.ucsc.edu
National Women's Law Center:
www.fairplaynow.org
P.E. Central:
www.pecentral.org
Women's Sports Foundation:
www.womenssportsfoundation.org

5

Management and Discipline in an Activity Setting

Learning Objectives

After reading this chapter, you will be able to . . .

○ Identify the essential teaching behaviors for managing children in a physical education setting.

○ List five steps for defining class procedures, rules, and consequences.

○ Identify management skills for starting and stopping a class, moving children into groups or formations quickly, and using equipment effectively.

○ Identify five levels of responsibility and explain how to teach and reinforce them with children.

○ Describe techniques to prompt, shape, and reinforce acceptable behavior.

○ Discuss strategies for decreasing unacceptable student behavior.

○ Identify the shortcomings of criticism and punishment when used to change and improve student behavior.

○ Contrast teacher-directed conflict resolution and peer-directed mediation.

Classroom Challenge

"We just can't play it that way!" Ms. Kirklian can hear the panic in Nikki's voice even from across the playground where she is working with a group on a game called "Fox Hunt." As she walks toward Nikki's group, she is struck by the fact that Nikki seems able to relax only when she is certain that she is following "the rules."

As Ms. Kirklian approaches the group, she sees another of her students, Peter, walk up to Nikki and confront her angrily.

"Peter," Ms. Kirklian asks gently, "why isn't your group playing 'Fox Hunt' with Nikki?"

"Because she's driving everybody crazy!" Peter fumes. "We've been trying to play for the last five minutes, but she keeps saying, 'It won't work! It won't work!' Why can't she just go along?"

Ms. Kirklian keeps her voice friendly. "So, Nikki, why are you doing this?"

Nikki's face is tense. "I'm not doing anything wrong! You told some of us to pretend we're hounds chasing foxes into their dens. But Peter wants to change it so that horses are chasing the foxes. That doesn't make any sense! Everybody knows in a real fox hunt the horses don't chase the foxes—they just follow the hounds!"

"That may be true, Nikki," Ms. Kirklian says, "but I set up a nice game, and all I'm getting are your arguments! I think you both need some time-out. I want you to go sit in silence on that bench until I say you can play again."

Peter scowls and the two walk off. Ms. Kirklian turns back to the group and has just finished instructing them when she hears Peter say, "You see what you've done! You think you're so smart, but you're not! You're a stupid idiot!" She turns just in time to see Peter shove Nikki off the bench and to the ground.

"Peter!" Ms. Kirklian shouts. "Just for that, your time-out will extend until the end of today's activity break! And the rest of you!" She turns to the others. "If you're not playing the game within 60 seconds, we're all going inside to work on fractions!" As the children scurry into their formations for the game, Ms. Kirklian regrets her outburst. She wonders how she could have handled this squabble more effectively.

anaging student behavior is an ongoing and ever-changing challenge. Although a classroom of children share roughly the same chronological age, each child, like Nikki and Peter, must be understood and treated as an individual. With 20 or more children in most elementary classrooms today, it's no wonder so many teachers doubt their ability to manage their students.

Management and discipline are interrelated, and one affects the other. Throughout this chapter, **management** is defined as organizing and controlling the affairs of a class. It refers to how students are organized, started and stopped, grouped, and arranged during class. Effective management means students are moved quickly, called by their names, grouped into appropriate formations, acknowledged for acceptable behavior, and so on. **Discipline** is defined as methods for discouraging non-adherence to rules and for changing unacceptable student behavior. When a student decides not to follow management requests, discipline techniques are required to create a constructive teaching environment. In a nutshell, effective management implies students follow class procedures, and when class procedures are not followed, discipline techniques are used.

It is unrealistic to believe that you will be able to offer children physical activity without encountering some type of discipline problem. Thus, you need to learn to manage student behavior with confidence and in a way that is acceptable to you and your students. A number of steps lead to a well-managed and disciplined class, each of which is discussed in detail throughout this chapter.

Use Proper Teaching Behaviors

Effective teachers make three assumptions: teaching is a profession, students are in school to learn, and the teacher's challenge is to promote learning. The basic reason that management and discipline are essential in education is that they protect children's freedom to learn. Our society is based on freedom partnered with self-discipline: we enjoy personal freedom as long as we do not infringe on the rights of others. In similar fashion, you may allow the children you teach to enjoy substantial freedom as long as their behavior is consistent with your educational objectives and does not prevent other students from learning. Students who choose to be disruptive and off task infringe on the rights of students who choose to cooperate. When a teacher has to spend a great deal of time working with students who are disorderly, those who want to learn are shortchanged. Effective management of behavior means maintaining an environment in which all children have the opportunity to learn.

Most children in a class are relatively easy to teach, but to make appreciable gains among children with emotional, behavioral, or cognitive problems, teachers should use the methods we discuss here. When you prevent problems from occurring, you spend less time dealing with deviant behavior and your students spend more time engaged in physical activity.

Develop an Assertive Communication Style

Generally, there are three ways a teacher communicates when faced with situations requiring management and discipline. Each style is discussed in detail here to help you develop and use an assertive style of communication.

Passive Communicator

A passive teacher hopes to make all children happy in order to avoid all conflict. Directly or indirectly, the passive teacher is constantly saying, "Like me. Appreciate what I do for you." Many passive teachers strive to behave perfectly themselves and in turn hope that their students will behave perfectly. When children behave like children and go off task, these teachers often let the behavior slide. This gives children permission to continue to misbehave, and they typically do so until the passive teacher "can't take it anymore." The teacher then loses his or her composure and lashes out at the class in anger. When the anger subsides, the passive teacher tries to make up for the outburst and again starts the cycle of letting things go and trying to be liked. This cycle is repeated throughout the school year.

Passive teachers typically exhibit other characteristic and unproductive behaviors.

- They often turn over power to students, particularly the least-cooperative students. For example, passive teachers might say, "We are not going to start the lesson until everyone is listening!" Students may hear, "We don't have to start the lesson until we finish our conversation."
- They ignore unacceptable behavior and hope it will disappear. Ignoring seldom causes behavior to disappear; rather, it becomes worse over time.
- They often say threatening things but fail to follow through, saying, for example, "If you do that one more time, I am going to call your parents." When there is no follow-through or it is impossible to follow through, the words are empty and meaningless and students soon learn disrespect for the teacher.
- They ask questions that elicit meaningless information, for example, "What did you do that for?" Or "Why are you doing this?" Or "Don't you

know better than that?" None of these questions elicit useful information, and the teacher soon becomes frustrated and angry with all of the "I don't know" responses.

Aggressive Communicator

Aggressive teachers come on strong in a desire to overpower students. To them, communication is a competition they must win at all costs. A common trait with aggressive communicators is their frequent use of the word *you* in statements, which keeps students feeling defensive and attacked. Examples are "you never listen to me," "you are always the one in trouble," "you are the problem here."

Aggressive communicators tend to view students' behavior as a personal attack. As a result, they may label the person rather than deal with the behavior. That's why aggressive communicators commonly use the words *always* and *never*. These are labeling words. They make students feel as if they are intrinsically bad people who cannot change their continually unacceptable behavior. This often causes students to become alienated from the teachers, from learning, and even from themselves.

Many aggressive teachers speak as if they are omniscient. For example, they may say to a student, "You think that because you got away with that last year, you can do it in my class." Obviously, no one knows what another person is thinking and to imply that one does undermines mutual respect and trust. On the other hand, aggressive communicators typically don't reveal how they feel about things, and they are unwilling to express their own thoughts and feelings. If students never know how a teacher feels, it is unlikely they will develop much empathy for their instructor. A guideline to keep in mind is this: Any statement about the student's feelings or thoughts, rather than your own, will give your communication an attacking and aggressive quality.

Assertive Communicator

An assertive teacher does not beg, plead, or threaten. Rather, he or she expresses feelings and expectations in a straightforward manner. Assertive people are not afraid to say what they want and do not worry about what others will think of them. Teachers who want to be liked are quite concerned about what their students think. An assertive teacher wants what is best for students and doesn't worry about what they think. Assertiveness comes across to students as a "no-nonsense" approach that is clear, direct, and very specific (requiring little interpretation to be carried out). For example, an assertive teacher might say to a student who has been talking out of turn, "It upsets me when you talk while I am talking." This teacher is expressing feelings and identifying the unacceptable behavior. The teacher would then continue with an assertive statement that expresses the acceptable behavior, for example, "That is your second warning; please go to time-out."

An excellent way to make messages more assertive is to use the word *I* instead of *you*. Talking about your own feelings and emotions will make the messages sound much more reasonable and firm. For example, say, "When you are playing with your equipment while I am talking, it bothers me and makes me forget what I planned on saying. Please put your equipment down when I talk." Assertive messages identify the behavior that is disruptive or annoying, state how you feel, and direct the student to behave in a proper manner. A valuable reference for becoming an assertive communicator is *Conscious Discipline* (Bailey, 2001).

How do you communicate? If you are uncertain, tape a class session. When you encounter a behavioral problem, do you respond in an assertive manner, or do you become aggressive or passive? A passive teacher may back away from the problem and plead with students to behave. An aggressive teacher will raise his or her voice and command students, for example, to "get back in line." Assertive communication is characterized by evenhandedness and clarity, rather than pleading or anger.

Back to Class

Overall, what kind of communication style does Ms. Kirklian have? Cite at least two examples from the chapter-opening scenario to support your answer.

Create a Personal Behavior Plan

One of the key elements of a management approach is to understand and plan how you will behave when disciplining students. Serious misbehavior may cause some teachers to become angry, others to feel threatened, and others to behave in a tyrannical manner. Part of your behavior plan is to remind yourself how you will act when misbehavior occurs. Personal behavior plans usually include the following points:

1. *Maintain composure.* Students don't know your trigger points unless you reveal them. If you "lose it," students lose respect for you and believe you are an ineffective teacher. They also have identified your "hot button," and may be able to upset you in the future.
2. *Personally acknowledge your feelings when student misbehavior occurs.* Teachers respond in different ways to misbehavior. How do you typically respond when a student defies you? Do you feel angry, threatened, challenged, or fearful?
3. *Design a response plan for yourself when you feel threatened.* For example, count to 10 before responding, or take five deep breaths. Avoid dealing with the student misbehavior until you are aware of how you feel.
4. *Know the options you have for dealing with deviant behavior.* It is always best to deal with deviant behavior in a quiet and personal manner. Calling out a

student across the classroom will put you in a vulnerable position. In-depth talking with students is best done after class if it is going to take more than a few seconds. Almost all options in class are time constrained. They include quietly correcting the behavior, gently and quietly moving the student into time-out, or seeking help if the situation is severe. More about this is covered later in the chapter.

Be a Leader, Not a Friend

Students want a teacher who is knowledgeable, personable, and a leader. They are not looking for a new friend; in fact, most students feel uncomfortable if they perceive that you want to be "one of them." So, don't look to be a part of their personal discussions. There must be a comfortable distance between you and your students. This is not to say that you shouldn't be friendly and caring; it is important to be concerned about students as long as your concern is expressed in a professional manner.

Being a leader means knowing where and how to direct a class. Let students know what they will learn during the semester. Communicate to them that you are taking responsibility for both the content of the lesson and how it is presented. Student input is important, but it is your responsibility to establish appropriate objectives.

Communicate High Standards

Students respond to your expectations. If you expect students to perform at high levels, the majority of them will strive to do so. A common expression is "you get what you ask for." If you expect students to perform to the best of their abilities, they probably will do so. On the other hand, if you act as if you don't care whether they try, many students will do as little as possible.

- The student may be testing the teacher.
- The student may have some type of learning disability that causes the behavior problem.
- The student may be looking for reinforcement from the teacher.
- The student may have low self-esteem, which causes the student to misbehave while trying to become the center of attention.
- The student may not understand the directions given.
- The student may be bored and unchallenged by the activities.
- Performing the activities may result in continuous failure, so the student misbehaves to avoid revealing a lack of ability.
- Parents may deal with their children in a manner completely unlike the methods used in physical education.
- The teacher may not like the student, thus forcing the student to be combative and angry.
- Failure in other subjects may carry over to physical education.

Figure 5.1 Typical causes of misbehavior.

Try to Understand Why Students Misbehave

Students might misbehave for any number of reasons, some of which are listed in Figure 5.1. The ability to identify these reasons as well as understand them will help you to anticipate and prevent behavioral problems in the future. For example, there are times when students misbehave because they didn't understand the instructions. Give clear instructions and proceed with the activity. If some students don't perform correctly, assume that they didn't understand. Clarify the instructions further and proceed. This two-tiered approach usually ensures that directions were clear and that ample opportunity was given for all to understand them.

Avoid Giving Feedback That May Cause Backlash

Teachers often evaluate the effectiveness of their teaching behaviors by asking themselves, "Did it work?" That is a poor way to evaluate behaviors, as some may seem to work in the short term but cause long-term negative consequences such as resentment or intimidation. When students become resentful, they may be deviant or disrespectful when the teacher is not around. Some examples follow.

- *Preaching, moralizing, or shaming.* The most common example is telling students they "should know better than that!" Students make mistakes because they are young and learning. A part of learning is making mistakes. Correct mistakes in a quiet and caring manner.

- *Threatening.* A threat is an ultimatum given in an attempt to terminate unacceptable behavior even though the teacher knows it is impossible to carry out. For example, saying, "If you don't stop that, I'm going to kick you out of class," sounds tough, but it is usually impossible to enforce. You are not in a position to expel students, and some students are aware of your inability to carry out the threat. If students hear enough idle threats, they will start to tune out and their respect for you will gradually wane.

- *Ordering and commanding.* If you are bossy, your students will begin to feel as if they are nothing more than pawns. Make requests, not demands, when you want students to carry out tasks, and don't neglect words such as *please* and *thank you*. Courtesy and politeness are requisites for effective teacher-student relationships.

- *Interrogating.* When there is a problem (such as a fight between students), the initial reaction of many teachers is to try to figure out "who started it." This is often impossible, since most students shirk the blame and suggest the other person was at fault. It's far more effective to deal with the feelings of the combatants. Try calmly saying, "You know fighting is not accepted in my class. You must have been very angry to place yourself in this situation." This encourages youngsters to talk about feelings rather than place blame. It also communicates to students that you care and are concerned about them even when they do something wrong.

- *Refusing to listen.* This commonly manifests itself as "Let's talk about it some other time." At times, for example when a child frequently interrupts you during instruction, this response is necessary. However, if you always refuse to listen, students avoid interaction with you and believe you don't care about their ideas or feelings.

- *Labeling.* As we noted earlier, some teachers label the child rather than deal with the behavior. For example, a teacher might say to an individual student, "You're always the troublemaker." Or a teacher may say to a class, "Stop acting like babies!" or "You're behaving like a bunch of first graders!" This is degrading and dehumanizes youngsters. Although teachers typically use labeling with the intent of improving perform-ance, it is usually destructive and reduces children's self-confidence.

Back to Class

Would you say that Ms. Kirklian behaved more like a leader or a friend? Why?

Define Class Procedures, Rules, and Consequences

Effectively managing a class depends on letting students know what you expect of them. They want to know what procedures are going to be used in class, as well as all rules and the consequences for breaking them. Without such information, students have to guess what the teacher wants or means. This leads to uneasiness, confusion, and incorrect guesses. Students feel more confident when they know your expectations.

An example illustrates the need for clear guidelines. Students are outside in a physical activity session. The teacher tells them not to get too far away because they need to be able to hear all the directions. Sure enough, some students stray beyond a distance the teacher deems acceptable and are reprimanded. This is unjust: the teacher set the students up for "misbehavior" by failing to establish clear guidelines. How are students to guess what distance their teacher thinks is too far away? What if they in fact could hear the directions? Can the teacher be consistent in applying this rule when even he doesn't know how far is too far? If cones had been set up around the perimeter of the area and students told to stay inside the cones, the problem would have been prevented.

In this section, we present some steps for defining class procedures, rules, and consequences. Carry them out at the start of the school year, and reinforce them on a regular basis throughout the year.

Step 1: Determine Class Management Routines

Students expect to follow established routines. At the beginning of the school year, explain your routines so that students understand why you've chosen them, and then practice them regularly until they're well established. Once they are part of the daily routine, you and your students will work together more comfortably. Following are examples of physical activity session tasks for which teachers often establish routines.

- How students enter the teaching area.
- How the teaching area is defined.
- How students group for instruction.
- Where and how students meet—in sitting squads, moving and freezing on a spot, in a semicircle, and so on.
- How students procure equipment.

What signal is used to freeze a class.

How students put away equipment.

How students line up and exit the area.

Step 2: Determine Rules for the School Year

Rules are general guidelines for expected behavior. They should not be overly specific nor should they be negative statements telling students what they shouldn't do. For example, "Use 'I care' language" is an appropriate rule for elementary school children. It is proactive and more widely applicable than a rule such as, "Never use the word 'hate,'" which could cause some children to wonder about the acceptability of saying something such as "I hate bananas!"

What rules should you choose, and how many? Most teachers want students to be respectful to them, to others, and to the school equipment and environment, thus rules requiring respect are essential. For example, the rule "Respect your neighbor" is a proactive one meaning many things, from not pushing to not swearing at another student. There should be a minimal number of rules. Try not to exceed three to five rules; more than this makes it difficult for students to remember all the details and makes you appear overly strict. In addition, too many rules make students engage in rule-specific thinking. A youngster may believe it is acceptable to chew gum in the multipurpose room because the rule says, "No gum-chewing in the halls." When students think in a rule-specific fashion, they do not learn to think about right and wrong and the spirit of the rule; rather, they often look for exceptions to the rule.

The following are examples of appropriate general rules that cover a wide range of behavior:

Stop, look, and listen. This implies freezing on signal, looking at the instructor, and listening for instructions.

Take care of equipment. This includes caring for equipment and distributing, gathering, and using it properly.

Respect the rights of others. This includes behavior such as not pushing others, leaving others' equipment alone, not fighting or arguing, and not physically or emotionally hurting others.

The following list of rules is useful with young children in an activity setting:

Be a mover.

Be kind.

Be safe.

Consider the following points when designing rules:

Select major categories of behavior rather than a multitude of specific behaviors.

Identify observable behavior. This makes it easy to determine whether a person is following a rule and does not involve subjective judgment.

State rules briefly and proactively. It is impossible to write a rule that covers all situations and conditions. Make the rule brief, yet broad.

Make rules reasonable for the age level of students. Meaningful rules cut across all ages and are suitable for all grades.

Limit the number of rules (three to five).

Post rules in the teaching area where all students can easily read them.

Step 3: Define Consequences When Rules Are Not Followed

When rules are broken, students must learn to accept the consequences of their behavior. Post the consequences for misbehavior in a prominent place in the teaching area. Discuss them with students to make sure they understand the consequences and appreciate their necessity. Then, apply them consistently and at the first infraction. When you fail to apply consequences at once, you encourage disrespect for rules and escalation of misbehavior.

Having agreed-on rules and consequences involves students in the development of an environment that, in part, they have designed. When a student chooses to break a rule, apply the consequences without making a derogatory statement about the student and without apology. The student made the decision to misbehave and trigger the consequences.

One of the best ways to earn students' respect is to treat them all fairly. One reason for defining consequences prior to misbehavior is that it allows you to administer them equitably. Most students are willing to accept the consequences of their misbehavior if they think they will be treated in the same way as others, but animosity occurs when students sense that you play favorites. Sometimes, teachers favor academically gifted students, cooperative students, athletes, or students who are physically attractive. You can prevent such favoritism by establishing and applying rules and consequences for all children.

Step 4: Share Your Rules with Parents, Teachers, and Administrators

It is not enough to share your rules with students. If it is true that "it takes a village to raise a child," it makes sense to ensure that all parties know and understand your rules. A newsletter to parents at the start of the school year explaining your approach to class management and listing your rules and consequences will set the appropriate tone immediately. Parents rarely complain about their child being disciplined if the routines, rules, and consequences are clearly identified in advance.

You should also share your rules with other teachers who work with your class, such as the music teacher, librarian, etc. This ensures a consistent approach to rules and consequences throughout the children's school day. Sharing your rules with administrators is also helpful. When you and your principal have the same understanding of rules and consequences, it is easier to work together to achieve common goals.

Step 5: Have the Class Practice Rules Systematically

Rules stipulate expected class behavior. If a rule is in place for proper care of equipment, students need the opportunity to practice how the teacher wants equipment handled. If a rule requires students to stop and listen, practice such behavior and reinforce proper responses. Children's behavior is not always correct, regardless of rules and how long such rules have been in place. It is common to hear teachers tell students, "I told you before not to do that." This assumes that telling students once will result in perfect adherence to rules. Obviously, this is not the case. Continue to allow time for students to practice acceptable behaviors throughout the school year.

> ### Back to Class
>
> When Peter confronted Nikki in our chapter-opening scenario, how did Ms. Kirklian handle it? What was the result of the way she dealt with his confrontational behavior?

Incorporate Efficient Management Skills

If a class is unmanageable, it is unteachable. Class management skills are prerequisites to effective instruction. However, in order to organize and move students quickly and efficiently, you'll need to master a variety of management skills and teach your students to follow and appreciate them. In truth, most students appreciate a learning environment that is organized and efficient because it allows a maximum amount of class time to be devoted to active learning.

As with physical skills, class management skills are learned through practice and repetition until they become second nature. Just as students make mistakes when performing physical skills, some will make mistakes performing management skills. Keeping this analogy in mind will help you maintain your empathy for students who do not perform well. A simple, direct statement such as, "It appears that you forgot how to freeze quickly; let's practice," is much more constructive than indicting a class for carelessness and disinterest.

Deliver Instruction Efficiently

If students are not listening when you give them instructions, they are not likely to learn much. And they are not likely to be listening if you deliver a long and involved instructional monologue. In a series of spoken items, people usually remember only the first and the last; thus, most students will be able to integrate and concentrate on only one or two points at a time. Deliver instructions in small doses, focusing on one or two specific points. Total instruction time should seldom exceed 20 to 30 seconds.

An effective approach is to alternate short instructional episodes with periods of activity. For instance, if you are teaching a classroom game that takes a lot of explanation, start the game and play it with minimal instruction. Once students understand the concept of the game, add a new rule or strategy. Minimizing the amount of content per instructional episode helps eliminate students' frustration and allows them to focus on stated goals. So, if you typically have a "tell it all at the start" instructional style, replace it with the more effective "input, practice, feedback, additional input" model.

When you are ready to deliver instructions, tell students "when" before "what." That is, tell the class *when* to perform the activity before stating *what* the activity is. An effective way to implement "when before what" is to use a keyword, such as *begin* or *go* to signal the class to start. For example, say, "When I say *Go!,* I want you to jog to a beanbag, pick it up, move to your own space, and practice tossing and catching. Go!" Since the keyword is not given until all directions have been issued, students must listen to all instructions before starting. To further illustrate, sometimes you'll want your students to work with a partner. If you don't say *when* before *what,* your students will immediately start to look for their favorite partner rather than listen to the rest of the directions.

Start and Stop a Class Consistently

The most basic and important management skill is to be able to start and stop a class quickly. To start a class, use a voice command. (See the previous discussion on keywords.) Be consistent in your instructions. For example, if students have learned that they are to remain in a single-file line until they hear your keyword *go,* you're likely to confuse them if you suddenly switch to a different word or a whistle.

To stop a class, pick a consistent signal. It does not matter what the signal is, as long as you always use it and it always means the same thing. Using both an audio signal (such as a whistle) and a visual signal (raising the hand overhead) is useful because some youngsters may not hear the audio signal when engrossed in activity. If children do not respond to the signal to stop, take time to practice the procedure.

Many teachers like to have students assume a specific position when they stop (**Figure 5.2**). Freezing in the ready position with hands on knees helps keep students' hands in their own space so they don't distract others. Keep in mind that being able

Figure 5.2 Class in freeze position.

to freeze a class quickly is a safety issue. Reinforce youngsters when they perform management skills properly. Behavior that is not reinforced regularly will not be performed well.

Expect 100 percent compliance when you ask students to stop. If some students stop and listen to directions and others do not, class morale is compromised. Students begin to wonder why they have to stop but other students don't. Scan the class to see if all students have stopped and are ready to respond to the next set of directions. If you settle for less than full attention, students will perform according to those expectations.

Move Students into Groups and Formations Quickly

It is often necessary to move students into partnerships, small groups, and instructional formations such as a circle or a single-file line. Simple techniques help you accomplish this in an enjoyable, yet rapid manner. Regardless of the technique used or the intended grouping, teach students to match up with someone near them rather than running around looking for their best friends. To facilitate this, delineate an area and call it the "friendship spot." Teach students that, when they need a partner or group, they should run to the friendship spot, raise their hands, and look for a partner or group members. After identifying a partner or group, they move out of the friendship spot.

Finding Partners

To help children locate partners quickly, teach them to get toe-to-toe (one foot only) with a partner as fast as possible. Other challenges are to get elbow-to-elbow or shoulder-to-shoulder. Students without a partner quickly go to the friendship spot and find someone else without a partner. This gives students a designated action to take when they're not partnered and prevents them from running around the area feeling unwanted.

Instruct children to take the nearest person for a partner rather than searching for a friend or embarrassing someone by avoiding them. If students insist on staying near a friend, tell the class to move throughout the area and find a different partner each time you call "Toe-to-toe!" If you still find children partnering with friends, implement the rule that a new partner must be selected each time. This will help avoid exclusive groupings and foster new friendships.

Other suggestions for finding partners are to ask students to find a partner wearing the same color, with a birthday during the same month, with a phone number that has two of the same digits, and so on. To arrange students in equal-sized groups, place an equal number of different-colored beanbags or other items on the floor. Ask students to move throughout the area. On signal, they sit on a beanbag. All students with a red beanbag are in the same group, green beanbags make up another group, and so on.

Dividing the Class in Half

To divide a class into two equal groups, have students get toe-to-toe with a partner. For kindergarten through second-grade students, have one partner sit down while the other remains standing. Those standing are asked to go to one side of the area, and then those sitting are moved to the other side. With grades three to six, one partner can raise a hand. Move the students with their hands up to one side of the area first.

Creating Small Groups

To arrange students in groups of a selected size, use the "Whistle Mixer" activity. Blow the whistle a certain number of times. Students then form groups—the number of people should be equal to the number of times the whistle was blown. Once they have the correct number of people, groups should sit down to signify that they are done. Students left out go to the friendship spot, find the needed number of members, and move to an open area. When this skill is mastered, students can move quickly into properly sized groups. Adding a hand signal to indicate the size of the group you want will make it even easier for all students to recognize the number required.

Creating Circles or Single-File Lines

To move a class into a circle, have them jog randomly throughout the area until you give the signal to "fall in." You will jog around the perimeter of the area and give the signal. Students then jog in the same direction as you and head toward the perimeter of the area, where they get in line behind someone until a circle is formed. As long as students continue to get in line behind another person, a circle will form automatically. Use a similar technique to move a class into a single-file line. Either you or a designated student leader then lead the line into the desired position.

Another method of moving a class into formation is to ask students to get into various formations without talking. Students may use non-verbal signals, but they cannot verbally ask someone to move. Groups hustle to see how quickly they can form the acceptable formation. In still another method, the teacher holds up a large card with a shape drawn on it to signal the desired formation. Young students learn various shapes through this technique.

Use Small Groups to Expedite Class Organization

Some teachers find that placing students into small groups helps them manage a class more effectively. For example, when using stations or limited equipment, small groups make for less waiting in line. Other teachers use small groups to place students in prearranged teams of equal ability for sports activities. Prearranged groups may also be used to separate certain students so they don't have the opportunity to disrupt the class. The following are guidelines for using small-group formation to maximize teaching effectiveness.

1. Pre-select groups to avoid embarrassing a child who might be chosen last. In all cases, avoid using an "auction" approach, where student leaders look over the group and pick those whom they favor. To group youngsters randomly, use the "Whistle Mixer" technique described previously.

2. Small groups provide opportunities for leading and following among peers. Assign leaders in each group so youngsters have an opportunity to learn leadership skills. Examples of leadership activities include moving to a specified location, leading the group through exercises or introductory activities, and appointing group members to certain positions in sport activities.

3. To ensure that students get to work with everyone in the class, change the group members on a regular basis.

4. In most cases, you'll find it helpful to establish an even number of groups so that you can quickly divide the class into halves for certain games. For example, you might initially divide a class of 30 students into six groups of 5 students each.

Use Equipment Effectively

In Chapter 3, we provided some general guidelines for using equipment. Here, we discuss skills for equipment management. As a reminder, when using small equipment such as balls, hoops, and jump ropes, be sure that every youngster has a piece of equipment to use.

Teach students to place equipment in the same (home) position when the class is asked to freeze and listen. For example, beanbags, jump ropes, and hoops are placed on the floor, and balls of all types are placed between the feet. Placing the equipment in home position avoids the problem of youngsters striking one another with the equipment, dropping it, or practicing activities when they should be listening. To prevent students from playing with the equipment when it is placed on the floor, ask them to take a giant step away from it.

Distribute equipment to students as rapidly as possible. When students have to wait in line for a piece of equipment, time is wasted and misbehavior occurs. For example, having student leaders get equipment for their group leaves the rest of the students sitting and waiting. A better and faster method is to have the equipment placed in different spots in the room. On signal, youngsters move to acquire a piece of equipment, take it to their personal space, and begin practicing the assigned skill. This approach takes advantage of the motivational value of the equipment and reinforces students who procure equipment quickly. Teach the reverse procedure to put equipment away.

Avoid placing the container of equipment in the middle of the area and telling students to "run and get a ball." This approach increases the chances that youngsters will be aggravated or hurt.

Clearly state what students are supposed to do with their piece of equipment. Waiting for all students to get a piece of equipment before allowing anybody to use it places control in the hands of the slowest and least-cooperative student. The students who hustled to get their equipment have to wait while the slowpokes take their time. Avoid this problem by allowing students to start practicing once they get their equipment. Privately prompt those students who are slow and less cooperative while the others are practicing.

Teach and Increase Acceptable Student Behavior

It is usually best to think of behavior in terms of acceptable and unacceptable rather than positive and negative. Unacceptable and acceptable speaks only to the behavior, not the child. In contrast, a child can easily interpret the words *positive* and *negative* as characterizing the child or class as good or bad. This is labeling, which you have learned is never an effective or constructive approach for improving student behavior. Thus, throughout this chapter, we use the terms *acceptable* and *unacceptable*.

Although you should avoid using the word *positive* to describe children's behavior, you should certainly be aware of **positive discipline**; that is, a discipline style that focuses on reinforcing acceptable behavior. When children receive approval for increasing acceptable behavior, they are likely to reduce unacceptable behavior. Lavay, French, and Henderson (2006) provide an excellent resource for the systematic approach to positive behavior management. They delineate three phases to such a program: (1) increasing acceptable behavior, (2) eliminating unacceptable behavior, and (3) maintaining acceptable behavior. There are a variety of strategies to help you implement the positive discipline program during physical activity sessions. We begin with teaching responsibility.

Teach, Post, and Reinforce Levels of Responsibility

The primary focus of a positive discipline program is teaching children *responsible* behavior. Hellison (2003) developed strategies and programs for teaching responsibility skills in a physical activity setting. A basic premise of Hellison's work is that responsibility skills must be planned, taught, and reinforced. Responsible behavior takes time and practice to learn, much like any other skill. Hellison suggests there is a hierarchy of five levels of responsible behavior that can be learned. Teaching responsible behavior as described here begins by presenting these five levels to your students. Each is defined below, followed by examples of typical student behavior at each level.

Level 0: Irresponsibility

Level 0 students are unmotivated and undisciplined. Their behavior includes discrediting other students' involvement and interrupting, intimidating, manipulating, and verbally or physically abusing other students and perhaps the teacher.

Behavior examples:

At home. Blaming brothers or sisters for problems; lying to parents.
On the playground. Calling other students names; laughing at others.
In physical education. Talking to friends when the teacher is giving instructions; pushing and shoving when selecting equipment.

Level 1: Self-Control

Students at this level do not participate in the day's activity or show much mastery or improvement. These students control their behavior enough so they do not interfere with other students' right to learn or the teacher's right to teach.

Behavior examples:

At home. Refraining from hitting a brother or sister even though angry.
On the playground. Standing and watching others play; not getting angry at others because they did something to upset them.
In physical education. Waiting until an appropriate time to talk with friends; having control and not letting others' behavior bother them.

Level 2: Involvement

These students show self-control and are involved in the subject matter or activity.
Behavior examples:

At home. Helping clean up the dishes after dinner; taking out the trash.
On the playground. Playing with others; participating in a game.
In physical education. Listening to instructions and performing the activity; trying even when they don't like the activity; doing an activity without complaining or saying, "I can't."

Level 3: Self-Responsibility

Level 3 students take responsibility for their choices and for linking these choices to their own identities. They are able to work without direct supervision, eventually taking responsibility for their intentions and actions.
Behavior examples:

At home. Cleaning up without being asked.
On the playground. Returning equipment after recess.
In physical education. Following directions; practicing a skill without being told; trying new activities without encouragement.

Level 4: Caring

Students behaving at this level are motivated to extend their sense of responsible behavior by cooperating, giving support, showing concern, and helping.
Behavior examples:

At home. Helping take care of a younger brother or sister or a pet.
On the playground. Asking others (not just friends) to join them in play.
In physical education. Helping someone who is having trouble; welcoming a new student; working with all students; defending a student who is being teased.

Responsible behavior is taught using a number of strategies. Post the levels of responsibility in the teaching area. Explain the different levels of behavior and identify examples of acceptable behaviors at each level. After students have received an introduction to responsible behavior, implement the program by reinforcing and redirecting actions: (1) catch students using responsible behavior and reinforce them, and (2) redirect students behaving at level 0 by asking, "At what level are you performing and what level would be more acceptable?" For example, see the following discussion between teacher and student.

You see a student behaving at level 0 and open dialogue with the student in a non-confrontational and non-adversarial manner:

"Johnny, it appeared you were making fun of someone."
"I wasn't making fun of anyone!"
"Maybe not, but if you were, what level of behavior would it be?"
"Zero!"
"Is that the kind of person you want to be or the level of behavior you want to show?"

"No!"

"If you were at level 0, do you think you could make some changes? Perhaps you could move to level 1 and have self-control even if someone else makes you mad or even if you do not like that person."

Back to Class

What level of behavior was Peter exhibiting? Write an imaginary dialogue that Ms. Kirklian might have initiated to move Peter toward more responsible behavior.

Employ Strategies for Increasing Responsible Behavior

Teacher feedback forms the core of Hellison's approach. Other strategies for increasing responsible behavior in the instructional setting include the following:

- *Model acceptable behavior.* Be aware of the impact your behavior has on students. What students learn reflects your personality, outlook, ideals, and background. Recognize that some of your personal habits and attitudes may affect youngsters negatively, and strive to model any behavior you desire from students. This means moving quickly if you demand that students do the same. It implies listening carefully to students when they want to share a thought. Students do not care about how much you know until they know how much you care. Treat youngsters with respect, and follow through with responsible actions and words. In return, expect students to treat you and others with the same respect. Bear in mind the old saying, "actions speak louder than words."

- *Use reinforcement.* Give students specific feedback about the quality of their behavior, identifying the acceptable level of behavior. If reinforcing acceptable behavior, be specific in identifying why the behavior is acceptable and that you appreciate such acts. In some cases, it may be beneficial to identify a super citizen or give a "happygram" card for special behavior.

- *Offer time for reflection.* Allow time for students to think about the attitudes and behaviors associated with each of the levels. Ask the students to fill out a self-responsibility checklist at different times of the year. See **Figure 5.3** for an example of a checklist.

- *Allow student sharing.* Offer students a chance to share their ideas about responsible behavior. Accept all students' feelings as important. Focus on ways to encourage higher levels of responsible behavior. Brainstorming to identify consequences of high and low behavior levels is an effective approach. Another practice is to ask different students to give examples of responsible behavior at different levels. Allow students time to share how they feel when someone uses a high- or low-level behavior around them.

Encourage goal setting. Help students set goals for the responsible behavior they want to exhibit. Do this at the start of the lesson by asking students to tell a partner the behavior they want to use today. At the end of the lesson, partners evaluate each other to see if the behavior was exhibited. Examples of behaviors are listening, hustling, following directions, being courteous, and complimenting others.

Offer opportunities for responsibility. There are a number of times when students may be given responsibility in a class setting. Being a group leader, team captain, referee, scorekeeper, rule maker, or dispute resolver are roles that encourage students to exhibit high-level behavior. Since responsible positions affect other students, effective leaders have to behave responsibly.

Allow student choice. Responsible behavior is learned when students make choices. Dealing with the natural consequences of self-selected choices is a good way to learn new lessons. Students may make choices about games they choose to play, fitness activities they select, and friends they choose.

My Self-Responsibility Checklist

Name: _____

Date: _____

Self-Control:

_____ I did not call others names.

_____ I had self-control when I became mad.

_____ I listened when others were talking.

_____ Other (describe)_____

Involvement:

_____ I listened to all directions before starting.

_____ I was willing to try all activities.

_____ I tried activities even when I didn't like them.

_____ Other (describe)_____

Self-Responsibility:

_____ I followed directions without being told more than once.

_____ I did not blame others.

_____ I worked on activities by myself.

_____ Other (describe)_____

Caring:

_____ I helped someone today.

_____ I said something nice to someone.

_____ I asked someone to do something with me.

_____ Other (describe)_____

Figure 5.3 Example of a Self-Responsibility Checklist.

Prompt Acceptable Behavior

Prompts are visual or verbal cues that remind students to perform acceptable behavior. Used appropriately, prompts help students become self-motivated to perform the prompted behavior. There are a number of ways to prompt children during physical activity. The most common are the following:

1. *Modeling.* You or another student performs the acceptable behavior with the expectation that students will respond in similar fashion. For example, placing your equipment on the floor reminds the class to do likewise. Modeling is an effective prompt for acceptable behavior because young students emulate their teacher.

2. *Verbal cues.* This common method of prompting uses cues such as "Hustle!" and "Eyes on me!" to remind students of acceptable behavior. Use verbal cues to maintain the pace of the lesson, increase the intensity of the performance, or motivate youngsters to stay on task.

3. *Nonverbal cues.* Gestures and other physical cues are helpful to communicate concepts such as "hustle," "move over here," "great performance," "quiet

down," and so on. Demonstrating an activity is a nonverbal physical cue that helps students visualize correct performance.

As a general rule, the weakest (least intrusive) prompt possible should be used to stimulate the desired behavior. For example, although you could give students a long lecture about the importance of staying on task, this approach is time-consuming and excessive. It is not suited for multiple (repetitive) use and is ineffective in the long run. Instead, select a short, concise cue that is closely identified with the acceptable skill.

If you use prompts too often and for too long, your students will either come to rely on them and not perform without them, or they will start to tune them out. The goal is to remove the prompt as soon as possible so that your students' behavior becomes self-motivated. This process is called *fading* and involves gradual removal of the prompt. For example, if you initially shouted, "Hustle!" and made a "boxing" gesture with your arms, you could gradually lower your volume, then remove the verbal cue altogether, then remove the gesture.

In addition to these points, be sure that the prompt is linked to a specific task. For example, if you prompt the class to hustle, and the prompt is not tied to a specific behavior, there may be confusion. Some children may think your prompt means to perform the skill as fast as possible; others may think it means to stop what they are doing and move to the teacher. Consistently tie the prompt to the desired behavior, and make sure that students clearly understand its meaning.

Reinforce Acceptable Behavior

"Catch them doing what you want them to do" is a subtle way to increase acceptable behavior. Behavior that is followed by appropriate positive reinforcement now occurs more often in the future. In this section, we discuss three types of reinforcers—social, activity, and extrinsic; how to select the type that is most appropriate for a given situation; and how to use social reinforcers effectively.

Social Reinforcers

Social reinforcers are words of praise, facial expressions and gestures, and physical contact that acknowledge acceptable behavior. Most children are familiar with social reinforcers because they live in a world filled with them: parents use praise, physical contact, and facial expressions to acknowledge acceptable behavior in their children, and teachers use the same in class when students perform acceptable behavior. **Table 5.1** shows examples of social reinforcers to use with students in a physical education setting.

Identify the type of social reinforcers students are accustomed to in the school setting. Certain reinforcers may embarrass students or make them feel uncomfortable. For example, some students

Table 5.1 Social Reinforcers

Words of Praise

Great job	Nice going
Exactly right	I really like that job
Perfect arm placement	That's the best one yet
Way to go	Nice hustle

Facial Expressions and Gestures

Smiling	Winking
Nodding	Clenched fist overhead
Thumbs up	Clapping

Physical Contact

Handshake	High five

may not want to be touched, even to the point of receiving a high five. Some students may not like to be reinforced in front of the class because it embarrasses them. If unsure, ask the school administrator to define the acceptable social reinforcers to which students respond positively.

Activity Reinforcers

Activity reinforcers are enjoyable activities that are used to reward acceptable behavior. An effective way to determine activities to use as reinforcers is to observe your students. Some examples of activities that might work with a class are free time to practice a skill, extra time at recess, and the opportunity to play a game. Examples of activities useful with individual students include helping hand out equipment, acting as a teacher's aide, or being a team captain. Or, you may give students special privileges such as being "student of the day," getting to choose the game to play, or having lunch with the teacher.

Extrinsic Reinforcers

Extrinsic reinforcers are tokens such as points, stickers, certificates, or trophies used to reward acceptable behavior. Since it is common in athletic competition to give awards to winners, some teachers believe that tokens should be used to motivate children in other types of physical activity. However, the practice of giving extrinsic rewards has its drawbacks: when such rewards are given only to winners, losers become less motivated to perform in the future. Some teachers give participation certificates or ribbons to all students; however, this practice gives the token little reinforcement value. In addition, there is evidence to show that extrinsic rewards may actually decrease a child's intrinsic desire to participate (Greene and Lepper, 1975; Whitehead and Corbin, 1991).

Extrinsic reinforcers work best with primary-grade children. Young children are typically motivated by the tokens they receive. However, after age nine, students begin to see the tokens as a form of bribery to get them to behave in a certain manner. Generally, it is best to use extrinsic reinforcers only if it appears that social reinforcers are ineffective.

Selecting Reinforcers

A common question among teachers is "How do I know what will reinforce my students?" It is impossible to know for sure until the reinforcement is administered. Fortunately, most children will respond to praise, attention, smiles, games, free time, and privileges. A practical way to identify effective reinforcers is to observe children during free time and analyze the things they appear to enjoy doing. Another solution is to ask them what they would like to do. Most youngsters will tell you that they would like more recess, free time, or another enjoyable activity.

Using Social Reinforcers

Words of praise and reinforcement can sometimes feel contrived and insincere. Although your students might not notice the difference, you may feel uncomfortable while learning to administer positive reinforcement if your behavior feels inauthentic. A common complaint from teachers learning how to reinforce behavior is "I do not feel real when I use this kind of language, and the children think I don't mean what I say." Any change in communication patterns may feel uncomfortable at first. Trying new ways of communicating with a class requires a period of adjustment. It is not necessarily the case that your personal speech patterns, which you acquired growing up, are the most effective ways to speak in an instructional setting. Teachers are made, not born, and they find success through hard work and the application of skills acquired throughout training and experience. If practiced regularly, new communication patterns will become a natural part of your repertoire.

As we said in Chapter 4, praise is effective when it refers to specific behavior. General and nonspecific statements such as "Good job!" do not tell the youngster what was done well. Instead, the student must guess what you are pleased about. If the student's guess does not align with your intent, incorrect behavior is reinforced. To improve the specificity and effectiveness of feedback, describe the behavior to be reinforced rather than judge it. For example, compare the following:

- *Describing:* "I saw your excellent forward roll, James; you tucked your head just right."
- *Judging:* "That's not right. You need to try it again."

In the first example, the youngster is identified and the specific behavior performed is reinforced. In the second, it is impossible to identify what is poorly done or to whom the feedback is directed. In most cases, if a question may be asked about delivered praise or criticism (such as what was good or what was not performed correctly), the feedback is nonspecific and open to misinterpretation. To increase acceptable behavior, verbally or physically describe what makes the performance effective, good, or noteworthy. This reinforces the student and communicates to the rest of the class what behavior is expected by the instructor.

Shape Acceptable Behavior

When acceptable behavior does not exist, you use shaping techniques to create new acceptable behavior. Use the following two techniques for shaping behavior.

- *Use differential reinforcement to increase the incidence of acceptable behavior.* Reinforce responses that reach a predetermined criterion and ignore those that do not meet the criterion. An example of this principle involves asking a class to put their equipment down quickly. You decide that students should put the equipment on the floor within five seconds. To use differential reinforcement, reinforce the students whenever they meet the five-second criterion and ignore their performance when it takes longer than five seconds.
- *Gradually increase the criterion standard that must be reached for reinforcement to occur.* In this step, you shift the criterion standard gradually toward the desired goal. For example, if the acceptable behavior is for the class to become quiet within 5 seconds after a signal has been given, it might be necessary to start with a 12-second interval. Why the longer interval? It is not reasonable to expect that—without previous drilling in this skill—an inattentive class will quiet down quickly. If you require a 5-second response initially, there is a strong possibility that you and your students will be

Changing behavior can be done if teachers are willing to experiment and be patient. Teachers want to change behavior quickly and on the spot and at times make incorrect decisions because they don't have time to think of an effective solution. In-class misbehavior can be temporarily stopped, but may often go unchanged for the future. Realize that change will require long-term action that must be planned ahead of time. The following steps can be used to develop a plan for changing behavior.

- Identify a single behavior that needs to be changed, improved, or strengthened. Don't pick more than one behavior as it will make it much more difficult to monitor change.
- Identify a behavior that will be substituted for the behavior to be changed.
- Determine what positively reinforces the student. Have a discussion with the student to see what is reinforcing.
- Decide whether a negative reinforcer is needed to give momentum to the change process.

- Develop a plan for getting the desired behavior to occur. This will generate a behavior that can be reinforced and used to replace the undesirable behavior.
- Put the plan into effect and set a time frame for evaluation of the plan. Decide what modifications are needed to make the plan more effective. This modification may demand a different set or schedule of reinforcers or negative consequences. If an entirely different plan is needed (because the behavior hasn't decreased or changed), make such changes and proceed.
- Continue evaluating and modifying the plan.

Figure 5.4 A plan for changing behavior.

frustrated by their lack of success. In addition, since this stringent standard of behavior will not be achieved very often, you'll have very few opportunities to reinforce the class. The result will be a situation in which both you and the class feel they have failed. To avoid this, gradually move toward the acceptable behavior goal. In this case, start with 12 seconds and use it until the class reaches this goal. Next, shift to a 10-second interval and ask the class to perform to this new standard. The process is gradually repeated until the desired terminal behavior is reached.

You may also shape students' behavior by taking a systematic approach. **Figure 5.4** offers a step-by-step plan for changing unacceptable behavior from an individual student. The figure may be adapted to use with a class, as well.

Decrease Unacceptable Student Behavior

Most effective techniques for improving class behavior are designed to guide the student away from behavior that is disrupting the class. Corrective feedback and application of consequences can be effective means for decreasing unacceptable behavior.

Deliver Corrective Feedback Respectfully

First, as described above, try using positive reinforcement to increase acceptable behavior and replace unacceptable behavior. For example, if a skilled student is always criticizing less-able youngsters, ask that student to help others and serve as a student assistant. The intent is to teach the youngster to deliver positive and constructive feedback rather than criticism.

If positive reinforcement does not work, deliver corrective feedback. An effective guideline for determining when to take this step is as follows: (1) Reinforce the acceptable behavior twice. (2) If this fails, deliver corrective feedback. For example, assume a youngster is slow to stop on signal, but the majority of other students are stopping and listening properly. Ask the class to move and freeze again. Reinforce students who are on task. (This doesn't work with students who are older; public reinforcement is usually not acceptable to students in grades four to six.) If the child is still slow to stop, try it again. Many primary-grade children will emulate those who are being reinforced. If this child does not, it may be necessary to use corrective feedback.

As always, corrective feedback should be specific and immediate. Students must understand exactly what behavior they are to stop and what acceptable behavior they are to start. Use corrective feedback as soon after the misbehavior as possible, just as positive reinforcement is delivered immediately following the acceptable behavior.

When students are disciplined or corrected, they may respond in a negative manner, causing class disruption if corrective feedback is not delivered correctly. The following steps prevent teacher-student conflicts from occurring in front of other students. When delivering corrective feedback or consequences, use these steps to avoid embarrassing students and yourself.

1. *Do not address the student publicly.* Buy some time for talking with the student privately by giving the class a simple task to perform, such as jogging around the area. This gives you time to discuss the situation privately with the misbehaving student. Calling out a student in front of other students may stop the behavior, but it may also prompt negative aftereffects. For example, the student being called out may be embarrassed, may get angry, may shout back, or may continue the behavior in defiance. When a student is called out in front of the class, you give the student the position of power. The rest of the class may even side with that student.

2. *Isolate the student and yourself.* Don't correct a student where others can hear what you are saying. The problem is a private matter between you and the student.

3. *Deal with one student at a time.* Often, a couple of students are misbehaving together. Separate them and deal with their unacceptable behavior one-on-one. In addition, avoid delivering feedback to an entire group of students when the misbehavior involved only one or a few. Shouting corrective feedback across the playground to the entire class may have a detrimental effect on uninvolved students. If you criticize the whole group, you risk losing the respect and admiration of students who were behaving properly.

4. *State your position once and repeat it once if you believe the student didn't understand.* Don't argue or try to prove your point. Take no more than 10 to 15 seconds to tell the student the unacceptable behavior and what acceptable behavior you would like to see.

5. *Do not insist on eye contact.* For example, do not say, "Look at me when I am talking to you!" Such behavior is confrontational, especially to older students. Stand beside the student and softly deliver your feedback.

6. *Don't threaten or bully the student, curse, raise your voice, or use sarcasm.* Such behaviors build resentment in students and may cause greater problems at a

later time. Instead, state clearly what you desire from the student in terms of acceptable behavior. Again, model the behavior you wish to promote.

7. *Avoid touching the student when correcting behavior.* Even if you have positive intentions, it may send mixed messages. Some students don't want to be touched and will aggressively pull away and make a scene in front of the class.

8. *Deliver your corrective feedback and move away.* Walk away after you have delivered the feedback. Don't look back at a student shortly after you have reprimanded him or her, as you may see things you don't want to see. To get yourself back on track, positively reinforce one or two students who are performing the acceptable behavior.

Back to Class

Now that you've learned how to deliver corrective feedback humanely, identify the steps in the process that Ms. Kirklian got wrong. What actions might have made her feedback more effective?

Apply Consequences

When corrective feedback fails to cause an acceptable change in behavior, consequences must follow. Students need to understand that unacceptable behavior brings consequences. Becoming responsible for one's behavior may be one of the most important social learning outcomes of the school experience. Consequences that may be used to decrease unacceptable behavior include reprimands, removal of positive consequences, and time-out.

Try Reprimands

Many teachers use reprimands to decrease unacceptable behavior. If done in a caring and constructive manner, reprimands serve as effective reminders to behave acceptably.

- Identify the unacceptable behavior, state briefly why it is unacceptable, and then explain what would be desired or acceptable behavior. For example, say, "You were talking while I was speaking, which bothers other students and me. That is unacceptable behavior. I expect you to be respectful and listen quietly when someone else is speaking."
- Avoid labeling. Ask the person to stop the misbehavior and do not comment on the person. For example, avoid telling a student "You are always causing problems in this class."
- As with corrective feedback, don't reprimand in front of other students. Not only does it embarrass students, it also can diminish their self-esteem. When students feel belittled, they may lash out in a manner more severe than the original misbehavior.

Reprimand softly. Studies (O'Leary and Becker, 1968) show that soft reprimands are more effective than loud ones.

After reprimanding and asking for acceptable behavior, reinforce it when it occurs. Be vigilant in looking for the acceptable behavior because reinforcing such behavior will cause it to occur more often in the future.

Remove Positive Consequences

Removing positive consequences is an approach commonly used by parents, so many students are familiar with it. The approach is to remove something positive from the student when misbehavior occurs. For example, students give up some of their free time, lose points toward a desired goal, or are not allowed to participate in an activity that is exciting to them. For removal of positive consequences to be effective, students must value the removal activity. A few key principles should be followed when using this technique.

Be sure that the magnitude of the removal fits the crime. In other words, children who commit minor infractions shouldn't have to miss recess for a week.

Be consistent in removal, treating all students and occurrences the same. Teachers are behaving unfairly if they are more severe with one student than another for the same misbehavior. In addition, a student penalized for a specific misbehavior should receive the same penalty for a later repetition.

Make sure students understand the consequences of misbehavior *before* the penalties are implemented. If students know what the consequences will be, they are making the choice to accept the consequences when they choose to misbehave.

It is helpful to chart a student's misbehavior to see if the frequency is decreasing. Regardless of the method used, if the behavior is not decreasing or is increasing, change methods until a decrease in frequency occurs.

Use Time-Out

Time-out is a consequence that moves youngsters who are misbehaving out of the class setting and places them in a pre-designated area. It is an equitable, socially acceptable behavioral management technique for dealing with individual children. It is also acceptable for children to voluntarily use the time-out area as a "cooling-off" spot if they become angry, embarrassed, or frustrated.

Time-out does not imply that the student is a "bad person," but rather that unacceptable behavior has occurred and there is a need for the child to reconsider and make the decision to behave acceptably. Being placed in time-out communicates to youngsters that they have disrupted the class and must be removed so the rest of the class can participate without interruption. When placing children in time-out, communicate to them that you care about them, but their behavior is unacceptable.

A common practice is to place time-out stations in each of the four corners of the instructional area. When outdoors, delineate the instructional area with four cones, and place a time-out sign on each cone. When directing students to go to a time-out area, inform them that they are allowed to return to class as soon as they have decided they are ready to behave in an acceptable manner. Some teachers have students stay in the time-out area for five minutes before returning. That works if you have a way to keep track of the time. However, it is difficult to manage when two or more students are sent to time-out at different times. Another method used by some teachers is the "you may return when I say you may return" method. The problem with this approach is that you may forget and leave a student in time-out longer than you planned. Also, if a student is a chronic offender, you may leave them in time-out for the same behavior longer than you would a student who seldom misbehaves. That sends a message that you like some students better than others. An effective behavior management system should be fair and consistent.

If youngsters are placed in time-out for fighting or arguing, they should be placed at opposite ends of the instructional area so that the high emotion does not escalate. In addition, when they come out of time-out, tell them to remain on their opposite sides until the physical activity session is over. This prevents contact between the two combatants and decreases the possibility of future hostility.

The implementation of this plan should be discussed with students so they know exactly what unacceptable behavior incurs a time-out. As discussed earlier, post a list of rules and consequences in the teaching area.

Time-out means time out from reinforcement; that is, it does not serve as a deterrent if the youngster is reinforced when placed in time-out. The physical location for time-out should provide *as little* reinforcement as possible. For example, imagine that a student who is not participating properly is told to sit in the hallway for time-out. Friends pass by, and they converse. Now the student not only gets to avoid participation, but gets to visit with friends. Note that being a spectator at an athletic event is an enjoyable experience for which many people pay money. Sitting on the side of the teaching area and looking on as a spectator may be more reinforcing for a student than participating in class activities. Therefore, if you put someone in time-out, make sure he or she is not facing the class and interacting with peers. Instead, position him or her facing away from the class, perhaps in front of a list of levels of responsibility or rules and consequences (**Figure 5.5**).

Finally, if class participation is a negative experience for students, taking them out of class will be a positive rather than negative consequence. Remember—if students don't enjoy participating in your class, time-out does not work.

Guidelines for Applying Consequences

As with corrective feedback, deliver consequences privately. Buy time for delivery by engaging the class in a task and then moving to the misbehaving youth. Avoid yelling across the teaching area. Not only does it embarrass and isolate the student, but evidence suggests it increases the general anxiety of the entire class. A proposed set of guidelines for applying consequences follows.

First Misbehavior: The student is quietly warned that the unacceptable behavior must stop. Students may not be aware they are bothering others, and a gentle reminder may be enough to refocus the youngster. In terms of "teacher talk," private conversation with the student would be as follows:

Figure 5.5 A student assigned to time-out should be alone and facing away from the rest of the class.

"John, you were talking while I was talking. That is unacceptable behavior. I expect you to listen respectfully in the future. This is your first warning."

Second Misbehavior: The student goes to one of the time-out spots and stays until ready to return and behave in an acceptable manner.

Third Misbehavior: The student goes to the time-out area for the remainder of the activity session. When the session is over, the student should rejoin the class with a clean slate.

Continual Misbehavior: If these consequences are ineffective, you will need to involve the school principal or other administrator. Most schools have an in-school suspension program to deal with continual misbehavior. In-school suspension typically requires the student to leave his or her class and move into another room of students at a different grade level. As a general rule, however, you should avoid asking the principal to solve your problems with misbehaving students. If you do this often, the principal will soon believe that you cannot effectively manage students. Ultimately, this erodes the principal's confidence in your teaching ability.

If in-school suspension is not effective, the last alternative is to call the parents in for a conference with you and the principal. This step is risky: if the parents respond to the conference with punishment at home, then there is a strong possibility that it will further alienate the student. Another possibility is that parents will disagree with your assessment. If they do, you will need to deal with the behavior in the school setting anyway.

> ## Back to Class
>
> Look back at the definition of a time-out and the guidelines for applying consequences. In your opinion, did Nikki's behavior warrant a time-out? Why or why not?

Use Criticism Sparingly

Use criticism with caution and good judgment. By definition, **criticism** is communication that identifies what is wrong or bad about somebody or something. Some teachers make criticism the behavior-control tool of choice because it usually stops misbehavior quickly, giving the appearance that the situation has been rectified. But when used too frequently, criticism becomes scolding and creates a negative-feeling instructional environment for both you and your students.

Teachers can hurt themselves, as well as students, when they use criticism too frequently because it can create in them a sense that they cannot handle their class without it, or that their class is incorrigible. This feeling of incompetence can lead to a destructive cycle in which the teacher's negative feelings about the class cause the students to feel badly about both the teacher and themselves, which in turn increases students' misbehavior.

In addition, too-frequent criticism is ineffective and may even be counter-productive. In a study by Thomas, Becker, and Armstrong (1968), a teacher was asked to stop praising a class. Off-task behavior increased from 8.7 percent to nearly 26 percent. When the teacher was asked to increase criticism from 5 times in 20 minutes to 16 times in 20 minutes, more off-task behavior was demonstrated—on some days more than 50 percent. This suggests that when attention is given to off-task behavior and no praise is offered for accomplishment, off-task behavior increases dramatically. This may be due in part to the fact that students are reinforced for their off-task behavior when they receive attention from the teacher. At the same time, since their on-task behavior is not reinforced, it decreases. The net result is exactly the opposite of what is desired.

Make Punishment a Last Resort

Punishment is defined as a penalty administered for severe or continual misbehavior; and it often involves some kind of action required of the student rather than simply removal of positive consequences or a time-out. For example, a teacher might require a student to complete a tedious math worksheet or pick up all of the trash on the playground. Bear in mind that a majority of U.S. states have passed laws banning corporal punishment in schools.

When debating the appropriateness of punishment, consider the long-term consequences of the situation. If a child is likely to be in a worse situation because you did not use punishment to deter his or her destructive behavior, then it would be unethical not to use it. For example, it may be necessary to punish a child in order to protect that child from self-inflicted harm (for example, walking on a balance beam without a spotter). Or, it may be necessary to punish a child in order to deter that child from hurting others. Punishment in these situations will cause discomfort to teacher and child in the short run, but it may allow the student to participate successfully in society later.

One reason for avoiding punishment whenever possible is that it makes your students fear and avoid you. Rather than deciding that they want to earn your favor with acceptable behavior, they may decide that their best strategy is to be more covert in their misbehavior so they won't get caught. In addition, if your punishment is particularly harsh, the child may act out with aggression toward others. This is a well-established effect of corporal punishment: children who are physically punished by parents or teachers are more likely to act abusively toward others. But this acting out may also be seen with other excessive forms of punishment, especially if they are public, such as making a child do 50 sit-ups in front of the class. Finally, it is often the case that as soon as the punishment stops, the behavior returns. Thus, little has been learned; the punishment has led only to short-term compliance.

If you decide that it is necessary to use punishment, adhere to the following guidelines:

1. *First, offer one warning.* This may prevent excessive use of punishment because many students will behave after receiving a warning. In addition, they will probably view you as caring and fair.

2. *Do not threaten students.* Threats have little impact on students and make them feel that you cannot handle the class. Threats rarely have follow-through, whereas one warning gives students the feeling that you are not looking for an opportunity to punish them. If the warning is ignored, follow through and apply the punishment.

3. *Be consistent and make the punishment "fit the crime."* Students quickly lose respect for a teacher who applies a punishment that is more harsh than that given to someone else or more severe than the infraction warrants. Peers often side with a student who is treated unfairly, causing a class morale problem for the teacher.

4. *The punishment should follow the misbehavior as soon as possible.* It is much less effective and more likely to be viewed as unfair if it is delayed.

5. *Punish softly and calmly.* Do not seek revenge or be vindictive. If you expect responsible behavior from your students, be sure you punish in a responsible manner.

If punishment is used, make sure that only those youngsters who misbehave are punished. Punishing an entire class for the deviant behavior of a few youngsters is unfair and often triggers unacceptable side effects. Students become hostile toward those who caused the loss of privileges, and this peer hostility lowers the level of positive social interaction with the students who have misbehaved.

Try to avoid developing negative feelings toward students for their misbehavior. Remember that applying consequences—including punishment—fairly and calmly contributes to the development of responsible, confident students who understand that people who function effectively in society must adjust to certain limits. At the start of each class, forget past incidents of unacceptable behavior and approach the student in a positive fashion. Expect acceptable behavior, and your students will learn to live up to your positive expectations.

Back to Class

Should Ms. Kirklian have punished Peter's behavior? In defending your answer, consider not only the nature of his infractions, but also Ms. Kirklian's responses.

Establish Procedures for Resolving Conflicts

Conflict between students often results in aggression and violence. About one in seven children is either a bully or a victim of bullying (Beane, 1999). Nobody wants to create a world where the strong dominate and the weak live in fear and submission.

Conflict is a part of daily life, and youngsters need to learn to deal with conflict in an effective manner. Students can learn ways to respect others' opinions and feelings while maintaining their own worth and dignity.

Of the many behaviors that children exhibit when approaching conflict, the most common are dominating, appeasing, and cooperating. Students who use the dominating style are often unsure about their standing in the group. They want things to be done their way but are afraid others will reject them. They often lack confidence and try hard to get others to accept their way of doing things.

Youngsters who are appeasers lack confidence but want to be accepted by others. They do not like conflict and are willing to set aside their feelings in order to placate others.

Some children are quite naturally cooperative. They are confident and secure in themselves and in the group, but at the same time they recognize that others' opinions are valid, too. When conflict arises, they know how to negotiate for what they want without dominating others or allowing others to dominate them.

Neither the dominating nor the appeasing approach for solving conflicts is effective in the long run. Conflict resolution can help students learn to solve conflicts in a peaceful manner, with no apparent losers. This cooperative approach to solving problems builds positive feelings between students and leads to better group cohesiveness. There are two general approaches to conflict resolution: the teacher-directed approach and the peer-mediated approach.

Use Teacher-Directed Conflict Resolution

Many teachers use the following steps to resolve conflicts (Gordon and Browne, 1996). These steps are effective with younger children or children without experience in conflict resolution. If children are experienced at conflict resolution, they may be able to carry out the steps without instructor intervention.

1. *Stop the aggressive behavior immediately.* Students in conflict are separated immediately and given an opportunity to cool down. Time-out areas are an excellent place to send students to relax and unwind.
2. *Gather data about what happened and define the problem.* Find out what happened, who was involved, and how each youngster is feeling. Ask open-ended questions such as "What happened?" and "How did you feel about . . . ?" so youngsters can talk freely about the problem.
3. *Brainstorm possible solutions.* Keep in mind that brainstorming is a nonjudgmental process in which all solutions are accepted regardless of their perceived value. Encourage youngsters to think of as many solution options as possible by asking open-ended questions such as "How could we solve this problem?" and "What other ways could we deal with this?"
4. *Test the solutions generated through brainstorming.* Ask a question such as "What solutions might work best?" Help students understand the implications of the solutions and how the solutions may be implemented. Accept solutions that may differ from your way of solving the problem.

5. *Help implement the plan.* Walk students through the solution so they develop a perception of the approach. Guide them through the steps by asking, "Who goes first?" "Who will take the next step?" As the solution is implemented, there may be a need to change it, which should be agreed on by the students involved.

6. *Evaluate the approach.* Observe the students to see if the plan is accomplishing the acceptable outcome. Encourage students to change the plan if necessary.

The conflict resolution process takes practice and time. It demands that you play certain roles and take an objective approach to resolution. An essential teacher behavior is listening to both parties. Both sides of the problem must be explored, and students must feel that the process was equitable. Avoid attempting to determine who is at fault. Placing blame only encourages defensive behavior, such as appeasing or being aggressive. Students have to trust that the process will be fair and objective and that they will receive a fair shake if they deal with the issue cooperatively.

Encourage Peer-Directed Mediation

Peer mediation is similar to conflict resolution except that it is student directed. Disputes and conflicts are resolved between students with a neutral peer acting as a moderator in the process. As with teacher-directed conflict resolution, the goal is to work out differences constructively. Moderators are trained to help their classmates identify the problems behind the conflicts and to find solutions. They do not attempt to discover who is right or wrong. Instead, students are encouraged to move beyond the immediate conflict and learn how to get along with each other. Mediation gets students involved in the problem-solving process, either as moderators or disputants, and teaches them a way of handling conflicts.

Situations involving name-calling, rumors, bumping into students in the hallways, and bullying are often best resolved through peer mediation. As discussed in the excellent text by Cohen (2005) on peer mediation, there are two parts to the mediation process: establish ground rules and follow mediation steps.

Ground Rules

All parties (including the mediator) participate in reviewing and agreeing to the ground rules. When there is agreement on the ground rules, mediation begins. Basic ground rules that must be agreed to are as follows:

- The problem will be solved. Participants have to agree that a solution will be found in the mediation session. It is not acceptable to leave the session without solving the problem.
- The truth will be told. Students must agree to tell the truth regardless of the impact it has on the situation. Since students will be solving the problem without adult supervision and the session will be confidential, telling the truth will not result in negative consequences.
- The full story will be heard without interruption. Each party must be able to tell his or her side of the story without interruption. Each person

Peaceable Playgrounds

News Clip

At Public School (PS) 217—a large, diverse elementary school in Brooklyn—teachers tell a simple story: A drop of honey falls from a rooftop in a kingdom. First a dog and cat fight over the drop. Then the neighbors get involved. Soon there's all-out war. The king realizes he should have dealt with the problem when it was just a drop of honey. This simple tale, just one tool in a schoolwide conflict resolution program, reminds children to solve small disagreements before they turn into large fights.

Nationwide, conflict resolution programs are offered in 15 to 20 percent of public schools. One of the most popular, a program called Resolving Conflict Creatively, was developed in 1985 by Educators for Social Responsibility. It offers lessons, discussions, and peer mediation training, all aimed at resolving disputes without aggression. As the program's philosophy statement states, "Avoidance is not the answer. In most cases, conflict should be dealt with head-on, with a focus on constructive problem solving."

Do such programs work? A recent study by the University of Washington in Seattle found a 29 percent decrease in incidents involving hitting and fighting in schools with conflict resolution programs. Another study from Columbia University found, however, that lessons must be frequent. Children exposed to 25 or more lessons show a decrease in aggression, but those who receive only a few lessons do worse than those who have none. And an analysis of 70 studies published in 2000 by the Washington-based Conflict Resolution Education Network found that many conflict resolution program studies are flawed and fail to follow students long enough to determine whether any behavioral changes noted are long-lasting.

And there are limits to what conflict resolution programs can accomplish. To date, no study shows that conflict resolution programs can reduce violent, high-risk behavior. Trish Jones, a professor in the Department of Communications Science at Temple University, found that the greatest impact is on mediators rather than those actually involved in conflict. Referring to the shootings at Columbine High School in Colorado in 1999, she cautions that conflict resolution programs cannot prevent all potentially dangerous actions but asserts that they can be effective for a majority of children who would benefit from better coping, communication, and life management skills.

Source: Adapted from The New York Times November 11, 2001, at: http://query.nytimes.com/ gst/fullpage.html?res=9C07E5DA1539F932A25752C1A9679C8B63&sec+&spon+&pagewanted

take action!

1. Check out the Pathways to School Improvement website (search under "conflict resolution") (see Web Resources). Download their "Hints for De-Escalating a Conflict," professional and parent information, and other materials and share them within your school community.

2. Find out how the elementary schools in the district in which you live approach conflict. Do teachers receive training in conflict resolution? Do children learn peer mediation?

3. Interview some elementary school teachers in your district to find out how they handle conflict in their classroom and how serious the problem seems to them. With the interviewees' permission, write an article summarizing your research and submit it to your local newspaper.

should feel that his or her side of the story was completely and fairly presented.

- All parties will act in a respectful manner. Students need to learn to state their case without excessive emotion and anger.
- All discussion will be confidential. Both the arbitrator and the parties in conflict agree not to discuss the situation with non-participants.
- The solution will be implemented. Both parties will carry out the agreement regardless of whom the solution favors.

Back to Class

If Ms. Kirklian had been using teacher-directed conflict resolution when she approached Nikki and Peter in our chapter-opening scenario, what is the first thing she would have done? How might she have used step 3 in the conflict resolution process?

Mediation Steps

After agreeing to the ground rules, mediation led by a trained peer begins. The problem is not discussed during the creation of ground rules. The mediation steps are intended to solve the actual problem and do so in a manner dictated by ground rules students agreed to follow. The following are steps to finding a mediated solution:

- *Tell your story or grievance.* Each student now has a chance to tell his or her side of the story. This should be an opportunity to "lay it on the table" and feel that both the other party and the mediator clearly understand the problem.
- *Verify the story.* The mediator and the other party have the opportunity to ask questions to clarify and verify the story. The mediator is responsible for trying to find out exactly what happened and how each party feels.
- *Discuss the conflict.* The mediator conducts a discussion about the situation and the emotions involved.
- *Brainstorm solutions to the problem.* All parties discuss ways the problem might be solved. Emphasis is placed on the need to find solutions that close the situation for both parties.
- *Discuss and implement the agreed-upon solution.* Both parties agreed previously to follow ground rules they developed. One of the rules was to solve the problem. Therefore, it is not acceptable to leave without a solution.
- *Sign a contract.* After agreeing to a solution, the offended parties must sign a contract agreeing to carry out the solution.

Chapter Summary

Use Proper Teaching Behaviors

Management is defined as organizing and controlling the affairs of a class. It refers to how students are organized, started and stopped, grouped, and arranged during class. *Discipline* is defined as methods for discouraging non-adherence to rules and for changing student behavior that is unacceptable.

Develop an assertive communication style. Assertive teachers want what is best for students and do not worry about what students think of them. Assertive messages identify the behavior that is unacceptable, offer how you feel, and direct the student to behave in a proper manner.

Create a personal behavior plan that includes the following points: maintain composure, acknowledge your feelings when misbehavior occurs, design a response plan for yourself when you feel threatened, and know your options for behavior management.

Other important teaching behaviors include being a leader, not a friend; communicating high standards; trying to understand why students misbehave; and avoiding feedback that could cause backlash.

Define Class Procedures, Rules, and Consequences

Students need clearly defined class procedures, rules, and consequences. Five steps to follow to define these include the following:

- Step 1. Determine class management routines.
- Step 2. Determine rules for the school year.
- Step 3. Define consequences when rules are not followed.
- Step 4. Share your rules with parents, other teachers, and administrators.
- Step 5. Have the class practice the rules systematically.

Incorporate Efficient Management Skills

Keep instruction short and specific, and tell students "when" before "what."

Use signals and management skills to start and stop a class quickly. Expect 100 percent compliance when you ask students to stop.

When students need to form groups, set aside a friendship spot where they can look for partners. Use toe-to-toe, the "Whistle Mixer," or other techniques to get students to partner or group quickly without looking for friends.

• When distributing equipment, place it in different spots around the area and have students move to acquire it, take it to their personal space, and begin practicing the assigned skill. Also teach children a home position in which to place equipment when you ask students to stop and freeze.

Teach and Increase Acceptable Student Behavior

• Positive discipline focuses on reinforcing acceptable behavior. When children receive approval for increasing acceptable behavior, they are likely to reduce unacceptable behavior.

• Strategies for positive discipline include teaching, posting, and reinforcing levels of responsibility; modeling acceptable behavior; using positive reinforcement; allowing time for reflection and sharing; encouraging goal setting; offering opportunities for responsible behavior; and allowing student choice.

• Prompts are visual or verbal cues that remind students to perform acceptable behavior. Used appropriately, prompts help students become self-motivated to perform the prompted behavior.

• Three types of reinforcers are social reinforcers, such as a handshake or words of praise; activity reinforcers, such as an enjoyable game; and extrinsic reinforcers, such as tokens.

• When acceptable behavior does not currently exist, shape it by using differential reinforcement and by gradually increasing the criterion that must be met for reinforcement to occur.

Decrease Unacceptable Student Behavior

• If positive reinforcement does not work, deliver corrective feedback. An effective guideline for determining when to take this step is as follows: Reinforce the acceptable behavior twice. If this fails, deliver corrective feedback.

• When delivering corrective feedback, address the student privately, one student at a time. State your position once, and repeat it once only if it seems the student has misunderstood. Do not insist on eye contact, threaten or bully the student, curse, raise your voice, or use sarcasm. Avoid touching the student when correcting behavior. As soon as you have delivered the feedback, move away.

• When corrective feedback fails to result in an acceptable change in behavior, apply consequences. Consequences that may be used to decrease unacceptable behavior include reprimand, removal of positive consequences, and time-out.

When directing students to go to a time-out area, inform them that they are allowed to return to class as soon as they have decided they are ready to behave in an acceptable manner. If youngsters are placed in time-out for fighting or arguing, each child involved should be placed at opposite ends of the instructional area so that the high emotion does not escalate.

Time-out does not serve as a deterrent if the student is reinforced by contact with peers, an opportunity to watch a game in progress, or by any other means while in the time-out area. It also does not work if the student does not enjoy participating in your class.

A first incident of misbehavior may usually be handled effectively with an immediate warning. If a second incident occurs, the student should be sent to time-out until ready to return and behave acceptably. Upon a third incident, the student goes to time-out for the remainder of the activity session. Continued misbehavior should be addressed with the school principal or other administrator.

Used frequently, criticism becomes counterproductive, actually increasing the incidence of off-task behavior.

Make punishment a last resort, for example, to protect a child from self-inflicted harm or to deter a child from hurting others.

Establish Procedures for Resolving Conflicts

Conflict resolution is a cooperative approach to solving problems that builds positive feelings between students and leads to better group cohesiveness.

Teacher-directed conflict resolution involves six steps that require you to take an objective approach to resolution. These steps are effective with younger children or children without experience in conflict resolution.

In peer-directed mediation, disputes and conflicts are resolved between students, with a neutral peer acting as a moderator in the process. Two steps in the process include establishing ground rules and following mediation steps led by a trained peer.

Review Questions

Content Review

1. Following the guidelines provided in the chapter, create your own personal behavior plan.

2. What rules would you have in your class? What consequences?

3. Identify at least two methods of moving students into partnerships or formations quickly and efficiently.

4. Create a table listing the five levels of responsibility and a classroom example of each. Do not use any of the examples given in the text.

5. Identify a step-by-step protocol for disciplining a child who teases another child three times within the same 20-minute session of physical activity.

Real World **1.** You have decided to work with your incoming first-grade class on their throwing and catching skills. Decide on the class management skills you will teach them for the following: leaving the classroom and walking to the gym, dividing into partners, acquiring a beanbag, starting the practice session, stopping the practice session, putting the beanbags away, and returning to the classroom.

2. As a teaching aide, you are assigned to Mrs. Baker's second-grade class. On the first morning, you notice a chart at the front of the room with each child's name above a column. In many of the columns are black check marks. You come to understand how Mrs. Baker uses the chart as throughout the day she reprimands different children for talking too loudly, getting up from their desk without permission, asking a question without first raising their hands, failing to share school supplies, and a seemingly endless variety of other infractions that are nowhere posted in the room. At each of the first four infractions, the child gets a check mark on the chart. If a child gets five check marks, he or she has to stay inside for recess. At lunchtime, Mrs. Baker asks you to supervise two rambunctious boys who have each been given five checkmarks and must stay inside for recess. You can't help feeling sorry for them on such a sunny winter day, and you ask them how they feel about staying inside. One of the boys bursts out, "It's rotten! I hate Mrs. Baker and I hate second grade!" The other boy just shrugs. "I used to mind it, but now it's no big deal anymore." You'll have an opportunity to talk with Mrs. Baker after the children have gone home for the day. Will you address her class management and discipline techniques? If so, what will you say?

References and Suggested Readings

Bailey, B.A. (2001). *Conscious discipline*. Oviedo, FL: Loving Guidance, Inc.

Beane, A. (1999). *The bully free classroom*. Minneapolis: Free Spirit Publishing.

Canter, L., and Canter, M. (1997). *Assertive discipline: Positive behavior management for today's classroom*. Santa Monica, CA: Lee Canter and Associates.

Cohen, R. (2005). *Students resolving conflict*. Tucson: Good Year Books.

Gordon, A., and Browne, K.W. (1996). *Guiding young children in a diverse society*. Boston: Allyn & Bacon.

Greene, D., and Lepper, M.R. (1975). Turning play into work: Effects of adult surveillance and extrinsic rewards on children's internal motivation. *Journal of Personality and Social Psychology*, 31, 479–486.

Hellison, D. (2003). *Teaching responsibility through physical activity* (2nd ed.). Champaign, IL: Human Kinetics Publishers.

Lavay, B.W., French, R., and Henderson, H.L. (2006). *Positive behavior management in physical activity settings* (2nd ed.). Champaign, IL: Human Kinetic Publishers.

What About You?

In this chapter, we described three styles of communication: passive, aggressive, and assertive. Which style would you say is most like your own? _____

If you're not sure, think of the last time someone disappointed or offended you. How did you respond?

_____

Which of the three styles most closely characterizes this response?

_____

Nelson, J. (1996). *Positive discipline.* New York: Ballantine.

O'Leary, K.D., and Becker, W.C. (1968). The effects of intensity of a teacher's reprimands on children's behavior. *Journal of School Psychology, 7,* 8–11.

Siedentop, D., and Tannehill, D. (2000). *Developing teaching skills in physical education* (4th ed.). Mountain View, CA: Mayfield Publishing Co.

Thomas, D.R., Becker, W.C., and Armstrong, M. (1968). Production and elimination of disruptive classroom behavior by systematically varying teachers' behavior. *Journal of Applied Behavior Analysis,* 1, 35–45.

Whitehead, J.R., and Corbin, C.B. (1991). Effects of fitness test type, teacher, and gender on exercise intrinsic motivation and physical self-worth. *Journal of School Health*, 61, 11–16.

Wolfgang, C. H. (1996). *The three faces of discipline for the elementary school teacher.* Boston: Allyn & Bacon.

Web Resources

Discipline by Design:
www.honorlevel.com/techniques.xml
Pathways to School Improvement, Conflict Resolution/North Carolina Regional Educational Library:
www.ncrel.org
P.E. Central: Creating a Positive Climate for Learning:
www.pecentral.org/climate

6

Teaching Children with Special Needs

Learning Objectives

After reading this chapter, you will be able to . . .

○ Identify the requirements of the Education for All Handicapped Children Act (EHA)/Individuals with Disabilities Education Act (IDEA) and discuss their implications for education.

○ Explain the concept of least restrictive environment.

○ Identify the due process procedures associated with special education assessment.

○ List the essential elements of an individualized education program (IEP).

○ Describe the formulation and implementation of an IEP.

○ Discuss guidelines for modifying instruction to children with special needs.

○ Describe ways of modifying physical activities for students lacking strength, endurance, coordination, balance, and/or agility.

Classroom Challenge

Bhakti was born with spina bifida, a birth defect affecting the spinal cord that can cause various degrees of paralysis. She wears leg braces and uses crutches to walk, but she is energetic and can usually **keep pace** with her classmates. Her first-grade teacher, Mr. Whitney, tries to include Bhakti in physical activity sessions but constantly worries that she might fall and hurt herself. Academically, Bhakti is well above grade level in math and problem-solving, but her reading skills are so poor that she has been scheduled for assessment for **special education** services.

One morning, Mr. Whitney brings the children onto the playground and organizes a game of kickball. He assigns his two most athletic children the role of team captains and has them choose team members. There are 19 children in the class, and after each captain has chosen eight teammates, Bhakti is the only child left unchosen. She looks uncertainly at Mr. Whitney, who calls out encouragingly, "That's all right, Bhakti! Come over here, and you can **keep score!**" Bhakti's head drops to her chest, and she makes her way slowly toward the sidelines. As she approaches Mr. Whitney, he notes the absence of her usual bright smile.

 s a teacher, you are responsible for providing a quality educational experience for all of your students. We hope you view this as an ethical and professional responsibility rather than something you must do simply because it is mandated by law. Effective teachers take pleasure in relating to their students as individuals; in getting to know their unique strengths, challenges, interests, and concerns; and in modifying their teaching methods to help each child succeed.

Since all children come to school with varying ability levels and environmental support, in a real way, all children have special needs. In this chapter, however, we focus our attention on children who face particular challenges that make it harder for them to participate in physical activity than most children their age. Some examples of these challenges include intellectual disabilities, behavioral disorders, psychiatric diagnoses, medical diagnoses, physical disabilities, communication disorders, and sensory impairments.

We begin by discussing the legal requirements for educating children with special needs. We then explore the process of screening and assessment for special needs and the development of an individualized education program (IEP). The chapter concludes by providing a systematic approach for accommodating children with special needs in classroom physical activity.

Legislative Requirements

Federal law mandates that every state develop a plan for identifying, locating, and evaluating all children with special educational needs and provide these children a free appropriate public education (FAPE). Here, we discuss this legislation and explore its main requirements.

Federal Legislation

Public Law 94-142, the Education for All Handicapped Children Act (EHA), was passed by Congress in 1975. The law was enacted ". . . to assure that all handicapped children have available to them . . . a free appropriate public education which emphasizes special education and related services designed to meet their unique needs, to assure that the rights of handicapped children and their parents or guardians are protected, to assist States and localities to provide for the education of all handicapped children, and to assess and assure the effectiveness of efforts to educate handicapped children." The term *handicapped* is used in PL 94-142 to include youngsters who are mentally retarded, hard of hearing, deaf, speech impaired, visually handicapped, seriously emotionally disturbed, orthopedically impaired, impaired in health in other ways, deaf-blind, multi-handicapped, or specific learning disabled. We prefer to use the phrases *students with special needs* or *students with disabilities* throughout this text to identify youngsters with such conditions.

Under the concept of zero reject, no child may be rejected from all educational services because of a disability. All children age 5 to 21 are entitled to a FAPE. Prior to 1975, students with significant disabilities had limited access to schools. They certainly did not have an equal opportunity to participate in school programs. With the passage of EHA, the U.S. Congress made a strong commitment to quality and comprehensive education programs for all children in the country. The law also ensured that funding would be made available to provide special education: it authorized a payment to each state of 40 percent of the average per-pupil expenditure in elementary and secondary schools for each disabled student receiving special education and related services.

EHA has been amended several times since its original passage into law. In 1986, it was extended to include children with disabilities beginning at age three. In 1990, Public Law 101-476 renamed the EHA as IDEA, the Individuals with Disabilities Education Act, and replaced the phrase "handicapped child" with "child with a disability." Autism and traumatic brain injury were added to the list of qualifying disabilities. IDEA was further extended and strengthened in 1997 to include consideration of the purchase of assistive technology devices if a child needs access to such devices to learn.

Physical education is the only curriculum area specifically mentioned in EHA/IDEA. The law defines the term *special education* as "specially designed instruction, instruction in physical education, home instruction, and instruction in hospitals and institutions." It also states that "physical education services, specially designed if necessary, must be made available to every child with a disability receiving a free appropriate public education."

Finally, EHA/IDEA introduced several new terms and concepts into schools and care facilities across the United States. These include *least restrictive environment*, *progressive inclusion*, *mainstreaming*, *due process*, and *individualized education programs (IEPs)*, all of which are discussed in this chapter.

Least Restrictive Environment

EHA introduced the term **least restrictive environment (LRE)** to identify the best placement of students with disabilities. The LRE is the educational setting providing the greatest level of interaction with students who are not disabled while still enabling the child to receive an appropriate education. The underlying goal, which is to prevent schools from segregating students with special needs, is secondary to the child's right to an appropriate education. In other words, a child's right to special services to promote progress in his or her learning has a higher value than the social benefits of learning in a general education classroom. Thus, when determining the LRE, the goal is to place students into settings that offer the best opportunity for their *educational* advancement. Just as it would be inappropriate to put a child into a setting that is more restrictive than necessary, it would be inappropriate to place a child in an environment where success is impossible.

Consistent and regular judgments need to be made about what constitutes the LRE because the type of activity and instructional approach can change the student's opportunity for success. For example, for a student in a wheelchair, a soccer activity might be impossible, whereas in basketball or Frisbee activities, the student could participate. For a student with a behavioral disorder, individual participation in a game might be a successful experience, while an activity requiring group cooperation might not be advisable.

Placing students with special needs into an LRE is an important initial step, but evaluation and modification of that environment needs to be ongoing. Through the process of *progressive inclusion*, students are continually evaluated to determine their readiness to progress to the next level of LRE. Over time, progressive inclusion enables children to experience more and more of the school's general educational programs. Again, the primary goal is for students to make progress as a result of their educational experiences.

Mainstreaming for Physical Activity

Mainstreaming is a term commonly used in public education delineating the process of placing students with disabilities in classrooms with non-disabled students. Effective mainstreaming is characterized by *normalization*; that is, the setting is as normal as possible while still ensuring that the student is able to achieve success in that placement.

Educators have identified several types of mainstreaming reflecting various levels of participation in academics and physical activity.

1. *Full mainstreaming.* Students with special needs function as full-time members in the regular school routine. They attend all classes with able students. Within the limitations of their disability, they participate in physical education with able peers (**Figure 6.1**). An example may be vision-impaired or auditory-impaired students, who, with a minimal amount of assistance, are able to participate fully.

2. *Mainstreaming for physical activities only.* Students with disabilities are not members of the regular academic classes but can still participate in physical activities with able peers. This setting may include students with emotional disabilities who are moved to the classroom for physical activity with other students.

3. *Partial mainstreaming.* Students participate in selected physical activity experiences but do not attend on a full-time basis because they can be successful in only a few of the offerings. Their developmental needs are usually met in special classes.

4. *Special developmental classes.* Students with disabilities are in segregated special education classes.

5. *Reverse mainstreaming.* Able students are brought into a special physical education class to promote intergroup peer relationships.

Back to Class

In terms of physical activity, which of the levels of mainstreaming listed would apply to Bhakti? Why?

Again, the goal is to place students in the LRE. Segregation denies children with disabilities opportunities to interact with their peers and to become a part of the social and academic classroom network; thus, it should be maintained only when it is in the best interests of the student. The purpose of segregation is to establish a level of skill and social proficiency that will eventually enable the student to be transferred to a less-restricted learning environment.

Students with disabilities need contact with support personnel during mainstreaming. Even though the teacher is responsible for the mainstreamed students during class time, these students may still require access to special education teachers, school psychologists, occupational therapists, speech therapists, etc. Support personnel are also a good source of information and support for the classroom teacher in charge.

Figure 6.1 Successful mainstreaming of children with disabilities into a session of physical activity.

Screening and Assessment

Screening is a process by which all children in a school setting are evaluated to determine whether they should be referred for a special education assessment. Recall that federal law requires states to identify children with special needs: screening is part of that "child find" process. Identifying special needs children often takes place at the start of the school year and is performed district-wide. In most situations, screening tests may be administered without parental permission.

After identified students have been referred to the director of special education, an **assessment** is conducted. Typically, a team of experts evaluates each child's needs as identified in the screening process. The team may include, in addition to an expert in special education, a speech therapist, an occupational therapist, and a child psychologist. Typically, the team also includes a classroom teacher. Although highly individualized, the assessment process often involves clinical and/or classroom observation as well as administration of a variety of tests (not necessarily written tests). It typically takes several weeks or even months to complete since the results of a particular assessment step may indicate the need for further evaluation in another domain. EHA/IDEA states that parents must be informed of the school's decision to conduct an assessment and must give their consent.

Due Process Procedures

The EHA mandates that a principle called **due process**, which is derived from the U.S. Constitution, must be followed when school districts conduct special education assessments. Due process demands respect for the legal rights of individuals in matters concerning the state or nation. In the context of special education assessments, it ensures the rights of parents (or legal guardians) to be notified of assessment proceedings involving their child, to be informed of their rights as related to such proceedings, to be heard at such proceedings, and to have the opportunity to challenge educational decisions they feel are unfair or incorrect.

To safeguard parents' rights to due process, the procedures listed here must be followed.

Written permission. A written notice must be sent to parents stating that their child has been referred for assessment. The notice must explain that the district requests permission to conduct an evaluation to determine whether special education services are required for their child. Also included in the letter must be the reasons for testing and the titles of the tests to be used. Before assessment may begin, the letter must be signed by the parents and returned to the district.

Interpretation of the assessment. The results of the assessment must be interpreted in a meeting with parents. Persons who are knowledgeable about the test procedures must be present to answer questions parents may ask. At the meeting, parents must be told of their child's assessment results and the services that will be provided for the child.

External evaluation. If parents are not satisfied with the results of the assessment, they may request an evaluation be performed outside the school setting. The district must provide a list of agencies that can perform such assessment. If the results differ from the school district evaluation, the district must pay for the external evaluation. However, if the results are similar, parents must pay for the external testing.

Negotiation and hearings. If parents and the school district disagree on the results of the assessment, the district is required to try to negotiate the differences. When negotiations fail, an impartial hearing officer listens to both parties and renders an official decision. This is usually the final review; however, both parties have the right to appeal to the state department of education, which must render a binding and final decision. Civil action through the legal system can be pursued should the district or parents still disagree with this action. However, few cases ever reach this level of long-term disagreement, and educators should not hesitate to serve the needs of children with disabilities based on this concern.

Confidentiality. As is the case with other student records, only parents of the child or authorized school personnel may review the student's records. Review by other parties may be done only after written permission has been given by the parents of the child under review.

The Impact of Diversity on Assessment

Diversity issues such as disabilities, language barriers, cultural differences, and poverty often interfere with standard assessment procedures. For example, many students have visual and auditory disabilities that prevent using tests that rely on these faculties. Students in an English as a second language (ESL) program must be tested in a manner that ensures that their reduced communication skills in their non-native language do not influence the test results. The probability of misdiagnosis is also increased when using certain types of tests with children from ethnic minorities such as Native Americans, African Americans, and Hispanic Americans. Children living in poverty may be malnourished and environmentally disadvantaged and therefore in need of adequate, nutritious food and cultural enrichment rather than special education. Since many tests are based on western European, middle-class standards, minority and poor children should be assessed only with instruments that have themselves been tested and shown to be valid with these populations.

Back to Class

Bhakti's parents moved to the United States from India when Bhakti was five years old. Her father is an engineer for a technology firm. Her mother, who speaks very little English, stays at home caring for Bhakti and her four-year-old brother. What diversity issues might affect Bhakti's special education assessment? What issues might affect her school experience?

Developing an Individualized Education Program

The EHA requires that an **individualized education program (IEP)** be developed for each disabled child receiving special education and related services. The IEP must be developed by a committee that must include the following members:

- A local education association representative who is qualified to provide and supervise the administration of special education.
- The child's parents.
- The teachers who have direct responsibility for implementing the IEP.
- The student, when appropriate.

Other individuals may be included at the discretion of the parents or the school district.

As noted earlier, screening and assessment identify the child's unique qualities and help committee members determine educationally relevant strengths and weaknesses. A plan is then devised based on the diagnosed strengths and weaknesses.

Content of the IEP

The IEP must contain the following material (**Figures 6.2A and 6.2B**):

1. Current status of the child's level of educational performance.
2. A statement of long-term goals and short-term instructional objectives.
3. A list of special education and related services that will be provided to the youngster. Also, a report on the extent to which the youngster will be able to participate in regular educational programs.

INDIVIDUALIZED EDUCATION PLAN

☐ Initial Placement
☐ Re-evaluation
☐ Change of Placement
☐ Review

A. STUDENT INFORMATION:

Student Name _____ Student No. _____ Home School _____
                  Last   First   Middle

Date of Birth _____ Chronological Age ___ (M___ or F___) Present Placement / Grade _____

Parent / Guardian Name(s) _____ Receiving School _____

Home Address _____ Program Recommended _____
                  Street   City / State   Zip

Home Phone _____ Work Phone _____ Starting Date _____

Emergency Phone _____ Three (3) Year Re-evaluation Due Date _____ / _____ / _____

Primary Language (Home) _____ (Child) _____ Interpreter Needed: Yes ___ No ___

B. VISION SCREENING RESULTS: Pass ____ Fail ____   **HEARING SCREENING RESULTS:** Pass ____ Fail ____

Date: _____ Comments: _____   Date: _____ Comments: _____

C. REQUIRED OBSERVATION(S): (All categories other than regular teacher)

_____ By: _____ _____ By: _____ _____ By: _____
  Date(s)   *Name(s)*   *Date(s)*   *Name(s)*   *Date(s)*   *Name(s)*

D. SUMMARY OF PRESENT LEVELS OF PERFORMANCE:

Educational: _____

_____

_____

_____

_____

_____

_____

_____

_____

_____

_____

Behavioral: _____

_____

_____

_____

_____

_____

_____

_____

_____

E. Additional justification. See comments _____ See addendum _____
                                              Initial   *Initial*

F. PLACEMENT RECOMMENDATION INDICATING LEAST RESTRICTIVE ENVIRONMENT:

Related services needed: Yes _____ No _____ (*List below.)

Placement Recommendation	Person Responsible	Amount of Time (Range)	Entry Date On/About	Review Reports On/About	Projected Ending Date	IEP Review Date
Primary:						
*Related Services:						

Transportation Needed? Yes _____ No _____ (If Yes, submit MPS Special Education Transportation Request Form.)

Describe extent student will participate in regular program: _____

_____

Page 1 of _____

(A)

Figure 6.2A and 6.2B Example of an individualized education program (IEP).

4. The dates for initiation of services and anticipated duration of the services.

5. Appropriate objective criteria for an annual determination of whether the short-term objectives are being reached.

INDIVIDUALIZED EDUCATION PLAN

REPORT OF MULTIDISCIPLINARY CONFERENCE
Date Held _____

Student Name _____ Student No. _____

G. PROGRAM PLANNING:

Long-Term Goals:

_____
_____
_____
_____
_____
_____
_____
_____
_____
_____
_____
_____

Short-Term Objectives (Goals):

_____
_____
_____
_____
_____
_____
_____
_____
_____
_____
_____
_____

H. EVALUATION:

Evaluation criteria are described in the Individual Implementation Plan (IIP) which is available in the classroom file.

I. PLACEMENT COMMITTEE:

The following have been consulted or have participated in the placement and IEP decisions:

Names of Members	Position	Present (Initial)	Oral Report	Written Report	Signatures
	Parents/Guardian				
	Parents/Guardian				
	School Administrator				
	Special Ed Administrator				
	School Psychologist				
	Nurse				
	Teacher(s) Receiving				
	Teacher(s) Referring				
	Interpreter				

Dissenting Opinion: Yes _____ No _____ If Yes, see comments _____ See addendum _____ .
                                                              Initial   *Initial*

J. PARENT (OR GUARDIAN) STATEMENT:

We agree to the placement recommended in this IEP. Yes _____ No _____

We give our permission to have our child counseled by the professional staff, if necessary. Yes _____ No _____

We understand that placement will be on a continuing trial basis and we will be contacted if any placement changes are contemplated. We are aware that such placement does not guarantee success; however, in order to help our child, we accept the responsibility to cooperate in every way with the school program. We acknowledge that we have been notified of and have received a copy of our due process rights pertaining to Special Education placement and have a basic understanding of these rights. We acknowledge that we have received a copy of the completed IEP Form.

_____   _____
Parent or Guardian Signature   Date

COMMENTS: _____
_____
_____
_____
_____
_____
_____
_____

Page 2 of _____

(B)

Formulating and Implementing the IEP

The first steps in formulating the IEP are developing and sequencing objectives for the student. Both short-term and long-range goals are delineated. The program also specifies the competencies that must be achieved before the student can progress to an LRE. These competencies include, for example, skills that are necessary to function in the new environment.

Materials and strategies to be used to implement the IEP are identified so parents (and the student, if appropriate) understand the instructional approach. In addition, data collection procedures, testing schedules, and other methods of evaluation are identified. These methods and procedures will be used to monitor the student's progress as well as the overall effectiveness of the program.

The IEP must state whether the child needs specially designed physical education. If not, the child should be held to the same expectations for physical activity as the peer group. A child who needs special physical education might be mainstreamed in regular physical education classes but have goals different from those of classmates. If the school doesn't have a physical education or adapted physical education specialist, classroom teachers need to provide the student with appropriate physical activity.

Because the child's progress needs careful monitoring, effective communication between special education and classroom teachers is essential. At the completion of the designated time period, a written progress report is filed by the special education teacher, along with recommendations for action during the next time period. Parents should receive a program to follow during summer months to ensure that improvement is maintained. Records should be complete so that information about the youngster's disability and the effects of long-term treatment is available to new teachers.

Back to Class

Imagine that Bhakti's assessment results indicate that she is an unusually intelligent child who is hampered in her reading skills by a visual-processing disorder and her ESL status. As a result of her assessment, she has begun wearing glasses and is scheduled to receive vision therapy from a local optometrist. She will also begin receiving ESL services as well as physical and occupational therapy to improve her motor skills.

In your opinion, should Bhakti remain in Mr. Whitney's first-grade general education classroom? Why or why not?

A Systematic Approach to Effective Mainstreaming for Physical Activity

Mainstreaming for physical activity is not only a legal issue but also a moral and ethical concern. As a teacher, you have a responsibility to offer all of your students the opportunity to take part in appropriate physical activity and its related social experiences. The issue is not *whether* to mainstream but *how* to mainstream effectively. To ensure that your students with disabilities are smoothly integrated into the activity session and accepted by other students as full participants, begin by determining what support you'll need and learn all you can about the student and the disability. What you learn will help you modify *how* you teach as well as *what* you teach. Few disagree that mainstreaming can increase the difficulty of instruction; however, teachers who support it show their concern for a child's spirit as well as the level of instruction.

Determine What Support Is Necessary

When a student is deemed ready for placement, consultation between the classroom teacher and the special education teacher is important. The reception and acceptance of students cannot be left to chance; rather, a plan has to be in place before the student is mainstreamed. First, the special education teacher needs to provide you, the classroom teacher, with full information about the needs of the student. You should discuss together what kind of help you think you'll need in order to integrate the child into your class. Negative feelings toward students with special needs often arise when teachers feel students are dropped into their class before they've been asked what kind of help is needed to integrate the students properly. It is possible that the special education teacher will need to participate in the classroom to ensure a smooth transition. Some children have full-time aides. When determining what support and aid is needed for participation in physical activity, the goal should be to challenge students to participate independently at whatever level they are capable of performing. Any approach that lowers expectations for students with disabilities is dehumanizing.

Learn About the Child

To work successfully with students with special needs, you need to understand their particular disability and how it affects their learning, including their ability to participate in activities you offer. Find out as much as possible about your student's disability. The child's parents often have information, so start by talking to them. Search the Internet, as well. As mentioned, you should consult the child's special education teacher, as well as the child's physical education teacher when possible, because they see the child in a variety of settings. These teachers can also help you judge when referral for additional services is in order. Study the child's permanent record so you have some insight into his or her strengths, health issues (including medications), academic performance, and emotional needs. List them on a card for quick reference. This helps you understand the youngster's needs and can help create a positive relationship. When you understand how the disability affects the student in a variety of domains, you'll have realistic expectations for the child's performance.

Teach Tolerance to All Students

An essential step toward effective mainstreaming is to teach your class tolerance. Able students need practical information about the disability and about the challenges the incoming student faces. Teach children that students with disabilities are functional and worthwhile individuals who have innate abilities and who can make significant contributions to society.

In general, there are three important teaching goals:

Helping students recognize the similarities among all people: their rights, hopes, aspirations, goals, doubts, fears, and challenges.

Helping students appreciate the differences among all people and the concept that all people are disabled in some way. For some people, the disabilities are of such a nature and severity that they interfere with activities of daily living or the ability to learn.

Exploring with your students ways to support those who differ without over-helping and accepting all students as worthwhile individuals. People with disabilities deserve consideration and understanding based on empathy, not sympathy.

With adequate preparation, your students will be ready to understand, accept, support, and learn side-by-side with their classmates with special needs.

Modify Your Instruction

Even though students with special needs may seem different upon first glance, bear in mind that they are much more similar to other students than they are different. They want to learn, be cared for, have friends, and participate with others. Although you might fear that your students with special needs will be difficult to teach, once you build a relationship with them, you will usually come to enjoy their contributions and to value the different experiences they bring to the classroom.

The following points will help you both as a person and a teacher when working with all students:

When giving explanations and directions, couch them in terms that all students can understand. Be sure that students with disabilities understand what is to be accomplished before the activity begins, especially when working with children who have an intellectual disability or an auditory impairment.

Use person-first language. For example, refer to students as "students with an emotional disability" rather than "emotionally disabled students." When addressing students directly, call all students by their first name and never refer to them by their disability.

Positively reinforce all students in your class. When a student with a disability accomplishes something, cheer it in the same manner you use when any other student accomplishes the same thing. Nothing makes students with disabilities feel better than to be treated the same as everybody else.

Accept that the personalities of students with similar disabilities vary widely. Some may be quiet and shy while others are outgoing and loud. Pay attention to each child's style to learn how each wants to be treated.

Let students talk about their disabilities if they want to. They know more about their strengths and limitations than you do. Also, if they want to talk to the class, support them in doing so. This may be an informative and bonding experience for all students.

In addition, there are many minor ways to modify your instruction that will not be obvious to your students but will improve the chances of success for those with special needs. For example, for a student with an auditory impairment, you could easily accompany verbal instructions with a handwritten poster listing the same instructions, or demonstrate the steps you want the students to take, or take a moment one-on-one with the student to repeat the instructions in sign language (**Figure 6.3**). For a student with attention deficit disorder, you could prepare the environment in advance by reducing visual clutter or auditory distractions. With some advance planning, you will probably be able to devise several easy ways to manipulate your instruction in a manner that improves the lesson for all.

Modify Activities for Student Success

The step of modifying activities for students' success involves identifying activities appropriate for your class, considering how the activities you've identified might affect your students with special needs, and planning ways to modify the activities to accommodate these students.

An initial consideration must be whether certain activities completely exclude certain students. Some activities might be so limiting that inclusion would not be in the best interest of a particular student no matter how the activities were modified. Or, a student might have such a severe developmental delay that he or she would be unable to experience success unless you modified the activity in a way that would make it inappropriate for other students. Of course, you should try to individualize activities as much as possible so that your students with disabilities are smoothly integrated; when this is not possible, you should choose other activities.

Students with disabilities need to build confidence in their own skills before they will want to participate with others. Individual activities give them a lot of time to practice without fear of failing in front of peers. Especially at the start of a school year, or whenever you introduce a new skill or type of activity, allow plenty of time for individual practice. When many students in the group have progressed in their skill development, consider offering the option of practicing individually or in pairs. This way, students who wish to continue practicing individually may do so without embarrassment.

Be aware of situations that devalue the student socially. For instance, avoid using the degrading method of having captains choose teams from a group of waiting students. Also, change elimination games so that points are scored or reduced instead of players being eliminated.

Offer activities in which all students can find success. Avoid placing students with disabilities in situations in which they are likely to fail. Offer participative opportunities that make the best use of their talents.

Plan carefully for accommodating your students with disabilities when you offer competitive team activities. This is especially true if the student's physical condition is poor or the disability is significant. All students like to win, and resentment may result if a team loss is attributed to

Figure 6.3 Using sign language to meet the needs of a student with an auditory impairment.

News Clip

Attitudes Start to Change as Special Olympics Come to China

Never before in the history of the Special Olympics had there been such an extravagant, star-studded opening ceremony. The government of China spent millions of dollars to host the games (held October 2–11, 2007) and to ensure that the 7,500 competitors were welcomed and cared for. Even China's President Hu Jintao was there.

As the Chinese reception illustrates, the Special Olympics has come a long way since its humble beginning in 1962. The movement got its start when Eunice Kennedy Shriver invited 35 boys and girls with intellectual disabilities to a day camp at her home in Maryland to explore their capabilities in a variety of sports and physical activities. Camp Shriver became an annual event, and in a few years more than 300 similar camps were underway, serving 10,000 children with intellectual disabilities. The First International Special Olympics games were held in Chicago in 1968. Today, Special Olympics is a global movement with 2.5 million athletes in 165 countries.

The mission of Special Olympics is to provide year-round sports training and athletic competition in a variety of Olympic-type events for children and adults with intellectual disabilities. Its vision is to improve the lives of people with intellectual disabilities and, in turn, the lives of everyone they touch.

Unfortunately, some discrimination against people with intellectual disabilities continues. Yin Yin Nwe, the head of UNICEF in China, noted that in contemporary Chinese culture, some people tend to be ashamed of children with disabilities, resulting in widespread neglect and discrimination. This is true not only in developing and transitioning nations such as China. Special Olympics star athlete Natalie Williams admits that in her home state of Kentucky she has never been treated on a par with other, normally-abled athletes. Still, Tim Shriver, chairman of the Special Olympics, is optimistic about the future, noting that in spite of obstacles in the past and still ahead, progress continues to be made.

Source: Adapted from the article by CNN, October 8, 2007, at http://cnn.com/2007/WORLD/asiapcf/10/08/special.olympics/index.html?iref=newssearch.

take action!

1. Log onto the Special Olympics website (see Web Resources) and request free copies of *Spirit*, a quarterly magazine that explores the dreams and accomplishments of people with intellectual disabilities. Share the magazine and its stories with colleagues and students.

2. Find out whether anyone in your community has attended the Special Olympics. If so, interview the athlete and his or her family. Videotape or record the interview and share it with teachers, administrators, and students, or invite the athlete and family to speak at your school.

3. Check out the Competition and Events Calendar on the Special Olympics website to find an event nearby. Organize a field trip or after-school activity to attend the event. Help students prepare by learning more about the Special Olympics and about children with intellectual disabilities. After the event, encourage students to share their feelings about the experience.

the participation of a student with a disability. A tactic called *equalization* helps reduce this source of friction: either modify the game rules or give a team a point advantage (such as a handicap in golf) so that the student with a disability has a chance to contribute to group success. Encourage your students to support and defend the principle that everyone has a right to play.

Determine the most desirable involvement for students with disabilities by analyzing participants' roles in game and sport activities. Assign roles or positions that make students with disabilities less conspicuous and keeps them integrated with able classmates. This makes the experience as natural as possible for everyone. Using students with disabilities as umpires or scorekeepers should be a last resort. Over-protectiveness benefits no one and prevents the student from experiencing both challenge and personal accomplishment. Avoid the tendency to underestimate students' abilities.

Back to Class

Identify at least two ways that Mr. Whitney could modify his instruction to increase Bhakti's opportunities to participate and succeed in physical activity.

A Reflection Check

It is relatively easy to modify activities for your special needs students, but it can be quite difficult to do so without reducing the educational value of the experience for others or placing too great a burden on yourself. When thinking about ways to accommodate everyone's needs, take some time to reflect on the total experience. Answer the following questions as you formulate modifications:

- Do the changes allow the student with differing needs to participate successfully yet still be challenged?
- Does the modification make the setting unsafe for the student with differing needs as well as for those students without disabilities?
- Does the change negatively impact the quality of the educational experience? Is learning seriously hampered because of the change that was made?
- Does the change place an undue burden on you? This is important to ask yourself because many teachers come to resent students with special needs if they feel the teaching burden is too great. Certainly, modifications need to be made, but you have to feel confident in your ability to teach and manage the modified activity.

All students have differing needs, thus teachers who seldom modify activities probably do not meet the needs of many students in their class. Effective teachers always examine an activity and know that it is their responsibility to make it work for all students. Next we discuss modifying activities in ways that can help all students.

Back to Class

In the chapter-opening scenario, would you say that Mr. Whitney had planned adequately for including Bhakti in the game? Why or why not? How do you think Bhakti felt about his method of team selection? What about his suggestion that Bhakti participate by keeping score?

Modifications for Students Lacking Strength and Endurance

The modifications listed here help students who lack strength and endurance.

- *Decrease or increase the size of the goal.* In basketball, the basket may be lowered; in soccer, the goal might be enlarged.
- *Modify the speed or tempo of the game.* For example, games might be performed using brisk walking rather than running. A way to modify tempo is to stop the game regularly for substitutions. Using auto-substitutions is also effective: students determine when they are fatigued and ask a predetermined substitute to take their place.
- *Reduce the weight and/or modify the size of the projectile.* A lighter object moves more slowly and will hurt less if misplayed. A larger, bright-colored object is much easier for students to track visually and catch. Beanbags and beanbag animals are excellent for tossing because they are soft and don't roll after a catch is missed.
- *Reduce the distance that a ball must be thrown or served.* Reduce the dimensions of the playing area or add more players to the game. In serving, others can help make the serve playable. For example, in volleyball, other teammates can bat the serve over the net as long as it does not touch the floor.
- *In games that are played to a certain number of points, reduce the number required for a win.* For example, play volleyball games to 7 or 11 points, depending on the skill and intensity of the players.
- *Modify striking implements by shortening and reducing their weight.* Racquets are much easier to control when they are shortened. Softball bats are easier to control when the player "chokes up" and selects a lighter bat.
- *If appropriate, slow the ball down by letting out air.* A softer ball reduces the speed of rebound and makes the ball easier to control in a restricted area. It also keeps the ball from rolling as far away from players when it is not under control.
- *Have students play the games in a different position.* Some games may be played in a sitting or lying position, which is easier and less demanding than standing or running.
- *Offer matching or doubling up.* Match a student wearing braces with a nondisabled student on borrowed crutches. Or match a student in a

wheelchair against a student seated in a desk chair with wheels. Assign two players to play one position together.

Allow students to substitute skills. For example, a student may be able to strike an object but may lack the mobility to run, in which case another student can be selected to run.

Modifications for Students Lacking Coordination

The modifications listed here can help students lacking coordination (including temporary lack of coordination due to injury).

Increase the size of the goal or target. Increasing the size of a basketball hoop will increase the opportunity for success. Another alternative is to offer points for hitting the backboard near a hoop. Since scoring is self-motivating, modifications should continue until the possibility of success is ensured.

Offer protection when appropriate. The lack of coordination makes students more susceptible to injury from a projectile. Use various types of protectors (such as glasses, chest protectors, or face masks).

When teaching throwing, allow students the opportunity to throw at maximum velocity without concern for accuracy. Use small balls that can be grasped easily. Fleece balls and beanbags are easy to hold and release. Don't have students throw to a partner; instead, have them throw at a wall or fence. Throwing and catching skills can't be practiced simultaneously if you expect students to learn proper form (throwing with velocity).

Use a stationary object when teaching striking, hitting, or kicking. Using a batting tee or tennis ball fastened to a string offers the student an opportunity for success. In addition, a larger racquet or bat and choking up on the grip can be used. A stationary ball is easier to kick than a ball in motion (**Figure 6.4**).

Make projectiles easily retrievable. If a great deal of time is spent recovering the projectile, students receive few practice trials and feel frustrated. Place students near a backstop or use a goal that rebounds the projectile to the shooter.

When teaching catching, use a soft, lightweight, and slow-moving object. Beach balls, balloons, and beanbags are excellent objects to use to teach beginning catching skills since they allow youngsters to more easily track them. In addition, foam-rubber balls eliminate a student's fear of being hurt by a thrown or batted projectile.

Figure 6.4 Modifying a kicking activity for successful participation.

Back to Class

Identify at least two ways that Mr. Whitney could have modified the kickball game to include Bhakti.

Modifications for Students Lacking Balance and Agility

The modifications listed here help students lacking balance and agility.

- *Increase the width of rails, lines, and beams when having students practice balance.* Having students carry a long pole helps minimize rapid shifts of balance and is a useful lead-up activity.
- *Have students increase the width of their base of support.* Students should be taught to keep their feet spread at least to shoulder width.
- *Emphasize use of many body parts when teaching balance.* The more body parts in contact with the floor, the easier it is to balance the body. Beginning balance practice should emphasize controlled movement using as many body parts as possible.
- *Have students increase the surface area of the body parts in contact with the floor or beam.* For example, walking flat-footed is easier than walking on tiptoe.
- *Have students lower their center of gravity.* A lower center of gravity increases a child's stability and balance. Teach children to bend their knees and lean slightly forward.
- *Make sure that surfaces offer good friction.* Floors and shoes should not be slick to avoid falls. Carpets or tumbling mats will increase traction.
- *Provide balance assistance.* A barre, cane, or chair can be used to keep the student from falling.
- *Teach students how to fall.* Students with balance problems inevitably fall. Offer practice in safe falling so that students learn how to absorb the force. Specifically, teach students to keep the wrists, elbows, and knees bent and to twist or roll their body to the side. The objective is to have as much of the body contact the floor as possible to spread out the impact of the fall. Instruct children to avoid trying to break the fall with their hands.

Integrate Students with Special Needs into the Activity Session

When correctly implemented, mainstreaming allows the student to make educational progress, achieve in those areas outlined in the IEP, learn to accept limitations, observe and model appropriate behavior, and experience acceptance by peers. Some final advice for successful integration follows.

- Help students with disabilities participate in regular classroom physical activities and meet target goals specified in the IEP. This may include physical education classes, after-school programs, and homework.
- Build ego strength by stressing the student's abilities. Eliminate established practices that unwittingly contribute to embarrassment and failure.
- Foster peer acceptance by accepting each student as a functioning, participating member of the class. Help all students experience the joy of participation (**Figure 6.5**).
- Concentrate on the student's physical activity needs and not on the disability. Give focused and continual attention to fundamental skills and physical fitness.

Figure 6.5 Children with disabilities can experience the joy of participation.

Provide continual monitoring and assess periodically the student's target goals. Document progress in the student's record frequently.

Maintain awareness of students' feelings and anxiety concerning their progress and integration. Provide positive feedback as a basic practice.

Chapter Summary

Legislative Requirements

Federal law mandates that every state develop a plan for identifying, locating, and evaluating all children with special educational needs and provide these children a free appropriate public education (FAPE).

The Education for All Handicapped Children Act (EHA), or Public Law 94-142, was passed by Congress in 1975. The law was enacted ". . . to assure that all handicapped children have available to them . . . a free appropriate public education." A 1990 amendment renamed the EHA as the Individuals with Disabilities Education Act (IDEA), or Public Law 101-476, and replaced the phrase "handicapped child" with the phrase "child with a disability."

Children with disabilities are to be placed in the least restrictive environment (LRE), that is, the educational setting providing the greatest level of interaction with students who are not disabled, while still enabling the child to receive an appropriate education.

Through the process of progressive inclusion, students with disabilities are continually evaluated to determine their readiness to progress to an LRE.

Mainstreaming is the process of placing students with disabilities in classrooms with non-disabled students.

Screening and Assessment

Screening is a process by which all children in a school setting are evaluated to determine whether they should be referred for a special education assessment.

Assessment is a thorough evaluation performed by a team of experts using clinical and classroom observation and a variety of tests to determine the child's unique challenges and make recommendations for special education services.

The EHA mandates that schools follow due process when initiating and conducting assessments. Parents have a right to grant or withhold their permission for the assessment, to be present at an interpretation of the assessment, to request an external evaluation, and to be granted hearings and other legal proceedings if they disagree with the school's evaluation and/or recommendations. In addition, the child's records must be kept confidential.

Diversity issues such as disabilities, language barriers, cultural differences, and poverty often interfere with standard assessment procedures. Minority and poor children should be assessed only with instruments that have been shown to be valid with these populations.

Developing an Individualized Education Program

The EHA requires that an individualized education program (IEP) be developed for each child with a disability receiving special education and related services.

The IEP must address certain mandated topics and include both short-term and long-range goals. It must also specify the competencies that must be achieved before the student progresses to an LRE. Materials and strategies to be used in implementing the IEP must be identified, as well as the evaluation procedures.

The IEP must state whether specially designed physical education is needed. If not, the child should be held to the same expectations for physical activity as the peer group.

A Systematic Approach to Effective Mainstreaming for Physical Activity

When a student is deemed ready for placement, consult with the special education teacher to determine what classroom support will be necessary.

To work successfully with your special needs students, you need to understand their particular disability and how it affects their learning, including their ability to participate in activities you offer. Find out as much as possible about your student's disability.

Prepare your class for the incoming student by teaching students tolerance. Modify your instruction as appropriate, and determine whether and how you should modify physical activities to promote the child's inclusion and success.

Review Questions

Content Review

1. Identify the implications of EHA/IDEA for classroom teachers offering physical activity.

2. List the due process procedures that must be followed for special education assessment.

3. Describe how individualized education programs are developed. Include comments on who is involved and what the IEP contains.

4. Identify five steps in mainstreaming a child for physical activities.

5. Do all children have disabilities? Explain your answer.

Real World

1. The results of a schoolwide screening for special education reveals that one of the children in your kindergarten class, Ryan, has been proposed for a full assessment. At your initial meeting with the special education teacher, you learn that Ryan is to have several different kinds of tests, including IQ tests, a comprehensive vision exam, and tests for attention deficit disorder. You are aware that Ryan receives free school breakfasts and lunches and that he lives with his grandmother, who is his legal guardian and who works full time in a minimum-wage job. Ryan's mother lives with her boyfriend in another state, and his father is unknown. What issues would be important to address regarding the up-coming assessment for Ryan?

2. Over lunch, a colleague apologizes that she won't be able to join you for a walk you'd planned after school because she has to attend an "IEP meeting" with a student's parents. "I dread it," she confesses. "This student is good-hearted and very athletic, but she's way behind academically, and the assessment shows she has a significant learning disorder." She sighs. "What parent wants to find out their kid has a disability?" What would you say?

What About You?

Earlier in this chapter, we talked about the importance of teaching your students tolerance. We suggested you introduce them to the concept that all people have a disability in some way. Imagine that your students were to ask you to explain some ways in which you are disabled. How would you respond?

_____

_____

References and Suggested Readings

Auxter, D., Pyfer, J., and Huettig, C. (2005). *Principles and methods of adapted physical education and recreation* (10th ed.). Boston: McGraw-Hill.

Bennett, T., Bruns, D., and Deluca, D. (1997). Putting inclusion into practice: Perspectives of teachers and parents. *Exceptional Children,* 64(1), 115–132.

Block, M.E. (2000). *A teacher's guide to including students with disabilities in regular physical education* (2nd ed.). Baltimore: Paul H. Brookes Publishing Co.

Block, M., Oberweiser, B., and Bain, M. (1995). Using classwide peer tutoring to facilitate inclusion of students with disabilities in regular physical education. *The Physical Educator,* Late Winter, 47–56.

Block, M., and Vogler, E.V. (1994). Inclusion in regular physical education: The research base. *Journal of Health, Physical Education, Recreation, and Dance,* 65(1), 40–44.

Bouchard, C., et al. (1990). The response to long-term overfeeding in identical twins. *New England Journal of Medicine,* 322, 1477–1482.

Brustad, R.J. (1993). Who will go out and play? Parental and psychological influences on children's attraction to physical activity. *Pediatric Exercise Science,* 5, 210–223.

Burton, A., and Miller, D. (1998). *Movement skill assessment.* Champaign, IL: Human Kinetics.

Cooper Institute. (2004). *Fitnessgram/activitygram test administration manual* (3rd ed.). Champaign, IL: Human Kinetics.

Davis, R.W. (2002). *Inclusion through sports: A guide to enhancing sport experiences.* Champaign, IL: Human Kinetics.

DePauw, K. (1996). Students with disabilities in physical education. In S. Silverman and C. Ennis (eds.), *Student learning in physical education.* Champaign, IL: Human Kinetics.

DePauw, K., and Goc Karp, G. (1994). Integrating knowledge of disability throughout the physical education curriculum: An infusion approach. *Adapted Physical Activity Quarterly,* 11, 3–13.

Dobbins, D.A., Garron, R., and Rarick, G.L. (1981). The motor performance of educable mentally retarded and intellectually normal boys after covariate control for differences in body size. *Research Quarterly,* 52(1), 6–7.

Dunn, J.M. (1997). *Special physical education: Adapted, individualized, developmental.* Madison, WI: Brown & Benchmark.

Education for All Handicapped Children Act of 1975, Pub. L. No. 94–142. Washington, DC: Government Printing Office.

Eichstaedt, C.B., and Kalakian, L.H. (1993). *Developmental/adapted physical education: Making ability count.* New York: Macmillan.

Epstein, L.H., et al. (1984). The modification of activity patterns and energy expenditure in obese young girls. *Behavior Therapy,* 15(1), 101–108.

Foster, G.D., Wadden, T.A., and Brownell, K.D. (1985). Peer-led program for the treatment and prevention of obesity in the schools. *Journal of Consulting and Clinical Psychology,* 53(4), 538–540.

Harter, S. (1985). *Manual for the self-perception profile for youth.* Denver: University of Denver.

Horvat, M., et al. (2003). *Developmental/adapted physical education: Making ability count* (4th ed.). San Francisco: Benjamin Cummings.

Jansma, P., and French, R. (1994). *Special physical education: Physical activity, sports, and recreation.* Englewood Cliffs, NJ: Prentice Hall.

Kauffman, J.M. (2001). *Characteristics of emotional and behavioral disorders of children and youth.* Upper Saddle River, NJ: Prentice Hall.

Lieberman, L., and Houston-Wilson, C. (2002). *Strategies for inclusion: A handbook for physical educators*. Champaign, IL: Human Kinetics.

Lohman, T.G. (1987). The use of skinfold to estimate body fatness on children and youth. *Journal of Physical Education, Recreation, and Dance,* 58(9), 98–102.

Sherrill, C. (2004). *Adapted physical activity, recreation and sport* (6th ed.). Boston: WCB/McGraw-Hill.

U.S. Department of Health and Human Services. (1995). *Asthma & physical activity in the school.* (NIH Publication No. 95-3651). Washington, DC: National Institutes of Health.

Vogler, E. (2000). Students with disabilities in physical education. In S. Silverman and C. Ennis (eds.), *Student learning in physical education* (2nd ed.). Champaign, IL: Human Kinetics.

Wilmore, J.H. (1994). Exercise, obesity, and weight control. *Physical Activity and Fitness Research Digest,* 1(6), 1–8.

Winnick, J.P. (2005). *Adapted physical education and sport* (4th ed.). Champaign, IL: Human Kinetics.

Winnick, J.P., and Short, F. X. (1999). *The Brockport physical fitness test manual.* Champaign, IL: Human Kinetics.

Yun, J., Shapiro, D., and Kennedy, J. (2000). Reaching IEP goals in the general physical education class. *Journal of Physical Education, Recreation, and Dance,* 71(8), 33–37.

Web Resources

Achievable Concepts, Ltd/Recreation and Sporting Equipment
for People with Disabilities:
www.achievableconcepts.us
Adapted Physical Education National Standards (APENS):
www.apens.org
Children's Disabilities Information:
www.childrensdisabilities.info
Education for All Handicapped Children Act of 1975/Public Law 94-142:
www.asclepius.com/angel/special
Individuals with Disabilities Education Act Amendments of 1997 (IDEA):
www.ed.gov/offices/OSERS/Policy/IDEA
The National Center on Physical Activity and Disability:
www.ncpad.org
PALAESTRA: Forum of Sport, Physical Education & Recreation
For Those With Disabilities:
www.palaestra.com
PE Central/Adapted Physical Education:
www.pecentral.org/adapted
Special Olympics:
www.specialolympics.org
Texas Women's University/Project INSPIRE:
www.twu.edu/inspire
U.S. Paralympics (Division of the U.S. Olympic Committee):
www.usolympicteam.com/Paralympics

7 Integrating Physical Activity and Academics

Learning Objectives

After reading this chapter, you will be able to . . .

- ○ Define integration and explain its importance.
- ○ Discuss the benefits and limitations of integrating physical activity and academics.
- ○ Identify three models of integration and describe how they are used.
- ○ Explain how you can integrate math, language arts, science, and social studies with classroom physical activity.

Classroom Challenge

It's a chilly winter day, but Mrs. Jefferson has brought her fifth-grade class outdoors for some physical activity to "wake them up." In a few weeks, they'll be taking their state exams, and Mrs. Jefferson worries about taking time away from academics; but she also knows that her math instruction this afternoon will be wasted if her students are lethargic and unfocused.

Because it's cold outside, Mrs. Jefferson has to keep her students moving, but she also wants to integrate into the activity a few math skills the class has been struggling with lately, especially calculating averages and converting to the metric system. So, after some quick stretching and calisthenics, she pairs students up and has each team member run around the perimeter of the playground. When each partner has run one lap, he or she is immediately replaced by the other partner, so the first has a chance to rest briefly before running again. When both partners have run the perimeter five times each, the second partner concludes the final lap by touching a cone in front of Mrs. Jefferson, who then records their time.

One of her students, Andrew, has asthma, so Mrs. Jefferson checks with him privately about his ability to participate. Andrew explains that he cannot run in the cold air and requests a different assignment. Mrs. Jefferson offers him a tape measure and the job of measuring the perimeter of the playground in yards and meters. He accepts the assignment with a smile of relief.

By the time Andrew has finished his measurements, all 12 teams have completed their laps. Mrs. Jefferson instructs them to form a single-file line and "Hustle back to class to find out which team is the winner."

Back in the warmth of their classroom, Mrs. Jefferson posts the 12 finish times on the board. She then invites volunteers to come to the board and identify the winning time, the class mean, the median, and the mode. She is surprised when nearly half her students raise their hands to come to the board, as normally she has to choose students herself. Next, she asks Andrew to report his measurements of the perimeter in yards and meters. Finally, she instructs students to work in two groups to calculate (1) how long it would take the first-place team to run 1 mile at their winning speed and (2) how long it would take the median team to run 1 kilometer at the mean class speed. The class engages in these calculations with enthusiasm, and the remainder of the afternoon passes quickly. As students are leaving for the day, one boy who has been struggling with math thanks Mrs. Jefferson for "that running game." He explains, "You've been talking about mean, median, and mode all year, but this is the first time it really sank in."

lassroom teachers often design lessons that combine two seemingly unrelated academic areas. For example, reading about the habitats of animals combines reading (language arts) and biology (science). Students calculating the distance from their town to the state capitol are using concepts from both math and social studies. Instruction that combines subjects in this way is often referred to as *integration*. More precisely, **integration** is instruction designed to combine two or more concepts from different areas to help students see the interrelatedness of knowledge. Some adjectives commonly used to describe this process are *interdisciplinary*, *multidisciplinary*, and *cross-disciplinary*.

In this chapter, our goal is to enable you to teach selected academic concepts using physical activity. We therefore present three types of integration and provide tips, topics, and sample activities to help you get started. But before we begin, let's quickly review the benefits of integration.

Why Integrate?

Classroom teachers are always seeking evidence-based strategies for increasing the effectiveness of their instruction. One such strategy is integration. Purcell-Cone et al. (1998) researched studies evaluating the effectiveness of integrating physical activity with a variety of academic subjects. Although more research is needed, it appears that such integration is effective for some students. These students may absorb academic concepts more readily when they are physically involved. Also, integration may help clarify areas of uncertainty or strengthen the students' retention. However, integration doesn't improve learning for all students. Therefore, you should view it as one more strategy to help some of your students reach their maximum potential.

We've just said that we need more research on the effectiveness of integrating physical activity and academics. But we also need to learn more about the impact of children's overall level of physical activity on their learning. Specifically, researchers are currently studying whether physically active children learn better and perform better academically than do physically inactive children. In a statistical review of numerous studies on children, Sibley and Etnier (2003) concluded that physical activity and cognition are positively related and that physical activity may aid in cognitive development. Tomporowski (2003) suggested that physical activity may improve cognitive performance. This article also suggests that behavior improves following bouts of activity. Similarly, Pellegrini, Huberty, and Jones (1995) found that recess periods taken throughout the day—thereby allowing short and regular bouts of physical activity—may improve children's attention and behavior. At the same time, the contribution of regular physical activity to children's health is well documented, and we also know that activity temporarily increases children's energy and alertness. These factors in turn contribute to learning: neither children nor adults learn well when they are ill or fatigued. In summary, although the evidence is not overwhelming at this point, there is enough to defend the assertion that, either directly or indirectly, physical activity can contribute to children's academic learning. For more information about how physical activity—in this case, playing dance video games—can influence children's academic success, see the accompanying News Clip.

In addition, classroom teachers see their students in an entirely different context when they use activity to promote academic learning. They often see students behave in new ways—for example, becoming more enthusiastic, cooperating with others, or expressing themselves more energetically. Finally, by allowing students to experience academics as fun, classroom physical activity can help you build a more effective learning environment.

Back to Class

List a few of the benefits you noted when Mrs. Jefferson integrated her math lesson with physical activity.

Types of Integration

You can use any of three general models when planning integration activities. You can work independently, consult with a partner, or collaborate with a group of teachers to develop theme-based learning experiences in a variety of settings.

Using the independent model, you would work individually to develop ideas for integrating physical activity and academic content. For example, you might have your students hold a stretch while counting to 20 or while reciting multiplication facts. Or, you might decide to teach concepts related to levers by having students practice throwing. This would require you to review beforehand information on levers related to throwing and plan how to integrate the information into the lesson.

For the partner model, you'd collaborate with the physical education teacher (or another specialist). This collaboration could be as simple as giving the physical education teacher your class vocabulary words for the week, or as complex as developing

News Clip

P.E. Classes Turn to Video Game That Works Legs

Children don't often shriek in excitement when they are let into class, but as the gymnasium doors open at schools across West Virginia, the noise can be deafening. Students rush to their places on plastic mats in front of two TV sets and, in less than a minute, are dancing furiously to the thumps of a techno song called "Speed Over Beethoven." It's all part of a video game called Dance Dance Revolution (DDR), which has been adopted for use in all public schools in West Virginia as well as in many other states.

A basic DDR system costs schools about $500–$800 dollars, but what are the benefits? First, it burns calories. A study from the Mayo Clinic found that children playing DDR expended significant energy, and a study from West Virginia University's School of Physical Education found that playing DDR improves children's blood pressure and overall fitness scores.

Second, proponents of DDR assert that regular use improves academics. Ron Ramspott, district coordinator of health and physical education for the Parkway School District in Chesterfield, Missouri, cited the high degree of teacher buy-in to DDR as a way to promote physical health and learning. Furthermore, because playing the game requires participants to both process the information and coordinate it with physical movements, some think it can help with brain development as well.

Although additional targeted research is needed, a number of related studies appear to support this claim. They include a 2005 study from the Appalachian Educational Laboratory, which showed improvements in reading and attention in children with attention deficit hyperactivity disorder (ADHD) who regularly played DDR. In addition, a 2007 study from Northwestern University's Neuroscience Laboratory suggests that music experience in general benefits children in a wide range of learning activities. And several research studies on a technique called *synchronized metronome tapping (SMT)* show significant improvements in attention, reading, and math fluency. Since dance video games incorporate the same elements of rhythm and timing essential to SMT, while also requiring visual processing and whole-body movement, promoters of dance video games claim that they may be even more effective than SMT at improving attention and learning.

Source: Adapted from the *New York Times,* April 30, 2007, available at http://www.nytimes.com/2007/04/30/health/30exer.html.

take action!

1.   Find out what all the fuss is! Locate a school, mall, or gym in your community that uses DDR, In the Groove, or another dance video game and try it out.

2.   After you've experienced dance video games for yourself, list their basic elements: for example, following directions, understanding patterns, moving the body in time to a beat, etc. Jot down some ideas for incorporating a few of these basic elements into non-video-based physical activities with elementary school children.

3.   Do your own research into the effects of music-based physical activity—or dance videos specifically—on children's academic success. Write a summary of your results and, if you find them convincing, submit them to your local school district to support your advocacy of increased music-based physical activity for the public school children in your community.

together an annual calendar that integrates similar concepts taught during the same time period. For example, the physical education instructor might teach students a Mexican dance during the same week that you teach a geography lesson on Mexico. While teaching the dance, the P.E. teacher could use Spanish terms and have students count their steps in Spanish. These changes enrich the educational experience for everyone, and physical educators are usually willing to implement them. Similarly, you could partner with the school's music teacher, art teacher, etc.

With group collaboration, you work together within a group of classroom teachers from a common grade level. This model usually centers on a theme. A considerable amount of planning is involved, because teachers use the theme to generate learning activities that cut across several academic areas. An example is the Olympic theme. For a set period of time, a majority of the students' activities are related to the Olympics. Each classroom represents a country. In social studies, students compare the culture, geography, economy, people, and/or government of their country with those of the other participating countries. For math, students calculate distances between cities in their country, calculate the population of the countries involved, determine the average population of the countries, and graph the number of Olympic medals each country earned during the most recent Olympics. During language arts, students read about their country and write a summary of their readings. They write letters to pen pals in other countries (other participating classrooms) and learn common phrases from their country's language. For science, concepts associated with the environment of the countries, their weather, geology, plants, animals, and inventions are covered. The technology teacher helps students research their country online. The music teacher teaches songs and dances from the countries being studied, and the art teacher helps students create the countries' flags or draw posters advertising the Olympics. During physical education, students learn the history of and participate in activities related to the Olympics. Track and field, gymnastics, volleyball, rhythmic gymnastics, basketball, tennis, badminton, and hockey are all examples of activities that are included in most curricula already and could be included in lessons taught during this time. A school assembly can be held to serve as the opening ceremonies, where students read aloud about each country, sing their national anthems, and display their flags.

Other examples of themes involving the group model might include ancient Egypt, the Vikings, or the Civil War. Although planning is necessary, the experiences for students can be exciting, educational, and remembered for a lifetime.

Back to Class

In our chapter-opening scenario, Mrs. Jefferson was working independently to integrate math and physical activity. How could she have taught the concepts of mean, median, and mode in the group model using the Olympics theme just described?

Academic Integration Activities

The remainder of this chapter presents tips, topics, and sample activities for teaching academic concepts using physical activity. These are organized into four academic areas: math, language arts, science, and social studies. These are the primary academic content areas in most elementary school curricula.

Each academic area is subdivided into integration tips, topics for integrated study, and sample activities.

- Integration *tips* are simple strategies you can use to teach academic skills through physical activity. For example, rather than saying "Freeze!" to get your students to stop in place, you might say, "15 degrees Fahrenheit!" This both signals a "freeze" and reinforces the fact that water freezes at or below 32 degrees Fahrenheit. Integration tips are not specific to a particular lesson; they may be used in a variety of lessons.
- *Topics* for integrated study are ideas for you to use to promote discussion, oral presentations, and written expression. These topics serve to trigger ideas that you can develop with your students.
- Three *sample activities* close each academic area. As in the activity cards included with this book, the following components are identified for each sample activity, where applicable: any academic concepts being taught or reinforced through this activity (i.e., tie-ins with math, language arts, social studies, or science curricula), specific physical development skills that students will practice or learn during the activity, and any supplies needed to perform the activity.

Math

During the early elementary years, students learn math concepts such as number recognition and meaning, counting, addition, subtraction, measuring, shapes, and patterns. As they progress through the grades, they learn numbers through one million, multiplication, division, fractions, percent, degrees, geometry, and statistics.

Integration Tips

Skip Counting   Whenever counting is used during an activity (e.g., for keeping score or timing a stretch), instruct students to count by a given number. For example, rather than keeping score such that one goal equals 1 point, make each goal worth 3 points. With this method, as the goals accumulate, students must skip count by threes to determine points.

Geometry Terms   Geometry terms such as *diameter, radius, perimeter,* and *area* are easy to integrate into many physical activities. For example, rather than instructing students, "Jog around the outside of the field," tell them, "Jog around the perimeter of the field." When discussing the influence of a ball's size on throwing, instead of asking, "Is a bigger ball easier or harder to throw?" ask, "If a ball has a larger diameter, is it easier or harder to throw? Remind me what the word *diameter* means before you answer."

Degrees and Fractions   In many physical activities, students are told, "Turn so that you are facing away from the teacher" or "Turn all the way around." Early in a child's education, these basic terms are necessary; however, as students mature, use more challenging directions to teach math concepts. For example, have students "turn 360 degrees" before catching a beanbag or "turn 90 degrees" when dismounting from a balance bench. Similarly, incorporate fractions by having students make a half turn or a three-quarter turn. For further challenge, instruct students to make a 4/4 turn or a 36/72 turn.

Estimating   Numbers are commonly used in physical activities. Therefore, there are many opportunities to integrate them into a variety of lessons. The following are two examples to help students practice estimating.

"Messy Backyard" is a game in which students attempt to rid their backyards (side of the court) of yarn balls (or beanbags or balloons) by throwing them over the net to the other team's side. Meanwhile, the other team tries to rid its side of the "mess" as well. After a set amount of time, the teacher stops the game and has the students count the yarn balls on each side. To teach estimation, before having students count the number of balls on each side, instruct them to estimate how many there are on each side and keep that number in their heads. When the actual number is announced, each child then self-assesses his or her estimate.

Another way to integrate estimating is to ask students to predict how many times within 30 seconds they can toss their beanbag a certain height and catch it. This activity can be repeated two or three times to allow students to make adjustments in their estimate.

Measurement   Measurement of distance, height, weight, and time can all be integrated into physical activity sessions. For example, ask students to jump as far as they can and then quickly measure the distance of their jump using 12-inch markings taped on the floor (**Figure 7.1**). Or, just count floor tiles, which are generally 12 inches square. Track and field lessons also offer numerous opportunities for students to measure. Have students time each other in a run, or measure the length of a person's long jump or the height of a high jump. They can also measure the distance that they run in a given amount of time, then calculate their rate of speed.

Figure 7.1 Checking the length of a long jump.

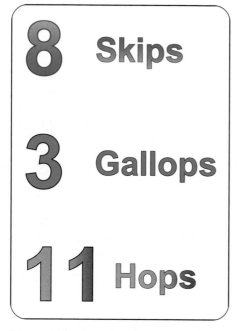

Figure 7.2 A number sign that may be used to accompany or expand activities.

Math Sample Activity 1

Math Concepts: Number Recognition and Number Sequencing
Physical Activity Skills: Locomotor Movements, Spacing, Sequencing Skills
Supplies: Laminated signs with numbers or sequences of numbers

- Hold one of the laminated signs so only students can see it.
- Instruct the students to perform their favorite locomotor skill the same number of times as written on the sign. When they finish, they should pick a different locomotor skill and perform it for the same number of times. For example, if the sign has the numeral 8 on it, a student may choose to walk eight steps, stop, and then skip eight times.
- The teacher (or a selected student) observes the class and tries to guess the mystery number.
- For older students, place a sequence of numbers on the sign, for example: 7, 13, 15.
- For each of the numbers, students select a locomotor movement and perform it. One student may choose to gallop 7 times, walk 13 steps, and jump 15 times.
- When the movements are completed, they start over with different movements to the number sequence of 7, 13, 15.
- Again, the teacher or a student tries to guess the number sequence on the card.

Teaching Tip: If desired, specific locomotor movements can be assigned for each number (as shown in **Figure 7.2**).

Topics for Integrated Study

Physical activity provides a wealth of opportunities for integrating math skills. Encourage your students to participate in any of the following activities:

1. Learn to measure physical performances. For example, use a tape measure for distance and height and a stopwatch to measure time.
2. After a self-test or standardized fitness test, calculate class averages. Identify the percentage of change from the last evaluation.
3. Learn percentages by working out batting averages, team standings, and field goal accuracy.
4. For a study of geometric principles, analyze the layouts of fields, playgrounds, and game areas. Rectangles, diamonds, and circles are used often as playing areas.
5. To help students better understand the metric system, compare European and U.S. performance in sports. Measure distances using the metric system.
6. Use math facts instead of numbers in games. For example, instead of saying "Eight," the scorekeeper could say, "Thirty-six divided by three, minus four."
7. Play number hopscotch to develop number recognition and memory. Draw a large square containing 16 or 25 smaller squares on the playground, and

Math Sample Activity 2

Math Concept: Odd and Even Numbers
Physical Activity Skills: Chasing, Fleeing, Locomotor Skills
Supplies: Large dice (optional)

- Establish two goal lines on opposite sides of the area.
- Divide the class into two groups—the Odds and the Evens. The groups face each other at the center of the area, about 5 feet apart.
- Call out either "Odds" or "Evens." The group called immediately chases the other group to the goal line. For example, if "Odds" is called, then the Odds chase. Any player caught goes to the other side and becomes a member of the opposing group.
- The goal is to try to capture the most players.

Teaching Tips: For added challenge, call out actual numbers so students have to determine if it is an odd or even number; for example, the call "Seven!" means that the Odds chase. Or, use simple math equations or math facts. Students solve the equation and then decide if the solution is odd or even and act accordingly.

Math Sample Activity 3

Math Concept: Odd and Even Numbers
Physical Activity Skills: Chasing, Fleeing, Locomotor Skills, Spacing
Supplies: None

- Arrange students in pairs. Partners stand facing each other on a line. One partner is designated Odd and one Even.
- As in the game "Rock, Paper, Scissors," students place one fist in the palm of the other hand. The game is played one-on-one and begins with both players hitting the palms of their hands with their fists twice, saying, "Math rocks!" On the third strike, rather than a fist, they extend one to five fingers. The partners quickly count the number of fingers on both hands.
- If the total is odd, the person designated Odd chases her partner. If she can tag him before he takes three steps, she gets a point. If the total number of fingers is even, the Even person becomes the chaser.
- The game ends when one of the partners reaches a designated number of points.

place a number in each of the smaller squares. A leader calls out a sequence of numbers and a player hops into each of the squares containing the numbers called.

8. Measure and lay out a playing field. Laying out a track and areas for field events could be a class project.
9. Use recorded pedometer data and stride length to calculate miles traveled. Convert miles to kilometers.
10. Estimate the number of steps that will be taken in a year based on one week, three weeks, and nine weeks of pedometer data. Which was the closest? Why?
11. Compare the relationship between time and number of steps accumulated. Calculate steps per minute.

Sample Activities

The following three sample activities will help you integrate math concepts with physical activities. Note that the samples used here have been modified to highlight key aspects of math integration. The activity cards that accompany this text use icons on the flip side of the cards to identify content area tie-ins, when they apply.

Back to Class

Mrs. Jefferson integrated concepts involving measurement, mean, median, mode, and the metric system into her students' physical activity. Identify at least one other math concept she could have integrated into this lesson.

Language Arts

In the elementary years, students explore language and learn to express ideas by writing, reading, speaking, listening, and using non-verbal communication. Concepts such as giving and following directions, critical thinking, taking notes, spelling, building vocabulary, and interacting with others are taught.

Integration Tips

Reading   Reading is easily integrated with physical activities. An effective strategy for integrating reading without sacrificing activity time is to use instructional task signs. For example, the sign in **Figure 7.3** requires simple word recognition. Students read the words, and then use the skill to move to one of the many other signs positioned throughout the teaching area. The sign in **Figure 7.4** requires students to read and follow more complex instructions. Again, in station format, students move from station to station reading and following instructions. The effective use of instructional signs efficiently integrates reading into physical activity and allows you to move about the teaching area to help those who need assistance.

Spelling   Earlier, we suggested having students count or skip count to a specified number to determine the length of time to stretch. But stretching can also be an

Figure 7.3 A simple instructional sign requiring word recognition. *Source: Deb Pangrazi, Mesa Public Schools, dlpangra@hotmail.com.*

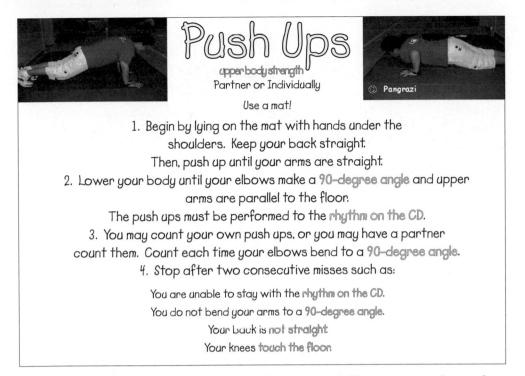

Push Ups

upper body strength
Partner or Individually

© Pangrazi

Use a mat!

1. Begin by lying on the mat with hands under the
shoulders. Keep your back straight.
Then, push up until your arms are straight.
2. Lower your body until your elbows make a 90-degree angle and upper
arms are parallel to the floor.
The push ups must be performed to the rhythm on the CD.
3. You may count your own push ups, or you may have a partner
count them. Count each time your elbows bend to a 90-degree angle.
4. Stop after two consecutive misses such as:

You are unable to stay with the rhythm on the CD.
You do not bend your arms to a 90-degree angle.
Your back is not straight.
Your knees touch the floor.

Figure 7.4 A fitness self-testing sign requiring students to read and follow a more complex set of instructions. *Source: Deb Pangrazi, Mesa Public Schools, dlpangra@hotmail.com.*

opportunity to teach the spelling of terms being used in the classroom (e.g., spelling words or vocabulary words from a specific content area). Instructions to implement spelling could be, "Choose your favorite lower body stretch from those you've learned in PE. Instead of counting while we hold the stretch today, we are going to spell words as we stretch. Since we are studying Antarctica, let's spell it while we stretch." The students then hold the stretch for as long as it takes them to spell *Antarctica*.

Parts of Speech   The action words such as *skip*, *run*, *throw*, and *roll* that you naturally use when instructing children in physical activity offer an excellent chance to teach them about verbs. An effective strategy is to quiz students as you give your instructions. For instance, after saying, "Everyone jump," immediately ask, "What was the verb in that sentence?" If the students do not respond at once with "jump," then quickly say, "It was *jump*. Remember, verbs identify action." The key to this strategy is to take no more than five seconds to determine the verb. As this process continues, students learn which words are verbs and begin responding quickly. This same process can be used to teach different parts of speech (i.e., nouns, adverbs, adjectives, prepositions).

Antonyms and Synonyms   Physical activity also offers many opportunities to use contrasting and similar words, thereby teaching antonyms and synonyms. For example, during a locomotor lesson, ask your students to skip at a low level. Next instruct them, "Skip at a level that is an antonym for *low*." Or, as part of a non-locomotor activity, ask students to "Stretch to make yourself large." While they are stretching, ask for examples of synonyms for *large*. If students have not learned the words *antonym* and *synonym*, use the words *opposite* and *same*.

Language Arts Sample Activity 1

Language Arts Concept: Parts of Speech
Physical Activity Skills: Chasing, Fleeing, Locomotor Skills
Supplies: None

- Establish two goal lines on opposite sides of the area.
- Divide the class into two groups—the Nouns and the Verbs. The groups face each other at the center of the area, about 5 feet apart.
- Call out either "Noun" or "Verb." The group called immediately chases the other group to the goal line. Any player caught goes to the other side and becomes a member of the opposing group.
- The goal is to try to capture the most players.
- After students have learned the difference between nouns and verbs, call out actual nouns or verbs such as *house* or *sing*.

Teaching Tip: When students are just beginning to learn to distinguish between nouns and verbs, point in the direction students should be moving when you call out a chase word to help those who are having difficulty. Use caution when choosing chase words! Many words, such as *jump, run, whisper,* etc., can be either a noun or a verb.

Language Arts Sample Activity 2

Language Arts Concept: Alphabetizing
Physical Activity Skills: Cooperation
Supplies: None

- The activity begins with the entire group standing on a line.
- Instruct students to arrange themselves in alphabetical order by first name while keeping at least one foot on the line at all times.
- Once students achieve this, instruct them to arrange themselves in alphabetical order by their last name without speaking. Players may use gestures, but they must keep one foot on the line at all times.

Teaching Tips: During this activity, students may be creative and use letters on their shirts, shoes, or jewelry. However, it is important to let students establish such strategies on their own. This is an excellent activity to use early in the school year to help students get acquainted.

Foreign Languages   Because many students are kinesthetic learners, integrating terms they are learning in a foreign language class with physical activity may help them better learn vocabulary. Consult with the foreign language teacher regularly to find out what vocabulary terms are being learned in the classroom and try to integrate them into activities. For example, have students count a stretch in the language they are studying. Translate key terms for the activity—such as *ball, bounce, roll,* or *jump*—and use them during instruction. Rather than say, "Hustle and get a tennis ball," you might say, "Hustle and get a *pelota de tenis*." Also, use the foreign language term for the activity (e.g., *gymnastics* is *gymnastique* in French and *gymnasia* in Spanish) when introducing the activity and whenever you refer to it during the lesson. If students are learning directional terms such as *above, below, in front of,* or *behind* in another language, these words can easily be included in instruction.

Peer Teaching   For fifth- and sixth-grade students, peer teaching can be an effective tool for learning the language concepts of listening and verbal instruction. Peer teaching simply involves one student teaching another a skill using the cues and strategies learned in class. For example, at the conclusion of a throwing activity, have students partner up. Instruct one student per pair to teach his or her partner how to

Language Arts Sample Activity 3
(based on Simon Says)

Language Arts Concepts: Listening and Following Directions
Physical Activity Skills: Non-Locomotor Skills, Locomotor
Skills, Manipulative Skills, Fitness Challenges
Supplies: None
In the traditional game of "Simon Says," the students remain
in one position. For our version, students should be moving
throughout the activity area.

- Choose one child as the leader. Explain that the leader gives students commands to perform physical actions, such as "Stretch your arms" or "Move like you're on a pogo stick."
- If the leader prefaces the command with "Simon says," the players must perform the command. However, if the leader does not preface the command with "Simon says," players must ignore the command.
- If students are fooled, they have a point scored against them or are eliminated from the round. The child who scores lowest or is the last left in the game becomes the leader for the next round.

Teaching Tip: At the end of the game, you might briefly comment, "When we think of language arts, we usually think of words that we write or say. However, an important part of language is being able to listen. Playing 'Simon Says' helped all of us practice listening skills."

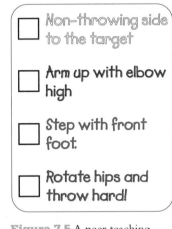

- Non-throwing side to the target
- Arm up with elbow high
- Step with front foot.
- Rotate hips and throw hard!

Figure 7.5 A peer teaching sheet.

throw, using the cues that were discussed in class. Students can also assess their teaching skills by using a self-assessment sheet such as that shown in **Figure 7.5**. This process requires partners to use listening and speaking skills.

Topics for Integrated Study

The topics of physical activity and sports make useful subjects for written and oral expression. Some suggestions include the following:

1. To increase your students' motivation to read, make use of game descriptions, rules of various sports, autobiographies of sports heroes, newspaper reports of game scores, and books oriented toward improvement in a given sport.

2. To add interest to spelling, teach words that occur in a variety of activity and sport settings. You could include the names of a few sports terms on the weekly spelling list or conduct a spelling bee using only terms and words found in sports and physical activities.

3. Study together the origin of terminology used in physical activity. Words such as *gymnasium, calisthenics,* and *exercise* have unique origins.

4. Get students writing about physical activity. They could write a summary of a game program the school has conducted; go to an intramural contest and

report the results for the school newspaper; find out as much as possible about a sports hero and write a short story about that individual to read aloud to the class; write about a favorite activity done outside of school, how they learned to swim, their favorite hiking trail, and so on.

5. Have students practice oral expression by giving demonstrations and describing various points of performance; explaining rules of various activities to other students; reporting the results of a school contest to students who were unable to attend; or evaluating each other's performances.

6. Have students write and perform plays about famous sports heroes, about the origin and development of games, or about imaginary athletes. They could also pantomime various sports and games activities and let other students guess the activity being pantomimed.

7. Conduct unison readings of well-known poems about sports, such as "Casey at the Bat."

8. After recording pedometer data for several different activities, challenge students to write a paragraph hypothesizing why some activities may be more active (more steps or time accumulated) than others.

Sample Activities

The following three sample activities will help you integrate language arts with physical activities. Note that the samples used here have been modified to highlight key aspects of language arts integration. The activity cards that accompany this text use icons on the flip side of the cards to identify content area tie-ins, when they apply.

Science

Elementary students are often fascinated by science. Thus, teaching concepts such as the human body, animals, plants, the environment, climate, the solar system, matter, and energy is often met with great enthusiasm.

Integration Tips

Freeze Signal   Successful teachers always make use of an effective signal to stop and "freeze" their classes. One strategy for teaching fourth-, fifth-, and sixth-grade students about temperature is to use "32 degrees Fahrenheit" as the freeze signal, since water freezes at 32 degrees. Similarly, you could say, "0 degrees Celsius." Once you've established this concept, you can say any number less than 32 degrees Fahrenheit or 0 degrees Celsius. For example, "11 degrees Fahrenheit" means "freeze."

Body Part Identification   A skill easily integrated with physical activity is the ability to identify body parts. Some teachers simply have students mimic them by performing the command as they give it. For example, "Touch your nose; your femur; your triceps." Or, you can give the commands without performing them yourself. This not only teaches body parts, but it also works on listening skills. Also, touching a specific body part can be the "Go" signal. For example, "When I touch my humerus bone, hustle to the line on the east side of the gym." Then immediately touch your humerus—or touch other bones first—to check for understanding.

Influence of Physical Activity on the Body   During a vigorous activity such as jogging, walking, or individual rope jumping, children often need a quick break. These breaks offer a great opportunity to teach about the influence of physical activity on the body. Concepts such as increased heart rate and why it happens, sweating and how it cools the body, why we get tired, and many others can be discussed during short breaks. Using the strategy throughout the year can be an effective method for teaching these concepts.

Topics for Integrated Study

Because all physical activities involve the body in generating force and movement, they provide ample opportunities for integrating science concepts. Here are some suggestions:

1. Think about the areas used in a variety of activities (a tennis court, a football field, a baseball diamond, a skating rink, a hiking trail, and so forth). Why do some activities use more space than others? Can the activities that use a lot of space be played in smaller areas? How?

2. Draw activities that require fast movement. Now draw activities that require slow movement. Why are these types of movements necessary during the activity?

3. Demonstrate light, weak, and gentle movements. Do these movements require a lot of force or not much force? In personal space, demonstrate the opposite of light, weak, and gentle movements.

4. Discuss activities that require different amounts of force. Similarly, act out a story that involves a variety of forces being exerted.

5. Diagram the different types of levers (**Figure 7.6**). Identify a joint in the body that represents each lever. For example, lifting a ball with the bicep is a third-class lever with the elbow as the fulcrum.

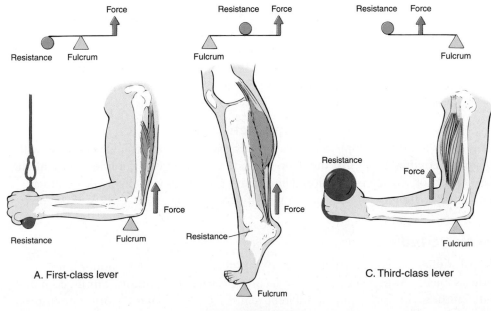

A. First-class lever

B. Second-class lever

C. Third-class lever

Figure 7.6 Types of levers in human joints.

Science Sample Activity 1

(Hand Wrestling)

Science Concepts: Force, Pushing, Pulling
Physical Activity Skills: Balance, Body Awareness
Supplies: None

- Players pair up and face each other, standing approximately 12 inches apart. Make sure they are matched by size.
- Partners place the palms of their hands together and must keep them together throughout the game.
- The object of the game is to get the opponent to move one of his or her feet by pushing, pulling, or performing other bodily movements while keeping both players' palms connected.

Teaching Tip: Following a few rounds, ask a few brief questions: How does force affect this game? Is it better to use a lot of force or not much? How could I use a little bit of force and still move my opponent off balance?

Science Sample Activity 2

(Finger Wrestling)

Science Concepts: Force, Pushing, Pulling
Physical Activity Skills: Balance, Body Awareness
Supplies: None

- Players pair up. Be sure that partners are matched by size for this game.
- Partners start balanced on one foot facing each other with their index fingers hooked. See **Figure 7.7** for starting position.
- The object is to push or pull the opponent off balance. If a person causes her opponent to lose his balance, she receives a point and the partners start over.

Teaching Tip: After a few minutes of play, stop the class and discuss strategies related to pushing and pulling. Which is more effective, pushing or pulling? Can you use both?

6. Determine which of the following two positions is more stable (best for balance): standing on your tiptoes with your legs together while reaching for the ceiling or standing with your feet flat on the floor, shoulder width apart, and knees bent? If it's true that being lower is more stable, in what position are you the *most* stable? (Lying down.) Explain why we naturally bend our knees when we are walking on slick surfaces.

7. Create diagrams of the human body and label bones, muscles, and organs. For each muscle identified, list one activity that uses that muscle. What activities use the most muscles?

Sample Activities

The following three sample activities will help you integrate science concepts with physical activities. Note that the samples used here have been modified to highlight key aspects of science integration. The activity cards that accompany this text use icons on the flip side of the cards to identify content area tie-ins, when they apply.

Social Studies

Social studies include geography, history, political science, and economics, among other subjects. At the elementary level, concepts such as directions, family, community, cultures, the geography of different regions, United States history, state history, political systems, and rules and laws are taught.

Figure 7.7 Starting position for Science Sample Activity 2 (finger wrestling).

Science Sample Activity 3

Science Concepts: Animal Locomotion
Physical Activity Skills: Animal Movements, Spacing
Supplies: None

- Designate a student as the Leader.
- The Leader calls out the names of different animals and methods of movement that may or may not correspond to that animal. For instance, the Leader might call out, "Pigs fly . . . Birds crawl . . . Salmon swim . . . ."
- When the Leader calls out a correct animal-movement relationship, the class must move accordingly. In this example, the children would make a swimming movement, ignoring the incorrect animal-movement relationships.

Teaching Tip: Rounds should be kept short so that all children have a chance to lead.

Integration Tips

Directions   Directions are an important part of geography and can easily be taught through physical activity. The first step is to place large directional signs, with the abbreviations N, S, E, and W clearly marked, on the appropriate walls. Early in the year, simply refer to these directions. For instance, "When I say, 'Go,' hustle to the line by the south wall." Initially, it may be helpful to point in the direction of the line as well. As students mature, your instructions may refer to the "southwest wall" or "the cone closest to the northeast basket." When you're outdoors, teach your students to use the sun to determine direction. In order to do this, students need to know the time of day and where the sun rises.

Games from Other Countries   When introducing games, dances, and other activities that originate in other countries, take a few minutes to discuss the country, show where it is on a map, and talk about the language spoken there.

Class Greeting   Prepare a list of greetings used in other countries and use a different greeting each week as the students arrive. The students attempt to determine the country in which the greeting is used. Gestures such as bowing or hand shaking may also be used.

Conversation and Courtesy   Often during physical activities, students work on skills with partners. During these activities, remind students to concentrate on the

Social Studies Sample Activity 1

Social Studies Concept: The Need for Rules and Laws
Physical Activity Skills: Classroom Management Skills
Supplies: None

- Discuss the importance of following directions. To reinforce this lesson, state the instructions for a simple example game, and then briefly explore why following the rules would ensure having a successful game.
- Say, for example, "When I say 'Toe-to-Toe,' quickly get toe-to-toe with the person closest to you. 'Toe-to-Toe' (pause). Thank you for doing that quickly. Now, one partner remain standing while the other partner sits. If you are standing, please report to the line by the south wall. If you are sitting, please report to the line by the north wall." Following the game, ask, "What would have happened if the class had decided not to follow directions?"
- After these directions, implement several actual games or activities to follow up on what you discussed with the group.

Teaching Tips: Early in the school year, establish basic ground rules for participation in physical activity and the consequences for not following them (see Chapter 5). Establish rules not only for classroom activities but also for games outside of class, such as during morning recess and the lunch break. It is important to reinforce early in the year the fact that following rules leads to more enjoyment for everybody.

Social Studies Sample Activity 2

Social Studies Concepts: Travel, Evolution of Transportation, Rural and Urban Settings
Physical Activity Skills: Locomotor Skills
Supplies: None

- Ask students to demonstrate how they would travel to a specific place if they lived during a given time in history. For example, "If I lived in a New England village during the 1700s and wanted to get to my neighbor's house, show me the different ways I could get there."
- Provide positive reinforcement to students walking, jogging, skipping, or galloping like a horse, which would have been a method of travel during this time.
- Depending on their age, some students will pretend to drive a car. This is a teachable moment for discussing the modes of transportation available in the 1700s and the distances between neighbors in different types of settlements during this time.

Teaching Tip: This activity can be implemented throughout the year to correspond with time period that students may be studying in the classroom.

skills, but also teach them how to have polite conversations. Identify courtesy words such as *please* and *thank you*. Discuss appropriate questions, how to ask questions, and how to apologize if they say something wrong. Many teachers assume that children have learned conversational skills at home, but these skills are often neglected.

Cooperative Activities   Cooperation is an important component of community, family, and relationships. Cooperative skills such as communicating, sharing, and listening can be reinforced in an active environment.

Topics for Integrated Study

Geography   Because the origins of physical activities are diverse, geographical associations provide another source of learning experiences. Find clues about the play and sports habits of people in different parts of the world and then consider how these habits are influenced by geographical factors.

1.   Study the climate in different areas of the United States to ascertain how climate affects physical activity habits. Factors such as altitude and weather could be studied.

2. Play and study games of different countries. Cultural factors such as dress, folklore, mores, and industries might be related to the games people play.

3. During a rhythmic unit in which folk dances are taught, discuss the origin of the dance and the characteristics of the country and its people. Design authentic costumes and discuss cultural implications.

4. Have students or local cultural groups from other countries visit the class to explain their play habits and games.

5. Study the Olympics to see how athletes from different countries perform in different sports. This offers a clue to the emphasis certain countries place on various sports and might offer insight into the types of physical activities taught in their schools.

6. Study geographical and climatic factors of various areas to see how they affect athletic performance. For instance, discuss how altitude at the Mexico Olympic Games in 1968 seriously affected long-distance runners but aided long jumpers.

7. Language barriers during international competition often cause problems for officials and referees. Discuss ways to help remedy this problem.

Social Studies Sample Activity 3

Social Studies Concepts: Cultures, Courtesy
Physical Activity Skills: Locomotor Skills
Supplies: None

- Have students perform traditional methods of greeting used in different cultures or regions.
- As students move about the teaching area, call out a method of greeting (e.g., shaking hands, bowing with palms together, embracing, or making a high five).
- Students perform this greeting with as many people as possible.
- Then, provide another example of other customs or culture-based activities (such as skiing for northern lands, surfing for island cultures, etc.).
- Be sure to identify the country or cultures from which various customs or activities originate.

Teaching Tip: For older children, simply call out the country name and have the class respond with the appropriate greeting/activity.

History   Many present-day activities are based in history and tradition. Develop students' knowledge of the historical aspects of physical activities.

1. Study the origin and evolution of various activities. Events such as the discus throw, the shot put, and the pole vault are performed now only because of tradition.

2. The history and development of sports equipment and facilities are often interesting and revealing to students. For example, compare the Roman Coliseum with present-day stadiums, or compare levels of performance with different types of poles used for vaulting.

3. Study the records and achievements of outstanding players in a particular sport. Examples of questions to guide discussion include the following: Who were well-known athletes and pioneers in sports? Who were outstanding individuals who set records? Who achieved outstanding performances internationally, including Olympic performances? Create a sports quiz to include items from each of the categories. Be sure to include achievements of both women and men.

4. Study the ethnic background, historical context, and meaning of dances to make them more interesting.

5. Compare how different cultures valued physical fitness and activity. The ancient Greek, Persian, and Roman civilizations placed significant emphasis on fitness.

6. Study the fascinating history of the Olympics. The evolution from the ancient games to the present-day Olympics offers many insights into the values of different societies.
7. Study medieval knights and their jousting tournaments.
8. Study the games and activities of a specific historic era (e.g., colonial, Civil War, Depression, and post–World War II) in the United States. Have the popular games changed throughout the history of the United States?

Sample Activities

The following three sample activities will help you integrate social studies with physical activities. Note that the samples used here have been modified to highlight key aspects of social studies integration. The activity cards that accompany this text use icons on the flip side of the cards to identify content area tie-ins, when they apply.

Back to Class

In Chapter 6, we talked about methods for including students with special needs into physical activities. Mrs. Jefferson's student Andrew could have suffered an asthma attack if he had run in the cold air. Do you think her method of including him in the activity was acceptable or not? Defend your answer.

Chapter Summary

Why Integrate?

- Integration is instruction designed to combine two or more concepts from different areas to help students see the interrelatedness of knowledge.

- Although more research is needed, it appears that integration of academics with physical activity is effective for some students. These students may absorb academic concepts more readily while they are physically active. Also, integration may help clarify areas of uncertainty or strengthen retention as well as contribute to a positive learning environment.

Types of Integration

There are three general models for integrating physical activity and academics. Using the individual model, you work independently to develop ideas for integration. Using the partner model, you collaborate with the physical education teacher or another specialist. Using the group model, you work within a group of classroom teachers at the same grade level, usually generating theme-based learning activities.

Academic Integration Activities

Physical activity provides a wealth of opportunities for integrating math skills such as counting, measuring, estimating, calculating, determining degrees and fractions, and studying geometric principles.

Language arts can easily be integrated with physical activities. An effective strategy for integrating reading without sacrificing activity time is to use instructional task signs. Use physical activity sessions to reinforce proper spelling, parts of speech, terms from a foreign language, and other language skills. Or, have students write about favorite sports teams, players, or after-school physical activities.

Science concepts easily integrated with physical activity include the human body, animal locomotion, force, and lever systems. Point out to students the physical effects they experience during strenuous activity, and explain the physiology behind these responses.

You can use physical activities to reinforce directions and other geography concepts, the need for rules and laws, history, travel, human cultures, and courtesy and cooperation. When teaching dances, games, and sports, integrate a bit of their history and their evolution over time.

Review Questions

Content Review

1. Why should teachers attempt to integrate academics and physical activity?

2. Identify a classroom teacher's potential partners in developing an interdisciplinary learning experience for students.

3. List and discuss at least five ways of integrating math concepts into physical activity.

4. Identify an easy way to promote reading skills during physical activity.

5. Explain how to integrate instruction about human anatomy and physiology into physical activity sessions.

Real World

1. At the end of Chapter 1, we asked how you would respond to a colleague who asserts that he doesn't have time for physical activity because he is too busy trying to improve his students' academic performance. Now that you've read this chapter, we'd like you to respond more specifically to this question. Refer to the research cited in this chapter on the influence of physical activity in general, as well as research on the effectiveness of integration.

2. In a planning meeting, two experienced teachers present an idea for a theme-based interdisciplinary learning experience that would involve the first through fifth grades at the elementary school where you have been hired to teach in the coming academic year. The theme they are proposing is "Every Day Is Earth Day." Topics they propose teaching include recycling, saving energy, global warming, endangered species, etc. You also know that there is a mandate in your school district to increase children's level of physical activity. What ways, if any, could physical activity be integrated into the "Every Day Is Earth Day" theme?

What About You?

In our chapter-opening scenario, a student thanks Mrs. Jefferson for using physical activity to teach math concepts he had been struggling with. Is there anything you are finding particularly challenging right now—perhaps an academic subject or something you're engaged in personally? If so, how might applying the concept of integration help you to tackle this challenge from a new angle?

_____

_____

_____

References and Suggested Readings

Blaydes-Madigan, J. (2004). *Thinking on your feet* (2nd ed.). Murphy, TX: Action Based Learning.

Christie, B.A. (2000). Topic Teamwork: A collaborative integrative model for increasing student-centered learning in grades K–12. *Journal of Physical Education, Recreation, and Dance,* 71(8), 28–32.

Cook, G. (1994). Topics and themes in interdisciplinary curriculum. *Middle School Journal,* 25(3), 40.

Jensen, E. (2000). *Brain based learning.* San Diego: Brain Store Publishing.

National Association for Sport and Physical Education (2004). *Moving into the future national standards for physical education.* Reston, VA: McGraw-Hill.

Pangrazi, R.P. (2007). *Dynamic physical education curriculum guide: Lesson plans for implementation* (15th ed.). San Francisco: Benjamin Cummings.

Pangrazi, R.P. Beighle, A., and Sidman, C. (2007). *Pedometer power* (2nd ed.). Champaign, IL: Human Kinetics.

Pellegrini, A.D., Huberty, P.D., and Jones, I. (1995). The effects of recess timing on children's playground and classroom behaviors. *American Educational Research Journal,* 32(4), 845–864.

Placek, J.H. (2003). Interdisciplinary curriculum in physical education: Possibilities and problems. In S.J. Silverman and C.D. Ennis (eds.), *Student learning in physical education: Applying research to enhance instruction* (pp. 255–271). Champaign, IL: Human Kinetics.

Purcell-Cone, T., et al. (1998). *Interdisciplinary teaching through physical education.* Champaign, IL: Human Kinetics.

Sibley, B.A., and Etnier, J.L. (2003). The relationship between physical activity and cognition in children: A meta-analysis. *Pediatric Exercise Science,* 15(3), 243–256.

Tomporowski, P.D. (2003). Cognitive and behavioral responses to acute exercise in youths: A review. *Pediatric Exercise Science,* 15, 348–359.

Werner, P. (ed.). (2003). Interdisciplinary learning [Special section]. *Teaching Elementary Physical Education,* 14(4).

Werner, P. (ed.). (2003). The integrated curriculum [Special section]. *Teaching Elementary Physical Education,* 10(1).

Web Resources

Language Arts Standards (National Council of Teachers of English):
www.ncte.org
Math Standards (National Council of Teachers of Mathematics):
www.standards.nctm.org
Science Standards (National Science Education Standards):
www.nap.edu
Social Studies Standards (National Council for Social Studies):
www.socialstudies.org/standards

8

Increasing Students' Activity Levels

After reading this chapter, you will be able to . . .

○ Distinguish between light, moderate, and vigorous physical activity.

○ Explain why even moderate physical activity is effective for promoting health.

○ Summarize the NASPE activity guidelines for elementary school children.

○ Identify the different levels of the Physical Activity Pyramid and explain how each level contributes to optimal health.

○ Explain how to structure the school playground to increase children's enjoyment of and engagement in physical activity.

○ Discuss the use of pedometers in monitoring children's levels of physical activity.

○ Teach students where to place the pedometer for highest accuracy and how to maintain personal responsibility for their assigned pedometer.

○ Describe the benefits of walking, especially for weight management.

○ Implement a schoolwide walking program.

Classroom Challenge

Ms. Estes is delighted with the spirit and enthusiasm of her second-grade class this year, but she is concerned about their health. In her 20 years of teaching, she has typically had no more than 1 or 2 overweight students in a class, but this year, of her 22 students, 5 are at least moderately overweight, and one girl, Stacy, is so significantly overweight that she easily becomes short of breath and cannot keep up with her peers in active games. With the goal of helping these children achieve a more healthful weight and instilling in all of her students a regular practice of physical activity, Ms. Estes decides to increase the amount of time she devotes each day to classroom physical activity.

This morning, she begins the day by asking her students to stand by their desks and "reach up to the sky." She then takes them through several stretches and follows this with three minutes of jogging in place. "Now that you're all warmed up," she says, "let's do our subtraction facts with jumping jacks! Take one step away from your desks to give yourselves plenty of room, and follow my lead!" As she leads the class in this activity, she notices that Stacy is sweating and breathing heavily, is not reciting with the others, and is only lifting her arms waist high instead of overhead. Before the rest of the children are halfway through their subtraction facts, Stacy slumps into her seat. For the remainder of the activity, she stares out the classroom window. Midmorning, when Ms. Estes has the children line up for a quick run around the school building, Stacy excuses herself, explaining that her sneakers are too tight. She stays behind in the classroom reading while the other children file out for their run.

Even with the best of intentions, Ms. Estes' efforts to turn her students on to physical activity backfired, discouraging a child who, with a different approach, might have discovered the joy of movement. This chapter will help you to increase your students' level of daily physical activity in ways that are appropriate for all of them. We begin by distinguishing between different levels of physical activity, then discuss recommendations for children's physical activity such as that shown in the Physical Activity Pyramid. We then identify ways to restructure the school playground to promote students' engagement in physical activity. Next, we provide suggestions for monitoring your students' level of physical activity using pedometers. Finally, we discuss some reasons and strategies for promoting walking, the "real" lifestyle activity.

Understanding Physical Activity

We've been using the term *physical activity* throughout this book in a general way, but for the purposes of this chapter, a technical definition might help: The National Association for Sport and Physical Education (NASPE) defines **physical activity** as bodily movement that is produced by the contraction of skeletal muscle and that substantially increases energy expenditure (NASPE, 2004). This definition encompasses the full range and process of moving, as well as all of its different forms, such as exercise, sports, labor, and leisure activity.

You can help children meet their need for physical activity by offering them short bouts of various types of activity throughout the day. To plan such opportunities, you need to understand what constitutes light, moderate, and vigorous physical activity.

Levels of Physical Activity

A unit of **metabolic equivalent**, or **MET**, is a ratio assigned to activities that identifies how much they increase an adult's metabolic rate above resting metabolic rate. That is, 1 MET equals the number of calories an average adult expends at rest (resting metabolism). Two METs indicates that an activity burns twice as many calories as resting. Three METs is three times as intense as being at rest, and so on. A study by Harrell et al. (2005) showed that children burn more calories at rest and during exercise than do adults. Therefore, when you are planning activities for your students and evaluating an activity's MET, you need to consider the greater overall energy expenditure of children.

Activities of 3 METs or fewer are classified as *light* physical activities. Examples are strolling (slow walking), slow stationary cycling, stretching, playing in a sandbox, pushing a doll carriage, bowling, playing croquet or miniature golf, and tidying up a classroom area.

Moderate activities range from 4 to 6 METs. Examples of moderate activities are climbing a rock wall, dancing a waltz, bicycling on level terrain, jogging, and walking at 2.5 mph.

Activity that expends more than six times the energy expended at rest (more than 6 METs) is considered to be *vigorous* (or high intensity). Examples of vigorous activities are speed walking, running, skipping, dancing a polka, stair climbing, and rope jumping.

Back to Class

Ms. Estes had her students stretch, jog, perform jumping jacks, and run. Classify each of these activities as light, moderate, or vigorous.

The Benefits of Moderate to Vigorous Physical Activity

Engaging in 60 minutes of moderate to vigorous physical activity each day burns 1,000 to 2,000 calories per week and achieves health benefits similar to performance-related fitness training. As we discuss shortly, experts recommend that children achieve a minimum of 60 minutes of activity each day. However, even 30 minutes a day of moderate physical activity expends about 150 calories and is associated with a reduced risk for chronic disease (USDHHS, 1996). In addition, although it was once believed that activity had to be performed in one long, continuous session (20 to 30 minutes) to be beneficial, it is now known that activity is beneficial even if accumulated in several shorter bouts throughout the day. For example, 15 minutes walking the dog both before and after school, a 5-minute mid-morning classroom activity break, 15 minutes playing tag at lunchtime recess, and 15 minutes of square dancing as part of an afternoon American history lesson exceed the 60-minute physical activity prescription. Table 8.1 identifies several *intermittent* and *continuous* physical activities.

As shown in the Lifestyle Activity Prescription for Children (Table 8.2), different standards of frequency, intensity, and time define lifestyle activity contributing to children's health. These recommendations are useful because they challenge the old adage, "No pain, no gain." The new recommendations make it easier for inactive children to see the value of participating in various types and levels of physical activity. Pleasurable activity is good activity.

Table 8.1 Different Types of Physical Activity

Intensity of Activity	Intermittent	Continuous
Moderate	Playing one-wall handball	Walking to a destination at 2.5 mph
	Playing catch with a friend	Hiking
	Raking the leaves or vacuuming	Riding a bike
	Playing four-square	Skateboarding
Vigorous	Playing tag games	Jogging
	Rope jumping	Track activities
	Playing softball or football	Soccer
		Swimming

Table 8.2 Lifestyle Activity Prescription for Children

Frequency	Daily, with frequent activity sessions (three or more) per day
Intensity	Moderate to vigorous activity. Alternating bouts of vigorous activity with rest periods as needed, or moderate continuous activity such as walking or riding a bike to school. Examples include walking, playing running games, doing chores at home, and climbing stairs.
Time	Duration of activity necessary to expend more than 6 to 8 kcal/kg/day. Equal to calories expended in 60 minutes or more of active play or moderate sustained activity, which may be distributed over three or more activity sessions.

Recommendations for Children's Physical Activity

The Lifestyle Activity Prescription provides some general parameters for children's activity. More specific recommendations include the NASPE guidelines and the Physical Activity Pyramid, discussed in this chapter (see **Figure 8.1**).

NASPE Activity Guidelines for Elementary School Children

The National Association for Sport and Physical Education (NASPE) has developed activity guidelines for elementary school children that call for 60 minutes or more of physical activity per day (NASPE, 2004). Why 60 minutes when the recommendation for adults is only 30 minutes a day? The primary reason is that the recommendation for adults is calculated on the energy expenditure necessary to achieve the reduced risk of chronic disease associated with what is commonly called *aerobic* or *cardiovascular fitness*. But children and youth need to gain experience in many types of physical activity and build total body fitness, including strength and flexibility, not just aerobic fitness. This broader need requires an additional time commitment.

The four major activity guidelines are briefly described here. For in-depth detail about the physical activity guidelines for children, see the NASPE document (NASPE, 2004).

Back to Class

Ms. Estes had her students stretch, jog, perform jumping jacks, and run. Classify each of these activities as intermittent or continuous.

Guideline 1: Children should accumulate at least 60 minutes, and up to several hours, of *age-appropriate* physical activity on all or most days of the week. This daily accumulation should include moderate and vigorous physical activity, of which the majority is intermittent in nature.

Although 60 minutes is the minimum amount of daily activity recommended for children, it is becoming increasingly clear that much more than 60 minutes is needed. For example, using data collected with a pedometer that measures activity time and steps, 60 minutes of physical activity equates to slightly fewer than 5,000 steps. The President's Council on Physical Fitness and Sports (2007) has established the Presidential Active Lifestyle Award (PALA) threshold of 11,000 and 13,000 steps for girls and boys, respectively. This makes it obvious that 60 minutes is a minimal level that youth should accumulate on a daily basis. Physical activity minutes accumulated each day should include both moderate and vigorous activity. For children, most activity will come in intermittent activity bursts ranging from a few seconds to several minutes in length alternated with rest periods. Continuous vigorous physical activity lasting several minutes, such as jogging around a track, *should not* be expected for most children, nor should it be a condition for meeting the guidelines.

Guideline 2: Children should participate in several bouts of physical activity lasting 15 minutes or more each day.

Much of a child's daily activity will be in short bursts accumulated throughout the waking hours. However, if optimal benefits are to accrue, much of the activity should be accumulated in bouts of 15 minutes or more. These bouts could include mid-morning and lunchtime activity breaks, physical education classes, active classroom games and dances, and sports practices. You can easily see why a 15-minute recess is vital to the health and development of children. It is indefensible to eliminate recess and time for physical activity—a trend all too common in today's schools.

Guideline 3: Children should participate each day in a variety of age-appropriate physical activities designed to help them achieve optimal health, wellness, fitness, and performance benefits.

Different levels of physical activity are described in the Physical Activity Pyramid (see **Figure 8.1**). It is recommended that children select from all of the first three levels of activities in the pyramid each week. These levels are discussed shortly.

Guideline 4: Extended periods (of two hours or more) of inactivity are discouraged for children, especially during the daytime hours.

Back to Class

Now that you've read the NASPE guidelines, comment on the appropriateness of Ms. Estes' morning activities for a group of second-graders.

Research suggests that people (including children) who watch excessive amounts of television, play computer games, work on computers for extended periods of time, or engage in other low-energy-expenditure activities will likely fail to meet guidelines 1, 2, and 3 (Gordon-Larsen, McMurray, and Popkin, 2000). Evidence suggests that reducing the average amount of daily sedentary time is effective in counteracting weight problems in children (Epstein et al., 1995). Thus, extended periods (two hours or more in length) of sedentary behavior both in and out of school are discouraged. Because many positive things can happen during times of relative inactivity (homework; studying; imagining; learning to read, write, and think; and family time), some periods of relative inactivity are important in a typical day. But children should be active before and after school, frequently during school, and on weekends.

The Physical Activity Pyramid

The Physical Activity Pyramid (Figure 8.1) is a fun visual tool you can use to teach children how much and what type of activity they need. It is especially useful for teaching children about the different categories of activity required for good health and total body fitness.

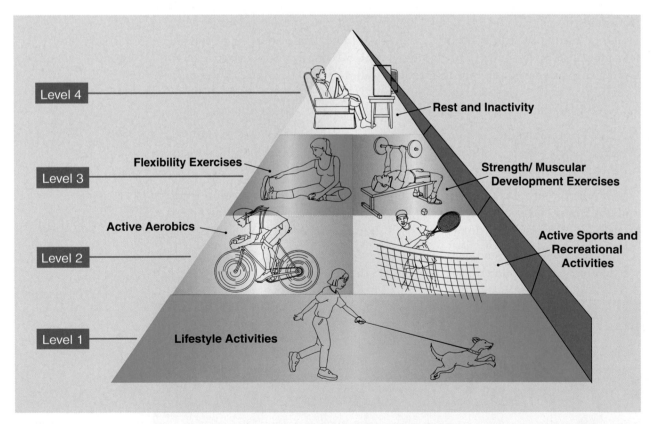

Figure 8.1 The Physical Activity Pyramid. *Source: C.B. Corbin and R.P. Pangrazi (1992). Are American children and youth fit? Research Quarterly for Exercise and Sport, 63(2), 96–106.*

The pyramid includes six categories of activities arranged into four levels that convey their relative importance and, thus, their suggested frequency. For example, lifestyle activities having broad general health and wellness benefits for large numbers of people are placed at level 1, the base of the pyramid, and should be engaged in several times every day. These benefits include a reduced risk of heart disease, diabetes, and cancer. The extra calories expended in doing these activities are also useful in controlling body fat and reducing the risk of obesity. Wellness benefits include increased functional capacity as well as improved quality of life.

Level 2 contains more vigorous activities: active aerobics and sports and recreational activities. **Aerobic activities** are those performed at a pace for which the body can supply adequate oxygen to meet the demands of the activity. (Because lifestyle activities meet this criterion, they are also aerobic.) Research suggests that active aerobics and active sports and recreation provide health and fitness benefits in addition to those provided by regular lifestyle activity. Thus, these activities are placed at level 2, and should be performed three to five times a week. Note that the more vigorous nature of the activities makes them difficult for some children to perform, and for this reason they may not be as appealing as the activities at level 1.

Level 3 exercises are designed to build flexibility and muscle fitness, qualities that contribute to improved performance in various jobs and sports. Muscle fitness has also been associated with reduced risk of osteoporosis (Shaw and Snow-Harter, 1995), and both types of exercises when performed appropriately are thought to contribute to reduced rate of injury and a lower risk of back problems (Plowman, 1993). They should be engaged in two to three times a week.

It is obvious why rest and inactivity are at the top of the pyramid (level 4). In general, they do not provide physical activity benefits, although rest is essential to health. Again, long periods of sedentary activity should be avoided.

The Physical Activity Pyramid was developed to guide people in choosing physical activities at all life stages. The following discussions will help you apply the pyramid's recommendations specifically to school-age children.

Level 1: Lifestyle Physical Activities

The greatest portion of accumulated minutes of physical activity for school-age children usually comes from lifestyle activities that children perform as part of their everyday routine. Examples include yard work, delivering newspapers, walking the dog, walking or riding a bike to school or elsewhere, and helping carry the groceries. Housework that requires using the large muscles of the body is also lifestyle physical activity.

Lifestyle activities for this age also include active play and games involving the large muscles of the body. Climbing, tumbling, and other activities that require lifting the body or relocating the body in space are desirable when they can be performed safely. Games such as tag or snowball fights are typically intermittent in nature rather than continuous and often include short bursts of vigorous activity.

Level 2: Active Aerobics

The second level of the pyramid includes active aerobics. Examples of moderate to vigorous aerobic activities popular with children are running, brisk walking, swimming, dancing, and biking. Participation in some aerobic activities is appropriate as long as children are not expected to participate in them continuously for a long duration. More appropriate are intermittent aerobic activities such as recreational swimming, family walking, or aerobic activities that are included in the lifestyle activity category, such as riding a bicycle to school or in the neighborhood. Participation in continuous aerobic activities of long duration is not recommended for this age group.

Level 2: Active Sports and Recreational Activities

Also on the second level of the Physical Activity Pyramid are active sports and recreational activities. Some examples of active sports are basketball, tennis, soccer, and hiking. Like active aerobics, this type of activity is typically more vigorous than lifestyle physical activity. Sports often involve vigorous bursts of activity with brief rest periods. Though they are often not truly aerobic in nature, when they are performed without long rest periods, they have many of the same benefits as aerobic activities.

When young children choose to be involved in sports, it is necessary for the sports to be modified to meet their developmental level. In general, active sports should not comprise the major proportion of activity for children in kindergarten through fourth grade. It is important that children in these grades have time to learn basic skills, such as catching, throwing, walking, jumping, running, and striking objects, which are prerequisite to performing sports and other recreational activities.

Fifth- and sixth-grade youngsters are more likely to be involved in active sports than younger children. Lead-up games and emphasis on skill development are necessary to make the activities suitable for this age. Age-appropriate recreational activities that have a lifetime emphasis or that can be done with family and friends are encouraged.

Level 3: Flexibility Exercises

As we noted earlier, *physical activity* is a term that describes virtually all types of human movement. In contrast, the term **exercise** is most commonly used to describe a type of physical activity done especially to maintain fitness. The flexibility exercises included at the third level of the pyramid are performed specifically to build the component of fitness called *flexibility*. **Flexibility** is the ability to use joints through a full range of motion as a result of having long muscles and elastic connective tissues. No doubt some activities from the first two levels of the pyramid can help build flexibility to some extent. Still, to fully develop this component of fitness, it is necessary to do special flexibility exercises that involve stretching the muscles and using the joints through their full range of normal motion.

In general, the amount of time spent on flexibility exercises for children in kindergarten through fourth grade should be minimal. Children are inherently more flexible than adults, and stretching is relatively easy for most of them. Teach some stretching exercises to illustrate the importance of flexibility. In addition, encourage play activities, such as tumbling and climbing, which can contribute to flexibility.

More time should be spent teaching and performing flexibility exercises when children reach the fifth and sixth grades. Children, especially boys, begin to lose some flexibility at this age. Some regular stretching is recommended either in the form of age-appropriate flexibility exercises or activities that promote flexibility.

Level 3: Strength and Muscular Development Exercises

Exercises and physical activities designed and performed specifically to increase *strength* (the amount of weight one can lift) and *muscular endurance* (the ability to persist in muscular effort) are included in this category. Some activities at lower levels in the pyramid may help children develop strength and endurance, so kindergarten through fourth-grade children who accumulate adequate daily physical activity at the lower levels of the pyramid do not need to participate in regular strength-training activities.

Upper-level elementary school children can successfully participate in strength development exercises that require them to move and lift their body weight, such as push ups and sit ups, or movements that include bending, stretching, swaying, and twisting. It is important to show children the relevance of such exercises. Participation in active play and games and sports that require muscle overload are also beneficial for these youngsters. Formal exercises and conditioning programs as part of youth sports or other activity programs should not typically constitute a major part of activity periods, though highly motivated children may benefit from exposure to these activities.

Level 4: Rest and Inactivity

At the top of the pyramid are rest and inactivity. Some types of inactivity are not detrimental to health. For example, musculoskeletal rest is important after vigorous exercise, and children need adequate amounts of sleep. Classroom learning is often sedentary, as is time spent playing with a train set or medieval castle, but no one would argue against the importance of such activities to children's intellectual and imaginative development.

Nevertheless, the Physical Activity Pyramid is designed to provide information about the benefits of regular physical activity. It therefore discourages inactivity *as a lifestyle choice*. Long periods of sedentary activity during the daylight hours should be limited. Youth who sit and watch hours of television or spend their free time playing video games or surfing the web are not getting the activity they need for good health.

Back to Class

Ms. Estes had her students stretch, jog, perform jumping jacks, and run. Place each of these activities on the appropriate level of the Physical Activity Pyramid. What do your findings reveal about this group of activities?

Structuring the Playground to Increase Physical Activity

One way to promote your students' participation in activities at different levels of the Physical Activity Pyramid is to structure their school playground in a way that makes recess active, safe, and fun. Although the term *recess* implies that students take a "recess from learning," an active, safe, and fun playground is an outdoor learning lab. While participating in playground games, students learn how to cooperate, compete, and negotiate for the success of the group, not to mention learn how much fun they can have simply being active.

Unfortunately, if playground activities are not structured and supervised properly, some students may injure themselves and others may learn inappropriate behaviors, such as how to dominate or exclude others. It's essential to structure a playground environment that contributes to all students' activity and health. The following steps are designed to make the school playground active, safe, and fun for all students. Some of the material in this section is adapted from the *Active and Healthy Schools Program* (Pangrazi, 2006), a total-school approach the author developed for Gopher Sport (see Web Resources).

Figure 8.2 Example of a sign designating the playground as an activity zone. *Source: Deb Pangrazi, Mesa Public Schools, dlpangra@ hotmail.com.*

Make an Activity-Friendly Playground

In this section, we identify some steps your school can take to make an activity-friendly playground.

Use New Terminology to Express New Ideas

You want your students to think of the playground as a place for everyone to be active. So, one of the first strategies you should implement is to change the name of the playground to the *activity zone*. This simple name change informs administrators, teachers, students, and parents that the primary goal for the playground is to encourage physical activity. To make the name change stick, place on or adjacent to all doors to the playground a large sign that designates the area as an activity zone. Make sure the signs are laminated so that they won't wear if exposed to the weather. **Figure 8.2** provides an example of an activity zone sign.

Zone the Playground

On unstructured playgrounds, if you observe the activity for a while, you'll notice that children move in all directions and often into situations where they are at risk of injury. For example, a group of second-graders playing a game of tag might run unrestricted into a sixth-grade football game. Injuries are likely to follow. In addition, the number of activities offered on the playground is typically limited, and there is little equipment available to increase play options. Imagine if you were to sign up for a health club only to discover it had just one stationary bike and one set of barbells! A playground without adequate equipment is just as frustrating for students. Some creative children will make up games with rocks and sticks, but others will stand around in the sun or the cold with nothing to engage them.

Structured playgrounds keep children safe and engaged. The first step is to delineate a variety of playground zones with different-colored cones. Leave at least 10 feet between zones. This helps ensure that students don't run into each other and that misplayed equipment doesn't interfere with another zone. Place a cone at each corner of each zone along with a sign that designates what activity will be conducted there. The signs may be laminated and attached to straps so they can be placed securely on the cones. Keep the zones flexible: change their size and activities every two to three weeks to keep the playground dynamic and exciting to children who like to see new activities and areas.

The following are a few examples of activities for playground zones.

1. Tennis beanbag station
2. Scoops and balls
3. Football passing
4. Tag games
5. Frisbee games
6. Long rope jumping
7. Hoop activities
8. Parachute games
9. Individual rope jumping

Use the School's "News Network" to Promote the Program

Most schools use a "news network," that is, a public address system or closed television system through which they make school-related announcements. Students often do the reporting. This network is an ideal medium for promoting the activity program and for announcing new activities offered in the playground zones. Announcements should be upbeat and fun to get children excited about participating.

Include a Learning Zone

Establish a zone that is always used for teaching new playground games. This learning zone should be a friendly place where students can expect to be taught how to play various games. In addition to the rules of games and sports, safety topics such as walking and bicycling safety may be taught in the zones.

Ideally, a new game should be presented every two weeks. This allows enough time for word of mouth to travel throughout the school and for many students to learn the game. The game being taught should be announced each day on the school news network.

Within the learning zone, use chalk, washable paint, cones, or other objects to designate lines and shapes related to the new activity. Use lines to serve as starting and finishing points and circles as standing places for children practicing simple passing and catching games.

Include a Social and a Low-Intensity Zone

We all experience times when we want to talk with friends, rest, or engage in activities at a gentler pace. So, even though the focus on the playground is to keep youngsters as active as possible, it is important to establish a zone for socializing and one for participating in a low-intensity activity such as shuffleboard or bowling. An obvious place for a social zone is an area where tables and benches are available. Students can do crafts, play board or card games, or just chat. Bear in mind that the social aspect of play is often a hook for getting youngsters more active.

One benefit of having many different zones on the playground is that it offers youngsters the opportunity to make choices. Unless they always select the social and low-intensity zones, offer children the freedom to pick and choose as they see fit. For children who do select the social zone frequently, you can gently suggest that they play in a more active zone for a while, then retire to the social zone for the last few minutes of recess.

Figure 8.3 Example of a walking and jogging trail sign. *Source: Deb Pangrazi, Mesa Public Schools, dlpangra@hotmail.com.*

Create a Walking/Jogging Trail

Establish a walking trail around the perimeter of the playground and place signs to clearly mark the route. It is important to place the signs where they are permanent and resistant to weather and vandalism. Mark off distances at regular intervals such as 1/8 mile or 200 meters. The markings make it easy for students to keep track of their progress and are especially helpful to students interested in accumulating mileage over a period of time. **Figure 8.3** shows an example of a walking/jogging trail sign.

Purchase Adequate Equipment

It is unrealistic to expect students to go outside and play without equipment. If you expect an increase in children's physical activity, then you must invest in adequate and appropriate equipment for the activity zones you create.

How do you pay for equipment? In many schools, each classroom teacher is given a small amount of money to purchase a small amount of equipment that children can take out to recess with them. This equipment is often quickly lost because no one has been assigned the responsibility for assuring that it is collected and returned to storage. A better alternative is for teachers to pool their money, purchase equipment that allows them to equip a number of zones, and appoint someone (e.g., a responsible student, a parent playground aide, or a teacher) to set out, collect, and return the equipment.

The following are points to consider when dealing with playground equipment.

1. Purchase equipment that is easy to identify as playground equipment. Equipment comes in many different colors, so it is easy to establish one color as playground zone equipment.
2. At the same time, purchase cones in a variety of colors to define the zones. Different-colored vinyl cones are excellent because they make it easy for children to identify different zone activities.
3. Identify someone who is responsible for seeing that the equipment is placed at the zones and put away at the end of outdoor activity. If an aide is not

available, use students to help monitor the equipment and move it on and off the playground.

4. When the zoning concept is first introduced on the playground, establish rules and consequences for keeping the equipment in the zones and returning it to storage (see Chapter 5). Establishing a new culture on the playground takes persistence. Maintain and convey high expectations that students will care for the equipment if they want to enjoy the privilege of using it.

5. Have a plan in place for returning equipment to storage at the end of each day. The storage area needs to be secure and accessible to the playground. One strategy is to store equipment in carts and place them in a locked storage closet inside the school building. On different weeks, different classes are responsible for wheeling out the carts and setting up the equipment. Another alternative is to use a small, lockable storage shed on the playground. Whatever the choice, the equipment must be secure or it will be damaged, lost, or stolen in a short time.

Establish an Activity Bulletin Board

Hang a bulletin board in a prominent place inside the school, and give students the option of recording their physical activity on a chart posted there. Make sure that participation in this activity tracking is optional: public posting of all students' performances may embarrass less-active students. Another use for an activity bulletin board is to announce upcoming games to be taught in the learning zones. Also use it to post photographs of children participating in playground activities, notices about after-school physical activities, team practice times, etc.

Supervise the Playground Actively

Too often, when teachers or aides are supposed to be supervising the playground, they actually spend the time chatting with each other or standing in one place without becoming actively involved themselves. Playground supervisors should be active, energetic, and enjoy encouraging students to participate in various activity zones. In addition to setting up the zones and managing the equipment dispersal, collection, and storage, supervisors should encourage activity, teach games, organize group activities, and make sure that the playground offers opportunities for both recreation and competition.

Encourage Activity

Many students are inactive during activity breaks. If asked why they're not participating, they will often reply, "There's no one to play with" or "There's nothing to do." In response, supervisors should be ready to teach inactive students simple games they can play with one or two friends. These games don't require that a team be formed, don't require sport skills, have simple rules, and are moderately to highly active. The *Gopher Sport Active and Healthy School Playground Game Card File* (see Web Resources) contains 40 such active playground games. Many of them are simple enough that older students can teach younger students how to play them, thus creating an active "school game culture."

Teach Playground Games

The supervisor is responsible for teaching playground games. The following are a few helpful tips:

- The games belong to the students. They can change the rules and modify them to make them more enjoyable. Ask them to agree on the rules before beginning play. If they want to modify the rules, all players must agree to the changes.
- Many of the games involve running. Since some students are faster runners, teach children a way to use a handicapping system so everybody has a chance of winning. Another alternative is to play the game in the speed walking mode rather than all-out running.
- Teach safe play. Play is only fun when nobody gets hurt. Set aside zones on the playground for youngsters, and align them so they run in the same direction and not in the path of other runners. Leave safety space between zones.
- Encourage youngsters to play games, but remember that not all students enjoy competition. Competition may be more enticing if players feel they are playing for fun rather than bragging rights.

Organize Group Activities

The lunchtime recess is usually the longest period of activity time students have during the school day. The supervisor can capitalize on this longer break by organizing and managing a variety of activities that are ideally suited to groups. These might include, for example, a walking club, a jogging club, a folk-dancing group, or any number of intramural sports teams.

Mix Recreation and Competition

Supervisors should ensure that the playground includes a mix of zones that offer opportunities for recreation and those that offer competition. This practice accommodates all students' needs and levels of ability.

Recreation emphasizes participation, often in lifestyle activities, so in a zone focused on a recreational game or sport, all children—no matter their ability level—are encouraged to play. Tournaments are avoided, and students play each game as an entity in itself. As noted in this chapter's News Clip, there is increasing evidence to support the effectiveness of promoting recreational as opposed to competitive physical activity.

In contrast, competition emphasizes practicing with peers, playing opponents who are equally skilled, avoiding mistakes as much as possible, identifying champions, and reinforcing winners and winning strategies. Thus, a zone dedicated to competition could offer a tournament.

When competition is the focus, it is the responsibility of the playground supervisor to ensure that teams have an equal chance of winning. One way to offer students a chance to play on a winning team is to change team players often. Short tournaments can be played and new teams formed each time a new tournament starts. Whatever method is used to form teams, the supervisor should maintain a balance of competition and should never allow students to select players themselves in such a fashion that the poorest player is chosen last. In playground games, all participants should feel welcome.

In New Approach, Physical Activity Trumps Sports

At Madison Junior High School in Naperville, Illinois, students wearing T-shirts proclaiming that they're "Gettin' Fit for Life!" work out on treadmills, stationary bikes, and elliptical machines. As they run, pedal, and flex to dance music, they check monitors and special watches to make sure they're staying in their target heart rate zone. If they don't, their grade suffers. It's all part of a program called PE4life that aims to give kids a foundation of skills and experiences that will keep them turned on to physical activity for life.

Ann Flannery, the president of PE4life, explains that in sports such as dodge ball, it's often the children who need exercise the most who are chosen last. Usually, the most athletic kids are the ones on the field, with everyone else just standing around. Other advocates claim that teaching sports skills is not a wise use of the limited time available for physical activity during the school day, since fewer than 3 percent of Americans continue to engage in a team sport after age 24.

These claims have some scientific support. Researchers at the University of Washington showed that overweight children lost more weight when they engaged in activities such as cycling and walking with pedometers than when they played sports during the same class period.

Source: Adapted from *The New York Times,* October 13, 2005, available at www.nytimes.com/2005/10/13/fashion/thursdaystyles/13Fitness.html.

News Clip

take action!

1. Check out the PE4life website (see Web Resources) and click on "Get Involved." Learn how you can become a Friend of PE4life, get your community involved, sign up for the PE4life newsletter, or communicate your concerns about children's physical activity to government leaders.

2. Interview the PE instructors at the elementary schools in your district. Find out how much they know about the benefits of lifestyle activity and active aerobics for kids and what they're doing to address childhood obesity. Summarize your findings and consider publishing them as an article in your local newspaper.

3. Follow the advice "Be the change you seek," and make a commitment to engage in at least 30 minutes of moderate to vigorous physical activity a day, at least five days a week. If you already do, encourage your kids or a friend to join you!

(Back to Class)

Imagine that Ms. Estes, from our chapter-opening scenario, is responsible for setting up activity zones in the school playground. Identify at least two zone activities she could offer that might appeal to a reluctant student such as Stacy.

Monitoring Physical Activity: The Case for Pedometers

All children can increase their current activity levels, so all children can experience success. But in order to see that success, they have to know where they're starting from and where they want to go. In short, they need to learn how to measure their baseline level of activity, set personal goals for improvement, monitor their increased activity, and evaluate their level of success. In all these steps, accuracy is vital, thus an objective measurement tool is very useful. That's where pedometers come in.

Pedometers are increasingly being used in schools to monitor physical activity. To appreciate the importance of using some type of monitoring device, ask yourself how active you were yesterday compared to the same day last week. You probably have no idea, nor would your students if asked the same question. When baseline values, goals, activities, and outcomes are not objectively measured, we cannot accurately determine if we are accumulating enough activity on a daily basis.

Pedometers are small, unobtrusive devices that are easily fastened to a belt or waistband. In their most basic form, they measure the number of steps a person takes. Of course, pedometers can't measure all types of activity, such as swimming, or activities on wheels, such as bicycling or in-line skating. Still, about 90 percent of the physical activity people accumulate is through walking, so counting steps is an effective way to measure how active a person is throughout the day. It's not surprising, therefore, that using pedometers to monitor children's physical activity levels is now an accepted instructional methodology (Beighle, Pangrazi, and Vincent, 2001; Crouter et al., 2003; Kilanowski, Consalvi, and Epstein, 1999).

A number of pedometers on the market not only count steps but perform other functions as well. Some can measure the distance covered and the calories expended if the child's stride length and weight are entered. Some newer pedometers can measure activity time: whenever the child moves, the pedometer starts accumulating time. When the child stops moving, the timing function stops. Pressing a button reveals the total hours and minutes of activity time accumulated throughout the day. A measurement of time spent in activity can be more valid than a step count in indicating overall physical activity level because it is not dependent on children taking steps of a minimum length.

Help Students Set Realistic Goals

There are two basic ways to set pedometer goals for your students: you can apply a single standard to everyone or have students determine their personal baseline and set their own goals accordingly. Many schools use the **single-standard goal**. For example, an often-referenced single standard is 10,000 steps per day (Hatano, 1993). It was originally used for cardiovascular disease prevention but is now much more widely applied. An often-cited goal for youth is 11,000 steps per day for girls and 13,000 steps per day for boys. This standard is used for the PALA (President's Council on Physical Fitness and Sports, 2007), which is awarded to students who meet these daily standards over a six-week period.

A basic assumption of the single-standard goal is that one goal can fit all students, regardless of chronological age, physical development, gender, or health. It thus fails to take into account the substantial individual differences among children and so can turn off students who need activity the most. For example, if a goal of 10,000 steps is applied to everyone, a predisposition to be active may make it much easier for some students to reach that goal, whereas others may find it next to impossible because they are naturally less active.

How many steps *should* be set as a standard? Should the goal be set high enough to provide a proven health-related benefit? If you accumulate 10,000 steps, is there any point in moving beyond this threshold? If you accumulate 4,000 steps each day, does 10,000 steps seem an impossible goal? As you can see, setting one goal that is appropriate across a large population is a difficult proposition.

The approach recommended here is the **baseline and goal-setting technique** (Pangrazi, Beighle, and Sidman, 2007). The first step in this technique is for each child to identify his or her average daily activity level (baseline). Research suggests that four days of monitoring provide adequate data (Trost et al., 2000). Middle and upper elementary children can incorporate math into this step by calculating the average of their four-day step counts (or activity time). Baseline data are then entered in a chart similar to the one shown in **Figure 8.4**.

After the baseline level of activity has been established, each individual has a reference point for setting a personal goal. The personal goal is established by taking the baseline activity level and adding 10 percent more steps (or time in whole minutes) to that level. For example, assume a student has a baseline activity level of 6,000 steps per day. Her personal goal for the next two weeks would be 6,000 steps plus 600 more steps for a total of 6,600 steps. If she reaches the goal for a majority of the days during this two-week period, another 10 percent is added to the goal, and the process repeated. For most people, a top goal of 4,000 to 6,000 steps above their baseline level is a reasonable expectation. Using the example of 6,000 baseline steps here, a final goal of 10,000 to 12,000 steps would be the goal.

This baseline and goal-setting approach takes into consideration the fact that all individuals are unique. It gradually increases personal goals so that they seem achievable to even inactive individuals. Most children are curious to discover their baseline levels of activity, and this can be a good way to motivate them to increase their current activity levels.

Step 1: Calculate Your Baseline Step Counts

Name:

Date:

Day 1 Step Count:

Day 2 Step Count:

Day 3 Step Count:

Day 4 Step Count:

Total Step Count: divided by 4 equals   . This number is your average **baseline step count** and will be used to determine your personal activity goal.

Step 2: Calculate Your Step Count Goal

The next step is to calculate your personal step count goal. A couple of examples are shown below. The first person discovered that she had a baseline step count of 4,000 steps. After 10 weeks her step count goal increases to 6,000 steps. For the person who has a baseline of 6,000 steps, her step count goal will increase to 9,000 steps by the final weeks. Thus, both individuals will increase their number of steps by one-third.

Baseline	Personal Goal (10 percent of your baseline plus your baseline)	Weeks	Total Step Counts
4,000 steps	$4,000 \times 0.10 = 400$; plus $4,000 = 4,400$ Every two weeks thereafter, the goal will be increased by 400 steps.	1 & 2 3 & 4 5 & 6 7 & 8 9 & 10	4,400 4,800 5,200 5,600 6,000
6,000 steps	$6,000 \times 0.10 = 600$; plus $6,000 = 6,600$ Every two weeks thereafter, the goal will be increased by 600 steps.	1 & 2 3 & 4 5 & 6 7 & 8 9 & 10	6,600 7,200 7,800 8,400 9,000
	$\times 0.10 =$; plus $=$ Every two weeks thereafter, the goal will be increased by steps.	1 & 2 3 & 4 5 & 6 7 & 8 9 & 10	

Figure 8.4 A log for setting personal activity goals using pedometers.

Teach Students About Pedometer Placement and Accuracy

The validity and reliability of pedometers have been confirmed by a number of researchers (Crouter et al., 2003; Schneider et al., 2003). That said, proper placement is essential to accuracy.

Two common placement points will provide accurate measurements for the majority of students. The first is at the waistline, directly in line with the midpoint of the front of the thigh and kneecap. The second point is at the waistline, on the side of the body over the hip. However, about 20 to 30 percent of users find that they have to establish a point that is unique to them. Therefore, students first need to learn the placement point where the pedometer measures accurately. Use the following protocol to help students find an accurate placement point.

1. Place the pedometer on the waistband in line with the midpoint of the thigh and kneecap. The pedometer must be parallel with the body and upright. If it is angled in any direction, it will not measure accurately. Teach students to open their pedometer (without removing it from the waistband) and reset it to zero steps. Have them walk at their normal cadence while counting the number of steps they are taking. Ask them to stop immediately when 30 steps are reached. Open the pedometer and check the step count. If the step count is within plus or minus 3 steps of 30, this placement is an accurate location for the pedometer. If the step count is less accurate, move the pedometer to the side position over the hip. If neither position is accurate, try step 2.

2. Move the pedometer on the waistband so it is positioned slightly closer to either the belly button or the hip. Open the pedometer, clear it, and take 30 steps (as described in step 1). Again, if the step count is within plus or minus 3 steps of 30, this new placement is accurate, and the child should always position the pedometer in that position. If not, try another placement and repeat the step test.

3. If it is still difficult to find an accurate measuring position, consider the following. Pedometers must remain in an upright plane (with the pedometer display perpendicular to the floor and parallel to the body) in order to accurately register step counts. Attaching the pedometer to loose-fitting clothing will reduce accuracy because the clothing will absorb the slight vertical force that occurs with each step. Excess body fat may also tilt the pedometer away from the body and reduce accuracy; in this case, placement at waist level behind the hip and on the back (where less body fat accumulates) may offer an accurate measurement point. Another alternative is to use a Velcro belt to ensure that the pedometer is maintained in an upright position. Placing the Velcro belt above the waist may be necessary to find a position where the pedometer remains in the vertical plane. Repeat the 30-step process until an accurate placement has been identified. One caveat is in order here: if Velcro belts are used, they should be used on all students in the class to avoid embarrassing any youngster.

Back to Class

Although she was not using pedometers, in what sense did Ms. Estes apply a single-standard goal to all of her students?

Using Pedometers in a Class Setting

There are a number of steps to work through once the decision to use pedometers has been made.

Acquiring Pedometers

The first step is to acquire a set of pedometers to use in class. Many schools have been successful in asking parent-teacher groups to fund pedometers. Create interest by making a presentation to the group and asking for support. Another approach is a "shareware" program in which pedometer companies sell pedometers to schools at a reduced price. Schools, in turn, sell the pedometers to parents and others to raise money. Selling pedometers is a much more healthful fund-raising activity than selling candy or cookies.

Introducing Pedometers to Students

Children are typically fascinated with pedometers, so it's important to plan for their enthusiasm to avoid disruptions in class time, breakage, and other problems. Using the following schedule can help you overcome common problems in the high-interest/novelty period. For the first six to eight weeks of school, use the pedometers for only short periods of time and only in the classroom. During this time period, children can handle the pedometers to gain familiarity with how they work and to check how active they are during an activity break.

Once the novelty wears off, have students wear their pedometers throughout the school day. Since students will be wearing the pedometers during recess, when attending special classes, and at lunch, you'll have an opportunity to evaluate whether they are behaving responsibly with their pedometers. If they lose their pedometer or break it, they may lose the privilege of further use.

After three or four months of use within the school setting, allow students to use their pedometers to carry out 24-hour monitoring. It may be necessary to limit 24-hour monitoring to students who have demonstrated responsibility for their pedometers. Students record their activity and reset the pedometers each morning at the same time. In most cases, it will be best to record activity Tuesday through Friday mornings because the chance of pedometers being lost increases when students take them home over the weekend.

Once the pedometers become a regular part of each student's lifestyle, fewer pedometers will be lost or misplaced. Many schools establish a replacement policy before giving students the privilege of taking the pedometers out of the school environment. Typically, the school sends a letter home

Figure 8.5 A method of storing pedometers.

explaining the activity program and the use of pedometers. The letter also specifies that if a pedometer is lost, it must be replaced for a fee.

Establishing Handling Procedures

Using pedometers requires teaching your class exactly what you expect of them. You'll quickly become frustrated with your students and avoid using the pedometers if you don't establish a standard procedure that students are to follow. In addition, if you fail to articulate clear rules for using, returning, and storing the pedometers, you will have a high rate of loss. The following is an example of a procedure that minimizes pedometer handling time and reduces class disruption.

Number each of the pedometers and store no more than six of them in a single container (Figure 8.5). Make sure that you have the same number of pedometers in each container so it is easy to see when a pedometer is missing (and which student has it).

Teach students to pick up their assigned pedometer first thing in the morning and put it on while moving back to their desks. When all students have their pedometers on, have them reset their pedometers (Figure 8.6). Class then begins as usual. At the end of the day, students remove their pedometers, put them back into the proper container, record their steps or activity time on the sheet next to their container, and prepare for dismissal.

Establish the following two rules for using pedometers: (1) "You shake it, I take it" and (2) "You take it off your waist, I put it away." Emphasize that shaking the pedometer to increase the step count is inappropriate behavior and that the consequence is loss of the pedometer for the day. In addition, if a student takes his or her pedometer off, the privilege to use it that day is removed. This rule is necessary to prevent students from taking off their pedometers and opening them during the normal routine. Also, the odds of pedometers being dropped and broken increase dramatically when students remove them from the waistband.

Suggested Pedometer Activities

Pedometers are valuable tools for hypothesis testing. Students can be challenged to answer questions such as, "Are students more active than parents?" or "Do you take more steps when you march down the hall or when you walk down the hall?" A further idea is to have students modify or invent a game based on pedometer-determined steps. Another use for the pedometer is to help students determine their leisure-time physical activity and establish personal goals for improvement (as described earlier).

The following activities illustrate a number of other ways to use pedometers in a school setting. They are explained in greater detail in the resource book *Pedometer Power* (Pangrazi, Beighle, and Sidman, 2007).

Figure 8.6 Students resetting their pedometers.

How Many Steps Does It Take? (Estimation)

Measure off a distance that is exactly 1/8 or 1/4 mile in length. Students put on their pedometers, clear them at the starting line, and walk at a normal pace to the end of the distance. Depending on the distance they walked, they multiply the number of steps they accumulated by eight or four. That is the number of steps it takes them to walk 1 mile.

Moving Across the State or United States

After performing "How Many Steps Does It Take?," challenge students to figure out how far they have traveled across a state or U.S. map. As they reach different checkpoints, discuss terrain, weather, local foods, industries, various cultural sites, etc.

Active or Inactive

Students participate in a variety of active games and try to predict which activities are highly active and which are less active. An enjoyable related activity is to have students try to guess how many steps they will take in the activity. Over time, they will begin to understand the activity value of different sports and games.

Safe Walk to School

Walking to school can add 1,000 to 2,000 steps each day to a student's activity level. This is an effective activity for teaching students about ways to walk that are safe, that increase the distance covered and steps taken, and that avoid traffic.

School Steps Contest

This is a schoolwide contest with all classes participating. Count the steps of all students in each class, as well as those of the teachers, then divide the total by the number of participants. Finding the average number of steps for the entire class makes this a group competition and prevents embarrassment to students who are less active. Another tactic for preventing embarrassment is to maintain children's anonymity. Have the students place their step counts anonymously on a tally sheet or have children pick a code name (an active animal, for example, greyhound, cheetah, etc.) from a hat and tally counts beside the code names.

The President's Council on Physical Fitness and Sports sponsors the PALA (Web Resources section), which has a website that allows students to log their activity time or steps. If students accumulate 60 minutes or 11,000 (girls) to 13,000 steps (boys) for most of the days of the week for six weeks, they earn the PALA. This award looks similar to the Presidential Fitness Award patch except that it is square instead of round. If 35 percent of the students in a school earn the PALA two or more times during the year, the school becomes an Active Lifestyle Model School. Such schools receive a certificate and are recognized on the website.

Back to Class

Ms. Estes was working with her students on subtraction. How might she have used pedometers to integrate subtraction with physical activity?

Promoting Walking: The Real Lifetime Activity

Walking forms the basis for nearly all lifestyle physical activity. Therefore, one of your most important goals in increasing your students' level of physical activity is to help them experience the joy of walking. Allied to this goal is teaching the many benefits of being a walker.

Benefits of Walking

Currently, the American College of Sports Medicine is promoting a new initiative, "Exercise Is Medicine," to teach the public the health benefits of physical activity. Walking, in particular, has so many health benefits that, if it could be put into the form of a pill to be swallowed, it would immediately become one of the most popular medicines on the market. These benefits include the following.

- *Weight management.* When combined with a healthful diet, walking is a lifetime approach to weight management. Proper weight management decreases the risks of many hypokinetic diseases such as type 2 diabetes, heart disease, stroke, cancer, and osteoarthritis. We discuss this important benefit in more detail shortly.
- *Blood pressure management.* Physical activity strengthens the heart and makes it more efficient so that it pumps more blood with less effort. This results in less pressure on the arteries and vital organs. Walking ap-pears to be as effective as some medications in reducing high blood pressure.
- *Boosting high-density lipoproteins.* High-density lipoproteins, or HDLs, help reduce low-density lipoproteins (LDLs) or destructive cholesterol. LDL cholesterol increases plaque buildup in the arteries, which is a major cause of heart attacks.
- *Reducing the risk of type 2 diabetes.* Type 2 diabetes is increasing at an alarming rate among young people. People at high risk of diabetes can cut their risk in half by combining walking with a balanced diet and a 5 to 7 percent decrease in weight.
- *Decreasing the risk of heart disease.* Three hours of walking a week is associated with a 30 to 40 percent lower risk of heart disease in women.

In addition to these health benefits, walking has a few advantages over some other forms of exercise. For instance, it does not require special equipment or a specific location, such as a gym or playing field. Neither does it require good weather: mall walking has become popular in many snowy regions. Walking also has a low injury rate. Finally, students will walk when they reach adulthood, probably more than any other activity.

Walking and Weight Management

Currently, it is estimated that over 17 percent of American youth are overweight (National Center for Health Statistics, 2007). It is also estimated that 70 percent of overweight adolescents grow up to be overweight adults; thus, it is critical to help elementary school children learn to maintain a healthful energy intake and increase their physical activity. Unfortunately, over the last 10 years, children's energy expenditure through physical activity has decreased while their energy intake has increased.

Weight management is achieved by balancing energy intake and expenditure; people who are successful in maintaining proper body weight have usually learned to maintain a balance between their caloric intake and their physical activity. A number of studies show that when a weight loss program addresses only caloric intake, the pounds that participants lose in the program are typically regained as soon as the intervention stops. There is no question that restricting diet in a highly controlled setting will result in weight loss. However, if this weight loss is not coupled with a new and more active lifestyle, success in weight management will be short lived.

Walking is an ideal activity for overweight students. It is easy on the joints, doesn't overly stress the cardiovascular system, and is not painful to perform. The old adage "No pain, no gain" makes no sense for these students, many of whom have turned off to physical activity because of negative past experiences. Students who have been forced to engage in inappropriately vigorous physical activity will usually push back to a sedentary lifestyle when they become old enough to make personal decisions. With kindness and sincerity, you can encourage your overweight students to choose walking and, especially when coupled with use of a pedometer, rekindle in them the joy of physical activity.

A practical question often asked is "Does walking really make a difference in weight management?" The answer is yes. However, it is easy to eat more calories than it is possible to expend. The number of calories burned during walking depends on a number of factors, the most important of which are the speed of walking and the person's body size. Thus, children burn significantly fewer calories than do adults walking for the same amount of time. Table 8.3 shows the number of calories burned during a 30-minute walk based on body weight.

Assume an 80-pound student takes a 30-minute walk at a moderate pace and burns about 86 calories. Wanting to reward himself, this student decides to eat a typical-size candy bar. Without looking at the nutrition label, the student eats the candy bar and quickly ingests 300 calories—a net gain of over 200 calories. In general terms, about 3,500 calories equals a pound of weight gained or lost, depending on the energy intake and expenditure balance. Within two to three weeks, if this student continues to walk 30 minutes a day but

Table 8.3   Approximate Calories Burned in 30 Minutes of Walking

Body Weight in Pounds	Approximate Calories Burned
40	43
50	54
60	64
70	75
80	86
90	96
100	107
110	118
120	129
130	139
140	150
150	161
160	172

adds a candy bar to his normal food intake, he will gain a pound of weight. This shows why it is necessary to keep an eye on both physical activity and diet. It also illustrates how easy it is to gain weight, even when we are increasing our physical activity. On the other hand, most people don't eat while they are engaged in an activity—or for a while afterward. Just being active may make it easier to decrease caloric expenditure.

Recently, walking (or trekking) poles have come into vogue. Similar to ski poles, they have been used for years in the Scandinavian countries. Walking poles may be a boon for fifth- and sixth-grade students who are overweight, as research has shown that 25 to 30 percent more calories are burned when walking with them as compared to walking without them (Church, Earnest, and Morss, 2002). Using the poles increases heart rate by 10 to 15 beats per minute and works more than 90 percent of the body's muscle mass. Additionally, the poles help absorb some of the impact on the knees and ankles, which results in an increase in upper body strength and a decrease in hip, knee, and foot injuries. Thus, using walking poles might reduce joint injuries in overweight children and help all students realize greater results from their walking (see Web Resources).

Back to Class

In our chapter-opening scenario, Ms. Estes had all of her students stretch, jog, perform jumping jacks, and run. Explain why these activities were more challenging for Stacy than for many of her classmates. Now identify the advantages of a walking activity for Stacy and other children who are moderately to severely overweight.

Recommendations for Walking

One of the things that make walking such a valuable skill for health maintenance is its simplicity. Any amount of walking is beneficial, but to receive the best health results, children should walk at least five times per week for 30 minutes. The 30 minutes can be accumulated in three bouts of at least 10 minutes. There are only a few things that students need to be taught to achieve maximum benefit.

1. They should walk at a brisk pace with a comfortable stride and a good arm swing.
2. Their walking pace should allow them to carry on a conversation without difficulty. If students find they can't walk and talk at the same time, encourage them to slow the pace slightly. For most youth in school, this will not be a problem, and the opportunity to socialize may be more important than the actual walk itself. The most important outcome is that they enjoy the experience and realize the benefits of walking.

3. All things being equal, the more steps students take in a specified time, the higher the intensity of their walk. In the upper grades, students are able to calculate the intensity of their physical activity.

Implementing a School Walking Program

When initiating a walking program, make sure to choose an area where all of your students are in full view, such as an outdoor track or field or inside the gym. When you're confident that your students have become comfortable with walking, provide them with more variety and distance. For example, with approval of the administration, set up one or more walking courses around the school's neighborhood. Map them out and write precise directions and mileage for each route. Before allowing students to follow them, drive along each route and check that each appears entirely safe; for example, there are sidewalks or wide shoulders alongside the roads, there is low traffic, and there are no snarling dogs, etc. In addition, teach and drill students in the following safety guidelines:

- Always use the sidewalk. If a sidewalk is not available, walk on the left side of the roadway facing traffic.
- Always walk in a small group. If someone is injured or needs help, one member of the group can return to the school for help.
- If you meet an aggressive dog, don't run. Because running from aggressive dogs only makes the problem worse, teach students to stop, face them, and give them a stern, "No!"
- Always sign out with your name and the path on which you will be walking. If a group has failed to return by the required time, it will be much easier to track its members.
- Always wear walking or running shoes. Encourage parents to purchase shoes for their youngsters with reflective tape built into them, which makes it much easier for automobile drivers to see them.
- Drink plenty of water. Whether it is cold outside or hot, students should drink 8 ounces of water 15 minutes before the walk. If it is hot and dry, they should drink 6 ounces every 15 to 20 minutes during the walk. At the end of the walk, they should drink another 8 to 16 ounces of water. Relying on the thirst signal as a reminder to drink is unwise, because the sensation of thirstiness usually comes after the body is in need of water.
- In cold weather, wear layers. Teach students to wear three or more layers of lighter clothing rather than one heavy layer so that they can remove a layer if they get hot. Students should wear a hat, gloves, and scarf, if necessary.
- In hot weather, wear loose, light-colored clothing, a hat, and sunglasses.
- Apply sunscreen. Teach students to apply sunscreen whenever they will be outside for more than a few minutes, because ultraviolet light from the sun causes skin damage.

Also, if students have a serious health problem, make sure the school nurse clears them to participate in the walking program. If the nurse requires them to wear a medical tag in case of an accident requiring emergency care, make sure they wear it.

Suggested Walking Activities

I Spy

On their walk, students take along a scorecard that has a challenge on it. For example, a scorecard may state, "Identify as many different makes of car as possible." Or, "List the different birds and animals you see on your walk." Or, "Find at least two trapezoids and two pentagons on your walk." Different cards may be designed to create varying challenges. When the students complete their walks, discuss the items they have identified.

Know Your Community

Have the class take different walks and identify the different types of businesses and professional offices along their route. Or, in a variation of the "I Spy" activity, ask students to spy particular businesses or other locations.

Learn About Your Friend

Give students a series of questions on a card that will help them get to know a group member better. The goal is for them to walk and discover new things about a friend while moving (**Figure 8.7**).

Figure 8.7 Walking in pairs gives children a chance to get better acquainted.

Mixed-Up Walks

For limited amounts of time, add some walking variations (e.g., backward; sideways slide with a left shoulder lead, then a right shoulder lead; skipping; galloping; marching) (**Figure 8.8**). For example, have students start with backward walking for one minute, then regular walking for one minute, then skipping for one minute, then regular walking, and so on. Tasks assigned can be different types of movement or varying challenges such as, "Complete your walk by making 10 left turns on your route." The location of where students make a turn must be documented.

Interval Walk

Set up a walking circuit on a football field, in a gym, etc., that includes stretching and strength activities at designated stations, such as at each corner. Posters at the stations instruct students to do a standing stretch for 30 seconds, then do a sitting stretch, then do some sit ups, then some push ups, etc.

Cross-Country Walking

Set up a cross-country walking race between two or more teams from your class. Try to balance the teams as evenly as possible in terms of athletic students versus sedentary students. Design a safe course with a nice variety of walking areas, such as through a park, beside a pond, etc. Draw and distribute a map of the course and discuss it with students to make sure they understand the route. Ideally, walk

Figure 8.8 Students marching to a beat.

the route with the class prior to the competition. During the race, students walk as quickly as possible along the route. At the finish line, they receive a number indicating their place. The team with the lowest number of points is the winner. This is a competitive activity, but it can be approached in a positive and fun manner.

Walking Golf

Set up a walking "golf" tournament around the gym, a field, or another large space. Use hula hoops for holes, cones for the tees, and a tennis ball for each student to throw. Students stand at the tee and try to toss the ball into the "hole," then walk to the ball, retrieve it, and try again. Students use a scorecard to keep track of the number of throws made at each hole.

Treasure Hunt

Set up a walking course with a set of clues leading to 10 sites. At the sites, tape a set of words that can later be arranged in a particular order to spell a popular saying or jingle. Examples of clues to follow on a playing field could include "a place for extra points on the south side," "a place for H_2O," "fans sit here on the west side," "stand under this for the score of the game," and "a place for trash."

Scavenger Hunt

Before students leave for a walk outdoors, give each group a list of things to find on their route, for example, "an acorn, a feather, and a triangular grey pebble." Or, have the children wear gloves, give each group a small trash bag, and ask them to collect any trash they find along their route.

Poker Walk

Set out several decks of cards at various locations around the teaching area. Students walk to an area and pick up one card without looking at it, then immediately walk to a different area and pick up another card. They walk to as many areas as possible within a time limit and then look at their cards and add up their points. (Score 10 points for face cards and 11 points for aces.) Ensure students don't return to the same area twice by using decks of cards with different designs and allowing only one card of each design. Give a prize for high- and low-point totals.

Weekly Walking Calendar

Each week give students a five-day calendar that stipulates different types of things to do on their walks. For example, tasks might include the following: Monday: Walk with a friend; Tuesday: Walk with walking poles; Wednesday: During your walk, stop and stretch periodically; Thursday: Walk 15 minutes in one direction and return to the starting spot by retracing your path; Friday: Walk using a pedometer to count your steps.

Off-Campus Walks

Students can gain extra credit by taking walks outside the school day. This can be an excellent opportunity for them to use pedometers to track their walks. They can record their steps and activity time and report back to class on both measures.

Walk to School

Children who walk to school accumulate an average of 2,000 more steps per day than children who are transported. So, it's not surprising that many organizations have developed programs encouraging children to walk to school. Perhaps the best known is *Kidswalk* (see Web Resources), which was developed by the Centers for Disease Control and Prevention. Materials, PowerPoint presentations, and training guides are available at the website.

Chapter Summary

Understanding Physical Activity

- *Physical activity* is defined as bodily movement that is produced by the contraction of skeletal muscle and that substantially increases energy expenditure. It is a general term that encompasses the full range and process of moving, as well as all of movement's different forms, such as exercise, sports, labor, and leisure activity.

- A metabolic equivalent (MET) is a ratio assigned to activities that identifies how greatly the activities increase an adult's metabolic rate above resting rate. When considering an activity's MET, bear in mind that children expend more energy than adults both at rest and during activity.

- Activities of 3 METs or fewer are light; 4–6 METs indicates moderate activity; activities that expend more than 6 METs are considered vigorous.

- Physical activity can be beneficial even if it is moderate and discontinuous, performed in several short bouts rather than in one continuous session.

Recommendations for Children's Physical Activity

- The National Association for Sport and Physical Education (NASPE) has developed activity guidelines for elementary school children that call for 60 minutes or more of age-appropriate physical activity on all or most days of the week. Activity should be intermittent rather than continuous.

- Children should participate in several bouts of activity, each lasting 15 minutes or more, every day.

- Activities should be varied to help children achieve health, wellness, fitness, and performance benefits.

- Extended periods of inactivity are discouraged, especially during daytime hours.

- The Physical Activity Pyramid is a fun visual tool you can use to teach children how much and what type of activity they need. It includes six categories of activities arranged into four levels that convey their relative importance and thus their suggested frequency.

- Level 1 includes lifestyle activities, such as walking the dog or riding a bike to a friend's house, that children should engage in every day.

- Level 2 includes active aerobic activities that should be engaged in three to five times a week. For children, intermittent aerobic activities are more appropriate, such as a game of tag, kickball, tumbling, etc. Also in level 2 are active sports and recreational activities such as tennis, soccer, etc.

- Level 3 includes flexibility and strength-training/endurance exercises. These exercises should be engaged in two to three times a week, but kindergarten through fourth-grade children usually do not need formal sessions. Upper-elementary-grade children can benefit from stretching and strength-development exercises that require them to move and lift their body weight.

- Level 4 is rest and inactivity. Although some sedentary activities are not detrimental to health, inactivity as a lifestyle choice is discouraged.

Structuring the Playground to Increase Physical Activity

- Post a sign identifying the playground as the activity zone, and divide the area into zones for learning, low-intensity play, socializing, walking and jogging, and sports and games. Purchase adequate equipment and establish a procedure for collecting, storing, and securing it at the end of each day. The most important responsibilities of playground supervisors are to encourage children to be active, teach them games, organize group activities, and make sure that the playground offers opportunities for both recreation and competition.

Monitoring Physical Activity: The Case for Pedometers

- Pedometers are small, unobtrusive devices that, when fastened to a belt or waistband, measure the number of steps the wearer takes. Some also measure distance covered, calories expended, or time spent in activity.

- Rather than applying a single step-count goal to all children, have each child determine his or her personal baseline and then set a personal goal of an increase of 10 percent during the next two weeks. If that goal is achieved, then the student sets a new goal of another increase of 10 percent.

- Research supports the accuracy of pedometers in measuring steps taken; however, proper placement is essential to accuracy.

- When introducing pedometers to a class, plan for children's curiosity and enthusiasm by taking a gradual approach. Establish procedures for handling and storing the pedometers and rules and consequences for inappropriate behavior.

Incorporate pedometers into a variety of games, such as "Moving Across the State," as well as activities involving the whole school, such as a school step contest.

Promoting Walking: The Real Lifetime Activity

Walking forms the basis for nearly all lifestyle physical activity.

The benefits of walking include weight management, blood pressure management, increased HDL, reduced risk of type 2 diabetes, and a reduced risk of heart disease.

Walking is an ideal activity for overweight students because it is easy on the joints, doesn't overly stress the cardiovascular system, and is not painful to perform.

Children should walk at least five times per week for 30 minutes. These minutes can be accumulated in two or three sessions. Children should walk at a brisk pace that allows them to carry on a conversation without difficulty.

Implementing a school walking program can help increase students' level of daily activity. Safety considerations are important, and students with health problems should be cleared for participation by the school nurse beforehand. Activities children can do on their walk include a game of "I Spy" or a variety of other games, learning about a classmate or their community, and varying the walk.

Children who walk to school accumulate an average of 2,000 more steps per day than children who are transported. One well-known walking program, called *Kidswalk,* has been developed by the Centers for Disease Control and Prevention.

Review Questions

Content Review

1. How many minutes of physical activity does NASPE recommend children engage in daily, and for how many days each week? Should continuous vigorous activity be expected of children?

2. Identify the levels of the Physical Activity Pyramid and the types of activities prescribed at each level. How much time should be spent in each type of activity on a weekly basis?

3. Identify the most important responsibilities of a playground supervisor.

4. Summarize the steps in the procedure for establishing a personal step-count goal.

5. Summarize at least four health benefits of walking.

Real World

1. In a strategy meeting addressing the problem of overweight among children at your school, you propose that the school approach the PTA for funding pedometers for a school walking program. Another teacher shakes her head dismissively. "Forget it. I tried pedometers with my third-grade class a couple of years ago, and it was a disaster. In the first couple of weeks, they couldn't keep their hands off them, and I barely got any teaching done for the distraction. Then, by the time the novelty wore off, they'd lost half of them. They're not worth the hassle." How might you respond?

2. At the same meeting, another teacher proposes beginning each school day with all of the students (K–5) in assembly in the school gym and having the PE teacher lead them in five minutes of calisthenics, five minutes of stretching, and five minutes of running. Would you support this proposal? Why or why not?

What About You?

If you do not currently own a pedometer, purchase or borrow one. Record your daily step counts for the next four days, and log them as shown in Figure 8.4. Then calculate and log your baseline and your new step-count goal. Finally, log your step counts for the next two weeks.

Were you surprised to discover how many steps you take on an average day? _____

_____

Why or why not? _____

_____

How successful were you in reaching your new step-count goal? _____

_____

Was it easier or harder than you'd anticipated? _____

_____

References and Suggested Readings

Beals, K.A. (2003). Addressing an epidemic: Treatment strategies for youth obesity. *ACSM Fit Society Page,* Spring 2003, 9–11.

Beighle, A., Pangrazi, R.P., and Vincent, S.D. (2001). Pedometers, physical activity, and accountability. *Journal of Physical Education, Recreation & Dance,* 72(9), 16–19.

Church, T.S., Earnest, C.P., and Morss, G.M. (2002). Field testing of physiological responses associated with Nordic walking. *Research Quarterly for Exercise and Sport,* 73(3), 296–300.

Corbin, C.B., and Pangrazi, R.P. (1992). Are American children and youth fit? *Research Quarterly for Exercise and Sport,* 63(2), 96–106.

Crouter, S.C., Schneider, P.L., Karabulut, M., and Bassett, D.R., Jr. (2003). Validity of 10 electronic pedometers for measuring steps, distance, and energy cost. *Medicine and Science in Sports and Exercise,* 35(8), 1455–1460.

Decker, J., and Mize, M. (2002). *Walking games and activities.* Champaign, IL: Human Kinetics.

Epstein, L.H., Valoski, A.M., Vara, L.S., McCurley, J., Wisniewski, L., Kalarchian, M.A., Klein, K.R., and Shrager, L.R. (1995). Effects of decreasing sedentary behavior and increasing activity on weight change in obese children. *Health Psychology,* 14(2), 109–115.

Gordon Larsen, P., McMurray, R. G., and Popkin, B.M. (2000). Determinants of adolescent physical activity and inactivity patterns. *Pediatrics,* 105, E83.

Harrell, J.S., McMurray, R.G., Baggett, C.D., Pennell, M.L., Pearce, P.F., and Bangdiwala, S.I. (2005). Energy costs of physical activities in children and adolescents. *Medicine and Science in Sports and Exercise,* 37(2), 329–336.

Hatano, Y. (1993). Use of the pedometer for promoting daily walking exercise. *International Council for Health, Physical Education and Recreation,* 29, 4–28.

Kilanowski, C.K., Consalvi, A.R., and Epstein, L.H. (1999). Validation of an electronic pedometer for measurement of physical activity in children. *Pediatric Exercise Science,* 11, 63–68.

Morgan, C.F., Jr., Pangrazi, R.P., and Beighle, A. (2003). Using pedometers to promote physical activity in physical education. *Journal of Physical Education, Recreation & Dance,* 74(7), 33–38.

National Association for Sport and Physical Education. (2004). *Physical activity for children: A statement of guidelines* (2nd ed.). Reston, VA: National Association for Sport and Physical Education.

National Center for Health Statistics. (2007). FastStats A to Z: Overweight. Available at www.cdc.gov/nchs/fastats/overwt.htm.

Pangrazi, R.P. (2006). *Active & healthy schools playground activities card sets.* Owatonna, MN: Gopher Sport.

Pangrazi, R.P. (2006). *Active & healthy schools program: A road map to make your school environment active & healthy.* Owatonna, MN: Gopher Sport.

Pangrazi, R.P., Beighle, A., and Sidman, C.L. (2007). *Pedometer power: Using pedometers in school and community* (2nd ed.). Champaign, IL: Human Kinetics.

Pate, R.R., Pratt, M., Blair, S.N., Haskell, W.L., Macera, C.A., Bouchard, C., Buchner, D., Ettinger, W., Heath, G.W., and King, A.C. (1995). Physical activity and public health. *Journal of the American Medical Association,* 273(5), 402–407.

Plowman, S.A. (1993). Physical fitness and healthy low back function. *Physical Activity and Fitness Research Digest,* 1(3), 1–8.

President's Council on Physical Fitness and Sports. (2007). *The president's challenge handbook.* Washington, DC: President's Council on Physical Fitness and Sports.

Sallis, J.F. (1991). Self-report measures of children's physical activity. *Journal of School Health,* 61, 215–219.

Sallis, J.F., and Patrick, K. (1994). Physical activity guidelines for adolescents: Consensus statement. *Pediatric Exercise Science,* 6(4), 302–314.

Schneider, P.L., Crouter, S.E., Lukajic, O., and Bassett, D.R., Jr. (2003). Accuracy and reliability of 10 pedometers for measuring steps over a 400-m walk. *Medicine and Science in Sports and Exercise,* 35(10), 1779–1784.

Shaw, J.M., and Snow-Harter, C. (1995). Osteoporosis and physical activity. *Physical Activity and Fitness Research Digest,* 2(3), 1–8.

Trost, S.G., Pate, R.R., Freedson, P.S., Sallis, J.F., and Taylor, W.C. (2000). Using objective physical activity measures with youth: How many days of monitoring are needed? *Medicine and Science in Sports and Exercise,* 32(2), 426–431.

U.S. Department of Health and Human Services. (1996). *Physical activity and health: A report of the Surgeon General.* Atlanta, GA: Centers for Disease Control and Prevention, National Center for Chronic Disease Prevention and Health Promotion.

U.S. Department of Health and Human Services. (2000). *Healthy people 2010. National health promotion and disease objectives.* Washington, DC: U.S. Government Printing Office.

Vincent, S.D., and Pangrazi, R.P. (2002). Does reactivity exist in children when measuring activity levels with pedometers? *Pediatric Exercise Science,* 14(1), 56–63.

Web Resources

AccuSTEP10,000.org:
www.accustep10000.org
Active and Healthy Schools Program:
www.activeandhealthyschools.com
America On The Move:
www.americaonthemove.org
Exerstrider Products:
www.walkingpoles.com
Gopher/PE, Health, Athletics, Recreation and Fitness Products:
www.gophersport.com
HealthTrackers 10,000 Steps Program:
www.10k-steps.com
Kidswalk/Centers for Disease Control:
www.cdc.gov/nccdphp/dnpa/kidswalk
National Association for Sport and Physical Education (NASPE):
www.aahperd.org/Naspe
PE4life:
www.pe4life.org

The President's Council on Physical Fitness and Sports/Presidential
Active Lifestyle Award (PALA):
www.presidentschallenge.org
Steptracker 2.0:
www.steptracker.com
TrekkingPoles.com:
www.trekkingpoles.com
Walking School Bus:
www.walkingschoolbus.org
Walkingabout.com:
www.walking.about.com
WalkSmart Active Schools:
www.walksmartactiveschools.com

9 Helping Students Develop Physical Fitness

Learning Objectives

After reading this chapter, you will be able to . . .

○ Differentiate between health-related and skill-related physical fitness.

○ Describe the fitness status of children in the United States.

○ Identify the factors that influence children's fitness.

○ Debate the effectiveness of fitness awards.

○ Discuss guidelines for promoting a positive attitude toward fitness.

○ Explain how to implement a fitness routine.

○ Plan and demonstrate numerous activities and exercises that can improve the physical fitness of children in grades kindergarten through two.

○ Plan and demonstrate numerous activities and exercises that can improve the physical fitness of children in grades three through six.

Classroom Challenge

It's mid-afternoon, and Mr. Kajiwara has brought his fourth-grade students out to the playground for a 10-minute activity break before the last class period of the day. He lines up the 12 girls and 11 boys in two rows and directs them in a series of stretches. He follows this with 50 jumping jacks, which leave some of his students panting and sweaty. Next he tells students he wants to see 10 push ups in one minute. Some students finish all of them easily, while others complete only three or four. A few children cannot manage even one push up. Wanting to avoid spending more than 10 minutes on the activity break, Mr. Kajiwara announces the final exercise without waiting for the slower students to finish: "I'm setting my stopwatch," he shouts. "You have three minutes to do 30 sit ups. Take your places, knees bent, hands clasped behind head, and go!" Once again, several students finish well ahead of time, while others have completed only a few sit ups by the time the three minutes are up.

It's time to go back to the classroom. Mr. Kajiwara orders his students to line up single file. "Some of you," he says, "have clearly been working on your calisthenics and are well on your way to earning your fitness badge at the end of the year. Others," he frowns, "need to work harder from now on, because you're not keeping up! I'll be testing you again next week, and I want to see some improvement! Back to class!"

At the end of the school day, after he has dismissed his class, Mr. Kajiwara is tidying up when he notices Rose lingering in the hallway. An exceptionally bright student, Rose was skipped forward a grade and thus is a year younger than her classmates. "Don't miss your bus, Rose," he warns her.

"I walk home," she answers. "Um ... Mr. Kajiwara ...?" Her voice trails off.

"Yes, Rose?"

"Mr. Kajiwara, it's not true what you said! I've been working on my calisthenics! I just don't know how to do push ups right! And I hate sit ups! And anyway, I don't care about getting a badge, and my mom says just do your best and that's good enough, and that's what I think, too!"

Rose's outburst takes Mr. Kajiwara by surprise. Before he can think of a reply, she has raced down the corridor out of sight.

As a classroom teacher, your primary emphasis in relation to your students' health should be on increasing the amount of physical activity they accumulate each day. Chapters 1 through 8 of this book have provided guidance in how to accomplish this goal. But in addition, you play a key role in helping your students gain a basic understanding of what physical fitness is, why it's important for them, how they can improve their fitness, and what exercises they can use for different areas of the body. This chapter provides information you need to take on this role. It describes the two types of physical fitness and components of each, how young people respond to fitness training, basic fitness principles, and easy exercises and games that can move students toward fitness. If you're concerned about how to incorporate fitness into your already-crowded teaching day, rest assured: a short activity break can refresh your students and offer you an opportunity to teach or reinforce a simple fitness concept.

Types of Physical Fitness

Physical fitness is a set of attributes that people have or achieve in relation to their ability to perform physical activity (U.S. Department of Health and Human Services [USDHHS], 1996). Physical *activity* is a process-oriented outcome related to behavior and lifestyles, whereas physical *fitness* is a product-oriented outcome with an emphasis on achieving a higher state of wellness. Physical fitness has a genetic component that strongly influences the level of fitness that can be achieved.

Physical fitness experts identify two types of physical fitness:

Health-related physical fitness is characterized by an ability to engage in moderate to vigorous physical activity (see Chapter 8) with vitality and without undue fatigue. Not surprisingly, it includes health-related components such as cardiovascular endurance and muscular strength.

Skill-related physical fitness is related to athletic ability and physical performance. Its components are physical qualities such as agility and speed that enable a person to succeed in sports activities.

Because health is essential to a high level of physical performance, the components of health-related physical fitness are considered a subset of skill-related fitness components, a concept illustrated in **Figure 9.1**.

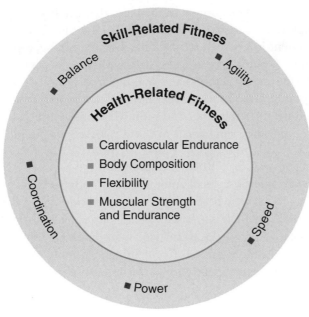

Figure 9.1 Components of skill-related physical fitness.

Health-Related Physical Fitness

Health-related physical fitness includes those aspects of physiological function that offer protection from diseases related to a sedentary lifestyle. It can be achieved and maintained through regular moderate physical activity. Teaching health-related fitness should be a priority in the classroom because it has the potential to leave students with positive activity habits that will benefit their health throughout their lifetime.

Because intensive workouts are not needed to achieve and maintain health-related physical fitness, for most students it is a more acceptable goal than skill-related fitness. In addition, all students can achieve health-related fitness regardless of their prior level of experience or genetic traits. This differs from skill-related fitness, which is performance-oriented and influenced by both previous experience and genetics.

Specific components of health-related physical fitness include cardiovascular endurance, body composition (ratio of leanness to fatness), flexibility, and muscular strength and endurance. Let's look at each in more detail.

Cardiovascular Endurance

Cardiovascular endurance is the ability of the heart, the blood vessels, and the respiratory system to deliver oxygen efficiently throughout the body over an extended period of time. It offers many health benefits, from a reduced risk of cardiovascular disease to an improved quality of life, and it is often seen as the most important element of health-related physical fitness.

In order to develop their cardiovascular endurance, children need to engage in activities that are aerobic in nature. Aerobic activities are continuous and rhythmic, requiring that the lungs take in ample oxygen and that the heart pump the oxygen-rich blood through the blood vessels for delivery to the muscle cells. Activities that stimulate development in this area are walking, jogging, biking, rope jumping, aerobics, and swimming. Aerobic activities also help with weight control; for example, activities such as low-impact aerobics and walking at a brisk pace burn about 2.5 calories per pound of body weight per hour, which is about twice the number of calories burned during stretching. And more vigorous aerobics, such as running, cycling, and dance-aerobics, can burn 4 or more calories per pound per hour.

Body Composition

Body composition is an individual's proportion of body fat to lean body mass. The most common way to evaluate body composition in children is to calculate their body mass index (BMI), which is a simple ratio of an individual's height to weight.

Regular physical activity helps to reduce fat and increase lean body mass. Because the body burns more calories maintaining lean body mass than maintaining fat, individuals who are lean expend more calories even at rest than do individuals who are overweight.

Flexibility

As noted in Chapter 8, *flexibility* is the ability to move a joint or sequence of joints through its full normal range of motion (ROM). Flexibility is important to fitness: a lack of flexibility can contribute to poor posture and muscle pain, whereas people who are flexible usually have good posture and less pain. Many everyday activities, from climbing stairs to making a bed, require flexibility, and it is essential for generating maximum force in athletic activities, such as serving a tennis ball or kicking a soccer ball.

Inactive individuals lose flexibility, whereas frequent movement helps retain full ROM. Stretching activities increase the length of muscles, tendons, and ligaments and are helpful for preventing tightness and pain. But as noted in Chapter 8, children in kindergarten through fourth grade are inherently more flexible than are older children and adults and do not usually need to stretch. Teach them some stretching exercises to illustrate the importance of flexibility, but focus on play activities such as tumbling and climbing that can contribute to flexibility. More time should be spent teaching and performing flexibility exercises when children reach the fifth and sixth grades.

Muscular Strength and Endurance

Muscular strength is the ability of muscles to exert force, and *muscular endurance* is their ability to exert force over an extended period. Endurance postpones the onset of fatigue so that activity can be performed for lengthy periods. Children need to engage in activities and exercises that help them build strength and endurance, especially in the arm-shoulder girdle and the abdominal-trunk region. This in turn will help them stay engaged in sports and games involving throwing, catching, striking, and kicking.

Skill-Related Physical Fitness

The ability to achieve skill-related fitness depends a great deal on genetics. Many children simply cannot excel in this area of fitness, and asking them to "try harder" only adds to their frustration, especially when they see their athletic friends perform well with little effort. So, before you teach skill-related fitness, take a moment to explain that some students will be able to perform an exercise well with a minimum of effort, whereas others will be unable to perform the same exercise well, no matter how hard they try. To illustrate genetic differences, use examples such as speed, jumping ability, strength, and physical size. Bear in mind that some students will want to work hard to improve their skill-related fitness, while others will be satisfied to enjoy less-demanding activity. For these students, health-related fitness is a valid outcome.

As noted earlier, skill-related fitness components are useful for performing motor tasks related to sports and athletics. They include the health-related components discussed above plus the following:

Agility

Agility is the ability of the body to change position rapidly and accurately while moving in space. Wrestling and football are examples of sports that require agility.

Balance

Balance refers to the body's ability to maintain a state of equilibrium while remaining stationary or moving. Maintaining balance is essential to all sports but is especially important in gymnastics.

Coordination

Coordination is the ability of the body to perform smoothly and successfully more than one motor task at the same time. Needed for football, baseball, tennis, soccer, and other sports that require hand-eye and foot-eye skills, coordination can be developed by repeatedly practicing the skill being learned.

Power

Power is the ability to transfer energy explosively into force. To develop power, the child practices activities that are required to improve strength but at a faster rate with sudden bursts of energy. Skills requiring power include high jumping, long jumping, shot putting, throwing, and kicking.

Speed

Speed is the ability of the body to perform movement in a short period of time. Usually associated with running forward, speed is essential for the successful performance of most sports and general locomotor movement skills.

Back to Class

In our chapter-opening scenario, Mr. Kajiwara asks his students to do 10 push ups in one minute and 30 sit ups in three minutes. Identify at least three components of physical fitness that are necessary for successfully completing these tasks and classify each one as either health-related or skill-related.

Common Questions About Children's Fitness

How effective is fitness training for children? Is it realistic to expect all children to reach specified standards of fitness, or do factors beyond the child's control influence fitness performance? Are rewards for high fitness scores good motivators? We explore these frequently asked questions in this section.

How Effective Is Fitness Training for Children?

In the 1950s, American children's low fitness levels became an issue of national concern. Educational leaders recommended fitness testing in an attempt to address the problem. When tests showed that children were unfit, the solution seemed simple enough: focus on physical fitness training and thereby achieve a fit society. Sadly, this approach to children's health has been a failure. Today's youth are showing greater deficits in personal health than their parents did decades ago. As we've noted elsewhere in this text, the percentage of youth who are overweight has more than tripled in the past 30 years (USDHHS, 2002), and fitness levels have not improved since testing began in the 1950s (Corbin and Pangrazi, 1992).

A primary reason for this lack of improvement in fitness appears to be that children don't respond as fully to fitness training as do adolescents. Payne and Morrow (1993) reviewed 28 studies examining training and aerobic performance in children and concluded that improvement is small to moderate in pre-adolescent children.

This does not mean that elementary schools should give up on the goal of physical fitness but rather that it be subsumed into a more comprehensive goal of increasing children's overall level of physical activity. Moreover, as we noted earlier, the goal of fitness programs should be to improve health-related fitness, as it is within this domain that we can bring the greatest benefits to the greatest number of children.

What Factors Influence Children's Fitness?

Lifestyle and environmental factors sometimes play a role in children's fitness test scores. For example, a child's nutrition over time, or even on the day of the test, is a lifestyle factor that can influence performance, as is the child's level of previous exposure to activities similar to those used for the test. Environmental conditions such as heat, humidity, and pollution also can affect test performances. That said, the most significant factors influencing fitness test performance are heredity, maturation, and body composition (Bouchard, 1999; Bouchard et al., 1992; Pangrazi and Corbin, 1990).

Heredity

One reason that heredity is thought to predispose some youngsters to high (or low) performance is the concept of trainability (Bouchard et al., 1992; Bouchard, 1999). *Trainability* means that some individuals receive more benefit from similar amounts of training than do others. For example, assume two youngsters perform the same amount and type of activity (workload) throughout a semester. Child A responds favorably to the training, showing dramatic improvement quickly, because she inherited a body that is highly responsive to exercise. She not only improves her fitness and scores well on the test, but she also gets positive feedback that "activity works—it makes me physically fit." Child B, who has performed the same workload, has a body that is not as responsive to exercise. She shows little improvement in fitness and scores poorly on the test; thus, she receives negative feedback and concludes that "activity doesn't improve my fitness, so why bother?" In truth, child B typically does become more fit but to a lesser degree than child A and over a longer span of time.

Maturation

Another factor that influences fitness performance is physical maturation. If two youngsters are the same age and sex, but one is physiologically older (advanced skeletal maturation), the more-mature youngster will usually perform better on a fitness test than the less-mature child. In fact, maturation can even override the effects of activity among young children: a skeletally mature, but inactive youngster might score higher than an immature but active child the same age.

Chronological age also plays a role in fitness performance (Pangrazi and Corbin, 1990). As little as three months' difference in age helps older children perform better than younger children, regardless of training. Thus, you can expect older classmates of younger students to perform better.

Body Composition

Currently, more than 17 percent of children 6 through 19 years old are overweight (National Center for Health Statistics, 2007), and another 31 percent are at risk for overweight (Hedley et al., 2004). Body fat is dead weight and does not contribute to muscular or cardiovascular performance; as an analogy, putting 20 pounds of sand on a child's back would certainly decrease the number of push ups he or she would be able to perform. Thus, most fitness measures show a decrease as body fat increases among children.

Level of Physical Activity Does Not Significantly Influence Fitness

Many teachers and parents believe that fitness in youngsters is primarily a reflection of the amount of activity (workload) children perform on a regular basis. They assume youngsters who score high on fitness tests are active and those who score low are inactive. This assumption is often incorrect. Physical activity is an important variable in fitness development for adults, but studies have shown that this relationship does not hold among children (Pate, Dowda, and Ross, 1990; Pate and Ross, 1987; Ross et al., 1987).

Youngsters try to behave in ways that please the teacher and impress their friends. When told that they can improve their fitness scores if they work hard each day, most take this challenge seriously, and therefore they naturally expect to perform well. Many teachers expect the same. But if, after working hard, these children achieve a low score, they become discouraged, especially if their teacher concludes that their low score reflects their efforts. So, it's important to avoid drawing the conclusion that scores on a fitness test necessarily reflect a child's overall activity level; instead, as advised earlier, explain to children the factors beyond their control (primarily heredity and maturation) that contribute to fitness scores.

It's also unwise to conclude that children who make high scores must have worked hard. As we just noted, many children perform well on fitness tests simply because of their genetic traits. If teachers do not teach otherwise, these children can get the message that they don't need to be active.

Are Fitness Awards Effective?

For years, award systems have been used to recognize students who demonstrate high levels of skill-related fitness. The original intent of the award systems was to motivate youngsters to improve. However, research shows that performance awards usually motivate only those youngsters who feel they have the ability to earn them (Corbin, Lovejoy, and Whitehead, 1988; Corbin et al., 1990). Students who don't believe they can earn such awards typically determine that there is no use in trying.

Another problem with fitness awards is that they focus on a single episode of accomplishment, making the act of participating in daily activity seem less important than earning the award. Children learn that the only thing that adults care about is performance on the test. At the same time, extrinsic awards can undermine intrinsic motivation; instead of engaging in physical activity just because it makes him or her feel good, a child learns to behave in ways that will win favor with adults.

For these reasons, generally, awards are not recommended. However, if your school chooses to use them, consider the following advice:

- Base awards on achievement of goals that are challenging, yet attainable (Locke and Lathan, 1985). Goals that are too difficult to attain may prompt a response called *learned helplessness* (Harter, 1978). This phenomenon occurs when children believe there is no use trying to reach the goals and that their efforts would be in vain. Learned helplessness often occurs when those in authority reward performance rather than participation or effort. Students with low self-esteem are among the most likely to experienced learned helplessness. These students can benefit significantly from positive feedback on their participation or effort.
- If an award system is used to motivate children's activity, the system should be phased out as soon as possible. Awards do motivate primary-grade children; however, by the age of 9 or 10 years, children start to see them as bribery (Whitehead and Corbin, 1991). Gradually removing awards helps students learn that participation is beneficial for intrinsic reasons—and for everyone.
- An approach that focuses on long-term behavior rather than a single outcome is to recognize students for regular participation in activity. This places the rewards in reach of all youngsters and helps establish activity habits that last a lifetime. In addition, this approach supports the research cited in the report of the Surgeon General on the benefits of regular moderate to vigorous physical activity (USDHHS, 1996).

Back to Class

In our chapter-opening scenario, Mr. Kajiwara has his students perform stretches, jumping jacks, push ups, and sit ups. In addition to Rose, his class includes a boy with type 1 diabetes who is smaller than his peers, and two boys who are overweight. Now comment on the appropriateness of Mr. Kajiwara's remarks to his students as he brings them in from the playground, including these additional students.

Promoting a Positive Attitude Toward Fitness

How fitness activities are presented determines to a great extent how students feel about them. The following strategies help students develop a positive attitude toward physical fitness.

Be a Role Model

Appearance, attitude, and actions speak loudly about teachers and their values regarding fitness. Teachers who display physical vitality, take pride in their own fitness, and participate in activities with their students provide a positive role model for maintaining an active lifestyle. Studies have shown that children's activity levels increase when classroom teachers are active with their classes.

Expose Students to a Variety of Fitness Activities

Some children like to sprint, others enjoy doing jumping jacks, and still others like to kick, jab, and lunge. Presenting a variety of fitness activities prevents monotony and increases the likelihood that students will find fitness sessions enjoyable. Youngsters are willing to accept activities they dislike if they know there will shortly be other routines they enjoy. Prevent boredom by offering a variety of activities, if not within a single activity break, at least from one activity break to the next.

Personalize Fitness Activities

Students who find themselves unable to perform an assigned exercise are highly likely to develop an aversion to physical fitness. Some children can become so fearful of failure in front of their peers that they avoid all activity sessions, insisting that they are ill or tired. You can prevent this kind of negative response by introducing fitness activities in a way that empowers children to discover their personal workload. For instance, use time (rather than repetitions or speed) as the variable and ask children to do the best they can within that time limit. When you allow children to control the intensity of their workouts, you help them develop internal motivation for participating in activity.

Challenge Children Appropriately

The fitness experience works best when it is a challenge rather than a threat. A *challenge* is an experience that participants feel they can accomplish. In contrast, a *threat* appears to be an impossible undertaking, one for which students believe there is no use trying. Keep goals within the realm of challenge. Bear in mind that whether an activity is a challenge or a threat depends on the perceptions of the learner, not on the instructor. Listen carefully to students rather than telling them they should do something "for their own good."

Start Easy and Progress Slowly

Fitness development is a journey, not a destination. Start students at a level that they can *accomplish* successfully. This usually means self-directed workloads within a short time frame. For example, ask students to "do their best" performing curl ups for 30 seconds. Starting out in this way assures success and avoids both discouragement and excessive muscle soreness. When students have proven to themselves that they can successfully accomplish a task, gradually increase the workload.

Encourage Activity of Low to Moderate Intensity

Make activity appropriate for children's developmental level. Most active adults participate in high-intensity–low-volume exercise because they have only a short period of time to devote to fitness each day. In contrast, as we noted in Chapter 2, most children participate in high-volume–low-intensity activity sporadically throughout a day. This naturally occurring activity is consistent with their developmental level. Children typically do not enjoy participating in high-intensity activities, nor do they need to do so to receive health benefits. They are the most active age group in our society (Rowland, 1990), and by encouraging their natural low-intensity activity, you promote their fitness.

Give Students Positive Feedback About Their Efforts

Teacher feedback contributes to the way children view fitness activities. Immediate, accurate, and specific feedback regarding effort encourages continued participation. Provided in a positive manner, this feedback can stimulate children to extend their participation habits. Reinforce all children, not just those who perform at high levels. All youngsters need feedback and reinforcement even if they aren't able to perform at an elite level.

Back to Class

How might Mr. Kajiwara have modified his instructions about the push ups and sit ups to help all his students experience success? How was his feedback? Was it immediate, accurate, and specific?

Avoid Harmful Practices and Exercises

When instructing students in fitness exercises, adhere to the following safety guidelines. For in-depth coverage of contraindicated exercises, see the texts by Lindsey and Corbin (1989) or Corbin, Lindsey, and Welk (2000).

1. Two types of stretching activity have been used to develop flexibility. *Ballistic stretching* (strong bouncing movements) formerly was the most common stretching used, but it has been discouraged for many years because it is thought to increase delayed onset muscle soreness and promote tissue damage. *Static stretching* involves increasing the stretch to the point of discomfort, backing off slightly to where the position can be held comfortably, and maintaining the stretch for an extended time. Static stretching has been thought to induce less muscle soreness than ballistic stretching and to prevent injury. However, one study (Smith et al., 1993) indicated that both ballistic and static stretching produced muscle soreness, but that the soreness following static stretching actually exceeded the soreness following ballistic stretching. Static stretching is still an excellent choice, but ballistic stretching may not be as harmful as once thought.

2. In a stretch, if forward flexion is done from a sitting position in an effort to touch the toes, the bend should be from the hips, not from the waist, and should be done with one leg flexed to reduce stress on the lower back. Avoid having students touch their toes from a standing position.

3. When doing stretching exercises from a standing position, the knee joint should be relaxed rather than locked. It is often effective to have students stretch with bent knees; this will remind them not to hyperextend the joint. In all stretching activities, participants should be allowed to judge their own range of motion.

4. Avoid the so-called hurdler's stretch, done in the sitting position with one leg forward and the other leg bent and to the rear. This stretch places excessive pressure on the knee joint of the bent leg. Instead, have students stretch with one leg straight forward and the other leg bent with the foot placed in the crotch area.

5. Avoid stretches that demand excessive back arching, for example, lying in prone position and reaching back to grab the ankles. By pulling and arching, it is possible to hyperextend the lower back. This places stress on the discs and stretches the abdominal muscles (which is not needed by most people).

6. When instructing students in performing abdominal exercises such as sit ups that lift the head and trunk off the floor, include these guidelines (Macfarlane, 1993):

   ● Avoid placing the hands behind the head or high on the neck. This may cause hyperflexion and injury to the discs when the elbows swing forward to help pull the body up.

   ● Keep the knees bent. Straight legs cause the hip flexor muscles to be used earlier and more forcefully, making it difficult to maintain proper pelvic tilt.

- Don't hold the feet on the floor. Having another student secure the feet places more force on the lumbar vertebrae and may lead to lumbar hyperextension.
- Don't lift the buttocks and lumbar region off the floor. This also causes the hip flexor muscles to contract vigorously.

7. Straight-leg raises from a supine position should be avoided because they may strain the lower back. The problem can be somewhat alleviated by placing the hands under the small of the back, but it is best to avoid such exercises.

8. Deep knee bends (full squats) and the duck walk (squatting and then walking forward and backward maintaining the squat position) are often advocated for strengthening the thigh muscles, but they should be avoided. They may damage the knee joints, and they have little developmental value. Much more beneficial is standing and flexing one knee joint to 90 degrees, then extending the knee to return to standing position again.

9. In general, activities that place stress on the neck—such as abdominal exercises with the hands behind the head—should be avoided.

Back to Class

Look back at the instructions for performing sit ups that Mr. Kajiwara gave his students in our chapter-opening scenario. What element of his instructions could promote injury?

Implementing Fitness Routines

A fitness routine is a group of exercises that target the fitness components identified earlier in this chapter. Before we describe fitness routines you can use with your students, let's review some suggestions for successful implementation.

1. Precede fitness instruction with a two- to three-minute aerobic warm-up period to help prepare the children's bodies for strenuous activity. Have students walk, jog, skip, or gallop for a few minutes to get them ready to be active.

2. The fitness routine, including warm-up, should not extend beyond 8 to 10 minutes. Some experts argue that more time is needed to develop adequate fitness; however, your goal as a classroom teacher is to teach students how to perform fitness activities rather than to improve their fitness level.

3. Include activities that exercise all body parts and cover the major components of fitness.

4. Vary the routine. Use a diverse array of activities that appeal to children's interests and developmental level to avoid boredom due to performing the same routine day in and day out.

5. Take advantage of circuit training with youngsters. **Circuit training** alternates stretching and strength development exercises with aerobic exercises. This gives youngsters a chance to recover from one type of activity while performing another. Most routines are effective when each segment is limited to 30 seconds. Beyond this length of time, students fatigue or become bored and go off task. Two specific circuit-training routines are described later in this chapter.

6. Use music to time segments so you are free to move throughout the area and offer individualized instruction. The easiest way to time segments is to alternate 30-second intervals of music and silence. When music is playing, it signals that students are to perform an aerobic activity. When the silence interval is on, it signals stretching or a strength development activity.

7. *Never* use fitness activities as a punishment! Such a practice teaches students that push ups and other activities are things you do when you misbehave. Also, avoid withholding physical activity from children if they don't finish academic work. This negative practice makes activity an option rather than a critical part of the curriculum. Instead, take a positive approach and offer students a chance to jog with a friend when they do something well. This gives both children an opportunity to exercise with a positive feeling. Be an effective salesperson: sell the joy of activity and the benefits of physical fitness to your students.

Back to Class

Mr. Kajiwara assigns his students four activities in 10 minutes: stretches, jumping jacks, push ups, and sit ups. Comment on the workload specified, the number and duration of activities assigned, and the order of the activities.

Fitness Activities for Children in Kindergarten Through Second Grade

In Chapter 2, we discussed the importance of understanding children's needs and readiness for physical activity. You learned, for example, that children in the primary grades have different body proportions from those of adults, making them top-heavy and short-legged. Because of this, they cannot successfully do push ups and sit ups. This is only one example of several such limitations. Before you instruct your students in fitness activities, make sure the activities you choose are developmentally appropriate, and review Chapter 2 if you have any doubts.

Present the following fitness challenges to primary grade children as *personal* challenges, for example, by introducing them with the instruction, "See if you can do this." Introduce all of them early in the year so that, later on, you can allow students to select the challenges they feel they can perform successfully. Again, the workload should be dictated by the student, not the teacher. Finally, alternate strength and flexibility activities with aerobic activities to avoid excessively fatiguing young children.

Arm-Shoulder Girdle Strength Challenges

The following are examples of challenges that can be used to help youngsters gradually develop arm-shoulder girdle strength. These challenges require less upper body strength than an actual push up, which requires lifting and lowering the entire weight and is difficult even for fit adults. Indeed, as discussed in the accompanying News Clip, the true push up is a frustrating task for many children.

1. Assume the crab position (tummy toward the ceiling, hands and feet on floor, knees bent at right angles, keeping the seat up so the body doesn't sag). Now keep your feet in place while you use your arms to make your body go in a big circle. Do the same from the push up position.
2. In crab position, go forward, backward, and to the side. Turn around, move very slowly, and so on.
3. Successively from standing, supine, and hands-and-knees positions, swing one limb (arm or leg) at a time in different directions and at different levels.
4. Combine two limb movements (arm-arm, leg-leg, or arm-leg combinations) in the same direction and in opposite directions. Vary the levels.
5. Make giant circles with your arms. In supine position, make giant circles with your legs.
6. In a bent-over position, swing the arms as if swimming. Try a backstroke or a breaststroke. What does a sidestroke look like?
7. Move your arms like a windmill. Turn the arms in different directions. Speed up and slow down.
8. How else can you circle your arms?
9. Pretend that a swarm of bees is around your head. Brush them off and keep them away.

Figure 9.2 Traditional push up position.

Keeping the body off the floor in the push up position (Figure 9.2) is another excellent way to help develop upper body strength. Allow students to rest with one knee on the floor in the up position. As youngsters develop strength, they can make a partial descent to the floor from the up position. This gradual approach allows students to experience success, whereas forcing them to do true push ups sets them up for failure. The following activities can be done with one knee down (beginning) or in the more challenging traditional push up position. Notice that many can also be done in the crab position.

1. Hold your body off the floor (in either the push up position or the crab position).
2. Wave at a friend. Wave with the other arm. Shake a leg at someone.

An Enduring Measure of Fitness: The Simple Push Up

In a 2001 study, researchers at East Carolina University administered push up tests to about 70 students ages 10 to 13. Almost half the boys and three-quarters of the girls didn't pass. Why not? One reason is children's increased weight. Since push ups use the upper torso and arms to lift the full body's weight, the more the body weighs, the more difficult the task. As the nation gains weight, arms are buckling under the extra load.

Another theory explaining kids' poor performance is schools' shrinking budgets for physical education classes—and the calisthenics that were once a childhood staple. In addition, the aerobics movement has emphasized cardiovascular fitness but has shifted emphasis away from strength-training exercises. At the same time, PE instructors want to make sure their classes give kids an opportunity to burn calories, which aerobic activities such as running and dancing do more efficiently and more entertainingly than a strength-training workout. Thus, the limited time kids do spend in PE class is likely to be focused on aerobic activities.

Why is it important to be able to perform push ups? A fundamental reason is that the ability to perform more than one with proper form is an important indicator of overall fitness. A second, more specific, reason is that push ups can provide the strength and muscle memory needed to reach out and break a fall. When people fall forward, they typically reach out to catch themselves, ending in a move that mimics a push up. The hands hit the ground, the wrists and arms absorb much of the impact, and the elbows bend slightly to reduce the force.

Both children and adults should learn to master push ups gradually. If traditional, on-the-floor push ups are too difficult, start by leaning at about a 45-degree angle against a countertop, heavy desk, or any stable structure at approximately waist height. Press up and down. Eventually, try it on stairs, then finally on the floor.

Source: Adapted from the *New York Times*, March 11, 2008, available at www.nytimes.com/2008/03/11/health/nutrition/11well.html.

News Clip

take action!

1. Can you do a traditional push up? If you're not sure, follow the instructions in this chapter and see for yourself. If you find yourself unable to perform the standard, on-the-floor push up, challenge yourself to build up to it using the gradual method described above.

2. If you're wondering whether or not strength-training exercises are really appropriate for children, check out the American Academy of Pediatrics policy statement, "Strength Training by Children and Adolescents" (see Web Resources). You might also want to read an informative discussion of the subject from the Mayo Clinic, "Strength Training: OK for Kids When Done Correctly."

3. Have the elementary schools in your district dropped strength training for children? Find out! If so, interview PE staff to discover why. Does their program focus on cardiovascular endurance, achieving and maintaining a healthy weight, sports skills, or some other aspect of health or fitness? How do instructors feel about their program's current emphasis?

3. Lift one foot high, then put it down. Now the other foot.
4. Bounce both feet up and down. Move the feet apart while bouncing.
5. Inch the feet toward the hands and then back again. Inch the feet toward the hands again and then inch the hands out.
6. Return to the starting position. Reach up with one hand and touch the other shoulder behind the back.
7. Lift both hands from the floor. Try clapping the hands.
8. Turn over, then complete the turn back to the starting position.
9. Walk on your hands and feet. Try two hands and one foot.
10. In push up position, with one knee on the ground, touch your nose to the floor between your hands. As you get stronger, move your head forward a little and touch your nose to the floor. (The farther in front of the hands the nose touches the floor, the greater the strength demands.)
11. Lower the body an inch at a time until the chest touches the floor. Raise the body back up again any way possible.
12. Pretending you are a tire, gradually lower yourself to the floor as if you were going flat.

Abdominal Strength Challenges

The basic position for exercising the abdominal muscles is supine on the floor or on a mat. Challenges should lift the upper and lower portions of the body from the floor, either separately or together. Since young children are top-heavy (large head, small body), they find it difficult to perform most abdominal exercises. Therefore, begin early abdominal development with youngsters lying on the floor and lifting their heads. Progress to a sitting position, followed by a gradual lowering (with head tucked) of the upper body backward to the floor. Challenges are as follows:

1. Lie down with your back to the floor. Lift your head from the floor and look at your toes. Wink your right eye and wiggle your left foot. Reverse.
2. "Wave" a leg at a friend. Use the other leg. Use both legs.
3. Lift your knees up slowly, an inch at a time.
4. Pick your heels up about 6 inches off the floor and swing them back and forth. Cross them and twist them.
5. Sit up any way you can and touch both sets of toes with your hands. Lie down again.
6. Sit up any way you can and touch your right toes with your left hand. Touch your left toes with your right hand.
7. In a sitting position, lean backward without falling. How long can you hold this position?
8. From a sitting position, lower the body slowly to the floor. Vary the positions of the arms (across the tummy, the chest, and above the head).
9. Curl up by pulling up on your legs. Hold. Lie down again.
10. Lift your shoulders off the floor. Hold. Lie down again.
11. Lift your legs and head off the floor. Hold. Lie down again.

Trunk Development Challenges

Movements that include bending, stretching, swaying, twisting, reaching, and forming shapes help develop trunk strength. Vary the child's position: standing, lying, kneeling, or sitting.

Bending

1. Bend in different ways.
2. Bend as many parts of the body as you can.
3. Make different shapes by bending two, three, and four parts of the body.
4. Bend the arms and knees in different ways and on different levels.
5. Try different ways of bending the fingers and wrist of one hand with the other. Use some resistance. (Explain resistance.) Add body bends.

Stretching

1. Keep one foot in place and stretch your arms in different directions; move with the free foot. Stretch at different levels.
2. Lie on the floor, and stretch one leg different ways in space. Stretch one leg in one direction and the other in another direction.
3. Stretch as slowly as you can and then snap back to original position.
4. Stretch with different arm-leg combinations in several directions.
5. See how much space on the floor you can cover by stretching.
6. Combine bending and stretching movements.

Swaying and Twisting

1. Sway your body back and forth in different directions. Change the position of your arms.
2. Sway your body, bending over.
3. Sway your head from side to side.
4. Select a part of the body and twist it as far as you can in one direction and then in the opposite direction.
5. Twist your body at different levels.
6. Twist two or more parts of your body at the same time.
7. Twist one part of your body while untwisting another.
8. Twist your head to see as far behind you as you can.
9. Twist like a spring. Like a screwdriver.
10. Stand on one foot and twist your body. Untwist.
11. From a seated position, make different shapes by twisting.

Leg Development and Cardiovascular Endurance Challenges

Leg development activities include a range of movement challenges that simultaneously help children develop cardiovascular endurance. Youngsters fatigue and recover quickly. Take advantage of this trait by alternating these activities with strength and flexibility exercises.

Running Patterns

Running in different directions
Running in place
Running and stopping
Running and changing direction on signal

Jumping and Hopping Patterns

Jumping in different directions, back and forth over a spot
Jumping or hopping in, out, over, and around hoops, individual mats, or jump
     ropes laid on the floor
Jumping or hopping back and forth over lines, or hopping down the lines

Rope Jumping

Individual rope jumping—allow choice

Combinations of Locomotor Movements

Many combinations of locomotor movements can be used to motivate youngsters.
The following are some challenges that you might try.

Run in place. Do some running steps in place without stopping.
Skip or gallop for 30 seconds.
Slide all the way around the gymnasium.
Alternate hopping or jumping for 30 seconds with 30 seconds of rest.
Jump in place while twisting the arms and upper body.
Do 10 skips, 10 gallops, and finish with 30 running steps.
Hold hands with a friend and do 100 jumps.
Jump rope as many times as possible without missing.
Hop back and forth over this line from one end of the gym to the other.
Try to run as fast as you can. How long can you keep going?

Animal Movements

Young children enjoy imitating the sounds and movements of animals. Most of the
animal movements are done with the body weight on all four limbs, which helps
develop the arms and shoulders. Challenge youngsters to move randomly throughout the area, across the gymnasium, or between cones delineating a specific distance.
Increase the distance or the amount of time each walk is performed to increase the
workload. To avoid excessive fatigue, alternate the animal movements with stretching activities. The following are examples of animal movements that can be used.
See the Basic Skills Activity Cards for descriptions of more animal movements.

Puppy Walk: Move on all fours (hands and feet, not the knees). Keep the head
     up and move lightly.
Lion Walk: Move on all fours (same as above) while keeping the back arched.
     Move deliberately and lift the "paws" to simulate moving without sound.
Elephant Walk: Move heavily throughout the area, swinging the head back and
     forth like an elephant's trunk.
Seal Walk: Move using the arms to propel the body. Allow the legs to drag
     along the floor much as a seal would move.

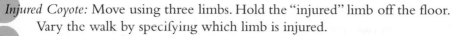

Injured Coyote: Move using three limbs. Hold the "injured" limb off the floor. Vary the walk by specifying which limb is injured.

Crab Walk: Move on all fours with the tummy facing the ceiling. Try to keep the back as straight as possible.

Rabbit Jump: Start in a squatting position with the hands on the floor. Reach forward with the hands and support the body weight. Jump both feet toward the hands. Repeat the sequence.

Jump Rope Exercises

Jump ropes are used in a number of exercises and aerobic activities. Playing music with taped intervals of silence is an excellent method for alternating periods of rope jumping and exercises. During the periods of silence, youngsters perform an exercise; during the music, children pick up their ropes and begin jumping. Use alternating segments (30 seconds in length) of silence and music to signal duration of exercise. Music segments indicate aerobic activity with the jump ropes, while intervals of silence announce using the jump ropes to enhance flexibility and strength development. Teach youngsters to space themselves so they don't hit others with their ropes.

1. Jump rope—30 seconds. If a student is unable to jump, practice swinging the rope to the side while jumping.
2. Place the rope on the floor and perform locomotor movements around and over the rope. Make different shapes and letters with the rope.
3. Hold the folded rope overhead. Sway from side to side. Twist right and left.
4. Jump rope—30 seconds.
5. Lie on your back with rope held with outstretched arms toward ceiling. Bring up one leg at a time and touch the rope with toes. Lift both legs together. Sit up and try to hook the rope over the feet. Release and repeat.
6. Touch toes with the folded rope.
7. Jump rope—30 seconds.
8. Place rope on the floor and execute various animal movements along or over the rope.
9. Do push ups with the rope folded and held between the hands.
10. Jump rope—30 seconds.

Fitness Activities for Children in Third Through Sixth Grade

With older children, the emphasis shifts to more structured exercises and routines. Most can be done in the classroom with a minimum of disruption. Exercises fall into the following five categories: (1) flexibility, (2) arm-shoulder girdle, (3) abdominal, (4) leg and agility, and (5) trunk twisting and bending. The purpose of placing the activities in categories is to help students learn to develop a balanced routine that covers all components of personal fitness.

Children with poor upper-body strength will not be able to perform some of the abdominal and arm-shoulder girdle exercises. Ensure that they have the opportunity to succeed and feel positive about fitness experiences by allowing them to select some of the modifications described in the Kindergarten Through Second Grade section of this chapter (pages 261–267).

Flexibility Exercises

Bend and Twist

Starting position: Stand with the arms crossed, hands on opposite shoulders, knees slightly flexed, and feet shoulder-width apart.

Movement: Bend forward at the waist (count 1). Twist the trunk and touch the right elbow to the left knee (count 2). Twist in the opposite direction and touch the left elbow to the right knee (count 3). Return to the starting position (count 4). Knees may be flexed.

Sitting Stretch

Starting position: Sit on the floor with one leg extended forward and the other bent at the knee, placing the foot in the area of the crotch. Touch the toes of the extended foot with the fingertips of both hands as the chest gradually moves forward (**Figure 9.3**).

Movement: Gradually bend forward, taking three counts to bend fully. Recover to sitting position on the fourth count.

Point to emphasize: Bend from the hips.

Figure 9.3 Sitting stretch position.

Partner Rowing

Starting position: Facing each other, partners hold hands with palms touching and fingers locked. Each student should spread and extend the legs to touch soles of the partner's feet.

Movement: One partner bends forward, with the help of the other pulling backward, to try to bring the chest as close to the floor as possible (**Figure 9.4**). Reverse direction.

Variation:

Steam engine. With both partners in the sitting position, alternate pulling hands back and forth like a pair of steam engine pistons. Do eight sets of right- and left-side pulls.

Lower Leg Stretch

Starting position: Stand facing a wall with the feet about shoulder-width apart. Place the palms of the hands on the wall at eye level (**Figure 9.5**).

Movement: Slowly walk away from the wall, keeping the body straight, until the stretch is felt in the lower portion of the calf. The feet should remain flat on the floor during the stretch.

Figure 9.4 Partner rowing.

Achilles Tendon Stretch

Starting position: Stand facing a wall resting the forearms on it. With the forehead on the back of the hands, back 2 to 3 feet away from the wall, bend, and move one leg closer to the wall.

Movement: Flex the bent leg with the foot on the floor until the stretch is felt in the Achilles tendon area. The feet should remain flat on the floor as the leg closer to the wall is flexed. Repeat, flexing the other leg.

Arm-Shoulder Girdle Exercises

Arm-shoulder girdle exercises for this age group include both arm-support and free-arm types.

Push Ups

Starting position: Assume the push up position (see **Figure 9.2**), with the body straight from head to heels.

Movement: Keeping the body straight, bend the elbows and touch the chest to the ground; then straighten the elbows, raising the body in a straight line.

Points to emphasize: Keep the movement in the arms. The head is up, with the eyes looking ahead. The chest should touch the floor lightly, without receiving the weight of the body. The body remains in a straight line throughout, without sagging or humping.

Variation: Some youngsters develop a dislike for push ups because they are asked to perform them without any modification. Also, as we noted in this chapter's News Clip, push ups are difficult even for fit adults. Make sure you allow youngsters to judge their own strength and choose a push up challenge they feel able to accomplish. Instead of asking an entire class to perform a specified number of push ups, personalize the workload by allowing each youngster to accomplish as many repetitions as possible of a self-selected push up challenge in a specified amount of time.

Teaching tip: Controlled movement is a goal; speed is not desirable. Push ups should be done at will, allowing each child to achieve individually within a specified time limit.

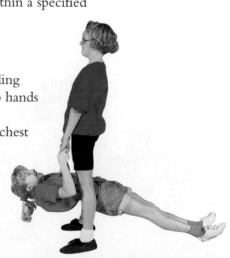

Figure 9.5 Lower leg stretch.

Reclining Pull Ups

Starting position: One pupil lies in supine position. Partner is standing astride, with feet alongside the reclining partner's chest. Partners grasp hands with interlocking fingers or with an interlocked wrist grip.

Movement: The pupil on the floor pulls up with arms until the chest touches the partner's thighs. The body remains straight, with weight resting on the heels (**Figure 9.6**). Return to position.

Points to emphasize: The supporting student should keep the center of gravity well over the feet by maintaining a lifted chest and proper head position. The lower student should maintain a straight body during the pull up and move only the arms.

Variation: Raise as directed (count 1), hold the high position (counts 2 and 3), return to starting position (count 4).

Figure 9.6 Reclining pull ups.

Figure 9.7 Arm circles.

Triceps Push Up

Starting position: Assume an inverted push up position with the chest to the ceiling and the arms and legs held straight.

Movement: Keeping the body straight, bend the elbows and touch the seat to the ground, then straighten the elbows and raise the body.

Points to emphasize: The fingers should point toward the toes or be turned in slightly. The body should be held firm, with movement restricted to the arms.

Arm Circles

Starting position: Stand upright, with feet apart and arms straight out to the side (Figure 9.7).

Movement: Do forward and backward circles with palms facing forward, moving arms simultaneously. Vary the number of circles executed before changing.

Points to emphasize: Avoid doing arm circles with palms down (particularly backward circles) as it stresses the shoulder joint. Correct posture should be maintained, with the abdominal wall flat and the head and shoulders held back.

Crab Kick

Starting position: Assume the crab position, with the body supported on the hands and feet and the back parallel to the floor. The knees are bent at right angles. As always with all crab positions, keep the seat up and avoid body sag.

Movement: Kick the right leg up and down (counts 1 and 2) (Figure 9.8). Repeat with the left leg (counts 3 and 4).

Crab Alternate-Leg Extension

Starting position: Assume the crab position.

Movement: On count 1, extend the right leg forward so that it rests on the heel. On count 2, extend the left leg forward and bring the right leg back. Continue alternating.

Abdominal Exercises

For most exercises stressing abdominal development, children should start from the supine position on the floor or on a mat. When lifting the upper body, they should begin with a roll-up (curling) action, moving the head first so that the chin touches or nearly touches the chest, thus flattening and stabilizing the lower back curve. The bent-knee position better isolates the abdominal muscles and avoids stressing the lower back region. When doing abdominal exercises, avoid moving the trunk up to the sitting position (past 45 degrees) since doing so increases the risk for pain and injury (Macfarlane, 1993).

Some youngsters develop a dislike for abdominal work in the early school years because it's difficult for them to lift their torso off

Figure 9.8 Crab kick.

the floor. As their body proportions change in the upper-elementary years, continue to allow students to choose an abdominal challenge they feel able to accomplish. For instance, instead of asking an entire class to perform a specified number of curl ups, personalize the workload by allowing youngsters to accomplish as many repetitions as possible in a specified amount of time using a self-selected abdominal challenge.

Figure 9.9 Knee touch curl up.

Reverse Curl

Starting position: Lie on back with the hands on the floor at the sides of the body.

Movement: Curl the knees to the chest. The upper body remains on the floor. As abdominal strength increases, the child should lift the buttocks and lower back off the floor.

Points to emphasize: Roll the knees to the chest and return the feet to the floor after each repetition. The movement should be controlled, with emphasis on the abdominal contraction.

Variations: Hold the head off the floor and bring the knees to the chin. Or, instead of returning the feet to the floor after each repetition, move them 1 to 2 inches off the floor. This activity requires greater abdominal strength as there is no resting period (feet on floor).

Pelvis Tilter

Starting position: Lie on the back with feet flat on the floor, knees bent, arms out in wing position, and palms up.

Movement: Flatten the lower back, bringing it closer to the floor by tensing the lower abdominals and lifting up on the pelvis. Hold for 8 to 12 counts. Tense slowly and release slowly.

Knee Touch Curl Up

Starting position: Lie on the back, with feet flat, knees bent, and hands flat on top of the thighs.

Movement: Leading with the chin, slide the hands forward until the fingers touch the kneecaps and gradually curl the head and shoulders until the shoulder blades are lifted off the floor (**Figure 9.9**). Hold for 8 counts and return to position. To avoid stress on the lower back, do not curl up to the sitting position.

Curl Up

Starting position: Lie on the back with feet flat, knees bent, and arms on the floor at the side of the body with palms down.

Movement: Lift the head and shoulders (**Figure 9.10**) to a 45-degree angle and then back in a

Figure 9.10 Traditional curl up.

Figure 9.11 Curl up with twist.

2-count pattern. The hands should slide forward on the floor 3 to 4 inches. The curl up can also be done as an 8-count exercise, moving up on count 1, holding for 6 counts, and moving down on the last count.

Points to emphasize: Roll up, with the chin first. Do not lift the hands off the floor.

Curl Up with Twist

Starting position: Lie on the back with feet flat and knees bent. Arms are folded and placed across the chest with hands on shoulders.

Movement: Do a partial curl up and twist the chest to the left. Repeat, turning the chest to the right (**Figure 9.11**).

Variations: Touch the outside of the knee with the elbow. Or touch both knees in succession. The sequence is up, touch left, touch right, and down.

Abdominal Cruncher

Starting position: Lie in supine position with feet flat, knees bent, and palms of hands cupped over the ears (not behind the head). An alternate position is to fold the arms across the chest and place the hands on the shoulders.

Movement: Tuck the chin and curl upward until the shoulder blades leave the floor. Return to the floor with a slow uncurling.

Variation: Lift the feet off the floor and bring the knees to waist level. Try to touch the right elbow to the left knee and vice versa while in the crunch position.

Leg and Agility Exercises

Recall that leg exercises also help children develop cardiovascular endurance.

Running in Place

Starting position: Stand with arms bent at the elbows.

Movement: Run in place. Begin slowly, counting only the left foot. Speed up somewhat, raising the knees to hip height. Then run at full speed, raising the knees hard. Finally, slow down. The run should be done on the toes.

Variations:

Tortoise and Hare. Jog slowly in place. On the command "Hare," double the speed. On the command "Tortoise," slow the tempo to the original slow jogging pace.

Marching. March in place, lifting the knees high and swinging the arms up. Turn right and left on command while marching. Turn completely around to the right and then to the left while marching.

Fast Stepping. Step in place for 10 seconds as rapidly as possible. Rest for 10 seconds and repeat fast stepping five or more times.

Jumping Jack

Starting position: Stand at attention.

Movement: On count 1, jump to a straddle position with arms overhead. On count 2, recover to starting position.

Variations:

Stride. Begin with the feet in a stride position (forward and back). Change feet with the overhead arm movement.

Cross. Instead of bringing the feet together when the arms come down, cross the feet each time, alternating the cross.

Quarter-turn. On the completion of each set of 8 counts, do a quarter-turn right. (After four sets, the child is facing in the original direction.) Do the same to the left.

Modified Jumping Jack. On count 1, jump to a straddle position with arms out to the sides, parallel to the floor, and palms down. On count 2, return to position.

Treadmill

Starting position: Assume the push up position, but with one leg brought forward so that the knee is under the chest (**Figure 9.12**).

Movement: Reverse the position of the feet, bringing the extended leg forward. Change back so that the original foot is forward. Continue rhythmically alternating feet.

Points to emphasize: The head should be kept up. A full exchange of the legs should be made, with the forward knee coming well under the chest each time.

Power Jumper

Starting position: Begin in a semi-crouched position, with knees flexed and arms extended backward.

Movement: Jump as high as possible and extend the arms upward and overhead.

Variations: Jump and perform different turns (quarter, half, and full). Or jump and perform different tasks (such as heel click, heel slap, clap hands, catch an imaginary pass, snare a rebound).

Figure 9.12 Treadmill.

Figure 9.13 Trunk twister.

Trunk-Twisting and Bending Exercises

Trunk Twister

Starting position: Stand with feet shoulder-width apart and pointed forward. The hands are cupped and placed loosely over the shoulders, with the elbows out and the chin tucked.

Movement: Bend downward, keeping the knees relaxed. Recover slightly. Bend downward again and simultaneously rotate the trunk to the left and then to the right (**Figure 9.13**). Return to original position, pulling the head back, with chin in.

Bear Hug

Starting position: Stand with feet comfortably spread and hands on hips.

Movement: Take a long step diagonally right, keeping the left foot anchored in place. Hug the right leg by encircling the thigh with both arms. Squeeze and stretch (**Figure 9.14**). Return to position. Hug the left leg. Return to position.

Point to emphasize: The bent leg should not exceed a right angle.

Side Flex

Starting position: Lie on one side with the lower arm extended overhead. The head rests on the lower arm. The legs are extended fully, one on top of the other.

Movement: Raise the upper arm and leg diagonally (**Figure 9.15**). Repeat for several counts and change to the other side.

Figure 9.14 Bear hug.

Body Circles

Starting position: Stand with feet shoulder-width apart, hands on hips, and body bent forward.

Movement: Make a complete circle with the upper body. A specified number of circles should be made to the right and the same number to the left.

Variations: Circle in one direction until told to stop, then reverse direction. Or change to a position in which the hands are on the shoulders and the elbows are kept wide. Otherwise, the exercise is the same.

Windmill

Starting position: Stand with feet shoulder-width apart and arms extended to the side with palms down.

Movement: Bend and twist at the trunk, bringing the right hand down to the left toes. Recover to starting position.

Figure 9.15 Side flex.

Bend and twist again, but bring the left hand to the right toes. Recover to starting position.

Back to Class

In our chapter-opening scenario, Mr. Kajiwara asked his students to perform 10 push ups in one minute. Instead of requiring that all his students do true push ups, what alternatives might he have allowed that could also have helped students develop arm-shoulder girdle strength? Be specific.

Examples of Fitness Routines

When planning fitness routines, establish variety in activities and include different approaches. This minimizes the inherent weaknesses of any single routine. The routines should exercise all major parts of the body. Teach students to avoid overloading the same body part with two sequential exercises. For example, if push ups (upper body strength) are being performed, the next exercise should not be crab walking, as it also stresses the arm-shoulder girdle.

Again, measure the workload for youngsters in *time* rather than in repetitions or speed (e.g., "Do your best for 20 seconds"). It is reasonable to expect a leaner youngster to be able to perform more repetitions in a certain amount of time than a child who is overweight. Develop positive attitudes toward activity by asking youngsters to do the best they can within the time allotted.

Student Leader Routine

Students enjoy leading their peers in single exercises or an entire routine. Students need prior practice if they are to lead their peers effectively in a stimulating exercise session. Don't force children to lead, because this can result in failure for both the child and the class. The routines in **Table 9.1** are examples of student leader exercises. Encourage youngsters to do the best they can within the specified time limit.

Table 9.1 Student Leader Exercises

Arm circles	30 seconds
Push-up challenges	30 seconds
Bend and twist	30 seconds
Treadmill	30 seconds
Sit up challenges	30 seconds
Single-leg crab kick	30 seconds
Knee to chest curl	30 seconds
Run in place	30 seconds
Standing hip bend	30 seconds

Conclude the routine with two to four minutes of jogging, rope jumping, or other aerobic activity.

Squad Leader Routine

In a squad leader routine, the class is divided into groups of four to five students. Each group is given a task card that lists 8 to 10 exercises grouped by how they impact different parts of the body. One of the group members begins leading the group through an exercise. Each time an exercise is completed, the card passes to a new leader. To ensure a balanced routine, each new leader must select an exercise from a different group. Use alternating intervals of music to signal exercising (30 seconds) and silence to indicate passing the card (5 to 10 seconds).

Squad leader routines give many students an opportunity to lead exercises in a small group. They are also effective for teaching students how to lead others and how to put together a well-balanced fitness routine.

Routine with Music

Music is highly motivating to children and increases the appeal of fitness routines. There are many commercial CD sets with exercise programs available. Pre-recorded music frees you from having to keep an eye on a stopwatch. A set of prerecorded music intervals on CD, titled *Physical Education Soundtracks, Vol. 1 and Vol. 2*, is available from Human Kinetics (see Web Resources).

A simple way to incorporate music is to let children move as long as music is playing and stretch whenever a silent interval occurs. A more specific routine using music follows. Notice that it alternates aerobic activities with strength and flexibility exercises. When the music is on, students perform the aerobic activities (for 30 seconds). Make sure you choose music with a strong rhythmic beat. When the silent interval is on, students perform the strength development and flexibility exercises (25 seconds). **Table 9.2** shows examples of various routines that could be used with music.

Table 9.2 Exercise Routines with Music	
Crab kicks	25 seconds
Rope jumping	30 seconds
Windmills	25 seconds
Walk and do arm circles	30 seconds
Abdominal crunchers	25 seconds
Jumping jack variations	30 seconds
Side flex	25 seconds
Two-step or gallop	30 seconds
Triceps push ups	25 seconds
Aerobic jumping	30 seconds
Push-up challenges	25 seconds
Leg extensions	30 seconds
Walking to cool down	30 seconds

Aerobic Fitness Routines

Aerobic exercises help develop cardiovascular endurance as well as strength and flexibility. Designate a leader to perform a series of movements that the other students follow. There are few limits to the range of activities a leader presents. The leader may integrate manipulative equipment (including balls, jump ropes, hoops, and wands) with the movement activities. The following are some teaching tips:

1. Use movement patterns that are organized by units of 4, 8, or 16 counts.
2. Vary movements so stretching and flowing movements are alternated with the more strenuous aerobic activities.
3. Keep steps relatively simple. Focus on activity rather than becoming competent rhythmic performers. Stress continuous movement (moving with the flow) rather than perfection of routines. Running and bouncing steps are easily followed and motivating.

4. Routines are best when they are not rigid. Youngsters shouldn't have to worry about being out of step.

5. Establish cue words to aid youngsters in following routines. Examples are "Bounce," "Step," "Reach," and "Jump."

The following basic steps and movements can be used to develop a variety of routines. The majority are performed to 4 counts, although this may vary.

Running and Walking Steps

Directional runs. Run forward, backward, diagonal, sideways, and turning.

Rhythmic runs. Run for three steps, then make a specific movement on the fourth beat. Examples of specific movements are knee lift, clap, jump, jump-turn, and hop.

Runs with variations. Run while lifting the knees, kicking up the heels, or slapping the thighs or heels; or run with legs extended as in the goose step.

Runs with arms in various positions. Run with hands on the hips, in the air above the head, and straight down.

Movements on the Floor

Side leg raises. Do these with a straight leg while lying on the side of the body.

Alternate leg raises. While on the back, raise one leg to meet the opposite hand. Repeat, using the opposite leg or both legs.

Rhythmic push ups. Do these in 2- or 4-count movements. A 4 count would be as follows: halfway down (count 1), nose touched to the floor (count 2), halfway up (count 3), and arms fully extended (count 4).

Crab kicks and treadmills. Do these to 4 counts.

Upright Rhythmic Movements

Lunge variations. Perform a lunge, stepping forward on the right foot while bending at the knee and extending the arms forward and diagonally upward (counts 1 and 2). Return to starting position by bringing the right foot back and pulling the arms into a jogging position (counts 3 and 4). The lunge can be varied by changing the direction of the movement, depth and speed of the action.

Side bends. Begin with the feet apart. Reach overhead while bending to the side. This movement is usually done to four beats: bend (count 1), hold (counts 2 and 3), and return (count 4).

Reaches. Reach upward alternately with each arm. Reach to the side for 2 counts. Fast alternating 1-count movements can be done, too.

Arm and shoulder circles. Make arm circles with either one or both arms. Vary the size and speed of the circles. Shoulder shrugs can be done in a similar fashion.

Jumping Jack Variations

Jump with arm movements. Alternately extend arms upward and then pull them in toward the chest.

Side jumping jacks. Use regular arm action while the feet jump from side to side or forward and backward together.

Feet variations. Try different variations, such as using forward stride with alternating feet or forward and side stride with alternating feet, adding kicks or knee lifts, crossing feet, or using heel-toe movements (turning on every 4 or 8 count).

Back to Class

If you were one of Mr. Kajiwara's fourth-grade students, do you think you would have found his fitness routine fun? If not, what changes would you make to the routine to make it more enjoyable for children?

Circuit Training Routine

A **circuit training** routine incorporates several stations, each with a designated fitness task. The student moves from station to station, generally in a prescribed order, completing the designated fitness task at each station. Exercises for the circuit should contribute to the development of all parts of the body. In addition, activities should contribute to the various components of physical fitness (strength, power, endurance, agility, and flexibility). Signs that include the name of the activity and any necessary cautions or stress points for execution should be placed at each station. The following are some suggestions for setting up this routine:

1. Each station provides an exercise task for the child to perform without aid. Exercises that directly follow each other should make demands on different parts of the body. This ensures that performance at any one station does not cause fatigue that could affect the ability to perform the next task.

2. Place an equal number of children at each station. This keeps demands on equipment low and activity high. For example, if there are 30 children for a circuit of six stations, place 5 children at each spot.

3. Music, whistle signals, and even verbal directions can be prerecorded to signal students to the next station. The tape provides time control and gives a measure of consistency to the circuit. Using tapes also allows you to help youngsters without worrying about timing each interval.

4. The number of stations can vary but probably should be no fewer than six (**Figure 9.16**) and no more than nine (**Figure 9.17**).

5. Use music segments (begin at 30 seconds) to indicate activity at each station; intervals of silence (10 seconds) announce it is time to stop and move forward to the next station. Ask students to do the best they can for 30 seconds at each station. This keeps fitness a personal rather than a competitive challenge.

6. Conclude circuit training with two to four minutes of walking, jogging, rope jumping, or other self-paced aerobic activity.

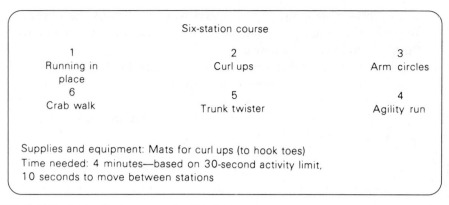

Figure 9.16 Example of a six-station circuit training course.

Fitness Games

Fitness games are excellent for cardiovascular endurance and create a high degree of motivation. When teaching these games to your students, emphasize that the object of the game is for them to *keep moving*. Structure these games so that they do not eliminate players. For instance, a player who is tagged doesn't leave the game; instead, that person becomes the tagger. This makes it difficult for players to tell who the tagger is, which is desirable since it ensures that players cannot safely stand around thinking the tagger is a significant distance from them. If various games stipulate a "safe" position, allow players to maintain this position for a maximum of 5 seconds. Because fitness games primarily focus on cardiovascular fitness, alternate the games with strength and flexibility activities. The following are examples of games that can be played.

Stoop tag. Players cannot be tagged when they stoop.

Train tag. Line up single file in groups of three or four and make a train by each player holding the hips of the player in front of him or her. Three

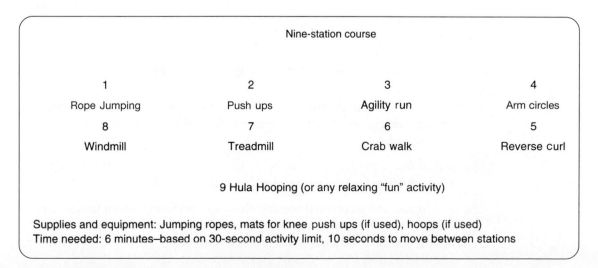

Figure 9.17 Example of a nine-station circuit training course.

or four players are designated as taggers who try to hook onto the rear of the train. If they are successful, the player at the front of the train must "get off" and become a new tagger.

Color tag. Players are safe when they stand on a specified color. The "safe" color may be changed by the leader at any time to keep children running from one spot to another.

Elbow swing tag. Players cannot be tagged as long as they are performing an elbow swing with another player.

Balance tag. Players are safe when they are balanced on one body part.

Push up tag. Players are safe when they are in push up position. Other exercise positions, such as bent-knee curl up and crab position, may be used.

Group tag: The only time a player is safe is when players are in a group (stipulated by the leader) holding hands. For example, the number might be "four," which means that students must be holding hands in groups of four to be safe.

Chapter Summary

Types of Physical Fitness

Physical fitness is a set of attributes that people have or achieve in relation to their ability to perform physical activity.

Health-related physical fitness is characterized by an ability to engage in moderate to vigorous physical activity with vitality and without undue fatigue. It includes cardiovascular endurance, body composition, flexibility, and muscular strength and endurance.

Skill-related physical fitness is related to athletic ability and physical performance. Its components include the health-related components as well as agility, balance, coordination, power, and speed.

Common Questions About Children's Fitness

In the 50 years since its widespread introduction into America's schools, fitness testing and training have not improved the health or fitness of America's schoolchildren.

The goal of fitness programs should be to improve health-related fitness and teach children fitness routines they can follow for a lifetime.

The most significant factors influencing children's performance on fitness tests are heredity, maturation, and body composition. Level of physical activity does not significantly influence fitness in children.

Fitness awards generally motivate only those students who feel they can earn them, and they promote extrinsic rather than intrinsic motivation. Thus, they are not recommended. They can be effective with primary-grade children for rewarding participation rather than achievement.

Promoting a Positive Attitude Toward Fitness

Introduce fitness activities in a way that encourages children to discover their personal workload. For example, use time rather than number of repetitions or speed as the variable and ask children to do the best they can within that time limit.

Present a variety of fitness challenges, that is, assignments that children can accomplish. Make sure you start easy and progress slowly, focusing on activities of low to moderate intensity. Stay active with your students, and reinforce their participation rather than achievement.

Avoid harmful activities such as those that place stress on the neck, lower back, or knee joint.

Implementing Fitness Routines

Fitness routines should not extend beyond 8 to 10 minutes, including a warm-up. Assume an active role, and use activities that exercise all body parts and cover the major components of fitness. Vary the routine from one day to the next, and use music to time segments.

Never use fitness activities as a punishment.

Fitness Activities for Children in Kindergarten Through Second Grade

Present fitness exercises to primary grade children as personal challenges, for example, by introducing exercises with the instruction, "See if you can do this."

Include activities to strengthen each body region, as well as activities to develop cardiovascular endurance; for example, jump-rope exercises, running games, etc.

Fitness Activities for Children in Third Through Sixth Grade

Upper-elementary children can handle more structured exercises for flexibility, strength, agility, and cardiovascular endurance.

Fitness routines for upper elementary students can include student leader routines, squad leader routines, routines with music, aerobics routines, and circuit training routines.

Fitness games are excellent for developing cardiovascular endurance. When presenting these games, make sure you convey to students that the object of the game is to keep moving.

Review Questions

Content Review

1. What type of physical fitness should a classroom teacher strive to help students develop, and why?

2. Why do so many students fail fitness tests? Defend your answer.

3. In what situations might it be appropriate for teachers to use fitness awards? In what situations should they not be used?

4. How can you, as a classroom teacher, make fitness activities fun for your students? Name at least three ways.

5. Design a fitness routine for 20 second-grade students. It should be 10 minutes in length, including warm-up and cool-down, with 30-second activities to develop strength in the major body regions and to promote cardiovascular endurance.

Real World

1. It's your first week of teaching, and you're packing up for the day when another teacher stops by your sixth-grade classroom. "I saw you leading your class through some calisthenics today," she says, referring to a 10-minute fitness routine you'd introduced to your students that afternoon. "You probably got a strong message in your teacher training about keeping kids active because of this obesity epidemic we're facing, but let me tell you, I've been teaching for 20 years, and I can guarantee kids don't like that fitness stuff. All they really want to do is run around, blow off some steam, you know? Their whole day is so structured, the last thing they need is us telling them what to do on the playground." How might you respond?

2. In a faculty meeting, the school's PE instructor proposes a six-week "Focus on Fitness" promotion. During the six-week period, he would provide classroom teachers with prescribed fitness routines, through which they would lead their students on days they did not have PE. He would lead them through the routines himself during the students' PE class. On the final day of the promotion, a competition would be held. Parents would be invited to watch children compete in various fitness activities for medals. "This would be highly motivating for kids," he explains, "and it would help parents see that our school cares about the health of their children." Would you support the proposal as described? If not, what aspects would you change?

What About You?

Throughout this text, we've emphasized the importance of being a good role model for your students. When you think about, for instance, performing jumping jacks with your students or demonstrating how to do a push up, how does this make you feel?

_____

_____

If you wrote that you feel less than confident about modeling fitness activities for your students, what steps could you take to increase your confidence level?

_____

_____

References and Suggested Readings

Bailey, R.C., Olson, J., Pepper, S.L., Porszaz, J., Barstow, T.J., and Cooper, D.M. (1995). The level and tempo of children's physical activities: An observational study. *Medicine and Science in Sport and Exercise*, 27(7), 1033–1041.

Bouchard, C. (1999). Heredity and health related fitness. In C.B. Corbin and R. P. Pangrazi (eds.), *Toward a better understanding of physical fitness & activity*. Scottsdale, AZ: Holcomb Hathaway Publishers.

Bouchard, C., Dionne, F.T., Simoneau, J., and Boulay, M. (1992). Genetics of aerobic and anaerobic performances. *Exercise and Sport Sciences Reviews*, 20, 27–58.

Corbin, C.B., Lindsey, R., and Welk, G. (2000). *Concepts of physical fitness and wellness: A comprehensive lifestyle approach*. Boston: McGraw-Hill.

Corbin, C.B., Lovejoy, P.Y., Steingard, P., and Emerson, R. (1990). Fitness awards: Do they accomplish their intended objectives? *American Journal of Health Promotion*, 4, 345–351.

Corbin, C.B., Lovejoy, P.Y., and Whitehead, J.R. (1988). Youth physical fitness awards. *Quest*, 40, 200–218.

Corbin, C.B., and Pangrazi, R.P. (1992). Are American children and youth fit? *Research Quarterly for Exercise and Sport*, 63(2), 96–106.

Corbin, C.B., and Pangrazi, R.P. (1998). Physical activity pyramid rebuffs peak experience. *ACSM's Health & Fitness Journal*, 2(1), 12–17.

Gortmaker, S.L., Dietz, W.H., Sobol, A.N., and Wehler, C.A. (1987). Increasing pediatric obesity in the U.S. *American Journal of Diseases in Children*, 14, 535–540.

Harter, S. (1978). Effectance motivation revisited. *Child Development*, 21, 34–64.

Hedley, A.A., Ogden, C.L., Johnson, C.L., Carroll, M.D., Curtin, L.R., and Flegal, K.M. (2004). Prevalence of overweight and obesity among US children, adolescents, and adults, 1999–2002. *Journal of the American Medical Association,* 291(23), 2847–2850.

Lindsey, R., and Corbin, C. (1989). Questionable exercises—Some safer alternatives. *Journal of Physical Education, Recreation, and Dance*, 60(8), 26–32.

Locke, E.A., and Lathan, G.P. (1985). The application of goal setting to sports. *Journal of Sport Psychology*, 7, 205–222.

Macfarlane, P.A. (1993). Out with the sit-up, in with the curl-up. *Journal of Physical Education, Recreation, and Dance*, 64(6), 62–66.

National Association for Sport and Physical Education. (2004). *Physical activity for children: A statement of guidelines* (2nd ed.). Reston, VA: National Association for Sport and Physical Education.

National Association for Sport and Physical Education. (2005). *Physical best activity guide* (2nd ed.). Champaign, IL: Human Kinetics.

National Association for Sport and Physical Education. (2005). *Physical education for lifelong fitness* (2nd ed.). Champaign, IL: Human Kinetics.

National Center for Health Statistics. (2007). FastStats A to Z: Overweight. Available at: www.cdc.gov/nchs/fastats/overwt.htm.

Pangrazi, R.P. (2007). *Dynamic physical education curriculum guide: Lesson plans for implementation* (15th ed.). San Francisco: Pearson Benjamin Cummings.

Pangrazi, R.P., and Corbin, C.B. (1990). Age as a factor relating to physical fitness test performance. *Research Quarterly for Exercise and Sport*, 61(4), 410–414.

Pate, R., Corbin, C.B., and Pangrazi, R.P. (1998). Physical activity for young people. *Physical Fitness and Sports Research Digest,* 3(3), 1–8.

Pate, R.R., Dowda, M., and Ross, J.G. (1990). Association between physical activity and physical fitness in American children. *American Journal of Diseases of Children*, 144, 1123–1129.

Pate, R.R., and Ross, J.G. (1987). Factors associated with health-related fitness. *Journal of Physical Education, Recreation, and Dance*, 58(9), 93–96.

Payne, V.G., and Morrow, J.R., Jr. (1993). Exercise and VO^2 max in children: A meta-analysis. *Research Quarterly for Exercise and Sport*, 64(3), 305–313.

Plowman, S.A. (1993). Physical fitness and healthy low back function. *Physical Activity and Fitness Research Digest*, 1(3), 1–8.

President's Council on Physical Fitness and Sports. (2007). *The president's challenge handbook.* Washington, DC: President's Council on Physical Fitness and Sports.

Ross, J.G., Pate, R.R., Caspersen, C.J., Damberg, C.L., and Svilar, M. (1987). Home and community in children's exercise habits. *Journal of Physical Education, Recreation, and Dance*, 58(9), 85–92.

Rowland, T.W. (1990). *Exercise and children's health*. Champaign, IL: Human Kinetics.

Smith, L.L., Brunetz, M.H., Chenier, T.C., McCammon, M.R., Hourmard, J.A., Franklin, M.E., and Israel, R.G. (1993). The effects of static and ballistic stretching on delayed onset muscle soreness and creatine kinase. *Research Quarterly for Exercise and Sport*, 64(1), 103–107.

U.S. Department of Health and Human Services. (1996). *Physical activity and health: A report of the Surgeon General.* Atlanta, GA: U.S. Department of Health and Human Services, Centers for Disease Control and Prevention, National Center for Chronic Disease Prevention and Health Promotion.

U.S. Department of Health and Human Services. (2002). *Prevalence of overweight among children and adolescents: United States, 1999.* Atlanta, GA: U.S. Department of Health and Human Services, Centers for Disease Control and Prevention, National Center for Health Statistics.

Whitehead, J.R., and Corbin, C.B. (1991). Effects of fitness test type, teacher, and gender on exercise, intrinsic motivation, and physical self-worth. *Journal of School Health*, 61, 11–16.

Williams, D.P., Going, S.B., Lohman, T.G., Harsha, D.W., Webber, L.S., and Bereson, G.S. (1992). Body fatness and the risk of elevated blood pressure, total cholesterol and serum lipoprotein ratios in children and youth. *American Journal of Public Health*, 82, 358–363.

Web Resources

Action for Healthy Kids:
www.actionforhealthykids.org
American Academy of Pediatrics:
www.aap.org
American Heart Association:
www.americanheart.org
Centers for Disease Control and Prevention:
www.cdc.gov/nccdphp/dnpa/physical/recommendations
The Cooper Institute:
www.cooperinst.org/products/grams
Healthy People 2010:
www.health.gov/healthypeople
Healthy Youth (CDC's Division of Adolescent and School Health):
www.cdc.gov/HealthyYouth/publications
Mayo Clinic:
www.mayoclinic.com/health
Medline Plus (National Library of Medicine and
the National Institutes of Health):
www.nlm.nih.gov/medlineplus/exerciseforchildren
PE4life.org:
www.pe4life.org
The President's Challenge:
www.presidentschallenge.org

10

Improving Students' Nutrition

Learning Objectives

After reading this chapter, you will be able to . . .

○ Describe the role of a school health committee in developing a schoolwide action plan for improving students' nutrition.

○ Summarize specific policies that schools should establish related to school breakfasts and lunches, point-of-decision prompts, classroom rewards, school celebrations, and school and club fundraisers.

○ Gather appropriate data about students' eating behaviors.

○ Identify reliable, age-appropriate resources for teaching students the basics of good nutrition.

○ Discuss the benefits of reinforcing students for making healthful food choices.

○ Identify strategies for helping parents understand their children's weight, increasing parents' nutrition knowledge, and inviting parents' participation in schoolwide nutrition initiatives.

Classroom Challenge

When Mr. Harding enters school this morning, he feels like a man on a mission. Yesterday, he received the results of some tests that his doctor had conducted as part of his annual checkup. He learned that his weight, blood pressure, and cholesterol levels are all above normal and that he has early signs of type 2 diabetes. He was advised to lose at least 15 pounds, adopt a diet low in saturated and trans fats, and perform at least 30 minutes of moderate to vigorous physical activity daily. Recognizing that his poor eating habits and low level of physical activity began in childhood, he is determined not only to take the prescribed actions to improve his own health but also to use his new awareness to help his students.

Greeting his third-grade class, he notices for the first time how many of his students already appear to be overweight. Later, when they get out their morning snacks, he observes that only 3 students out of 24 have brought a piece of fruit: the others are eating cookies, chips, or candy. Worse, when he congratulates one of his students for getting 100 percent on his spelling test, he automatically nods to the candy jar on his desk that he's been using for rewards for years. And when he monitors the cafeteria at lunch, he notes that the menu choices are hot dogs or macaroni and cheese.

At the end of the day, he stops instruction early to tell his class that, beginning the following week, he is going to begin teaching them the basics of good nutrition. He also says that he'll be sending information home to their parents about what constitutes an acceptable morning snack. Finally, as a display of his new focus on nutrition, he ceremoniously picks up the candy jar from his desk and spills its contents into his wastepaper basket.

His students gasp. Miguel, the student who'd been rewarded that morning for his perfect spelling score, shouts out, "Don't do that, Mr. H! You won't have anything to give us for a reward!"

After his students leave, Mr. Harding sits at his desk and stares at their empty seats. Thinking about the enormity of the task that he's set himself— improving his students' nutrition—he feels suddenly deflated. Sure, he can teach them the basics of good nutrition and tell their parents not to send them to school with junk food for snacks, but will that really make a difference when even the choices in the school cafeteria are full of empty calories? Where should he begin?

hen initiating any project, one of the toughest tasks for teachers is getting started. Often, great ideas get lost because teachers feel overwhelmed by the enormity of a given subject and cannot conceive of where to begin. This is especially true of ideas that tackle public health concerns such as children's nutrition: because health is influenced by many factors, including age, culture, socio-economic level, and social-political issues, the issue seems almost impossible to address. But the key with any project is to break down the work into a series of manageable tasks. This chapter explores a number of specific actions that can be taken to improve students' nutrition and teach them the basics of sound nutritional habits.

The approach is twofold: the first step involves creating a team to develop a schoolwide initiative to bring attention to students' nutrition and to change school policies and procedures to support improved nutrition. The second step occurs at the classroom teacher level—good teachers making good things happen. You can implement the action items described in this section independently, or in cooperation with other teachers and your administration. When you do, you'll be sending the message to students, parents, and the broader community that you value children's health.

Schoolwide Strategies for Improving Students' Nutrition

Just as "it takes a village to raise a child," the goal of improving students' nutrition demands an approach involving the total school environment. Why?

Let's say you have taught your students the basics of good nutrition and have watched them make healthful food choices at breakfast and lunch today. But that afternoon, you watch the school librarian awarding your top reader a box of jelly beans. Later on, a parent arrives for a birthday celebration with cupcakes, a bag of cheese curls, and several two-liter bottles of soda. And finally, after school is dismissed, there is a "Fun Friday" fundraiser for which the student body is selling candy and chips. At this point, you'd probably be feeling more than a little frustrated.

To be effective, any program for improving students' nutrition must be coordinated throughout the school. Only then will there be some assurance that the value of good nutrition and healthy eating habits is being consistently reinforced. Here we discuss strategies for making improved nutrition the goal of a schoolwide initiative.

Form a School Health Committee

The first step in developing a schoolwide initiative for improving students' nutrition is to form a school health committee. You need a dedicated committee because, as just noted, you cannot improve students' nutrition alone. The combined talents, experience, resources, and relationships of many people in the school and broader community are essential to success. Don't assume that, as an individual teacher, you don't have the clout to bring such a group together. Instead, talk to your school administrator: by convincing him or her of your concern for your students' health, you will have made a strong ally who can help make your vision a reality. Here are a few more networking strategies to increase the sphere of your influence.

- Ask advice from other teachers and administrators, as well as friends. Often, your contacts will know others whom you should meet who will be sympathetic to your cause. The more people who become informed about your desire to improve students' nutrition, the easier it will be to convince the decision makers.
- Get involved in other schoolwide projects. Attend PTA meetings, talk with youth sport leaders, and visit local youth clubs. Volunteer to help with projects in these groups. If you want people to help you, you have to help them.
- Take your cause to the local newspaper. Explain that you want to form a school health committee and why. Invite interested community members to contact you.

To increase the potential influence of your committee, invite key personnel in the community to become members. Other teachers and staff, district administrators, parents, students, nutrition or PE faculty from a nearby university, healthcare providers, police and fire department staff, local business owners, and leaders of community organizations such as the local YMCA are just some of your potential partners. Also, at the initial meeting of this group, it is important to encourage attendees to invite other people they think should be members.

Finally, be patient and persistent. It has often been said that it takes three years to implement change within a school system. Things move slowly, but they do move. Even though your efforts will probably be turned down many times, remember that you are doing this for kids; sooner or later, people will come to see the benefit of your proposal.

Conduct Some Initial Research

Appropriate goals and effective interventions require some initial research. One successful strategy to help generate and maintain a quality schoolwide nutrition program is to meet with other schools that have existing programs. The phrase "Don't
reinvent the wheel" applies here. Learning what has been successful at other schools
may save your committee time and effort. Keep in mind that the demographics of
the school may contribute to the success of some activities. Therefore, an activity
that wasn't effective at Franklin Elementary may be effective at Monroe Elementary
and vice versa. When working with other schools, it is important to keep an open
mind, collect as much information as possible, and allow the committee to discuss
future directions based on the experiences of other schools.

Your initial research should also include data. Check out the United States
Department of Agriculture's (USDA's) consumer information online (see
Web Resources), and find out about levels of nutrition in your state by
clicking on "How Is Your State Doing?" This community-mapping feature
provides state-by-state data on several health indicators, including nutrient in-
takes for most vitamins and minerals, percentages of overweight children, etc.
If you find out, for instance, that a minority of children in your state consume adequate calcium, you can use that data to help shape your objectives.

In addition, download the following kit of materials from the
USDA—*Changing the Scene: Improving the School Nutrition Environment* (see
Web Resources)—which can serve as a starting point for developing an
effective plan of action. It offers general guidelines for planning for
change, offers six components of a healthy school environment, and provides ways to evaluate the success of the program. Material from the kit is
also available on overhead transparencies.

Develop an Action Plan

Once the committee has done some initial research, the next step is to develop an
action plan. As the force behind the plan, you or someone you have asked for help
should provide the committee with the background information you've gleaned
from your research and your desired vision for the school. Then invite the committee
to help you develop short-term and long-term objectives for the program. As always,
measurable objectives are more useful: "Increase students' consumption of fruits and

vegetables by 25 percent by the end of the school year" is an objective that can be evaluated for its success or failure, whereas "Improve students' diet" cannot.

Next, the committee needs to brainstorm for ideas about policy changes and activities that will help the school achieve its objectives, then prioritize those ideas with the greatest promise. Lastly, it is important to be satisfied with moving forward in small steps. This prevents overwhelming teachers, students, and communities.

For example, the committee may decide that their first activity will be to give a short presentation about the program objectives at the school's open house. They may decide to set up a booth at the front door from which members can survey and provide information to parents. After reviewing the results of the survey, committee members can determine the next steps to take. Another school may begin by mailing questionnaires home to parents or giving students fliers about the program to take home. The key is to keep the tasks manageable and aligned with desired goals.

Back to Class

Mr. Harding logs onto www.nutrition.gov and, using the Community Nutrition Mapping Project, finds out that only 16 percent of the residents of his state consume the recommended number of servings of vegetables daily. How could he use this information to develop an objective and an activity for his students?

Establish Policies Promoting Healthful Nutrition

Children's eating behaviors can be improved readily in the school environment because it offers opportunities to influence youngsters in a variety of ways. The school health committee can take the lead in promoting policy changes that will then be approved by the school board or other key decision makers. The following are general policy guidelines adopted in most schools that advocate a quality nutrition environment.

- All students must have access to nutritious foods. Hungry children cannot perform well academically. For this reason, programs that ensure students receive a nutrient-dense breakfast and lunch should be developed. School breakfast and lunch programs are discussed in more detail shortly.
- The eating environment should be clean, safe, and attractive.
- Lunch should be served as close to noon as possible. More and more schools are serving lunch to students as early as 10 a.m.
- If vending machines are on campus, they must serve only nutritious, healthy choices.
- Nutrition education content should be integrated into classroom activities. See the Activity Cards on Nutrition and Sun Safety for examples of nutrition-related activities.

Feedback should be gathered from parents and other community members regarding their feelings about the nutrition environment at the school or the changes being made.

In addition, most schools that advocate a quality nutrition environment have specific policies related to school breakfast and lunch menus, posting point-of-decision prompts, the use of food as rewards, the choice of foods used in school celebrations, and the sale of foods for fundraisers. Let's look at each of these policies in more detail.

Develop Healthful School Breakfast and Lunch Menus

Educational experts realize that to keep children healthy, schools need to provide ample amounts of nutritious food (Anspaugh and Ezell, 2004). Research also suggests that healthy and well-nourished students perform better academically than students who are hungry (Hanson et al., 2005), and the USDA cites studies showing increased attention span and fewer behavioral problems in children who eat breakfast (USDA, 2003). Public schools are required by law to provide breakfasts and lunches at low cost to all students and free of charge to low-income students. For this reason, many students consume both breakfast and lunch at school; in other words, the school provides a majority of their meals during the school week. Thus, it's critical that the meals schools provide are of high quality.

School breakfasts and lunches should be made up of a variety of foods high in **nutrient density**. This means the foods provide the highest amount of nutrients for the lowest amount of energy (number of calories). For example, a large bowl of fruit provides fiber-rich carbohydrates plus essential vitamins and minerals for fewer than half the calories in a commonly offered alternative dessert: a large chocolate-chip cookie. When cookies *are* served, they should be made with whole-grain flour, oats, shredded carrots, applesauce or mashed banana, and healthful plant oils instead of butter. Foods high in "empty calories," such as French fries and cupcakes, should not make up even a small portion of school meals. Recommendations for nutrition standards and instructional materials are available from the USDA (see Web Resources).

In most schools, the breakfast and lunch programs are operated by private businesses driven by economic realities: they must sell an adequate volume of food to stay in business. Processed food is cheaper than fresh food, has a longer shelf life, and is more appealing to many students. Thus, food service directors worry that if they offer "healthy" foods, they will only increase their costs and end up with surplus perishable food that students didn't want. So, it's not surprising that breakfast menus are often dominated by white breads, waffles, and sugar-laden cereals, and lunch menus offer hot dogs and French fries.

Fortunately, across the United States, schools are proving that this worry is unwarranted. A recent survey conducted by the Centers for Disease Control and Prevention (CDC) found that more schools are offering salads and vegetables, removing the skin from poultry before cooking, and substituting low-fat cheeses than when the same survey was conducted six years earlier (Sack, 2007), and children are choosing them. For example, changes in cafeteria offerings in Mesa, Arizona, schools have shown that children will choose healthier foods when given the options. There, the food and nutrition director chose to experiment with different menu options to see if youngsters would select them. Fruit and yogurt soon became a best seller at breakfast and lunch. Mandarin chicken salad, sandwiches, and turkey wraps also were popular choices. The following are some of the other healthy choices that were offered: six new entree salads, two versions of a grilled chicken sandwich on whole wheat bread, two different tortilla wraps, and fish items. The student salad bar was modified to include fresh vegetable salads that included a broader selection of greens such as broccoli, bean sprouts, peas, and jicama. Not only did youngsters make healthy selections, but total cafeteria revenue actually increased.

In addition, the school garden movement is teaching schoolchildren across the United States how to grow, harvest, and prepare nutritious school breakfasts and lunches. When children begin to understand how seeds, soil, sunshine, water, and their own labor produce fresh and nourishing foods, they are more likely to choose those foods at school and ask for them at home. For more information on the school garden movement, visit The Edible Schoolyard online (see Web Resources).

Back to Class

Mr. Harding also discovers that 27 percent of the children in his state are clinically overweight. How might the school health committee use this statistic to influence the school's food services provider to offer more healthful menu choices?

Post Nutrition Point-of-Decision Prompts

Point-of-decision prompts are bulletin boards, signs, and other prompts placed at locations where people make decisions with the goal of influencing those decisions—for example, decisions about what to eat. Schools dedicated to improving students' nutrition should post point-of-decision prompts in the cafeteria to complement the nutrition messages that students are receiving throughout the school.

The effectiveness of using signs to prompt individual choices was first evaluated in a study of people using stairs versus elevators. When signs were placed near the elevators encouraging users to take the stairs, the use of the stairs increased by 54 percent. In addition, evidence showed that tailoring the prompts to appeal to specific populations increased their effectiveness (Kahn et al., 2002).

Figures 10.1 and 10.2 Point-of-decision prompts include signs encouraging students to eat five fruits and vegetables per day, and to balance their energy intake and expenditure.

Point-of-decision prompts about principles of good nutrition and eating habits placed in the school cafeteria can be used to remind students to choose healthy foods. For example, prompts may remind students to eat five fruits and vegetables a day and to balance food and physical activity (**Figures 10.1 and 10.2**). Such prompts can also serve as discussion starters for teachers.

Don't Use Foods as Rewards

Many teachers hand out candy bars or other sweets as rewards for correct answers, good behavior, etc. Some teachers allow students to pick from a candy jar when they do well. Nutrition experts caution against such practices, saying that they link these foods to self-esteem and comfort and send young people the message that they can use sweets to lift their spirits or to forget things that are bothering them. Thus, a schoolwide policy should be established prohibiting teachers from giving students sweets (and other junk foods) as a reward.

A new rewards policy, which should be developed by the school principal, would allow teachers to use stickers, pencils, and other non-food items as rewards. The Center for Science in the Public Interest's report, *Constructive Classroom Rewards: Promoting Good Habits While Protecting Children's Health*, offers many ideas for using rewards other than food (see Web Resources).

Another alternative is to allow teachers to give food to students as long as it is nutritious. Think of the positive message sent to children about eating healthy foods if an apple is the reward for a correct answer. An apple would be viewed as a treat. This method is particularly effective if implemented during the students' first few years of school.

Implement a Healthful Celebrations Policy

Many schools allow teachers to celebrate holidays and students' birthdays in the classroom. Typically, parents bring in the food for such events, and wanting to please the class, offer cupcakes and sugar-filled drinks. But because they attend only a few holiday parties and their own child's birthday celebration, parents usually don't realize how often cupcakes and sodas are offered in the classroom. When they're informed that their child eats these types of foods 40 to 60 times during the school year, many are willing to offer healthy alternatives.

Schools should establish a policy on acceptable foods to offer during celebrations. Many foods that are appealing to youngsters are also nutritious. For example, the brochure *Healthy Celebrations: Promoting a Healthy School Environment*, from the Connecticut Department of Education, offers alternatives; download it to share with parents and students (see Web Resources).

The following are examples of foods and drinks that the brochure recommends serving at school celebrations:

- Low-fat or nonfat plain or flavored milk, 100 percent juice, water, flavored/sparkling water (without added sugars or sweeteners), sparkling punch (seltzer and 100 percent fruit juice)
- Fruit smoothies (blend berries, bananas, and pineapple)
- Fresh fruit assortment, fruit and cheese kabobs, fruit salad, fruit with low-fat whipped topping
- Dried fruit (raisins, cranberries, apricots, banana chips), 100 percent fruit snacks
- Vegetable trays with low-fat dip, celery and carrots with peanut butter and raisins
- Whole-grain crackers with cheese cubes, string cheese, or hummus
- Waffles or pancakes topped with fruit
- Pretzels, low-fat popcorn, rice cakes, bread sticks, graham crackers, and animal crackers
- Angel food cake, plain or topped with fruit
- Bagel slices with peanut butter or jam, fruit or grain muffin (low-fat), whole wheat English muffin, hot pretzels
- Pizza with low-fat toppings (vegetables, lean ham, Canadian bacon), pizza dippers with marinara sauce
- Ham, cheese, or turkey sandwiches or wraps (with low-fat condiments)
- Low-fat pudding, low-fat yogurt, squeezable yogurt, yogurt smoothies, yogurt parfaits, or banana splits (yogurt and fruit topped with cereal, granola, or crushed graham crackers)
- Quesadillas or bean burrito with salsa
- Low-fat breakfast or granola bars
- Low-fat tortilla chips with salsa or bean dip
- Trail/cereal mix (whole-grain, low-sugar cereals mixed with dried fruit, pretzels, etc.)
- Nuts and seeds

Focus Fundraising Events on Healthful Foods

Another event where unhealthy foods are offered to youngsters is the school or club fundraiser. Some schools schedule Fun Fridays, where students bring money to school to purchase candy bars and sugar-filled drinks at the end of the day. The money raised funds for school equipment and events. Other schools and clubs hold bake sales or have students sell boxes of cookies, candies, or chocolates door-to-door. Certainly, schools and clubs need to raise funds for projects; however, schools should establish a policy stating that they may do so only by offering non-food items or foods that have been approved as nutritious.

Reflect, Evaluate, and Progress

Once the committee has established the policies for the schoolwide nutrition initiative, reflection and evaluation are essential to ensure progress and improvement. For instance, perhaps the committee offers a family cooking class, and it is met with low attendance. Was this because the class wasn't appealing to children and families? Or was it poorly advertised? Or was it scheduled on the same day as the Little League opening or the school play? Similarly, if the cafeteria increases its healthful menu choices and eliminates hot dogs, French fries, and sodas, are students purchasing and eating the new foods? If not, why not? Without thoughtful reflection and honest evaluation, the desired initiatives run the risk of becoming stale, dormant, and possibly nonexistent. With quality reflection, programs continue to evolve to meet the needs of the school and community.

Back to Class

The health committee at Mr. Harding's school has decided to hold a fundraiser to raise money for the purchase of pedometers for all students. Which of the following should the committee decide to sell to families and community members? You may choose more than one item, but explain the reasons behind your choice(s):

- Boxes of cookies
- Packets of vegetable seeds
- Reduced-fat chocolate bars
- Pedometers
- Scenic calendars
- Shares in the harvest from the school's garden

Classroom Strategies for Improving Students' Nutrition

Although we've discussed the importance of a schoolwide initiative to improve students' nutrition, there remains a great deal you can do to promote healthy eating right in your classroom. It is often the case that children are most strongly influenced to change their behavior because of the efforts of their classroom teacher. If you give the topic of nutrition consistent attention over time, you'll succeed in shifting your students' eating behaviors.

This section discusses strategies for improving students' nutrition that you can accomplish in your classroom. They are not difficult and don't take too much time away from academic pursuits, yet implementing these steps can improve the health of children throughout their lifetime.

Gather Data About Students' Eating Behaviors

Classroom teachers spend the school day close to their students so are in a position to observe students' eating behaviors. Carefully observe students at snack time and at lunch. What foods do they choose? What portion sizes? Do they actually eat what they put on their plate? Taking notes will help you remember the types of information some students may require to improve their nutritional status. If you notice that a child has an abnormal appetite, excessive or poor, you'll need to investigate further. Changes in appetite can be caused by depression, anxiety, or other emotional issues, and occasionally they are symptomatic of an underlying physical disorder.

In addition to observation, you can gather data by conducting a survey of your students. The following are examples of questions that you might ask:

- Are there foods you don't like or won't eat?
- Did you drink any milk yesterday? Do you like cheese and yogurt?
- Do you eat fruit every day? What fruits are your favorites? Which do you eat the most?
- Do you eat vegetables? What vegetables do you eat the most? How many do you eat each day?
- What are your favorite foods? If you could pick what you want to eat for every meal tomorrow, what would you choose for breakfast, lunch, and dinner?
- Do you like to snack between meals? What are your favorite snacks? Do you snack alone or with friends and parents?
- Does your family eat together at dinner? With whom do you eat most often? Do you ever prepare your own meals?
- Do your parents remind you to eat certain foods? What foods do they encourage you to eat?
- Do you go grocery shopping with your parents? Do you help them select healthy foods?

Such questions elicit information that may help you guide your students toward healthier eating and improved nutrition. For example, if students were to respond that they don't drink milk or eat yogurt or cheese, you would know that you'd need to teach them that these foods are important for building strong bones. Students who say they eat at irregular intervals and skip meals may be deficient in essential nutrients and overall caloric intake. On the other hand, students who report that they eat and snack alone, especially when in front of the television, may eat more than they need because of boredom and inattention. When a family eats

together, parents have an opportunity to model proper eating behaviors and encourage children to share their thoughts and feelings. Another way for children to learn about nutrition is to go grocery shopping with parents and help them select healthy foods.

As a classroom teacher, you are in a unique position to observe children and identify unhealthy behaviors. The goal of observation and questioning about eating habits is not to diagnose problems and prescribe remedies, but rather it is to help you determine what information your students require, and in appropriate cases, to alert parents and healthcare professionals about children in need.

Teach the Basics of Good Nutrition

For students to be able to make healthy eating choices, they need to understand the basics of good nutrition. You should plan to cover a number of topics, including how to select food from every food group, how to get the most nutrition from the calories consumed (nutrient density), how to choose an appropriate portion, and how to balance food and physical activity. Keep the information basic, simple, and easy to understand. An excellent starting point is to become familiar with the USDA website MyPyramid (see Web Resources). For students, this site contains a colorful poster of MyPyramid for Kids (**Figure 10.3**), worksheets, coloring pages, and an interactive computer game titled MyPyramid Blast Off. The material is available free of charge at the website, and you can get all the materials, including the Blast Off game, on a CD as well.

For teachers, the MyPyramid website contains a series of lesson plans for three grade levels: kindergarten through second grade, grades three and four, and grades five and six. The lessons include all the necessary materials to teach a quality lesson, including reproducible worksheets, instructional objectives, and expected skill outcomes. They offer a well-organized plan for teaching basic nutrition and eating skills.

Another excellent teaching tool for upper-grade students tackles the subject of portion control. The two-part presentation, called *Portion Distortion I and II*, is part of the Obesity Education Initiative of the National Heart, Lung, and Blood Institute (see Web Resources). This interactive presentation demonstrates the dramatic increase in food portion sizes in the last 20 years.

Back to Class

In conducting his initial research, Mr. Harding discovers that more than 13 percent of his state's population have a median household income below the poverty line. How could he use this data to make his instruction in nutrition effective for all his students?

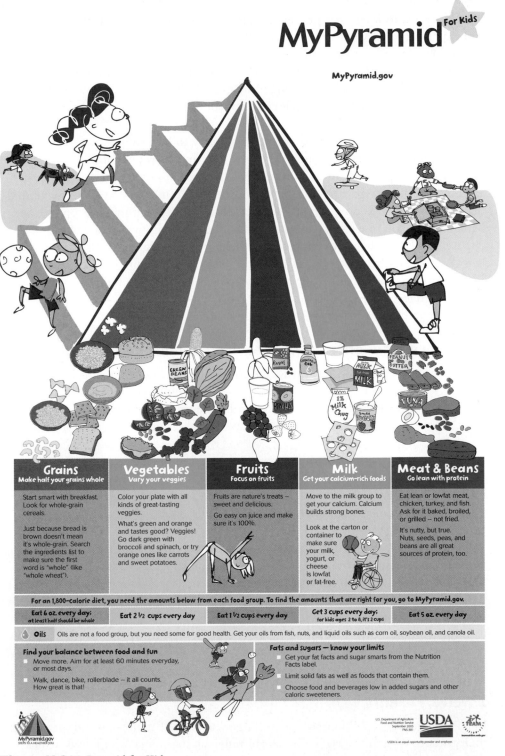

Figure 10.3 MyPyramid for Kids.

Teach Age-Appropriate Weight Management

Students need to learn that proper weight management is a result of caloric intake and expenditure. As you can see in the illustration of energy balance in Figure 10.4, when the calories you consume match those you expend each day, you neither gain nor lose weight. With children, the energy equation is not as straightforward as with adults because it is confounded by growth; however, as a general rule, if children eat substantially more calories than they burn, they are likely to gain weight.

For years it was common to ask students to try to lose weight or to maintain their current weight, even though they were growing. This unrealistic expectation often frustrated parents and students. Dieting is a health issue that should be managed by a healthcare professional; therefore, make it your policy to avoid suggesting that your students go on a weight-loss diet. However, it is entirely appropriate and beneficial for you to encourage healthy food choices and physical activity for all children, and these behaviors in turn may help resolve weight-management problems. Also remember that as a classroom teacher, you are an important role model; use not only words but also your behavior to encourage all students to eat wisely and stay active.

Reinforce Students in Making Healthful Food Choices

You cannot always watch what students choose to eat, but when you do observe healthy food choices, offer a few words of positive reinforcement in private, so as not to embarrass the student. As always, make the reinforcement short and specific: "Yogurt is a great choice, Anne, because it helps your body build strong bones."

You can also use stickers to promote the selection of healthy foods. When schools place "Good Nutrition" stickers inside packaged healthy food choices to make them attractive to students, many students learn to look for the stickers. This positive reinforcement can quickly change students' choices from favorite foods to healthy foods.

Students who bring lunches to school can create problems for the whole school if those lunches are filled with candy, chips, soda, and other junk food. Students who have resolved to eat healthy foods may feel their willpower vanish when friends offer to share their "treats" or sell them on the schoolyard "black market." To help promote a healthy eating environment schoolwide, ask lunchroom monitors to give stickers to students who bring healthy brown bag lunches to school.

Involve Parents

In an average week, children eat an evening meal, as well as all weekend meals, with their parents. If parents serve high-calorie, nutrient-sparse meals, children will eat them. Thus, if you are to be successful in improving your students' nutrition, you will need to include their parents in your objectives and your interventions. That means offering both information and opportunities to get involved.

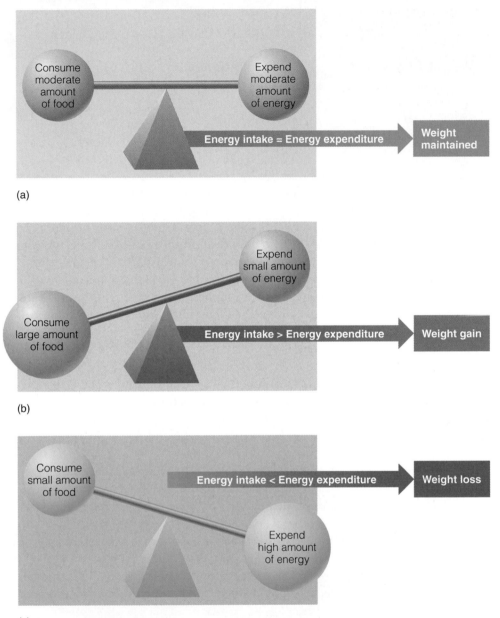

Figure 10.4 The energy balance equation shows that (a) when you consume as many calories as you expend each day, you neither gain nor lose weight. (b) When you consume more calories than you expend, you gain weight. (c) When you consume fewer calories than you expend, you lose weight. Because children use nutrients not only for basal metabolism and physical activity, but also to fuel growth, the equation is somewhat more complex in this population.

Help Parents Understand Their Children's Weight

Body mass index (BMI) is a number representing the ratio of a person's weight to his or her height. BMI does not measure body fat directly, as does, for example, underwater weighing. However, BMI is a popular alternative to direct measures of body fat because it is inexpensive, easy to perform, and research has shown that it correlates well to direct measures.

Table 10.1 **Weight Status and Percentiles for Children**	
Weight Status	Percentile
Underweight	Less than the 5th percentile
Healthy Weight	5th percentile to less than the 85th percentile
At Risk of Overweight	85th to less than the 95th percentile
Overweight	Equal to or greater than the 95th percentile

When used with children, the BMI value is usually plotted on a percentile graph indicating where a child's BMI falls in relation to those of his or her peers of the same gender and age. Percentiles are the most commonly used indicator to assess the height, weight, and growth patterns of individual children in the United States: a child's BMI percentile measurement is referred to as his or her *BMI-for-age*. For example, a child whose BMI falls within the 40th percentile is considered normal weight: 60 percent of children of the same gender and age weigh more, and 39 percent weigh less. **Table 10.1** identifies weight status for all possible percentiles.

The easiest way to determine a child's BMI is to use the CDC's Calculator for Teens and Children (see Web Resources). The calculator requires a child's date of birth, date of measurement, sex, height without shoes, and weight. The calculator outputs the BMI, the BMI-for-age percentile, and the child's weight status category.

Some states and individual school districts are now requiring that each student's BMI be calculated and the result sent home to parents. The point of this practice is to share with parents the status of their child's weight, as many parents fail to perceive the fact that their children are overweight. For instance, in a survey from the University of Michigan of more than 2,000 parents, more than 40 percent appeared unaware of their child's obesity, instead reporting that their child was "about the right weight" (Nagourney, 2007). The survey results suggest that some nutritional interventions might be ineffective with children because their parents do not perceive they need to make changes.

CDC BMI-for-age charts offer a visual tool for showing parents how their child's BMI score compares to other students the same age (**Figures 10.5 and 10.6**). These growth charts can be used to communicate to parents what are considered to be healthy weight percentiles or to suggest they may want to consult their healthcare provider if their child falls into the other categories. As a teacher, it is important to remember that the BMI is an *estimate* of levels of body fat that is reliable for most, but not all, children. The child's healthcare provider will do further analysis and use different methods to determine whether there are any issues that need to be addressed. Thus, the main reason school districts share children's BMI with parents is not to intervene, but simply to alert parents to potential issues

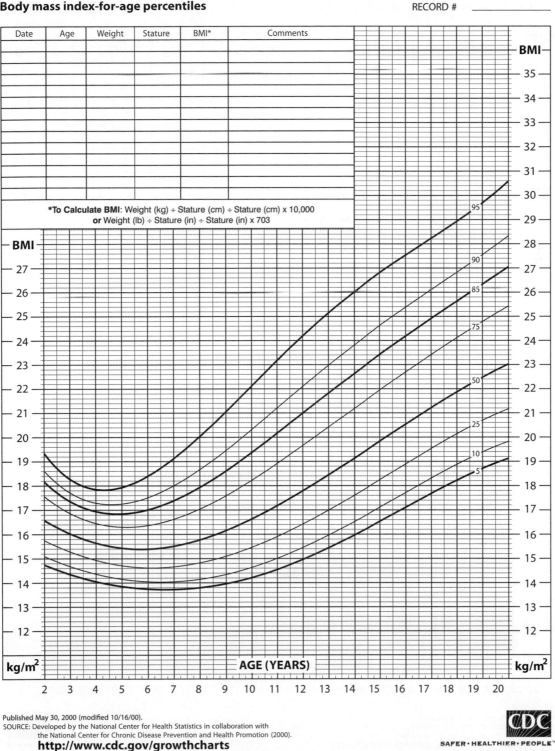

2 to 20 years: Boys
Body mass index-for-age percentiles

NAME _____

RECORD # _____

*To Calculate BMI: Weight (kg) ÷ Stature (cm) ÷ Stature (cm) x 10,000
or Weight (lb) ÷ Stature (in) ÷ Stature (in) x 703

Published May 30, 2000 (modified 10/16/00).
SOURCE: Developed by the National Center for Health Statistics in collaboration with
the National Center for Chronic Disease Prevention and Health Promotion (2000).
http://www.cdc.gov/growthcharts

CDC
SAFER · HEALTHIER · PEOPLE™

Figures 10.5 and 10.6 Body mass index–for-age percentile charts for boys and girls from the
Centers for Disease Control and Prevention (CDC).

2 to 20 years: Girls
Body mass index-for-age percentiles

NAME _____

RECORD # _____

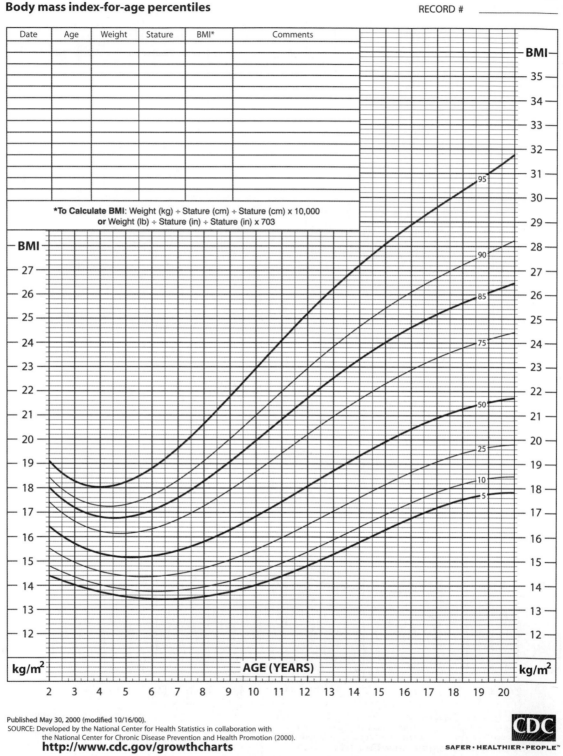

*To Calculate BMI: Weight (kg) ÷ Stature (cm) ÷ Stature (cm) x 10,000
or Weight (lb) ÷ Stature (in) ÷ Stature (in) x 703

Published May 30, 2000 (modified 10/16/00).
SOURCE: Developed by the National Center for Health Statistics in collaboration with
the National Center for Chronic Disease Prevention and Health Promotion (2000).
http://www.cdc.gov/growthcharts

Figures 10.5 and 10.6 (Continued)

so that they can make an informed decision about consulting their healthcare provider.

Nevertheless, reporting of children's BMI is a controversial issue among parents, educators, and healthcare professionals. Some people worry that the reports could prompt teasing, eating disorders, low self-esteem, and a sense of helplessness. For more on the controversy surrounding BMI "report cards," see the accompanying News Clip.

Send Home Nutrition Newsletters

As mentioned earlier, if parents' eating habits do not change, you cannot expect their children's diets to improve. A series of newsletters can be a source of regular information about nutrition and healthy meal planning. The newsletters should be positive in nature, short, and practical, describing not only the essentials of good nutrition, but also tips for choosing foods at the grocery store, for dining out, and for cooking quick, nourishing meals at home.

Another alternative is to send home a brochure from a professional nutrition society. Some excellent web-based resources for parents include the following (see Web Resources for links).

- *Healthy Habits for Healthy Kids: A Nutrition and Activity Guide for Parents.* Produced by Wellpoint and the American Dietetic Association, this 16-page, richly illustrated color brochure can be purchased online for approximately $12.00 for 25 copies. The brochure also contains a nutrition quiz and a goal-setting module.
- *Help Your Child Grow Up Healthy and Strong.* A resource from the U.S. Department of Education, this brochure offers parents many tips for designing healthy meals for their children and encouraging adequate physical activity.
- *Lunch and Learn.* Since lunches taken to school are generally made by parents, this engaging and informative brochure from David Thompson Health Resource should be welcome. This handout offers parents simple and straightforward ideas for constructing a healthy lunch for their kids.

Back to Class

In Mr. Harding's state, fewer than 3 percent of the population are Hispanic or Latino, and Mr. Harding's only Hispanic student is Miguel. He invites Miguel's parents to participate in the school health committee, but neither speaks English very well, and they decline his offer. What are some other ways he might encourage participation and/or support for Miguel?

News Clip

As Obesity Fight Hits Cafeteria, Many Fear a Note from School

When six-year-old Karlind Dunbar read the school note saying her BMI was in the 80th percentile, she became convinced that her teachers were faulting her for overeating. After reading it, her mother complained to the school, noting that Karlind was now refusing to eat regular meals.

She is not alone in her concern. Across the United States, school districts are sending home reports on their students' BMIs . . . and responding to outraged parents. Marlene Schwartz, director of research and school programs at the Rudd Center for Food Policy and Obesity at Yale, also questions the practice. She argues that to successfully change students' eating habits, schools would need to counsel each child and provide thorough nutrition and physical activity assessments. She points out that the practice of reporting BMI scores has gone from pilot program to mass weigh-in despite the fact that no solid research exists on either the physical or psychological impacts, and there have been no controlled randomized trials. Instead, states are adopting a policy that has not been tested or substantially evaluated.

However, Dr. David Ludwig, director of the Optimal Weight for Life program at Children's Hospital Boston, contends that BMI is an effective, low-cost screening tool. He notes that many families don't have an accurate perception of the issue, and he points out that in many regions the prevalence of overweight children is so great that perceptions about what's normal and healthy are effectively distorted. However, Ludwig acknowledges the potential for sending conflicting messages as long as schools continue serving low-quality meals and snacks and offering few if any opportunities for exercise at school.

Source: Adapted from *The New York Times,* January 8, 2007, available at www.nytimes.com/2007/01/08/health/08obesity.html.

take action!

1.   Log onto the website of the Optimal Weight for Life (OWL) program at Children's Hospital Boston (see Web Resources) and click on the "Overweight Experience Journal." Here you can read journal entries from their patients and learn what it's like to be a kid who is struggling with overweight. You can also access entries from healthcare professionals.

2.   Find out if your school district sends students home with BMI "report cards." If so, assess the quality of the school's nutrition environment. Does the school have a health committee? What are its policies on using food as rewards, school celebrations, etc.? What menu choices are offered in the school cafeteria each month? How does the school promote physical activity? Interview school administrators as well as parents about the BMI notifications. Then write a point–counterpoint essay for your school newsletter or local newspaper presenting your findings.

Invite Parents to Join the School Health Committee

Although parents determine what their children will eat for dinner and on weekends, the school food and nutrition departments decide what food choices will be offered to students during the school day. That's one reason parents should join the school health committee (discussed earlier). Also, school committees addressing complex issues such as children's health are typically more successful when they involve parents rather than exclude them. Furthermore, parents have a right to be informed about the school's objectives and how policy changes will affect the school environment. Finally, if a parent has a concern about the foods offered in the school or the proposed policies, he or she may feel more comfortable addressing the concern with one or more of the parents on the committee rather than a teacher or administrator.

Food choices are driven in part by culture, ethnicity, and socioeconomic bracket, so all groups in the school community should be represented. If no parent from a particular group volunteers to join the committee, members should talk with parents from this group, explaining the goals of the health committee and the value of community-wide participation, and encourage parents to volunteer.

Chapter Summary

Schoolwide Strategies for Improving Students' Nutrition

- To be effective, any program for improving students' nutrition must be coordinated throughout the school. Only then can there be some assurance that the value of good nutrition and healthy eating habits is being consistently reinforced.

- The first step in developing a schoolwide initiative for improving students' nutrition is to form a school health committee. Invite other teachers and staff, district administrators, parents, students, nutrition or PE faculty from a nearby university, healthcare providers, and other community members to join the committee.

- Appropriate goals and effective interventions require some initial research. One successful strategy to help generate and maintain a quality schoolwide nutrition program is to meet with other schools that have existing programs. Also check out the USDA's materials for improving the school nutrition environment (see Web Resources).

- The committee should develop specific and measurable short-term and long-term objectives, as well as policy changes and schoolwide and community activities that can help the school achieve these objectives.

Most schools that advocate a quality nutrition environment establish specific policies related to serving healthful school breakfast and lunch menus, posting point-of-decision prompts, avoiding the use of food as rewards, offering only healthful foods during school celebrations, and selling non-food items or healthful foods for fundraisers.

The school health committee should meet regularly to evaluate the effectiveness of activities and policies and implement any appropriate changes.

Classroom Strategies for Improving Students' Nutrition

There are many steps you can take to improve your students' nutrition right in your own classroom.

First, you need to gather data about your students' eating behaviors, so you can use it to help you target your teaching to your students' needs. Observe their food choices, and ask them direct questions about their eating behaviors away from school.

Teach your students about food selection, nutrient density, portion control, and how to balance food and physical activity for weight management.

Reinforce students for making healthful food choices. Make supportive statements in private so as not to embarrass the student or use stickers or other reinforcements.

If you are to be successful in improving your students' nutrition, you will need to include their parents in your objectives and your interventions. That means offering both information, such as nutrition newsletters, and opportunities to get involved, for example, on the school health committee.

Body mass index (BMI) is a number representing the ratio of a person's weight to his or her height. Notifying parents about their children's BMI is a controversial intervention, but it can help parents see where their child's weight falls in comparison to peers so they can choose to consult their healthcare provider, if necessary, or make other appropriate changes to the child's energy consumption or physical activity.

Review Questions

Content Review

1. Identify five steps for establishing a school environment dedicated to improving students' nutrition.

2. Define the term *nutrient density;* provide two examples of lunchtime menu choices that are high in nutrient density and two examples of choices that are low in nutrient density.

3. Design a point-of-decision prompt that could be placed near a vending machine to encourage students to choose milk over sodas.

4. Provide a rationale for gathering data via observation and interviews about your students' eating behaviors.

5. Identify two effective methods for involving parents in improving students' nutrition.

Real World

1. At a PTA meeting, a mother requests that the school establish a policy whereby parents would be allowed to bring only healthful foods to classroom birthday parties and other celebrations. The mother explains that her son is seriously overweight and that she is attempting to help him manage his weight, but that her efforts are thwarted when cupcakes, soda, and other treats are offered in the classroom. When she is finished, another parent shrugs and says, "I don't see this as a big deal. An occasional treat doesn't hurt. It's the day-to-day diet that matters." Which parent's position do you support, and what would you offer in defense of your position?

2. You are monitoring lunch in the school cafeteria today, and you notice that one of your fourth-grade students takes from his lunchbox a can of grape soda, a bag of potato chips, a peanut butter sandwich with marshmallow fluff, and a two-pack of chocolate cupcakes. The school has no policy on lunches brought from home, and there has been no schoolwide initiative to improve students' nutrition. What might you do?

References and Suggested Readings

Anspaugh, D.J., and Ezell, G. (2004). *Teaching today's health.* San Francisco: Pearson Benjamin Cummings.

Hanson, T.L., Muller, C., Austin, G., and Lee-Bayha, J. (2005). Research findings about the relationship between student health and academic achievement. In California Department of Education, *Getting results: Developing safe and healthy kids update 5.* Sacramento: CDE Press.

Kahn, E.B., Ramsey, L.T., Brownson, R.C., Heath, G.W., Howze, E.H., Powell, K.E., Stone, E.J., Rajab, M.W., Corso, P., and the Task Force on Community Preventative Services. (2002). The effectiveness of interventions to increase physical activity. *American Journal of Preventive Medicine,* 22(4S), 73–107.

Nagourney, E. (2007). Many parents fail to see obesity in children. *The New York Times,* December 18, 2007, p. D6.

Pangrazi, R.P., Beighle, A., Vehige, T., and Vack, C. (2003). Evaluating the effectiveness of the State of Arizona's Promoting Lifestyle Activity for Youth program. *Journal of School Health,* 73(8), 317–321.

Pellegrini, A.D., Huberty, P.D., and Jones, I. (1995). The effects of recess timing on children's playground and classroom behaviors. *American Educational Research Journal,* 32(4), 845–864.

Sack, K. (2007). Schools found improving on nutrition and fitness. *The New York Times,* October 20, 2007. Available at www.nytimes.com/2007/10/20/health/20junkfood.html.

What About You?

Below, jot down everything you ate for breakfast, lunch, dinner, and snacks yesterday. If you cannot remember everything you ate, make your best estimate. For example, if you can't remember what you had for breakfast yesterday, record what you ate this morning or what you know is your typical breakfast meal.

_____

_____

_____

_____

Now log onto the USDA's website at www.MyPyramid.gov and enter your personal data. How many servings of each type of food should you eat each day? Fill in the second column of the table below. Now look back at yesterday's diet and determine how many servings you actually consumed for each food group. Fill in the third column of the table.

Food Group	Recommended Number of Servings	Number of Servings Yesterday
Grains		
Vegetables		
Fruits		
Milk		
Meat and Beans		

Are you pleased with your results, or do you need to consume more or less of a particular food group?

_____

_____

Tudor-Locke, C., Lee, S.M., Morgan, C.F., Beighle, A., and Pangrazi, R.P. (2006). Children's pedometer–determined physical activity patterns during the segmented school day. *Medicine and Science in Sports and Exercise, 38*(10), 1732–1738.

USDA. Food and Nutrition Service. 2003. School Breakfast Program. Healthy eating helps you make the grade. Available at www.fns.usda.gov/cnd/Breakfast/SchoolBfastCampaign/theresearch.html.

Web Resources

Center for Science in the Public Interest (CSPI), Constructive Classroom Rewards: Promoting Good Habits While Protecting Children's Health: *www.cspinet.org/nutritionpolicy/constructive_rewards.pdf*

Centers for Disease Control and Prevention (CDC), Body Mass Index (BMI) calculator:
www.cdc.gov/nccdphp/dnpa/bmi/index.htm
Changing the Scene: Improving the School Nutrition Environment (USDA):
www.teamnutrition.usda.gov/Resources/changing.html
Children's Food Pyramid:
www.MyPyramid.gov/kids/index.html
Children's Hospital Boston, Optimal Weight for Life (OWL):
www.childrenshospital.org/clinicalservices/Site1896/mainpageS1896PO.html
Connecticut Department of Education, Healthy Celebrations: Promoting a Healthy School Environment:
www.sde.ct.gov/sde/lib/sde/PDF/DEPS/Student/NutritionEd/
Healthy_Celebrations.pdf
Consumer Information (USDA):
www.nutrition.gov
The Edible Schoolyard:
www.edibleschoolyard.org
Gopher Sports Active and Healthy School Program:
www.gophersport.com
Healthy Habits for Healthy Kids: A Nutrition and Activity Guide for Parents:
www.wellpoint.com/healthy_parenting/index.html
Help Your Child Grow Up Healthy and Strong:
www.ed.gov/parents/academic/health/growhealthy/growhealthy.pdf
Lunch and Learn:
www.dthr.ab.ca/resources/documents/nutrition/ParentHandout_Lunch.pdf
MyPyramid for Kids:
www.mypyramid.gov/kids
Nutrition.gov:
www.nutrition.gov
Portion Distortion I and II, National Heart, Lung, and Blood Institute, Obesity Education Initiative:
http://hp2010.nhlbihin.net/portion
School Nutrition Association:
www.asfsa.org
United States Department of Agriculture (USDA):
www.teamnutrition.usda.gov/resources/changing.html

11

Teaching Sun Safety

Learning Objectives

After reading this chapter, you will be able to . . .

- ○ Identify the different types of ultraviolet radiation and the factors that influence the intensity of exposure.
- ○ Teach students how to interpret the UV index.
- ○ Explain the role of sunlight in vitamin D synthesis.
- ○ Identify the risks of excessive sun exposure.
- ○ Explain the effects of sunscreens on sun exposure.
- ○ Identify schoolwide initiatives for promoting sun safety.
- ○ Instruct children in sun-safety behaviors.
- ○ Access teaching materials from the EPA SunWise website.

Classroom Challenge

Mrs. Collins teaches in the full-day kindergarten program in an inner-city school. It's a bright late April afternoon, and the children have been back in the classroom for about an hour since their noontime recess on the asphalt parking lot they use as a playground. As Mrs. Collins hands out boxes of crayons for a small-group activity, she notices that one of her students, Erik, is squirming in his seat and his face looks flushed. "Erik," she asks, "Are you okay?"

Erik fans his face with his hands. "I guess so," he answers. "But I'm sort of hot."

Mrs. Collins' class includes many students of African, Hispanic, and Middle Eastern descent with dark coloring, but Erik's blue eyes and pale blond hair reflect his Scandinavian origins. Usually, his skin is nearly the color of milk, but now Mrs. Collins notices that his face, neck, and forearms below his sleeves look pink and dry, as if his exposed skin had been vigorously scrubbed. "Let's get you to the school nurse," she says, and asks her aide to manage the class while she takes Erik to the nurse's office.

When she and Erik walk through the door, Mr. O'Connell, the school nurse, shakes his head. "Erik," he says, "you look like a tomato in a T-shirt! Did you get too much sun today?"

"I don't know," Erik answers softly. "Is that why my face feels hot?"

Mrs. Collins sighs. "It's my fault, Erik, not yours. I should have brought you kids in from recess sooner."

Mr. O'Connell sits Erik on his examining table and gently examines his skin. "Don't be too hard on yourself," he says to Mrs. Collins. "Erik and me, we're northern types. It doesn't take much to fry us. And besides, today was the first day this year that the UV index went into the red zone. So the strength of the sun probably caught you by surprise."

"What's the UV index?" Mrs. Collins asks. "And the red zone?"

Mr. O'Connell points to his computer. "Click on my SunWise bookmark," he says. "While I make Erik some cold compresses, you look up the UV forecast for tomorrow!"

ost of us know that we should limit children's exposure to the sun, but like Mrs. Collins, we might not know exactly when, why, or how. This chapter begins by defining exactly what ultraviolet (UV) radiation is and then identifies the factors that affect the level of UV radiation in the environment. We'll also show you how to predict the risk of sun exposure in your area using the UV index. We then identify the benefits and risks of sun exposure, who is at greatest risk of over- and underexposure, and discuss the role of sunscreen in protecting skin from UV radiation. The second half of the chapter explains how to implement a sun-safety program through both schoolwide initiatives and classroom instruction using sun-safety teaching tools.

Understanding Ultraviolet Radiation

The spectrum of the sun's rays includes visible light and two types of light that can't be seen: *infrared rays* are longer than visible light and are given off by the sun as heat. *Ultraviolet rays* are shorter than visible light and have more energy. They are so named because their frequencies are just higher than the last band of visible light, which humans identify as the color violet. The spectrum of **ultraviolet (UV) radiation** is divided into three bands:

- *Ultraviolet A (UVA)*. UVA radiation travels through the atmosphere unfiltered and unabsorbed, but its energy level is lower than UVB or UVC, and it is less harmful; for example, it does not cause sunburn, but it can indirectly damage DNA.
- *Ultraviolet B (UVB)*. Although much UVB radiation is absorbed in the ozone layer of the earth's atmosphere, its high-energy rays are destructive to DNA and can cause skin cancer.
- *Ultraviolet C (UVC)*. UVC rays are the highest-energy type of UV light and potentially the most damaging; fortunately, all UVC radiation is absorbed in the ozone layer of the atmosphere.

Factors Affecting UV Exposure

A number of factors affect the level of UV radiation to which we are exposed. In general, we can group these into environmental factors and intrinsic factors.

Environmental Factors

The following factors have the greatest impact on the amount of UV radiation in the environment on any given day, at any given place and time:

- *Time of day*. Most of the radiation is received during the hours of 9 a.m. and 3 p.m. The greatest amount of UV radiation occurs between 11:00 a.m. and 1:00 p.m. (about 30 percent of the daily total). This is a time of day when children have an opportunity to be outside playing and are subject to intense sun rays.

Geographical location. As the distance from the equator increases, the solar radiation decreases.

Season. The angle of the sun changes throughout the year and causes an increase or decrease in the intensity of UV radiation. UV radiation is greater in the summer months.

Altitude. The atmosphere is thinner at higher altitudes, making it less able to absorb UVB and thus increasing the amount of total UV radiation.

Weather conditions. Sunny days have higher levels of UV radiation. Although cloudy weather decreases the heat from the sun's rays, clouds do not completely protect the skin from UV radiation.

Ozone in the atmosphere. Ozone in the upper atmosphere helps protect us from UV radiation. Unfortunately, the ozone layer has been depleted in some areas by airborne chemicals such as CFCs (chlorofluorocarbons). The use of these chemicals has been restricted in recent years, but the atmosphere has not yet recovered.

In addition, UV radiation can be direct (straight from the sun) or indirect (scattered and reflected). Scattered UV radiation occurs as the sun's rays travel through the atmosphere and are moved around by atmospheric dust and water drops. It is possible, but not as common, to receive more radiation indirectly than directly. For example, on a cloudy day, more UV radiation will be accumulated indirectly. UV radiation is also reflected off the ground, buildings, bodies of water, and objects, so even in a shaded area, exposure can be significant. Smooth surfaces such as concrete or asphalt reflect more UV radiation than rough surfaces such as grass or soil. Sand and fresh snow reflect a great deal of radiation. In fact, snow reflects nearly 90 percent of the UV radiation compared to grass, which reflects around 3 percent.

Intrinsic Factors

Our skin color significantly affects the amount of UV radiation our skin cells absorb. Skin color is largely determined by a pigment called *melanin* produced by skin cells called *melanocytes*. Melanin protects skin by absorbing UV rays, and production varies according to our genetic makeup: people whose ancestors lived in regions closer to the equator have melanocytes that produce more melanin, and their skin tone is darker. People whose ancestors lived farther away from the equator have melanocytes that produce less melanin, and their skin is fair.

The UV Index

Because of variations in the factors just identified, UV radiation varies from one region to another and throughout the year. To help Americans reduce their risk of overexposure to the sun, the Environmental Protection Agency (EPA) and the National Weather Service created the **UV index**, which predicts the next day's UV radiation levels throughout the United States. The index rates UV intensity levels on a scale of 1 (low) to 11+ (extremely high) and is calculated using National Weather Service data for every zip code throughout the United States. After logging onto the EPA's SunWise website, you can access a UV index forecast map of the United States or find the day's UV index for your own city or town simply by typing in your zip code or city and state name.

Table 11.1	UV Index of Risk for Skin Damage and Sun Protection Behaviors	
UV Index Risk of Skin Damage	**Behaviors to Prevent Skin Damage**
2 or Less—Low	Wear sunglasses on bright days or in snow-covered areas. Use sunscreen if you burn easily.
3 to 5—Moderate	Wear protective clothing outdoors. Stay in the shade as much as possible.
6–7—High	Use sunscreen with SPF of 15 or more. Stay out of sun or in shade between hours of 10 a.m. and 4 p.m. Wear protective clothing regardless of skin type.
8–10—Very High	Stay out of sun or in shade between hours of 10 a.m. and 4 p.m. Wear protective clothing regardless of skin type. Unprotected skin burns quickly—use plenty of sunscreen.
11 or More—Extreme	Avoid sun exposure during hours of 10 a.m. to 4 p.m. Apply sunscreen a minimum of every two hours. Sand and water reflect sunlight and increase the risk of sun exposure.

Source: United States Environmental Protection Agency SunWise Program, available at www.epa.gov/sunwise/uvindex.html.

Table 11.1 shows how the index numbers correspond to the level of risk of skin damage. It also identifies the sun-protection behaviors that are recommended at that level. When the UV index is 6 or over (high risk), the National Weather Service issues a UV alert. This is a warning to take special steps to protect yourself and your students from the sun. Sun-safety behaviors are discussed in detail later in this chapter.

An excellent resource for teaching students about the UV index is the *SunWise Meteorologist Tool Kit* developed by the EPA, National Weather Service, and American Meteorological Society (see Web Resources).

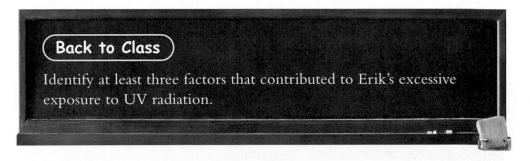

Back to Class

Identify at least three factors that contributed to Erik's excessive exposure to UV radiation.

Benefits of Exposure to UV Radiation

In addition to lighting and warming the earth and providing energy for plants to grow, the sun's radiation benefits human health. For instance, sunlight is prescribed clinically as a treatment for certain skin disorders, and inadequate sunlight is implicated in a form of clinical depression called *seasonal affective disorder* (*SAD*). Most significantly, our bodies synthesize vitamin D, a nutrient essential to health, using energy from exposure to sunlight.

Vitamin D is essential for the body's maintenance of bone health. Breast milk contains inadequate vitamin D, so breast-fed infants and toddlers who don't get adequate exposure to sunlight or receive adequate vitamin D in their diet are at high risk for developing a bone disorder called *rickets*. This condition is characterized by poor growth, skeletal deformities, muscle weakness, and seizures (**Figure 11.1**). In addition to its role in bone health, vitamin D has many other functions: it improves muscle function; helps regulate blood pressure and insulin levels; contributes to immunity; and is believed to regulate cell growth, including controlling abnormal cell growth, which thereby reduces our risk for cancer.

Controversy exists among healthcare advisors over whether children should get their vitamin D primarily from supplements or from exposure to sunlight. The EPA advises that all children avoid the sun and take a vitamin supplement providing 100 percent of the Dietary Reference Intake (DRI) (EPA, 2006). Vitamin D is also obtained from fortified milk and certain other foods, though at a level unlikely to meet a child's daily needs. Other experts contend that brief sun exposure on bare skin (no sunscreen) is "the most physiologic way to prevent vitamin D deficiency" (Holick, 2006). These experts advise regular brief exposure to sunlight. For more information on this controversy, see the accompanying News Clip.

The number of minutes of sunlight per day needed for vitamin D synthesis by any one individual is determined by several factors, including skin color/pigmentation, the time of day, the season, and the latitude at which the person lives. At or above latitudes of 40 degrees north in the United States, the sun does not rise high enough in the sky between October and March for any vitamin D synthesis to occur. Thus, children living in northern states need to build up adequate stores of vitamin D during the summer months to last them throughout the winter. For example, a child with light-colored skin living in Chicago can build up adequate levels of vitamin D by exposing his or her bare arms and legs to sunlight for as little as 10 minutes a day throughout the summer (Brody, 2003). After 10 minutes, the child should cover up and apply sunscreen.

Children with darker skin need longer exposure to sunlight because their higher melanin levels block more of the sun's rays and thus inhibit vitamin D synthesis. Indeed, many studies have shown that darker-skinned populations are at increased risk for vitamin D deficiency; for example, a study by the United States Centers for Disease Control and Prevention (CDC) showed that 48 percent of African American women ages 15–49 throughout the United States were deficient (Looker et al., 2002). At the same time, the higher melanin levels in dark-skinned people mean they are at a lower risk for skin damage from UV exposure.

Figure 11.1 This child exhibits the bowed legs characteristic of rickets, a bone-deforming disease in children caused by vitamin D deficiency.

Risks of Exposure to UV Radiation

There are both immediate and long-term risks for excessive exposure to UV radiation. Immediate risks include sunburn and heat illness. If youngsters are not taught to avoid excessive UV radiation at an early age, serious long-term consequences can include skin cancer and vision loss.

News Clip

Shining a Light on the Health Benefits of Vitamin D

Dr. Michael Holick of the Boston University Medical Center has spent 30 years researching the many benefits of vitamin D. A 56-year-old endocrinologist and a professor of dermatology, biophysics, and physiology, his research into the way skin converts sunlight into vitamin D has led him on a crusade to encourage people to let some sun shine on their skin.

According to Holick, vitamin D is critically important for maintaining normal calcium in the blood and for bone health. It plays a crucial role in most metabolic functions and also muscle, cardiac, and neurological functions. In addition, there is evidence that vitamin D may have subtle but profound effects on regulating cell growth and on our cardiovascular and immune systems. There is a strong association of sunlight exposure and increased blood levels of vitamin D with a decreased risk of many common cancers: colon, breast, prostate, and ovarian. And vitamin D deficiency has been associated with an increased risk for type 1 diabetes. The converse is also true. Overall, adequate vitamin D level equals less risk for diabetes, all of which makes this a very important vitamin.

Holick explains that about 80 to 100 percent of our vitamin D requirement comes via our exposure to sunlight. Fish, such as salmon and mackerel, provide vitamin D, but for an adequate intake, people would have to eat such fish three times a week. Milk is fortified with vitamin D, but an average person would have to drink six to eight glasses a day to get enough.

Thus, Holick contends that many people, especially those living in northern regions, are not getting adequate vitamin D. He cites a study he conducted among Boston medical students that found that 36 percent were vitamin D deficient at the end of the winter and 11 percent were deficient at the end of the summer. Other studies indicate that up to 60 percent of adults over age 65 are deficient. Holick suspects this is true for many younger people who spend most of their day indoors, too. His recommendations?

Go outside and get the 5–15 minutes of exposure it takes to synthesize vitamin D in your skin. Then make sure to wear sunscreen with an SPF of at least 15 to prevent the effects of chronic excessive exposure to sunlight. New research shows that African Americans may require more time outdoors to synthesize vitamin D. But whatever your ethnicity or skin tone, it's important to be aware of your body's need to metabolize vitamin D through sun exposure as well as to take reasonable precautions against potential skin damage from overexposure—and to stay informed.

Source: Adapted from *The New York Times*, January 28, 2003, available at http://query .nytimes.com/gst/fullpage.html?res=9402E2DA1239F93BA15752C0A9659C8B63&sec+&spon

take action!

1.   What steps could you take to help a class of diverse students to both reduce their risk of harm from excessive exposure to UV radiation and reduce their risk of vitamin D deficiency?

2.   What schoolwide policies could you promote to address these dual concerns?

Sunburn

The most common immediate risk is sunburn, which ranges from mild to severe. Mild sunburn injures the top layer of the skin and is characterized by redness and heat over a small percentage of the body. Peeling of the damaged layer usually follows one or more days after the burn. Treatment with cold compresses and a soothing gel is usually sufficient. Severe, blistered sunburns over a large percentage of the body can be serious enough to require hospitalization. A key risk of all serious burns is infection.

As we noted earlier, a person with fair skin, hair, and eyes will burn more easily than a person with dark eyes and skin because melanin shields skin cells from UV radiation. Different parts of the body are also more sensitive to burning; for instance, the upper body is much more sensitive than the legs.

Heat Stress

Although not specifically due to UV exposure, another immediate risk of outdoor activity on a hot day, especially when the humidity is high, is *heat stress*. Its signs and symptoms include heavy sweating, weakness, dizziness, headache, and nausea. The condition can progress rapidly to *heat stroke*, in which the person experiences vomiting, diarrhea, and/or a dangerously rapid heart rate. If heat stroke progresses, it can be fatal. As we discussed in Chapter 2, several factors contribute to making children more vulnerable to heat stress than adults.

Because dehydration significantly increases the risk of heat stress, it is essential to ensure children are well hydrated before they begin physical activity in hot weather and have fluid breaks during any activity lasting longer than 20 minutes. Sports drinks, which replace lost fluids, carbohydrates, and electrolytes, may be helpful. For more information, see Chapter 2.

Skin Cancer

Skin cancer is the most commonly diagnosed cancer in the United States, accounting for as many as half of all cancer diagnoses. About 20 percent of all Americans will develop skin cancer in their lifetime. Most cases of skin cancer are thought to be preventable, because excessive exposure to UV radiation is considered the primary contributing factor in most cases. Three types of skin cancer occur:

- *Basal cell carcinoma* arises from cells in the deep (basal) layer of the skin. It is the most common form of skin cancer and very rarely spreads. Thus, surgical removal, usually in a dermatologist's office, is the only treatment typically required.
- *Squamous cell carcinoma* is the second most common form of skin cancer, and like basal cell carcinoma, it rarely spreads. It arises in cells in the top layer (epidermis) of the skin, usually on sun-exposed areas of the neck, face, or back of the hands. As with basal cell carcinoma, excision usually cures this cancer.
- *Malignant melanoma* is cancer arising from the melanin-producing cells, the melanocytes (**Figure 11.2**). It is by far the most serious form of skin cancer. Although it accounts for only about 3 percent of skin cancer cases, it causes nearly 80 percent of skin cancer deaths. That is because, unlike basal and squamous cell carcinomas, malignant melanoma can spread throughout the body. After an initial phase of superficial growth, the tumor begins to grow vertically, invading the deeper layers of the skin

Figure 11.2 Malignant melanoma is character-ized by a skin lesion that is asymmetric, with uneven borders, varied coloration, and a diameter larger than a pencil eraser (6 millimeters).

and gaining access to blood and lymph vessels. Malignant cells that spread via the bloodstream can invade the lungs and the brain. In 2004, nearly 8,000 people died of malignant melanoma. Although genetic factors have also been implicated, the American Cancer Society (2007) suggests that between 68 percent and 90 percent of all melanomas result from excessive exposure to UV radiation.

On average, the majority (80 percent) of sun damage that occurs to a person's skin occurs during the school-age years. Five or more blistering sunburns in child-hood can double the lifetime risk of developing some form of skin cancer. These are valid reasons for you to view excessive sun exposure as an experience that might shorten the lifespan of the students in your care. The second half of this chapter identifies steps you can take to instill in your students the fundamentals of sun safety.

Other Long-Term Risks

Chronic, excessive exposure to the sun can cause premature aging of the skin; that is, the skin becomes thick, toughened, and wrinkled. These skin changes are not a part of normal aging and can be substantially avoided with proper sun protection (EPA, 2006).

In addition, research suggests that overexposure to UV radiation can alter the distribution and function of disease-fighting white blood cells for up to 24 hours after the exposure. Mild sunburns can suppress immune function in people of all skin types (EPA, 2006).

Repeated overexposure to UV radiation is also a risk factor in two types of vi-sion impairment, cataracts and macular degeneration. *Cataracts* are damaged areas in the lens of the eye, which cause cloudiness of vision (**Figure 11.3**). *Macular degenera-tion* is deterioration of the central portion of the retina, the membrane at the back of the eye that receives light (**Figure 11.4**). As the macula breaks down, the person loses the ability to see details, especially in the center of the visual field. In both dis-orders, the risk increases with repeated exposure over many years and is present for people of all skin colors and ethnicities. Wearing sunglasses that protect against UV radiation is important for reducing the risk of vision damage.

Effects of Sunscreens on UV Exposure

Sunscreens are products that protect human skin by absorbing UVA and UVB rays. The product label on all sunscreens is required to identify the product's *sun protection factor (SPF)*. The SPF identifies the amount of protection that the sunscreen will deliver on an average skin type. An SPF of 15 protects the skin from 93 percent of UVB radiation and is the level recommended for adequate protection. An SPF of 30 provides 97 percent protection; thus, when the SPF is doubled from 15 to 30, there is only a 4 percent increase in sun protection. Even though the SPF factor applies only to UVB radiation, many of the newer sunscreens are broad-spectrum and will filter UVA as well. Incidentally, not only sunscreens, but many types of make-up, moisture lotions, and lip balms now offer sun protection.

Sunscreens use chemicals that absorb the sun's rays. In contrast, sunblocks use ingredients that reflect the sunlight. Both products work effectively; however, there are considerations for and against each choice.

Figure 11.3 Excessive exposure to UV radiation can increase our risk for vision impairment. Cataracts cause general cloudiness of vision.

Sunscreens that contain chemical ingredients to absorb UV radiation can cause skin reactions in a small percentage of users. Reactions include itching, dryness, rash, burning, and tightening of the skin. Some users report red, stinging eyes. All of these reactions are most commonly associated with PABA-based sunscreens (PABA is an abbreviation for para-aminobenzoic acid), and those containing benzophenones.

Blood vessels   Macula   Optic disk

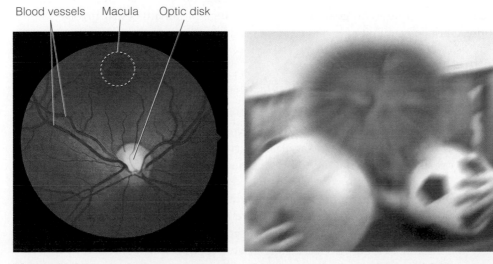

Figure 11.4 Macular degeneration causes vision loss in a centralized area of the visual field.

If students have a reaction to chemical-based sunscreens, recommend that they switch to a sunblock. Titanium dioxide and zinc oxide are ingredients in sunblocks that act as physical barriers to reflect the sun's rays. Very few youngsters experience any reaction to these ingredients, but because they are bright white and easy to see, some children resist using them. Fortunately, many of the newer sunblocks use nanoparticles that make them transparent.

Finally, some words of caution. Sunscreens inhibit the skin's ability to synthesize vitamin D, so some experts advise that they be applied only after children have had a few minutes of "unblocked" time in the sun (Holick, 2006). As noted earlier, children with darker skin need longer periods of sun exposure without sunscreen to synthesize adequate vitamin D. Fortunately, their increased skin pigmentation offers them increased protection against sunburn as well. On the other hand, the use of sunscreens does not ensure that children will not develop skin cancer. In fact, there is no evidence that sunscreens protect from melanoma. That's why another important sun-safety behavior is to cover up. We discuss this and other protective behaviors next.

Back to Class

Erik is at greater risk for sunburn than his darker-skinned classmates, but at lower risk for vitamin D deficiency. Identify the common physiologic factor behind each of these differences.

Implementing a Sun-Safety Program

Sun safety requires more than just offering students a few facts about protecting their skin. This important goal merits a broad range of initiatives that involve the entire school community.

Schoolwide Initiatives

The following are outcomes characteristic of schools with a quality sun-safety program.

- Students know when, where, and how to apply sunscreen or sunblock and lip balm. Products are made available to students free of charge, or parents are asked to provide them. Teachers and staff reinforce children for applying sun protection.
- Students learn to wear protective hats, clothing, and sunglasses. School policies are changed if necessary to make it acceptable to wear sun hats and dark glasses during outside play at peak UV hours. Concerns about children wearing hats with gang-related logos can be addressed by

holding a fundraiser to purchase identical hats for children, and concerns about sharing hats (spreading head lice) can be addressed by insisting that children write their names inside their hats and wear only their own hats.

Playgrounds have adequate areas of shade. Shade structures are becoming more commonplace on school grounds, where they help prevent sun damage and contribute to the children's overall activity levels. The amount of activity students accumulate outdoors decreases in climates where it is hot and humid and without shade areas.

Children play in indoor areas when the National Weather Service issues UV alerts. Just as students are required to stay inside when it is excessively cold or wet, they should stay inside when the UV index is extreme.

Parents and community members are involved in sun-safety efforts. Much of the success of the sun-safety program depends on parents' understanding the importance of sun protection and their willingness to provide sun-protective clothing, sunglasses, lip balm, and sunscreen, if not provided by the school. Newsletters to parents and informational meetings should be a part of the program.

Sun-Safety Behaviors for Students

Too often, students attend a single workshop on sun safety and then quickly forget what they've learned. Unless there are refresher lessons and continual classroom reinforcement, students will regard the behaviors as unimportant and forget them. So, teach your students sun-safety behaviors at the beginning of the year and practice them throughout the school year. Topics that are refreshed and practiced regularly contribute to an institutional value set.

The following are concepts and behaviors that students should learn, practice, and be able to share with others.

Understand the UV index. Students should know how to interpret the rating scale for the UV index (see Table 11.1).

Use sunscreen properly. Students not taking vitamin D supplements can benefit from a few minutes of "unblocked" exposure to sunlight when the sun is high in the sky, which allows their skin to synthesize adequate stores of vitamin D. But as noted earlier, fairer-skinned children need less sun exposure, and darker-skinned children need more. After this period of brief exposure, students should apply sunscreen (or if they experience a reaction to sunscreen, a sunblock). They should apply sunscreen 20 minutes before outside sun exposure so that the skin has time to absorb it. It should be applied generously and often, about every two hours while outdoors. It should be put on all body parts that are exposed, including lips, ears, feet, hands, and the back of the neck. Sweating, swimming, and toweling off will quickly remove a sunscreen's protection, so even water-resistant sunscreens need to be reapplied regularly. When first teaching students how to use sunscreen, monitor them closely for skin reactions.

Wear protective clothing. Children should wear wide-brimmed hats to protect their face, eyes, and neck. Baseball caps are inadequate. In addition, clothing that covers most of the skin helps prevent sun damage. Tightly woven fabrics will offer protection similar to SPF 30 sunscreen. (Many manufacturers of children's clothing today identify their clothing's SPF rating on the tags.) Darker clothing absorbs more of the UV radiation than light-colored fabric. However, dark fabric will also be hotter to wear because of heat absorption.

Wear sunglasses. All children, no matter their skin color, need to protect their eyes from UV radiation. Sunglasses that filter out virtually all the UVA and UVB radiation will help prevent cataracts and other eye problems. In addition, by protecting the delicate skin around the eyes, sunglasses help prevent premature wrinkles.

Play in the shade. Encourage students to seek shade for outdoor activities. Give them a tour of the play area and point out areas of shade. Instruct children to move their activities into the shade whenever the sun is overhead and UV radiation is at its peak.

Limit time in the sun at midday. To help students avoid overexposure, teach them to use the shadow index. If your shadow is taller than you are, the sun is low in the sky and your chance of overexposure to UV radiation is also low. If your shadow is shorter than you are, the sun is high in the sky and your chance of overexposure is also high. That means you need to play in the shade or indoors.

Back to Class

Of the sun-safety actions just listed, how many did Erik and his classmates take the day that Erik was sunburned? Assuming that there is no shade on their asphalt playground, and that neither the school nor the children had sunscreen, sunglasses, or protective hats and clothes, what is the one step that Mrs. Collins could have taken to protect her students on this "red zone" day?

Sun-Safety Teaching Tools

A number of online resources are available for teaching sun-safety skills. The list that follows offers a brief synopsis of the materials offered at each website.

SunWise

The EPA has developed an excellent sun-safety program called SunWise. This environmental and health education program aims to teach children and their caregivers how to protect themselves from overexposure to sun. The program has several components.

- School administrators and teachers can start by downloading the *SunWise School Program Guide* (see Web Resources), which explains how to make their school "SunWise." The guide describes available teaching materials, action steps for sun protection, and additional resources that are available for schools. These additional resources include, for example, information on how to create a sun-safe infrastructure, including shade structures (e.g., canopies, trees), and policies (e.g., using hats, sunscreen, sunglasses) that promote sun protection in a school setting.
- Teachers can access the SunWise website for lesson plans, instructional materials, and evaluation instruments. The lessons do not take a great deal of teaching time, and the benefits can be dramatic. The materials encourage cross-curricular classroom learning.
- The educator resources also include two PowerPoint presentations, one for primary grades and one for grades three through six (see Web Resources). The presentations are colorful, age appropriate, and convey basic facts. In addition, there is a downloadable teacher's guide that supplements the presentations. This minimizes the amount of preparation time needed to present a comprehensive lesson. Topics included in the presentation include good and bad effects of the sun, UV radiation and how it is measured, how to become SunWise, and finally, a brief quiz and fun facts section.
- For parents, SunWise has a poster (**Figure 11.5**) in English and Spanish (see Web Resources). Included in the same file are four newsletters for

Figure 11.5 The EPA's SunWise poster. *Source: United States Environmental Protection Agency.www.epa.gov/sunwise/doc/poster.pdf.*

teachers to duplicate and send home to parents. Topics include sun facts, a crossword puzzle about sun safety, and a short quiz to find out if you are SunWise or sun foolish.

Back to Class

Identify a few schoolwide initiatives that Mrs. Collins and Mr. O'Connell could propose together to further protect students from excessive exposure to UV radiation during their recess breaks.

Other Sun-Safety Teaching Tools

You should also check out these other sun-safety teaching tools.

- The Sun Safety Alliance has produced an excellent guide called *Block the Sun, Not the Fun* (see Web Resources). This booklet contains a number of lessons and activities for teachers, including an exam to give students to see if they are "sun-certified."
- The National Safety Council has a comprehensive website that includes many games and learning activities for youngsters (see Web Resources). Follow the *Kids Sun Fun* link.
- The Sun Safety for Kids website (also in Web Resources) contains sections on sun protection, school policies, and securing resources. For example, in the securing resources section, topics include sun-protective hats, sunscreen, shade trees, shade structures, curriculum materials, and letters to parents. The section on shade structures lists a number of companies that manufacture shade structures.
- The CDC has produced a document titled *Shade Planning for America's Schools.* This document provides comprehensive information on planning or retrofitting a playground to provide more shade for play and activity. Also included are case studies of school districts and organizations that have successfully developed shade areas.
- The Activity Cards for Nutrition and Sun Safety that accompany this text include a number of games for teaching sun-safety skills. They are designed to provide activity in the classroom while reinforcing the concepts related to safe exposure to the sun.

Chapter Summary

Understanding Ultraviolet Radiation

- Ultraviolet (UV) rays are emitted from the sun. They are shorter than visible light rays, have more energy, and are capable of damaging skin cells.

- Factors affecting the level of UV radiation in the environment include time of day, geographical location, season, altitude, weather conditions, and ozone in the atmosphere. UV radiation can be direct or indirect (scattered or reflected, e.g., off buildings, the ground, sand, or snow).

- The level of melanin pigment in a person's skin affects their sensitivity to UV radiation. Darker-skinned children have more melanin and are at reduced risk of skin damage from UV radiation, whereas fairer-skinned children have less melanin and are at increased risk.

- The UV index rates UV intensity levels on a scale of 1 to 11+ for every zip code in the United States.

- The primary benefit of exposure to UV radiation is synthesis of vitamin D, a nutrient essential for bone health, normal cell growth and differentiation, and other body functions. Melanin pigment blocks UV radiation and inhibits vitamin D synthesis, so children with dark skin are at increased risk for vitamin D deficiency.

- Immediate risks of overexposure to UV radiation include sunburn and heat illness. Long-term risks of chronic overexposure include skin cancer, premature aging of the skin, reduced immunity, and vision impairment.

- Sunscreens are creams and lotions containing chemical ingredients that protect human skin by absorbing UVA and UVB rays. A sun protection factor (SPF) of 15 protects the skin from 93 percent of UVB radiation.

- Sunblocks contain ingredients such as titanium dioxide and zinc oxide, which reflect the sun's rays.

Implementing a Sun-Safety Program

- In a sun-safe school, students know how, when, and where to apply sunscreen and lip balm. They learn to wear protective hats, clothing, and sunglasses. Playgrounds have adequate areas of shade, and children play indoors when the National Weather Service issues UV alerts. Parents and community members are also involved in sun-safety initiatives.

Topics for classroom teaching include understanding the UV index; proper use of sunscreen, protective clothing, and sunglasses; and the importance of playing in the shade or moving indoors when the sun is overhead.

A number of online resources are available for teaching sun-safety skills. One of the most comprehensive is the EPA's SunWise program.

Review Questions

Content Review

1. All other things being equal, who is at greater risk for overexposure to UV radiation on the same sunny day: a child playing at the beach or a child playing on a grassy field? Why?

2. In a 2004 study, 42 percent of African American and Hispanic adolescents living in Boston were found to be deficient in vitamin D (Gordon et al., 2004). What factors were likely contributors to the level of deficiency in this population?

3. Malignant melanoma accounts for only about 3 percent of skin cancer cases, yet it causes nearly 80 percent of skin cancer deaths. Explain why.

4. A tanning oil with an SPF of 8 is on sale at your local drugstore. Is this product an effective sunscreen? Why or why not?

5. Explain how children can use the "shadow index" to protect themselves from overexposure to UV radiation.

Real World

1. At a community health fair, you visit the booth of a local charitable organization. They're selling zebra-striped sunglasses to raise money for a weeklong camping and kayaking adventure they're sponsoring for underprivileged kids. You pick up a pair of the sunglasses, but decide not to buy them because the lenses are narrow, they seem cheaply made, and they have no UV rating tag. A poster from last year's camp shows children wearing the sunglasses steering their kayaks down a river. What—if anything—would you say?

2. You are visiting a friend and her two-year-old son, Quincy. It's a warm day, but hazy, and the two of you are planning to go for a walk to the town center with Quincy in the stroller. A few minutes before you leave, you put on some sunscreen and, noticing Quincy's fair complexion, offer to put some on him as well. Your friend shrugs. "It's so hazy today, I don't think he'll need it." How would you respond?

What About You?

Before you read this chapter, how much thought had you given to sun-safety behaviors?

_____

Do you plan to change anything about your own approach to UV exposure, based on the information in this chapter? If so, what? _____

_____

References and Suggested Readings

American Cancer Society. (2007). "What are the key statistics about melanoma?" Revised 05/30/2007. Available at www.cancer.org/docroot/CRI/content/CRI_2_4_1X_What _are_the_key_statistics_for_melanoma_50.asp?sitearea.

Brody, J.E. (2003). "A second opinion on sunshine: It can be good medicine after all." _The New York Times,_ June 17, 2003. Available at http://query.nytimes.com/gst/fullpage.html?res= 9A03EFD61538F934A25755C0A9659C8B63.

Environmental Protection Agency. (2006). _The Sun, UV, and You: A Guide to SunWise Behavior._ EPA 430-K-06-002, September, 2006. Available at www.epa.gov/sunwise.

Gordon, C.M., DePeter, K.C., Feldman, H.A., Grace, E., and Emans, S.J. (2004). Prevalence of vitamin D deficiency among healthy adolescents. _Archives of Pediatrics & Adolescent Medicine,_ 158, 531–537.

Holick, M.F. (2006). Resurrection of vitamin D deficiency and rickets. _Journal of Clinical Investigation,_ 116, 2062–2072.

Looker, A.C., Dawson-Hughes, B., Calvo, M.S., Gunter, E.W., and Sahyoun, N.R. (2002). Serum 25-hydroxyvitamin D status of adolescents and adults in two seasonal subpopulations from NHANES III. _Bone,_ 30, 771–777.

Robinson, J.K., Rigel, D.S., and Amonette, R.A. (2000). Summertime sun protection used by adults for their children. _Journal of the American Academy of Dermatology,_ 42(5), 746–753.

Task Force on Community Preventive Services. (2004). Recommendations to prevent skin cancer by reducing exposure to ultraviolet radiation. _American Journal of Preventive Medicine,_ 27(5), 467–470.

Westerdahl, J., Olsson, H., and Ingvar, C. (1994). At what age do sunburn episodes play a crucial role for the development of malignant melanoma? _European Journal of Cancer,_ 30A(11), 1647–1654.

Web Resources

National Safety Council (follow the Kids Sun Fun link):
www.nsc.org/resources/factsheets/environment/sun_safety.aspx
Shade Planning for America's Schools, Centers for Disease Control and
Prevention (CDC):
www.pubweb.epa.gov/sunwise/doc/cdc_shade_planning.pdf
Sun Safety Alliance (*Block the Sun, Not the Fun* guide):
www.sunsafetyalliance.org/user-assets/Documents/TeachingGuide.pdf
Sun Safety for Kids:
www.sunsafetyforkids.org
SunWise Meteorologist Tool Kit, Environmental Protection Agency, National
Weather Service, and American Meteorological Society:
www.epa.gov/sunwise/doc/met_kit.pdf
SunWise educator resources:
www.epa.gov/sunwise/educator_resources.html
SunWise materials for teachers:
www.epa.gov/sunwise/doc/guide.pdf
SunWise poster (English):
www.epa.gov/sunwise/doc/poster.pdf
SunWise poster (Spanish):
www.epa.gov/sunwise/doc/spanishposter.pdf
SunWise School Program Guide:
www.epa.gov/sunwise/doc/guide.pdf
UV index teaching materials for teachers:
www.epa.gov/sunwise/doc/met_kit.pdf

12

Promoting Children's Health Beyond the School Day

Learning Objectives

After reading this chapter, you will be able to . . .

○ Identify the benefits of using homework to promote children's activity, nutrition, and sun safety.

○ Create homework assignments that promote children's activity, nutrition, and sun safety.

○ Identify the main benefits and challenges of developing an after-school program.

○ List six standards recommended for a quality after-school program.

○ Discuss ideas for selecting an existing after-school program.

○ Identify five guidelines for developing your own after-school program.

○ List some simple behavioral changes that can greatly increase a family's level of physical activity.

○ Explain how pedometers can be used to promote family activity.

○ Describe ways of getting the whole community involved in improving children's health.

Classroom Challenge

It's 2:30 on a May afternoon, and Miss Dixon is monitoring the lines for the school buses after releasing her sixth-grade class for the day. While the children wait for the first bus to arrive, she chats with a group of friends waiting for bus 5: Alonzo, Rudy, and Lyza all live in the housing project on the west side of town. "Goodness, the sunshine feels great after all the rain we've been having," Miss Dixon says. "Do you three have any plans for the afternoon?"

Alonzo shrugs. "Guess we'll go to Lyza's place and hang," he says.

"It's always my place," Lyza smiles, "'cause I'm the only one with food in the fridge!"

Rudy tackles her. "Hey, I got food in the fridge, too! Problem is, I'm the one who fixed it! Lyza's the only one's got real grandma food!"

"Why don't you all do your activity homework together by walking into town?" Miss Dixon asks. "They're showing *National Treasure* at the West Branch Library at 5 o'clock."

Alonzo puts an arm around his teacher's shoulders. "Miss Dixon," he says, "it's my turn to be the teacher. If Lyza and Rudy and me walked from the projects to the West Branch Library, our mommas would whip our butts."

Miss Dixon frowns, recalling the shooting incidents that frequently occur in the vicinity of the West Side Housing Project. "I get it," she stammers.

Bus 5 pulls up. "See you tomorrow, Miss Dixon," Lyza shouts. She smiles and waves as she gets on the bus. "Enjoy the sunshine!"

As she walks back to her classroom to grade papers, Miss Dixon keeps thinking about her students spending this bright spring afternoon cooped up in Lyza's apartment. She stops by the principal's office. "Tom," she asks him, "what would it take to start an after-school program here at Douglass Elementary?"

Throughout this text, we've emphasized the vital role that classroom teachers play in promoting the health of their students throughout the school day. You've come to see that a school that really cares about children's health will have a comprehensive plan that includes classroom activity breaks, a quality physical education program, playgrounds organized to promote activity, a schoolwide nutrition policy, and a sun-safety program. But for many children, something vital is still missing: when they get off the bus at the end of the school day, they have limited options for physical activity and healthy snacks. Indeed, thousands of children across the United States come home to an empty house or apartment, sit in front of a TV or computer, and snack on junk food.

To help address this problem, we've identified in this chapter three key ways in which you can promote children's health outside the school environment. These include assigning health-promoting homework, helping to develop structured after-school programs, and encouraging family and community involvement.

Health-Promoting Homework

In a study by Morgan, Pangrazi, and Beighle (2003), 24-hour activity surveillance showed that elementary school children gathered the majority (60 percent) of their daily steps outside of school. They gathered only about 30 percent during the course of a normal school day, and the remainder, about 10 percent, in dedicated physical education. The message from this study is that classroom physical activity is not enough: teachers need to capitalize on methods for promoting activity beyond the school day. Similarly, children eat one or two meals a day at school. Teachers have no control over what students consume for after-school snacks and evening and week-end meals. And obviously, they cannot monitor their students' sun safety after school hours. Fortunately, one thing classroom teachers *can* do to promote children's activity, nutrition, and sun safety is assign them health-promoting homework.

What do we mean by health-promoting homework? Although it can consist of written work, puzzles, and coloring pages on topics such as fitness, nutrition, and sun safety, what we're really advocating here is homework that actively engages students in healthy activities. Here are a few simple examples:

- Assign your students to go for a 20-minute walk wearing a pedometer and recording their step counts.
- Have your students complete a fitness routine that you send home with them. Structure it as a checklist so that they can check off each component as they complete it (**Figure 12.1**).
- Have students present a brief oral report about a healthy extracurricular activity they are engaged in, such as karate, skating, or a cooking class. Hearing about their classmates' experiences can prompt other students to try new activities.

Name: _____   Date: _____

At-Home Workout #1

❑ Circle your arms in big windmills while you count to 20, then go in the other direction for 20.

❑ Jump rope for 20 jumps.

❑ Lie on the floor and stretch as slowly as you can. See how much space on the floor you can cover by stretching, then snap back to your original position.

❑ Go up one flight of stairs in your house or apartment building. Go back down again.

❑ Place hands against a wall, then walk your feet out from the wall until you feel a stretch in your lower legs. Count to 20 while you hold.

❑ Run around your house or apartment building one time.

❑ Jump rope for 20 jumps.

❑ Standing up, bend as many different parts of your body as you can. Now do it lying down.

❑ Now curl up slowly any way you can and touch both sets of toes with your hands. Curl back down slowly.

❑ Walk around your house or apartment building imitating one of the following animals. Check off which animal you chose to imitate:

  ❑ Elephant with long, heavy trunk

  ❑ Lion stalking prey

  ❑ Excited puppy

  ❑ Jumping rabbit

  ❑ Galloping horse

  ❑ Long-necked giraffe

  ❑ Monkey

Figure 12.1 Example of a simple fitness routine that children can do at home.

Give your students a set of healthy, kid-friendly recipes. Keep most of them simple, requiring only assembly of familiar foods: for example, apple slices dusted with cinnamon, or celery sticks spread with peanut butter or hummus. For recipes requiring cooking or baking, such as a veggie pizza, state on the recipe card, "Ask an adult to help!" Ask children to choose one of the recipes to make during the week and then have them report back to the class on its appearance, taste, and how easy it was to make (**Figure 12.2**).

Send your students on a nutrition quest at the grocery store. While their parents shop, students complete a simple assignment, such as the following:
- Find three fruits or vegetables that are blue or purple.
- Find out which kids' brand of yogurt contains the lowest amount of sugar per serving. Report the name of the yogurt to the class on Monday.
- Identify three kids' cereals that are made with whole grains. Be prepared to share the names of the cereals with the class.

Benefits of Health-Promoting Homework

Health-promoting homework has many benefits. First, it helps children integrate physical activity and healthy eating behaviors into an overall healthy lifestyle and thereby reduces the risk of developing chronic diseases such as hypertension and type 2 diabetes. As we discussed in Chapter 8, the report of the U.S. Surgeon General on physical activity found that just 30 minutes of moderate to vigorous activity a day reduces the risk for chronic disease (USDHHS, 1996). Activity-related homework helps children achieve this minimum every day.

Figure 12.2 A child who helps prepare healthful foods is more likely to enjoy them.

Second, health-promoting homework gives children an opportunity to develop intrinsic motivation for adopting healthy behaviors. As they play tag, jump rope, or wash carrot sticks, they experience the pleasures of movement and healthy eating unfiltered by the message from adults that "this is good for you." Left on their own to explore how their bodies want to move and what their bodies want to eat, children develop greater self-awareness, self-expression, and self-discovery (Gabbei and Hamrick, 2001).

Third, health-promoting homework provides an opportunity to influence family members' lifestyle choices. As they watch their child perform exercises on a fitness routine checklist or help their child assemble a veggie burrito, they learn about healthy lifestyle choices—and can be motivated to incorporate more of them into their family's routine.

Guidelines for Assigning Health-Promoting Homework

If your homework assignments are to be effective, you'll need to ensure that you follow certain guidelines. Make sure that the assignment is specific, that students understand what you expect of them, and that students appreciate the value of what you ask them to do. For example, if they need to report back to the class, specify whether their report will be oral or written. If you ask them to evaluate the calcium content of milk versus soda, make sure they understand what calcium is and that their bodies need it to build and maintain healthy bones.

As with any homework assignment, make sure that students understand the consequences of failing to complete the work. That said, you must also accept the fact that a child could easily tick off components on a fitness routine that she has not actually completed or report enjoying a recipe that he has not actually made. Just as they have different levels of skeletal maturation, elementary school children have varying levels of moral development, and it is best to communicate to them that you trust their word.

Back to Class

Miss Dixon's activity-related homework assignment required students to walk 1 mile outdoors every sunny afternoon during the week. Was this a good choice for her students? Why or why not? If not, how could she have modified the activity to accommodate the unique concerns of her students and their families?

Because it is vital that parents appreciate the value of health-promoting homework, make sure that you use school newsletters and other channels of communication to inform them of the benefits to their child. In addition, request that, whenever possible, they monitor their child's completion of assignments. Finally, encourage their participation: urge them to exercise with their child, help their child prepare healthy recipes, and practice sun safety. In addition, the Centers for Disease Control and Prevention (CDC) advocates that at least some of the child's health-promoting homework assignments *require* parental involvement (CDC, 2005).

After-School Programs

After-school programs are school-based, private, or community programs that offer children opportunities to improve their academics; work on their homework together; learn a musical instrument, craft, or hobby; engage in sports or other forms of physical activity; or simply socialize after school has been dismissed for the day. They offer significant benefits to students, families, and communities but also present some challenges.

Benefits and Challenges of After-School Programs

The most significant benefits of after-school programs include increased safety, improved academic performance, increased physical activity, and closer interpersonal ties.

According to the U.S. Census Bureau, more than 28 million children have both parents working outside the home, and 15 million of these children have no place to go when school ends. A study by Snyder and Sickmund (1999) found that violent crimes committed by and against juveniles peaked during the after-school hours. After-school programs keep youngsters in a safe environment and ease the anxiety of working parents regarding their children's safety.

After-school programs also improve academic achievement. Studies show that students in after-school programs get better grades and have better school attendance records than students who do not attend such programs.

Figure 12.3 In an after-school program, children have a chance to form lasting friendships.

Many after-school programs provide opportunities for children to engage in physical activity. From sports activities such as swimming, soccer, and rock-climbing, to recreational activities such as walking, playing active games, and working in a school garden, these opportunities can contribute to children's health.

Finally, after-school programs provide a place where students can form lasting friendships, both with other students and with program staff (**Figure 12.3**). Few programs for youth offer so many benefits at such a low cost to society. Many teachers and school administrators feel that in America today schools are unfairly asked to do everything for everybody. In such a climate, developing a quality after-school program may seem like another burden, but the payoff of safer and more successful students makes it worthwhile.

After-school programs are not without their challenges, the most considerable of which is funding. Costs for start-up and maintenance—for staff, space, utilities, equipment and supplies, and marketing—are expensive, and as we discuss in the accompanying News Clip, fund-raising may seem like a constant strain. Both public and private sources of funding should be sought, including federal, state, and city grants and donations from community associations, local businesses, philanthropic groups, and individuals.

Transportation is an often-overlooked challenge. As we said in Chapter 1, often the success of an after-school program is strongly influenced by the availability of transportation for students (Jago and Baranowski, 2004). School buses are scheduled to bring children home once each day. If children stay for after-school programs, does the burden of transporting them home fall on parents? What if parents don't drive or work later than the program is open and no public transportation is available? If parents feel that transporting their child home is their personal responsibility, they may not allow their child to participate in a program. Many programs must raise additional funds to support the cost of transporting children home safely. Others facilitate ride sharing among families within the same neighborhood or find other solutions that work for their communities.

A final common challenge is staffing. Teachers who have worked a full day and have homework to grade and after-school meetings to attend often simply cannot staff after-school programs. But talented people experienced in working with children may not be available to work just a few hours each afternoon. Some programs overcome this challenge by offering after-school staff positions to undergraduates majoring in education, AmeriCorps volunteers, and grandparents and other retirees in the community.

Assuring a Quality After-School Program

As a classroom teacher, you might not want to run an after-school program; however, you are in a unique position to advocate for a quality program. Of the many models of programs being used in schools, some are run by teachers while others are operated by private contractors or community organizations such as the YMCA or city recreation departments. These vary widely in their offerings and their quality—from

Back to Class

What benefits would you rate as most important for an after-school program serving Alonzo, Rudy, Lyza, and their classmates? What challenges would Miss Dixon most likely face in trying to develop such a program?

challenging academic or sports programs to those that offer little more than afternoon day care. Thus, it is important to have standards to use when reviewing programs and selecting those that best match your students' needs. After a program is selected, it is also important that it be carefully monitored to ensure that it continues to meet the needs of all students who choose to participate.

The National AfterSchool Association (see Web Resources) offers six major standards that a quality after-school program should address. In brief, they include the following:

- *Human relations.* The program must focus on ensuring that interactions and relationships are positive and caring.
- *Indoor environment.* The space must be large enough to meet the physical needs of children and offer the opportunity to explore personal interests.
- *Outdoor environment.* The play area should meet the needs of children and contain equipment that allows them to be independent and creative.
- *Activities.* An activity schedule should be flexible and the variety of activities broad. There should be adequate equipment and supplies to support the activities.
- *Safety, health, and nutrition.* The safety of youth should be uppermost and the environment must be safe and enhance the health of participants. The program should serve food and drink that meets the needs of children.
- *Administration.* Specific guidelines regarding staff, group sizes, parents, and training of the staff are offered in the original document.

Selecting an After-School Program

As a classroom teacher, you may not make the final selection of an after-school activity program, but your input is often expected and valued. When seeking an after-school program to increase your students' physical activity, make sure that any program you consider provides experiences appropriate for students of all physical types and skill levels, including students with disabilities. The after-school program should offer students an opportunity to develop interest and competence in a wide range of recreational activities. Evidence has shown that if people do not develop competence and confidence in their ability to participate in recreational activities during their school years, they seldom participate in later life. In the after-school program, students can learn to play and cooperate in an environment with little at stake in terms of winning and losing.

News Clip

Financing After-School Programs: A Tough Challenge

In the 1990s, Intermediate School 238 in Hollis, Queens, was considered the worst school in its district. Today, test scores and attendance have improved; the school has an orchestra, a theatre group, and a dance troupe; and it regularly sends several dozen graduates to specialized high schools. At a school where over 70 percent of kids come from families living below the poverty level, Principal Joseph Gates credits much of the improvement to the variety of academic and cultural activities offered after school. It's a similar story at 118 other schools with after-school programs that serve more than 20,000 children in New York City.

Lucy Friedman, executive director of the nonprofit After-School Corporation, explains that after-school programs offer children a safe environment where they receive academic tutoring, physical activity, and classes in subjects, like art and music, that have been cut from the regular school day. Because in recent years, the dynamics have changed regarding whether parents are home after school, the hours from 3:00 to 6:00 p.m. are increasingly a period where kids need constructive places to go.

Yet, funding for such programs is precarious. After-school programs are typically funded through a patchwork of public and private sources. Jim O'Neill, executive director of the Sport and Arts in Schools Foundation, notes that the problem with programs funded this way lies in the funding award cycle and time period. Once programs are established and running, the question becomes how to sustain them with no consistent funding sources.

Public money exists, but is often difficult to manage or is pulled after an initial program start-up period. Private foundations, therefore, can be a critical source of revenue for after-school programs, such as the Charles Stewart Mott Foundation's support for an after-school initiative from the Institute for Youth, Education, and Families. Under this program, eight U.S. cities will participate in a three-year, $1.5 million initiative to nurture support for after-school programs. Check the Foundation's website (see Web Resources) for more information.

Source: Adapted from the *New York Times*, June 18, 2007, at www.nytimes.com/2007/06/18/nyregion/18citywide.html.

take action!

1.   Do the schools in your local district offer after-school programs to the children in your community? Find out! If they do, ask if you can visit the program to observe it in action. Interview the director and ask where their funding comes from. Volunteer to help with fund-raising efforts, or write a letter to your local newspaper appealing for funding from the community.

2.   If the schools in your district don't offer after-school programs, find out what the stumbling block is and ask what you can do to help get a program started.

3.   For assistance with your efforts, check out the website of the After-school Alliance (see Web Resources). Click on *Program Tools: Funding,* and get involved!

It's also important to keep in mind the innate needs of children, which we identified in Chapter 2. Elementary school children are high energy and, after a day at school, need an opportunity for vigorous activity. Most children like large-muscle activities such as running, jumping rope, and playing hopscotch (**Figure 12.4**). They like games with simple rules so time is spent playing rather than learning how to play.

Hall and Gruber (2006) investigated after-school physical activity and nutrition programs. The review was funded by the National Institute on Out-of-School Time to see how well some popular after-school programs aligned with the standards of the National AfterSchool Association identified earlier in this chapter. This document is an excellent resource for finding existing programs that could meet the needs of your school. Programs selected for the Hall and Gruber review had to meet the criteria of being easily implemented in a school setting. If specialized professional help, such as a physician, nutritionist, or nurse, were required for implementation, the programs were not included. Twenty programs were selected and evaluated by the authors. Some of those included were as follows:

Figure 12.4 After a structured school day, many young children enjoy engaging in vigorous activity, such as running.

- CATCH Kids Club Nutrition
- Eat Well & Keep Moving
- Generation Fit
- Get in the Game for Good Health
- Hearts N' Parks
- Just for Kids
- KidShape
- Operation Fitkids
- Planet Health
- School Health Index Incentive Program (SHIIP)
- Slimkids
- Team Nutrition

Most of these programs have an active website where information and materials can be downloaded.

Developing an After-School Program

If your school wants to develop an after-school activity and sports program, an excellent reference is the NASPE document, *Guidelines for After-School Physical Activity and Intramural Sport Programs* (see Web Resources). This document offers teachers and administrators excellent information regarding how to develop a quality program that uses existing staff. Some basic guidelines to consider for a school-directed program are as follows:

- Use all available times. After-school hours are most common, but the hour before school, the noon hour, and Saturdays merit consideration. Some evening participation might be a possibility.
- Ensure that the program is open to all interested students. Regardless of the activities offered, all participants should receive an equal amount of time for

participation. Set a minimum playing time for each team member, with the goal being to have players share the playing time equally. Rotating positions can help prevent domination by the more skilled participants.

- Modify rules according to facilities, equipment, and level of skill. Elimination games should be avoided so that participation is stressed.
- Emphasize safety awareness and procedures to participants.
- Post a bulletin board with pertinent information and update it regularly. Post rules of play governing each activity and list individual and team rosters. Display tournament information and progress. Locate after-school program information at or near the bulletin board.

In addition, the Afterschool Alliance has created an action kit to help those developing a quality, affordable after-school program. It explains how to find programs, contact influential people, secure funding, and structure a new program. Download the kit from the web (see Web Resources); it is available in both English and Spanish.

Back to Class

Would you suggest that Miss Dixon find an existing after-school program to bring into her school or develop a program tailored to the unique needs of her students? What might be some advantages and disadvantages of each approach?

Family and Community Involvement

As we've stressed throughout this text, it is impossible to assure adequate physical activity for children by focusing only on the school setting. Families and communities must be enlisted as allies.

Include Education for Families in Children's Health Initiatives

The CDC advocates including education for parents and other family members as part of health-promotion activities for children (CDC, 2005). Specifically, the CDC notes that family members can:

- encourage their children to be active on a regular basis;
- be role models for physical activity and healthy eating;
- encourage the family to eat meals together (**Figure 12.5**);
- set limits on the amount of time children spend watching television and playing video or computer games;

- plan and participate in family activities that include physical activity, such as walking, biking, and playing outdoors, and include physical activity at birthday parties, picnics, and vacations, etc.;
- facilitate participation by their children in school and community physical activity and sports programs; and
- advocate for quality school and community physical activity programs.

Help Families Increase Their Activity Level

By making some simple changes in their everyday behaviors, families can increase their level of physical activity. Use a newsletter or other forum to share the following active behaviors:

Figure 12.5 Parents promote their children's health when they emphasize shared family mealtimes.

- Include family walks in the weekly schedule of events.
- Take the dog for a walk twice a day.
- Use stairs instead of escalators and elevators.
- Walk to activities such as games, shopping, church, and school.
- When you must drive, park at the end of the lot and walk together into the store or other business.
- Work out as a family by joining a health club that specializes in family activities, such as the YMCA and YWCA.
- Encourage children to play outdoors. Very few indoor activities are active in nature.
- Avoid drive-up windows in banks and fast-food establishments—instead, park the car and walk in.
- Log family activity by writing it down in an activity journal or, better yet, use a pedometer and record steps.

A recent study showed that people who wore pedometers accumulated 2,000 more steps per day. Because users receive feedback about the number of steps they take, they are often more motivated to incorporate some of the suggestions above.

Promote Family Pedometer Activities

In Chapter 8, we discussed how to introduce pedometers to your students and explored reasons why pedometer use increases children's motivation to engage in physical activity. The same is true for families. This section identifies a variety of activities that use pedometers to help families increase their physical activity.

Open House on the Move

Most schools have an open house sometime during the year. These events offer an excellent chance to educate parents about pedometers and increase awareness about the importance of living an active lifestyle. Set up a booth at the location where most families will enter the school. As families enter, invite them to check out a pedometer

Back to Class

When sending a newsletter home encouraging families to walk in their neighborhood or join a fitness club, teachers need to remain sensitive to families' personal and financial pressures. If you were Miss Dixon, which of the suggestions listed earlier would you feel comfortable sharing with your students' families?

to wear during the open house. If students have already been using pedometers during the school day, they will be happy to teach parents how the pedometer works. Parents wear the pedometer while they are participating in the open house. Before parents leave, collect the pedometers and hand out a physical activity newsletter that explains how pedometers work and describes schoolwide efforts to promote physical activity. You can also offer parents the opportunity to purchase the pedometer they have been wearing so that they can continue to keep track of their steps at home.

Guess and Share

Families can use this activity when walking the dog, participating in a charity walk, or engaging in any other family event that involves physical activity. Assuming there is one pedometer for a family, each person gets to wear the pedometer for three to five minutes. When time is up, family members guess how many steps the person wearing the pedometer accumulated. The pedometer is passed on to another family member who wears it for three to five minutes, and the process continues. After each person has used the pedometer, the family guesses either the total steps accumulated by everyone (don't reset the pedometer) or the steps accumulated by the last person to wear it.

Active Chores

Wearing a pedometer and monitoring steps while doing chores is another way to measure the amount of activity accumulated during lifestyle activity. Make a chart of family chores with a space for "steps taken" while doing the chores. Family members wear a pedometer while performing their tasks and then record the number of steps they took while completing them. This chart may be kept on the refrigerator and used for future reference. After all chores are finished, the family discusses which chores are active and which are less active. Also, families can brainstorm about ways to increase the number of steps taken during relatively inactive chores.

Errands with a Pedometer

Often, families feel they are too busy to exercise because they are constantly running errands. Pedometers allow parents and children to see how much activity they can accumulate while completing errands. In a day of walking to the post office, shopping at the mall, etc., many steps can be accumulated.

How Active Are My Activities?

Many favorite activities—from gardening to shooting hoops—can be put to the test by using a pedometer. This test allows both parents and children to see the number of steps accumulated while doing their favorite activities. Each family member gets to pick an activity for family participation. The steps accumulated during that activity are recorded so that the family can evaluate the activity level of their favorite pastime. A chart of the activities they participated in and the corresponding steps for that activity should be displayed on the refrigerator or in another prominent place in the home. Family members should seek new and enjoyable activities to evaluate.

Household Goal Setting

The purpose of this activity is to make every member of the family an important part of the family activity goal. Moving together toward a common physical activity goal is a way for a family to promote lifestyle activity. Each family member wears a pedometer for four days and records his or her activity each day. At the end of four days of tracking activity, the average of the four days of activity is computed for each family member. The average scores are added together to determine the baseline family activity level. A goal of increasing the baseline activity level by 10 percent is set, and family members try to achieve the group goal. If the family reaches the goal for the majority of days over a two-week period, they can increase the goal another 10 percent.

Walk the Talk

Walking and talking is a good way for parents and children to learn about each other without interference and distractions. Each family member pairs with another family member to take walks on specified days or evenings. A rotating list should be posted on the refrigerator, and every effort should be made to ensure that all family members have an opportunity to walk with each other at least once a week. The walk should last at least 10 minutes, and each person should actively participate in a discussion (e.g., about their day's activities). One night a week, the entire family walks and talks together.

One Small Step

In recent years, many schools and communities have organized a Step-a-Thon to raise funds, promote physical activity, facilitate a sense of community, and enhance multiple dimensions of wellness (i.e., physical, emotional, spiritual, intellectual, and social). Typically, sponsors contribute a set amount for every 1,000 steps. Parents are encouraged to participate actively, or help their children collect sponsors, or staff the event.

In addition, some schools designate a day as "Step It Up Day." On this day, typically a Saturday, students and their families actively engage in as much lifestyle, recreational, and leisure activity as possible, recording their steps with their pedometers.

An excellent resource from the U.S. Department of Health and Human Services, called SmallStep and SmallStep Kids (see Web Resources), provides information and resources on other ways to incorporate small changes into the lifestyles of kids and their families.

Community-Based Efforts to Promote Children's Health

In Chapter 1, we acknowledged that "it takes a village" to raise a healthy child. The following are just a few examples of efforts to improve children's health that involve the entire community.

- *Walk to school day.* As we stated in Chapter 8, walking to school is an easy way for some children to start the day actively. International, national, and local programs exist to encourage walking or bicycling to school to promote health, conserve the environment, and/or rally for safer streets. Pedometers can be used to record step counts, and classes, entire schools, or neighborhoods can compete to encourage greater participation and motivation for continuing the program.

- *Open parks and playgrounds.* Does your community have a public park or playground? Are school playgrounds open to the public? If so, are they safe, shaded, well-maintained, and available for children to use outside of school hours? If not, gather a group of concerned teachers and parents to lobby your town planning commission, department of parks and recreation, or other office to make the necessary improvements and keep playgrounds accessible before and after school, on weekends, and throughout the summer. Publish a list of addresses of all local open parks and playgrounds and send it to parents in a school newsletter. You can also include public beaches, recreation centers, etc.

- *Kids' menu challenge.* Get in touch with your local restaurant association and invite their members' to participate in a kids' menu challenge. How does it work? By a specified deadline, head chefs at participating restaurants submit a proposed menu for kids' entrees. A panel of experts, which should include at least one registered dietitian and several kids, evaluates the menus on criteria including nutritional quality, variety, value, taste, and kid appeal. The winning restaurant receives free publicity with the menu featured in local press releases, in school newsletters, etc. You can even invite the winning chef to share his or her menu with the manager of your school cafeteria!

- *Community gardens.* Many communities across the United States have established gardens where seniors, middle adults, and children work side-by-side growing nourishing food for their families. Before you dig the first hole, check out the website of the American Community Gardening Association (see Web Resources), where you'll learn how to form a planning committee; approach sponsors; find, prepare, and develop a site; manage the garden; and much more.

- *Safe summers.* Most communities have numerous organizations that offer summer camps for children, including beach camps, arts camps, hiking adventures, and so on. Before the end of the school year, gather a list of these organizations and mail to each of them a letter urging them to make their camp SunWise; provide them with the FDA's SunWise web address (see Web Resources).

- *Networking.* Coordinate your efforts to promote children's health by networking with the administrators of your local YMCA, Boys and Girls Clubs, recreation centers, community centers, Boy Scout and Girl Scout troops, Little League teams, hockey leagues, and other kid-friendly community organizations and sports teams. Also, contact professional organizations and businesses such as Rotary International, HMOs, banks, and your local chamber of commerce. They may be willing to partner with your school to develop programs, to donate funds directly, or to participate in fund-raising efforts.

Back to Class

Provide some examples of ways in which Miss Dixon could network with community members to help develop an after-school program for her students.

Chapter Summary

Health-Promoting Homework

- Teachers can promote children's physical activity, nutrition, and sun safety by assigning homework that actively engages them in performing healthy activities.

- Health-promoting homework helps children integrate physical activity and healthy eating behaviors into an overall healthy lifestyle, thereby reducing their risk for chronic disease. It can also help children develop intrinsic motivation for adopting a healthier lifestyle and motivate family members to engage in similar healthy behaviors.

- Make sure that homework assignments are specific, that students understand your expectations, and that they appreciate the value of what you are asking them to do. Also make sure they understand the consequences for not completing the assignment.

- Communicate to parents the value of the homework, ask them to monitor the child's completion of the assignments, and urge their participation.

After-School Programs

- After-school programs are school-based, private, or community programs that offer children opportunities to improve their academics; work on their homework together; learn a musical instrument, craft, or hobby; engage in sports or other forms of physical activity; or simply socialize after school has been dismissed for the day.

- The most significant benefits of after-school programs include increased safety, improved academic performance, increased physical activity, and closer interpersonal ties. Serious challenges include funding, transportation, and staffing.

- The National AfterSchool Association sets standards for several aspects of a quality after-school program, including human relations, indoor environment, outdoor environment, activities, safety, health and nutrition, and administration.

- Guidelines for developing a school-directed after-school program include using all available times, including before school and weekends; ensuring the program is open to all students; modifying rules according to facilities, equipment, and level of skill; emphasizing safety; and using a bulletin board to communicate information about the program.

Family and Community Involvement

- The CDC recommends that parents be actively involved with efforts to improve their children's health through a variety of actions, such as limiting TV time, planning physical activity involving the whole family, etc.

- Classroom teachers can share with families some simple behavioral changes they can make to increase their overall level of physical activity.

- Teach families to incorporate pedometers into their activities to help them monitor and increase their physical activity.

- Involve the community in your efforts to improve children's health. Some ideas include organizing walk to school days; lobbying for open parks and playgrounds; sponsoring a kids' menu challenge; starting a community garden; notifying summer camp organizations about SunWise summer activities; and networking with community and business organizations that can help you meet your health-promotion goals.

Review Questions

Content Review

1. Explain how health-promoting homework can help children develop intrinsic motivation to make healthy lifestyle choices.

2. Using the information you learned in Chapter 9 on physical fitness, design an appropriate fitness routine for early-elementary students similar to that given in Figure 12.1 to use as a homework assignment.

3. Identify four primary benefits of after-school programs. Can you think of any others?

4. Explore the website of at least one of the after-school programs studied by Hall and Gruber and listed in this chapter. What does it offer? How does it address each of the six standards set by the National AfterSchool Association?

5. Identify several steps that parents and guardians can take to improve their own health as well as the health of their children.

Real World

1. You send your second-grade class home with a newsletter for parents explaining your intention to start sending the children home with physical activity homework. As an example, you mention a 20-minute walk in the neighborhood or a game of tag outside with other family members or friends. The next day, a single mother who is dropping off her child at school confronts you. She states that she does not allow her daughter to go outside without adult supervision, and as she comes home from work after dark every night, she has no opportunity to walk with her daughter or supervise a game of tag. What would you say?

2. The elementary school where you teach fifth grade has a successful after-school program that has been running for the past five years. You overhear two teachers talking in the lunchroom about federal and state budget cuts slashing the program's annual funding by half. One of the teachers insists that the funding cuts will mean the death of the program. What steps could you and your colleagues take to prevent the loss of the program?

References and Suggested Readings

Beighle, A., Pangrazi, R.P., and Vincent, S.D. (2001). Pedometers, physical activity, and accountability. *Journal of Physical Education, Recreation, & Dance,* 72(9), 16–19.

Centers for Disease Control and Prevention (CDC). (2005). *Healthy Youth! Promoting Better Health: Strategies: Families.* Available at www.cdc.gov/HealthyYouth/physicalactivity/promoting_health/strategies/families.html.

Gabbei, R., and Hamrick, D. (2001). Using physical activity homework to meet the national standards. *Journal of Physical Education, Recreation, & Dance,* 72(4).

Hall, G., and Gruber, D. (2006). *Health Choices AfterSchool: Investigation of the Alignment of Physical Activity and Nutrition Programs/Curricula and the National AfterSchool Association Program Standards.* New York: Robert Wood Johnson Foundation, The After School Project. Available at www.niost.org/publications/healthy%20choices%20afterschool.pdf.

What About You?

Throughout this text, we've emphasized the value of forming wide networking relationships in your community. Through such ties, you can help build the committees and get the funding you need to improve the health of your community's children. How many people are in *your* network? List everyone you can think of.

Family members:

_____

Friends:

_____

Teachers and staff at your college or university:

_____

_____

People from companies where you have been employed:

_____

People at places where you frequently conduct business, such as banks, the post office, insurance agencies, grocery stores, hairdresser, drug store, YMCA or fitness club, restaurants and coffee shops you frequently visit, etc.:

_____

People from nonprofits you belong to or support, such as church groups, local charities, the public library, community associations, political parties, community theatre groups, local museums, etc.:

_____

_____

Now that you've listed all of the people in your network, how do you feel about your list? Were you surprised by how many people you know? Now think about the fact that everyone on your list has his or her own network, which you can tap into simply by inviting your contact to spread the word about your goals. Next time you feel powerless to make a difference in children's lives, go back to your list, and start talking!

Jago, R., and Baranowski, T. (2004). Non-curricular approaches for increasing physical activity in youth: A review. *Preventive Medicine,* 39(1), 157–163.

Morgan, C.F., Pangrazi, R.P., and Beighle, A. (2003). Using pedometers to promote physical activity in physical education. *Journal of Physical Education, Recreation & Dance,* 74(7), 33–38.

Pangrazi, R.P. (2006). *Active & Healthy Schools Program: A Road Map to Make your School Environment Active & Healthy.* Owatonna, MN: Gopher Sport.

Pangrazi, R.P., Beighle, A., and Sidman, C.L. (2007). *Pedometer power: Using pedometers in school and community* (2nd ed.). Champaign, IL: Human Kinetics.

Snyder, H.N., and Sickmund, M. (1999). *Juvenile Offenders and Victims: 1999 National Report.* Washington, DC: National Center for Juvenile Justice and the Office of Juvenile Justice and Delinquency Prevention.

U.S. Department of Health and Human Services. (1996). *Physical activity and health: A report of the Surgeon General.* Atlanta, GA: Centers for Disease Control and Prevention, National Center for Chronic Disease Prevention and Health Promotion.

Web Resources

Afterschool Alliance:
www.afterschoolalliance.org
American Community Gardening Association:
www.communitygarden.org
American Heart Walk (American Heart Association):
www.americanheart.org
Be Active (steps program):
www.beactivenc.org
Charles Stewart Mott Foundation (funding for after-school programs):
www.mott.org
Child Care and Development Fund and Temporary Assistance to Needy Families program:
www.afterschool.gov/docs/federalfunding.html
Eat Better, Eat Together program (Washington State University, Cooperative Extension, the Nutrition Education Network of Washington, and USDA Food and Nutrition Service):
www.nutrition.wsu.edu/ebet/toolkit.html
International Walk to School:
www.iwalktoschool.org
NASPE, Guidelines for After-School Physical Activity and Intramural Sport Programs:
www.aahperd.org/naspe
National AfterSchool Association:
www.njafter3.org
National YMCA:
www.ymca.net
Project ACES (All Children Exercise Simultaneously):
www.projectaces.com
Safe Routes to School Programs:
www.saferoutesinfo.org
Small Step Kids (U.S. Dept. of Health and Human Services):
www.smallstep.gov/kids/flash/index.html
SunWise (FDA):
www.epa.gov/sunwise
Walk to School Events:
www.walktoschool.org

Appendix A

Sample Curriculum Guide–Lesson Plan

Manipulative Skills Using Beanbags
Grades K–2

Instructional Objectives:

To move in a large group without bumping into others

To freeze on signal

To learn tossing and catching skills

To cooperate in game activities

NASPE National Standards:

Introductory Activity: 1, 5

Fitness Activity: 1, 4, 5

Lesson Focus: 1, 2, 4, 5

Game: 1, 5

Equipment Required:

Tambourine or tom-tom

Music for Fitness Games & Challenges

One beanbag per student

Instructional Activities	Teaching Hints

Introductory Activity — Bend, Stretch, and Shake

1. Bend various body parts individually and then bend various combinations of body parts.

2. Stretch the body in various levels. Encourage stretching from various positions such as standing, sitting, and prone position.

3. Practice shaking individual body parts when the tambourine is shaken. Progress to shaking the entire body.

4. Bend body parts while doing different locomotor movements. Bend limbs while shaking.

Use a tambourine to signal changes between bending, stretching, and shaking.

Encourage smooth movements in bending and stretching activities.

Encourage creative responses.

Fitness Development Activity — Fitness Games and Challenges

1. Stoop Tag - 45 seconds.

2. Freeze; perform stretching activities.

3. Back-to-Back Tag - 45 seconds.

4. Freeze; perform Abdominal Challenges using Curl-up variations.

5. Balance Tag - 45 seconds.

6. Freeze; perform Upper Body Strength Challenges using Push-up variations.

7. Elbow Swing Tag - 45 seconds.

8. Freeze; perform Trunk Development challenges.

9. Color Tag - 45 seconds.

Tape alternating segments of silence and music to signal duration of exercise. Music segments indicate fitness game activity while intervals of silence announce flexibility and strength development activities.

Choose any of the tag games. The names of the tag games indicate a "safe" position when one cannot be tagged, i.e., back to back with a partner or balancing on one foot.

Avoid getting caught up in rule infractions. The purpose of the tag games is to encourage locomotor movement.

Lesson Focus — Manipulative Skills Using Beanbags

Stand in place and practice tossing and catching.

1. Toss and catch with both hands.

2. Toss and catch with the back of hands. This will encourage children to catch with "soft hands."

3. Toss the beanbag to an increasingly high level, emphasizing a straight overhead toss. To encourage straight tossing, have the child sit down.

Stand in place, toss and catch while performing stunts.

1. Toss overhead and perform the following stunts and catch the bag.

   a. Quarter and half turns, right and left

   b. Full turn

   c. Touch floor

   d. Clap hands

   e. Clap hands around different parts of body, behind back, under legs.

   f. Heel click

   g. Sit down, get up.

   h. Look between legs.

Each student must have a beanbag for practice.

Give students two or three activities to practice so you have time to move and help individuals. Alternate activities from each of the categories so students receive a variety of skills to practice.

Emphasize tosses that are straight up and about 12 inches above the head.

Toss, move to a new spot, and catch the beanbag

1. Toss overhead, move to another spot, and catch.

2. Toss, do a locomotor movement, and catch.

3. Toss and move from side to side.

4. Toss overhead behind self, move, and catch.

Balance the beanbag

1. Balance on the following body parts:

   a. Head

   b. Back of hand

   c. Shoulder

   d. Knee

   e. Foot

   f. Elbow

   g. Exploratory activity

2. Balance and move as follows:

   a. Walk

   b. Run

   c. Skip

   d. Gallop

   e. Sit down

   f. Lie down

   g. Turn around

   h. Combinations of the above

   i. Exploratory activity.

Beanbag challenge activities

1. Hold the beanbag between knees and play tag with a partner or small group.

2. Place the beanbag on tummy and shake it off.

3. Place the beanbag on back and "mule kick" it off.

4. Push the beanbag across the floor with different body parts.

5. Toss the beanbag up and touch specified body parts.

6. Put beanbags on floor. Rotate various body parts on a beanbag.

7. Beanbag Balance Tag: Balance a beanbag on selected body parts. Announce a color to identify those who are it.

This is an excellent activity for teaching students to track (keep their eyes focused on) the beanbag. Remind them not to look away while tossing and catching.

Students should be encouraged to see how long they can balance the beanbag.

Movements should be controlled with as little bounce as possible.

These are body control activities. Students must be able to concentrate on moving slowly and keeping the beanbag in place.

Use the challenge to motivate students. These activities will be exciting and should be integrated throughout the lesson.

Hand-eye coordination is slowly learned after many repetitions. Encourage students to repeat their attempts.

Game Activities

Midnight

Supplies: None

Skills: Running, dodging

A safety line is established about 40 feet from a den in which two or three players, the foxes, are standing. The others stand behind the safety line and ask, "What time is it, Mr. Fox?" One of the Foxes is designated to answer in various fashions, such as "one o' clock," "four o' clock," etc. When the Fox says a certain time, the class walks forward that number of steps. For example, if the Fox says, "six o'clock," the class has to move forward six steps. The Fox continues to draw the players toward him or her. At some point, the Fox answers the question by saying, "Midnight," and chases the others back to the safety line. Any player who is caught becomes a Fox in the den and helps to catch others.

Leap the Brook

Supplies: None

Skills: Leaping, jumping, hopping, turning

A brook is marked off on the floor for a distance of about 30 feet. For the first 10 feet, it is 3 feet wide; for the next 10 feet, it is 4 feet wide; for the last 10 feet, it is 5 feet wide. Children form a single file line and jump over the narrowest part of the brook. They should be encouraged to do this several times, using different styles of jumping and leaping. After they have satisfactorily negotiated the narrow part, they move to the next width, and so on. The selection of the distances is arbitrary, and the distances can be changed if they seem unsuitable for any particular group of children.

Variation: Children can use different means of crossing the brook—leaping, jumping, hopping. They also can vary the kinds of turns to be made—right or left; or quarter, half, three quarter, or full. They should use different body shapes, different arm positions, and so on.

Appendix A

Sample Curriculum Guide–Lesson Plan

Manipulative Skills Using Frisbees
Grades 3–4

Objectives:

To learn the unique throwing style required with Frisbees

To learn the rules of Frisbee Golf

To perform continuous fitness activity

NASPE National Standards:

Introductory Activity: 1, 5

Fitness Activity: 1, 4, 6

Lesson Focus: 2, 3, 5

Game: 2, 3, 5

Equipment Required:

Tom-tom or tambourine

Signs and music for Aerobic Fitness

One Frisbee per student

Cones and hoops for Frisbee Golf

Instructional Activities	Teaching Hints

Introductory Activity—European Rhythmic Running with Variations

Students clap to the beat of the tambourine and run in single-file formation. Practice some of the following variations:

1. Clap hands the first beat of a four beat rhythm.
2. Stamp foot and clap hands on the first beat.
3. On signal, make a complete turn using four running steps.

Encourage students to originate different variations of rhythmic running.

After the rhythm is learned, stop striking the tambourine and let the class maintain the rhythm.

Fitness Development Activity — Aerobic Fitness

1. Rhythmic run with clap
2. Bounce turn and clap
3. Rhythmic 4-count curl-ups (knees, toes, knees, back)
4. Rhythmic crab kicks (slow time)
5. Jumping Jack combination
6. Double knee lifts
7. Lunges (right, left, forward) with single-arm circles (on the side lunges) and double-arms circles (on the forward lunge)
8. Rhythmic trunk twists
9. Directional run (forward, backward, side, turning)
10. Rock side to side with clap
11. Side leg raises (alternate legs)
12. Rhythmic 4-count push-ups (If these are too difficult for students, substitute single-arm circles in the push-up position.)

Use music to stimulate effort. Any combination of movements can be used.

Keep the steps simple and easy to perform. Some students will become frustrated if the learning curve is steep.

Signs that explain the aerobic activities will help students remember performance cues.

Don't stress or expect perfection. Allow students to perform the activities as best they can.

Alternate bouncing and running movements with flexibility and strength development movements.

Lesson Focus — Manipulative Skills Using Frisbees

Throwing the Disk

Backhand Throw

The backhand grip is used most often. The thumb is on top of the disk, the index finger along the rim, and the other fingers underneath. To throw the Frisbee with the right hand, stand in a sideways position with the right foot toward the target. Step toward the target and throw the Frisbee in a sideways motion across the body, snapping the wrist and trying to keep the disk flat on release.

Underhand Throw

The underhand throw uses the same grip as in the backhand throw, but the thrower faces the target and holds the disk at the side of the body. Step forward with the leg opposite the throwing arm while bringing the Frisbee forward. When the throwing arm is out in the front of the body, release the Frisbee. The trick to this throw is learning to release the disk so that it is parallel to the ground.

Catching the Disk

Thumb-Down Catch

The thumb-down catch is used for catching when the disk is received at waist level or above. The thumb is pointing toward the ground.

Use the following instructional cues to improve skill performance:

a. Release the disk parallel to the ground. If it is tilted, a curved throw results.

b. Step toward the target and follow through on release of the disk.

c. Snap open the wrist and make the Frisbee spin.

If space is limited, all Frisbees should be thrown in the same direction.

Thumb-Up Catch

The thumb-up catch is used when the Frisbee is received below waist level. The thumb points up, and the fingers are spread.

Throwing and Catching Activities:

a. Throw the Frisbee at different levels to partner.

b. Throw a curve—to the left, right and upward. Vary the speed of the curve.

c. Throw a bounce pass—try a low and a high pass.

d. Throw the disc like a boomerang. Must throw at a steep angle into the wind.

e. Throw the Frisbee into the air, run and catch. Increase the distance of the throw.

f. Throw the Frisbee through a hoop held by a partner.

g. Catch the Frisbee under your leg. Catch it behind your back.

h. Throw the Frisbees into hoops that are placed on the ground as targets.
   Different-colored hoops can be given different values. Throw through your partner's legs.

i. Frisbee bowling—One partner has a bowling pin which the other partner attempts to knock down by throwing the Frisbee.

j. Play catch while moving. Lead your partner so he or she doesn't have to break stride.

k. See how many successful throws and catches you can make in 30 seconds.

l. Frisbee baseball pitching—Attempt to throw the Frisbee into your partner's "Strike Zone."

Children can develop both sides of the body by learning to throw and catch the disk with either hand. The teacher should design the activities so that the students get both right-hand and left-hand practice.

Since a Frisbee is somewhat different from the other implements that children usually throw, devote some time to teaching form and style in throwing and catching. Avoid drills that reward speed in throwing and catching.

Frisbee Game Activities

Frisbee Keep Away

Supplies: Frisbees
Skills: Throwing and catching Frisbees
Students break into groups of three. Two of the players in the group try to keep the other player from touching the Frisbee while they are passing it back and forth. If the Frisbee is touched by a defensive player, the person who threw the Frisbee becomes the defensive player. Begin the game by asking students to remain stationary while throwing and catching. Later, challenge can be added by allowing all players in the group to move.

Frisbee Golf

Supplies: One Frisbee per person, hoops for hole markers, cones
Skills: Frisbee throwing for accuracy
Frisbee Golf or disk golf is a favorite game of many students. Boundary cones with numbers can be used for tees, and holes can be boxes, hula-hoops, trees, tires, garbage cans, or any other available equipment on the school grounds. Draw a course on a map for students and start them at different holes to decrease the time spent waiting to tee off. Regulation golf rules apply. The students can jog between throws for increased activity.
Disk golf is played like regular golf. One stroke is counted for each time the disk is thrown and when a penalty is incurred. The object is to acquire the lowest score. The following rules dictate play:
Tee-throws: Tee-throws must be completed within or behind the designated tee area.
Lie: The lie is the spot on or directly underneath the spot where the previous throw landed.
Throwing order: The player whose disk is the farthest from the hole throws first. The player with the least number of throws on the previous hole tees off first.
Fairway throws: Fairway throws must be made with the foot closest to the hole on the lie. A run-up is allowed.
Dog leg: A dog leg is one or more designated trees or poles in the fairway that must be passed on the outside when approaching the hole. There is a two-stroke penalty for missing a dog leg.
Putt throw: A putt throw is any throw within 10 feet of the hole. A player may not move past the point of the lie in making the putt throw. Falling or jumping putts are not allowed.
Unplayable lies: Any disk that comes to rest 6 feet or more above the ground is unplayable. The next throw must be played from a new lie directly underneath the unplayable lie (one-stroke penalty).
Out-of-bounds: A throw that lands out-of-bounds must be played from the point where the disk went out (one-stroke penalty).
Course courtesy: Do not throw until the players ahead are out of range.
Completion of hole: A disk that comes to rest in the hole (box or hoop) or strikes the designated hole (tree or pole) constitutes successful completion of that hole.

Appendix A

Sample Curriculum Guide–Lesson Plan

Long Rope Jumping Skills
Grades 5–6

Objectives:

To jump a rope turned by others

To know the difference in long-rope jumping between entering front and back doors

To understand how to enter and exit in Double Dutch rope jumping

NASPE National Standards:

Introductory Activity: 1, 4

Fitness Activity: 1, 4, 6

Lesson Focus: 2, 3, 4, 5

Game: 1,2,5

Equipment Required:

Music for exercises and rope jumping

6–12 long jump ropes (16 ft long)

Cageball and 12–15 throwing balls for game

Instructional Activities	Teaching Hints

Introductory Activity — Move and Freeze

1. Review the run, walk, hop, jump, leap, slide, gallop, and skip with proper stopping.
2. Practice moving and stopping correctly—emphasize basics of proper movement.

Add variety by asking students to respond to some of the following movement factors such as high, low, zigzag, large, small, square, triangles and circles.

Fitness Development Activity — Teacher Leader Exercises

Arm Circles	35 seconds
Bend and Twist	35 seconds
Treadmill	35 seconds
Abdominal Challenges	35 seconds
Single-Leg Crab Kick	35 seconds
Knee to Chest Curl	35 seconds
Run in Place	35 seconds
TrunkTwister	35 seconds

Follow each exercise with of aerobic activity.

Tape altering segments (35 seconds) of silence and music. The music signals aerobic activity. During the silent segments, the exercises are performed

Allow students to adjust the workload to their personal ability and fitness level. This means that some students may perform more repetitions than others.

Move and help students with the exercises.

Lesson Focus — Long Rope Jumping Skills

Single Long-Rope Activities

1. Review previously learned jumping skills. Teach the difference between entering front and back doors. *Front door* means entering from the side where the rope is turning forward and toward the jumper after it reaches its peak. *Back door* means entering from the side where the rope is turning backward and away from the jumper. To enter front door, the jumper follows the rope in and jumps when it completes the turn. To enter back door, the jumper waits until the rope reaches its peak and moves in as the rope moves downward. Learning to enter at an angle is usually easier, but any path that is comfortable is acceptable.
2. Have more than one student jump at a time. Students can enter in pairs or triplets.
3. Jump while holding a beanbag or playground ball between the knees.
4. While turning rope, rotate under the rope and jump. Continue jumping and rotate back to the turning position.
5. Play catch with a playground ball while jumping.
6. Do the Egg Beater: Two or more long ropes are turned simultaneously. The ropes are aligned perpendicular to each other; the jumper jumps the rope where they cross.
7. Try combinations of three or four ropes turning. The ropes are aligned parallel to each other and students jump and move through to the next rope.

Four children is an appropriate group size for practicing long-rope skills. Two members of the group turn the rope while the others practice jumping. A plan for rotating turners is important so that all children receive similar amounts of practice jumping.

Long ropes should be 16 feet in length.

Instructional cues to teach long-rope jumping skills are:
a. Turn the rope with the forearm.
b. Lock the wrist and keep the thumb up while turning.
c. Stand perpendicular to the rope.
d. Barely touch the floor with the turning rope.
e. Don't cross the midline of the body with the forearm while turning the rope.
f. Jump on the balls of the feet.

Double Dutch (two ropes) Activities

1. Teach entering and exiting. Basic jump on both feet. Land on the balls of the feet, keeping ankles and knees together with hands across the stomach.

   Entering: When entering, stand beside a turner and run into the ropes when the back rope (farther from the jumper) touches the floor. Turners should be taught to say "Go" each time the back rope touches the floor.

   Exiting: Exit the ropes by facing and jumping toward one turner and exiting immediately after jumping. The exit should be made as close to the turner's shoulder as possible.

2. Jogging Step. Run in place with a jogging step. Increase the challenge by circling while jogging.

3. Scissors Jump. Jump to a stride position with the left foot forward and the right foot back about 8 inches apart. Each jump requires reversing the position of the feet.

4. Straddle Jump. Jump to the straddle position and return to closed position. Try a Straddle Cross Jump by crossing the legs on return to the closed position. The straddle jumps should be performed facing away from the turners.

5. Turnaround. Circle left or right using the basic jump. Begin circling slowly at first and then increase speed. To increase the challenge, try the turnaround on one foot.

6. Hot Peppers. Use the Jogging Step and gradually increase the speed of the ropes.

7. Half Turn. Perform a half turn with each jump. Remember to lead the turn with the head and shoulders.

8. Ball Tossing. Toss and catch a playground ball while jumping.

9. Individual Rope Jumping. Enter Double Dutch with an individual rope and jump. Face the turner and decrease the length of the individual jump rope.

Arm positions and turning motions are similar to turning a single long rope. In short, keep the upper arm stationary, rotate at the elbow with locked wrist, and keep the thumb up. Avoid crossing the midline of the body, and establish an even cadence. Rotate the hands inward toward the midline of the body (right forearm counterclockwise and left forearm clockwise).

Double Dutch turning takes considerable practice. Take time to teach it as a skill that is necessary for successful jumping experiences.

Students should concentrate on the sound of the ropes hitting the floor so that they make an even and rhythmic beat.

Concentrate on jumping in the center of the ropes facing a turner. Use white shoe polish to mark a jumping target.

Game Activity

Cageball Target Throw

Supplies: A cageball (18- to 30-in.), 12 to 15 smaller balls of various sizes

Skill: Throwing

An area about 20 feet wide is marked across the center of the playing area, with a cageball in the center. The object of the game is to throw the smaller balls against the cageball, thus forcing it across the goal line in front of the other team. Players may come up to the line to throw, but they may not throw while inside the cageball area. A player may enter the area, however, to recover a ball. No one is to touch the cageball at any time, nor may a ball in the hands of a player push the cageball. If the cageball seems to roll too easily, it should be deflated slightly. The throwing balls can be of almost any size—soccer balls, volleyballs, playground balls, for example.

Sunday

Supplies: None

Skills: Running, dodging

Two parallel lines are delineated at each end of the playing area. Three or more players are "it" and stand in the center of the area between the two lines. The rest of the class is placed on one of the designated lines. The object is to cross to the other line without being tagged or making a false start. All line players stand with their front foot on the line. The line players must run across the line immediately when one of the taggers calls "Sunday." Anyone who does not run immediately is considered caught. The Tagger can call other days of the week to confuse the runners. No player can move if another day of the week is called. "Making a start" must be defined clearly. To begin, it can be defined as a player moving either foot. Later, when children get better at the game, any movement of the body constitutes a start.

Wolfe's Beanbag Exchange

Supplies: One beanbag per child

Skills: Running, dodging, tossing, catching

Five or six children are identified as Taggers. The remaining players start scattered throughout the area, each with a beanbag in hand. The Taggers chase the players with beanbags. When a tag is made, the tagged player must freeze, keeping his or her feet still and beanbag in hand. To unfreeze a player, a nonfrozen player can exchange his or her beanbag for a beanbag held by a frozen player. If two frozen players are within tossing distance, they can thaw each other by exchanging their beanbags through the air using a toss and catch. Both tosses have to be caught or the beanbags are retrieved and tried again from their previous location. After students have learned the game, Taggers can interfere with the tossing of beanbags between two frozen players by batting them to the floor. The toss is tried again and the players remain frozen until both players make successful catches.

Appendix B

Activity Cards Quick Reference Guide

Grade Level	Activity Card Section	Activity Name	Equipment	Additional Skills Emphasized	Academic Concept Tie-Ins
K-2	Classroom-Based Activities	Partner Mixer	None		Math
K-2	Classroom-Based Activities	High Medium Low	Music	Fitness	Language Arts Math Science
K-2	Classroom-Based Activities	Simon Says	None		Language Arts
K-2	Classroom-Based Activities	Teacher Leader	Music	Fitness Locomotor	
K-2	Classroom-Based Activities	Do This, Do That	None		Language Arts
K-2	Classroom-Based Activities	One Behind	Music	Fitness	Language Arts
K-2	Classroom-Based Activities	Bubbles	None		Science
K-2	Classroom-Based Activities	O'Malley Says	None		Language Arts
K-2	Classroom-Based Activities	Do As I Say	None		Language Arts Science
K-2	Classroom-Based Activities	Animal Signs	Simple instructional signs	Fitness Animal movements	Language Arts Science Social Studies
K-2	Classroom-Based Activities	Frozen Balance	None	Fitness	Language Arts Science
K-2	Classroom-Based Activities	Pigs Fly	None	Animal movements	Science
K-2	Classroom-Based Activities	Crows and Cranes	None		
K-2	Classroom-Based Activities	Movement Mystery	Pictures of people or animals	Animal movements	Science
K-2	Classroom-Based Activities	Rock/Paper/Scissors	None		Math
K-2	Classroom-Based Activities	Come with Me	None		Language Arts
K-2	Classroom-Based Activities	Shuffle Foot	None		Math
K-2	Classroom-Based Activities	High Low Jackpot	Whiteboard, markers		Math
K-2	Classroom-Based Activities	Circle Buzz	1-2 medium-sized balls, clock		
K-2	Classroom-Based Activities	Switch-A-Rooski	None		
K-2	Classroom-Based Activities	BPI	None	Locomotor	Science
K-2	Classroom-Based Activities	Group Orienteering	None		Social Studies
K-2	Classroom-Based Activities	Follow the Leader	None		
K-2	Classroom-Based Activities	Pop Up	None		Math
K-2	Classroom-Based Activities	Dandy Dice	2 dice (regular or large foam)		Math
K-2	Classroom-Based Activities	Classroom Parade	Music		
K-2	Classroom-Based Activities	Marching Mixer	None		Math
K-2	Classroom-Based Activities	Paper Ball	1 piece of paper per student		
K-2	Classroom-Based Activities	Volley Relay	1 balloon per team		
K-2	Classroom-Based Activities	Color Hunt	Color-coded cards		Science Math

Grade Level	Activity Card Section	Activity Name	Equipment	Additional Skills Emphasized	Academic Concept Tie-Ins
3-6	Classroom-Based Activities	In A Line	None		Language Arts Social Studies Math
3-6	Classroom-Based Activities	Balloon Foosball	Balloon or beach ball		Science
3-6	Classroom-Based Activities	Balloon Volleyball	Balloon, rope		Science
3-6	Classroom-Based Activities	Pass the Buck	1 silver dollar or other small object		Social Studies Math
3-6	Classroom-Based Activities	Mouse Snap	None		
3-6	Classroom-Based Activities	Hide the Beanbag	1 beanbag		Social Studies
3-6	Classroom-Based Activities	Human Compass	None		Science Social Studies
3-6	Classroom-Based Activities	Student Leader	Music	Fitness	
3-6	Classroom-Based Activities	Duo Balance	None		Science
3-6	Classroom-Based Activities	Found It	An eraser or other medium-sized object		
3-6	Classroom-Based Activities	I Am a . . .	None		Social Studies
3-6	Classroom-Based Activities	Stations	Eight signs with an exercise on them, music	Fitness	
3-6	Classroom-Based Activities	Slap, Clap, Snap	None		
3-6	Classroom-Based Activities	Tangle	None		Social Studies
3-6	Classroom-Based Activities	Is That True?	None	Locomotor	Language Arts Science Social Studies Math
3-6	Classroom-Based Activities	Who's in Charge?	None		Social Studies
3-6	Classroom-Based Activities	Flag Relay	4 erasers, 4 flags		
3-6	Classroom-Based Activities	Clapping Relay	1 small object (e.g., beanbag or eraser) per row		
3-6	Classroom-Based Activities	Occupation Charades	None		Social Studies
3-6	Classroom-Based Activities	Who's Missing?	None		
3-6	Classroom-Based Activities	Tongue Twister Tango	None		Language Arts
3-6	Classroom-Based Activities	Evens	None		Math
3-6	Classroom-Based Activities	Keep it Up . . . Or Sit Down	Balloon		Social Studies
3-6	Classroom-Based Activities	Card Find	Deck of cards		Social Studies
3-6	Classroom-Based Activities	Which Corner?	None		
3-6	Classroom-Based Activities	Row Volleyball	1-2 beach balls		
3-6	Classroom-Based Activities	Find a Seat	Music		
3-6	Classroom-Based Activities	Jump and Jog	An eraser and a pen, or other medium-sized objects		
3-6	Classroom-Based Activities	Move That Ball	1 balloon or beach ball for every 4-5 students		Social Studies
3-6	Classroom-Based Activities	Veggie Salad	None		Science
3-6	Classroom-Based Activities	Twenty Questions	None	Fitness	Language Arts Science Social Studies Math
3-6	Classroom-Based Activities	Finger/Hand Wrestling	None	Fitness	Science
3-6	Classroom-Based Activities	Partner Tipping	None		Science Social Studies

(continued)

Grade Level	Activity Card Section	Activity Name	Equipment	Additional Skills Emphasized	Academic Concept Tie-Ins
3-6	Classroom-Based Activities	Paper Golf	1 piece of paper per student		Social Studies Math
3-6	Classroom-Based Activities	Bicycle Race	None	Fitness	
3-6	Classroom-Based Activities	Keep it Up	1-2 balloons or beach balls		
3-6	Classroom-Based Activities	Beanbag Pitch	Several cardboard boxes and beanbags		
3-6	Classroom-Based Activities	Chair Quoits	1 chair per group of 4-5 students, 5 deck tennis or rope rings		Math
K-2	Large Area Activities	Boundaries	Cones or other makeshift markers		
K-2	Large Area Activities	Fall In	4 markers		
K-2	Large Area Activities	Everybody's It	None		
K-2	Large Area Activities	Help Me Tag	None		
K-2	Large Area Activities	Sneak Attack	None		
K-2	Large Area Activities	Crazy Crows	None		Math
K-2	Large Area Activities	Midnight	None		Math
K-2	Large Area Activities	Squirrels	None		Science
K-2	Large Area Activities	Dog House	1 marker per student		Science
K-2	Large Area Activities	Swap Sides	None		Math
K-2	Large Area Activities	Roller Ball	4-5 roughly 80" foam balls		Math
K-2	Large Area Activities	Pilots	None		Social Studies Science
K-2	Large Area Activities	Where Did You Go?	None		
K-2	Large Area Activities	Musical Ball Pass	1-2 roughly 80" foam balls, music		Math
K-2	Large Area Activities	Mouse Trap	None		Science
K-2	Large Area Activities	Quack Quack	Blindfold		Science
K-2	Large Area Activities	Red Light Green Light	None		Social Studies
K-2	Large Area Activities	Flippers and Floppers	1 flying disk or paper plate per student		Social Studies
K-2	Large Area Activities	Pretend	None		Science
K-2	Large Area Activities	Pirate's Loot	15-20 beanbags or other similar-sized safe objects		Social Studies
3-6	Large Area Activities	Inside/Outside	Cones or other markers		Social Studies
3-6	Large Area Activities	Circle Up	Four markers		Social Studies
3-6	Large Area Activities	Nouns and Verbs	None		Language Arts
3-6	Large Area Activities	Duck Duck Goose	None		
3-6	Large Area Activities	Amoeba Tag	None		Science
3-6	Large Area Activities	Tadpole Relay	One ball		Science
3-6	Large Area Activities	Division Tag	None		Math
3-6	Large Area Activities	ABC	None		Language Arts
3-6	Large Area Activities	Odds and Evens	None		Math
3-6	Large Area Activities	Twins	None		
3-6	Large Area Activities	One Step	1 ball per set of partners		

Grade Level	Activity Card Section	Activity Name	Equipment	Additional Skills Emphasized	Academic Concept Tie-Ins
3-6	Large Area Activities	Walkie Talkie	A list of interview questions per set of partners		Language Arts Math Science Social Studies
3-6	Large Area Activities	Find Your Home	6 poly spots or other similar markers		
3-6	Large Area Activities	Partner Rock/Paper/Scissors	4 markers		Math
3-6	Large Area Activities	Walking Cards	3-4 decks of playing cards		Math
3-6	Large Area Activities	Grab It	1 beanbag or similar object per set of partners		
3-6	Large Area Activities	Guard the Treasure	1 cone and beanbag per 4-5 students		Social Studies
3-6	Large Area Activities	Fire in the Woods	None		Science
3-6	Large Area Activities	Loose Caboose	None		
3-6	Large Area Activities	Flag Grab	6-8 handkerchiefs or bandanas		Social Studies
3-6	Large Area Activities	Marking	None		
3-6	Large Area Activities	Three Deep	None		Math
3-6	Large Area Activities	Circle Tag	None		
3-6	Large Area Activities	Game Inventors	Various available classroom equipment or objects		Social Studies
3-6	Large Area Activities	Map a Trail	1 piece of paper per group, pencils, portable writing surfaces		Language Arts Math Science Social Studies
3-6	Large Area Activities	Right Left	None		Math Social Studies
K-2	Basic Skills	Pathways	None	Spatial awareness	
K-2	Basic Skills	Levels and Speeds	None	Spatial awareness	
K-2	Basic Skills	Elephant Space	None	Spatial awareness Animal movements	
K-2	Basic Skills	Walking	None	Locomotor	
K-2	Basic Skills	Jogging/Running	None	Locomotor	
K-2	Basic Skills	Galloping	None	Locomotor	
K-2	Basic Skills	Sliding	None	Locomotor	
K-2	Basic Skills	Hopping	None	Locomotor	
K-2	Basic Skills	Jumping	None	Locomotor	
K-2	Basic Skills	Skipping	None	Locomotor	
K-2	Basic Skills	Leaping	None	Locomotor	
K-2	Basic Skills	Throwing	1 medium-sized bouncy ball per student	Manipulative	
K-2	Basic Skills	Catching	1 handkerchief, beach ball, or yarn ball per student	Manipulative	
K-2	Basic Skills	Kicking	One 8" foam ball or beach ball per student	Manipulative	

(continued)

Grade Level	Activity Card Section	Activity Name	Equipment	Additional Skills Emphasized	Academic Concept Tie-Ins
K-2	Basic Skills	Trapping	One 8" foam ball or beach ball per student	Manipulative	
K-2	Basic Skills	Rolling	1 paper ball per student	Manipulative	
K-2	Basic Skills	Rocking	None	Non-locomotor	
K-2	Basic Skills	Bending	None	Non-locomotor	
K-2	Basic Skills	Stretching	None	Non-locomotor	
K-2	Basic Skills	Twisting	None	Non-locomotor	
K-2	Basic Skills	Turning	None	Non-locomotor	
K-2	Basic Skills	Puppy Walk	None	Animal movements	
K-2	Basic Skills	Bear Crawl	None	Animal movements	
K-2	Basic Skills	Alligator Crawl	None	Animal movements	
K-2	Basic Skills	Kangaroo Jump	None	Animal movements	
K-2	Basic Skills	Inch Worm	None	Animal movements	
K-2	Basic Skills	Crab Walk	None	Animal movements	
K-2	Basic Skills	Frog Jump	None	Animal movements	
K-2	Basic Skills	Rabbit Jump	None	Animal movements	
K-2	Basic Skills	Elephant Walk	None	Animal movements	
K-2	Basic Skills	Abdominal Challenges	None	Fitness	
K-2	Basic Skills	Upper Body Challenges	None	Fitness	
K-2	Basic Skills	Lower Body Flexibility Activities	None	Fitness	
K-2	Basic Skills	Upper Body Flexibility Activities	None	Fitness	
K-2	Basic Skills	Individual Rope Jumping I	1 jump rope per student	Fitness	
K-2	Basic Skills	Individual Rope Jumping II	1 jump rope per student	Fitness	
3-6	Sports on the Playground	Fives	None	Locomotor	
3-6	Sports on the Playground	Knee Tag	None		
3-6	Sports on the Playground	Copy Me	None	Locomotor Non-locomotor	
3-6	Sports on the Playground	Athletic Position	None		
3-6	Sports on the Playground	Twenty-One	1 basketball and basket per group of 4-5 students		
3-6	Sports on the Playground	Five In A Row	One or two 8" foam balls		
3-6	Sports on the Playground	Knockout	2 balls and a basket per group of 6-8 students		
3-6	Sports on the Playground	Basketball Tag	2 basketballs (or similar-sized playground balls)		
3-6	Sports on the Playground	Offense Defense	1 ball per group of 6-8 students		
3-6	Sports on the Playground	Line Passing	1 ball per group of 8 students		
3-6	Sports on the Playground	Sideline Basketball	1 basketball court and a basketball (or similar ball)		

Grade Level	Activity Card Section	Activity Name	Equipment	Additional Skills Emphasized	Academic Concept Tie-Ins
3-6	Sports on the Playground	Fast Football	1 football or similar-sized ball		
3-6	Sports on the Playground	End Zone	A paperclip or similar-sized object		
3-6	Sports on the Playground	Hot Box	1 softball-sized ball and 2 poly spots per group of 4-5 students		
3-6	Sports on the Playground	Speed Baseball	1 softball and 2 poly spots per group of 4–5 students		
3-6	Sports on the Playground	Over The Line	1 softball-sized ball and 2 makeshift markers		
3-6	Sports on the Playground	Base Stealing	4 hoops and 1 ball per group of 16 students		
3-6	Sports on the Playground	Five Hundred	1 ball per group of 4-5 students		
3-6	Sports on the Playground	All Touch Baseball	1 softball-sized ball		
3-6	Sports on the Playground	Train Baseball	1 softball-sized ball, 2 makeshift markers		
3-6	Sports on the Playground	Disk Golf	1 flying disk per student		
3-6	Sports on the Playground	Paperball	1 piece of paper per student		
3-6	Sports on the Playground	Zigzag Race	1 medium-sized ball per group of 8 students		
3-6	Sports on the Playground	Shadows	None		
3-6	Sports on the Playground	Hand Soccer	One or two 8" foam balls		
3-6	Sports on the Playground	Kentucky Ball	One or two soccer-sized balls		
3-6	Sports on the Playground	Wall Ball	1 playground-type ball and a wall per group of 4-5 students		
3-6	Sports on the Playground	Keep It Up	1 beach ball per group of 4-6 students		
3-6	Sports on the Playground	Catch Volleyball	1 beach ball per group of 16 students		
3-6	Sports on the Playground	Casual Volleyball	1 beach ball per roughly 16 students, 3-4 poly spots		
3-6	Sports on the Playground	Four Goal Soccer	4 soccer balls (or similar), 8 mini-cones (or makeshift markers)		
3-6	Sports on the Playground	Circle Soccer	1-2 foam soccer balls per group of 10 students		
3-6	Sports on the Playground	Soccer Keep Away	1 foam soccer ball per group of 6 students		
3-6	Sports on the Playground	Diagonal Soccer	1-2 beach balls		
3-6	Sports on the Playground	Sideline Soccer	1 soccer ball, 4 small cones		

(continued)

Grade Level	Activity Card Section	Activity Name	Equipment	Additional Skills Emphasized	Academic Concept Tie-Ins
3-6	Sports on the Playground	Pentagon Keep Away	1 ball per group of about 8-9 students		
3-6	Sports on the Playground	Track Meet	10 beanbags, 5 flying disks, 6 cones		
K-6	Multicultural Activities	Varra (Albania)	3 × 3' square divided into nine 1' squares using chalk or tape		Social Studies
K-6	Multicultural Activities	Balon En El Aire (Argentina)	1 medium-sized ball, 2 cones or makeshift markers		Social Studies
K-6	Multicultural Activities	Peteca (Brazil)	1 badminton birdie per group of 3-4 students		Social Studies
K-6	Multicultural Activities	Chinese Wall (China)	None		Social Studies
K-6	Multicultural Activities	Countries (Czech Republic)	1 medium-sized ball per group of 7-8 students		Social Studies
K-6	Multicultural Activities	Cascade Juggling (Egypt) (Part 1 of 2)	3 handkerchiefs, scarves, or bandanas per student		Social Studies
K-6	Multicultural Activities	Cascade Juggling (Egypt) (Part 2 of 2)	3 handkerchiefs, scarves, or bandanas per student		Social Studies
K-6	Multicultural Activities	Spear the Disk (Ethiopia)	1-3 hoops, 1 beanbag per student		Social Studies
K-6	Multicultural Activities	Da Ga (Ghana)	None		Social Studies
K-6	Multicultural Activities	British Bulldog (Great Britain)	None		Social Studies
K-6	Multicultural Activities	Skyros (Greece)	One 6-8" ball per group of 20 students		Social Studies
K-6	Multicultural Activities	Pebble Tossing (Guinea)	1 flying disk per group of 5 students, 1 beanbag per student		Social Studies
K-6	Multicultural Activities	Kabaddi (India)	None		Social Studies
K-6	Multicultural Activities	Main Karet Gelang (Indonesia)	5-6 rubber bands per student		Social Studies
K-6	Multicultural Activities	Hora Dance (Isreal)	Music ("Hava Nagila")		Social Studies
K-6	Multicultural Activities	Modified Ishikera (Japan)	Chalk or marking tape, beanbags (optional)		Social Studies
K-6	Multicultural Activities	Mexican Kick Ball (Mexico)	1 medium-sized ball and 6 makeshift markers per group of 6 students		Social Studies
K-6	Multicultural Activities	Bolan Maldecida (Mexico)	One 8" foam ball per group of 2 students		Social Studies
K-6	Multicultural Activities	Days of the Week Hopscotch (Netherlands)	Chalk or marking tape, beanbags (optional)		Social Studies
K-6	Multicultural Activities	Catch the Tail (Nigeria)	One handkerchief, or paper towel per group of 2 students		Social Studies
K-6	Multicultural Activities	Modified Hoppe-Strikk (Norway)	Two 12" pieces of electric tape per group of 5 students		Social Studies
K-6	Multicultural Activities	Left or Right (Pakistan)	None		Social Studies
K-6	Multicultural Activities	Bola (Peru)	1 medium-sized ball, 3 makeshift bowling pins per group of 4 students		Social Studies

Grade Level	Activity Card Section	Activity Name	Equipment	Additional Skills Emphasized	Academic Concept Tie-Ins
K-6	Multicultural Activities	El Reloj (Peru)	1 long jump rope per group of 4-5 students		Social Studies
K-6	Multicultural Activities	Buwan, Buwan (Philippines)	Chalk or marking tape		Social Studies
K-6	Multicultural Activities	Tick Tack (Scotland)	None		Social Studies
K-6	Multicultural Activities	Modified Ka Fao Jai (Thailand)	1 cone and 1 small ball (or beanbag) per group of 4 students		Social Studies
K-6	Multicultural Activities	Maika Stone (Hawaii)	1 deck ring, 2 makeshift markers per group of 4 students		Social Studies
K-6	Nutrition and Sun Safety Activities	Food Group Hustle	Pictures of food, 6 boxes		
K-6	Nutrition and Sun Safety Activities	Meal Planners	Pictures of food, 6 hula hoops		
K-6	Nutrition and Sun Safety Activities	High/Low Nutrient	Index cards with pictures of high- and low-nutrient foods		
K-6	Nutrition and Sun Safety Activities	Anytime and Sometimes	None		
K-6	Nutrition and Sun Safety Activities	Nutrition Volleyball	1 balloon per group of 4 students		
K-6	Nutrition and Sun Safety Activities	Foods and Benefits	Index cards with pictures and descriptions of foods		
K-6	Nutrition and Sun Safety Activities	Red Light/Green Light Foods	Pictures of a variety of foods		
K-6	Nutrition and Sun Safety Activities	Food Labels	Various food labels		
K-6	Nutrition and Sun Safety Activities	Sun Safety Tag	Umbrella, hat, sunglasses, sun screen, long-sleeved shirt		
K-6	Nutrition and Sun Safety Activities	Sun Safety Scavenger Hunt	Index cards with pictures of sun protection items		
K-6	Nutrition and Sun Safety Activities	Sun Safety Ball	1 ball per group of 5-6 students		
K-6	Nutrition and Sun Safety Activities	Sun Shuffle	1 index card per student with beneficial or harmful effect of the sun listed on it		
K-6	Nutrition and Sun Safety Activities	Good Sun/Bad Sun	Index cards with images of good and bad sun effects		
K-6	Nutrition and Sun Safety Activities	Sunny Mimes	Music		
K-6	Nutrition and Sun Safety Activities	Sun Science Search	1 container per set of 3 students		
K-6	Nutrition and Sun Safety Activities	Dressed-for-Sun Relay	Various articles of clothing		
K-6	Nutrition and Sun Safety Activities	Sun Safety Blitz	Index cards with pictures of sun safety items		
K-6	Nutrition and Sun Safety Activities	Sun Protection	None		

(continued)

Grade Level	Activity Card Section	Activity Name	Equipment	Additional Skills Emphasized	Academic Concept Tie-Ins
K-6	Health and Fitness Activities	Emotional Freeze and Go	None	Mental and emotional health	
K-6	Health and Fitness Activities	Emotional Movement	None	Mental and emotional health	
K-6	Health and Fitness Activities	Mystery Emotion	Pictures of faces with different expressions	Mental and emotional health	
K-6	Health and Fitness Activities	Stress Tag	Several stress balls or bean-bags	Mental and emotional health	
K-6	Health and Fitness Activities	No! Tag (Refusal Tag)	None	Personal health	
K-6	Health and Fitness Activities	Relax to the Max	Music (optional)	Personal health	
K-6	Health and Fitness Activities	Splish Splash	Music ("Splish Splash, I Was Taking a Bath")	Personal health	
K-6	Health and Fitness Activities	Hygiene Move and Go	None	Personal health	
K-6	Health and Fitness Activities	Healthy Choices	Signs with pictures displaying healthy and unhealthy activity choices	Personal health	
K-6	Health and Fitness Activities	Germs Everywhere	Glow-in-the-dark gel, black light	Personal health	
K-6	Health and Fitness Activities	Clogged Artery	None	Personal health	
K-6	Health and Fitness Activities	Risk Factor Tag	Index cards describing various cardiovascular disease risk factors	Personal health	
K-6	Health and Fitness Activities	Cardiovascular Obstacle Course	Red and blue paper balls, pictures of the body, lungs, and heart	Personal health	
K-6	Health and Fitness Activities	Strong Heart	None	Personal health	
K-6	Health and Fitness Activities	Senses	Paper balls, blindfolds (optional)	Personal health	
K-6	Health and Fitness Activities	Who Helps Us?	None	Family and social health	
K-6	Health and Fitness Activities	That's My Family	Lists of interview questions	Family and social health	
K-6	Health and Fitness Activities	Help a Friend	Index cards listing various physical disabilities, 1 paper ball per pair of students	Family and social health	
K-6	Health and Fitness Activities	Stop, Drop and ROOOLL	None	Safety	
K-6	Health and Fitness Activities	Medicine or Candy? Shuffle	Index cards with pictures of over-the-counter medications and candy that resembles medicine	Safety	
K-6	Health and Fitness Activities	Get Low and GO!	None	Safety	
K-6	Health and Fitness Activities	Hand Signals	None	Safety	
K-6	Health and Fitness Activities	Stop, Look and Listen	None	Safety	
K-6	Health and Fitness Activities	Smokers' Aerobics	None	Personal health	

Appendix C

Definitions of Academic Concepts

Academic Concept	Definition of Academic Concept	Integration Area
1/4, 1/2, 3/4 full turns	Turning the body or body parts a specified amount	Math
Accelerate/decelerate	Gradually move faster/slower	Language Arts
Action verbs	Words such as skip, run, twist, leap, shake	Language Arts
Addition	Finding the sum of two or more numbers; combining a number of movements and actions	Math
Adjectives	A word that describes a noun or pronoun	Language Arts
Aerobic intensity	How hard the body is working to move such as brisk walking, jogging, and running	Science
Angles	Space formed by two lines such as right, 45 degrees; trajectory of release (throwing)	Math
Animal recognition	Identifying animals by name and movement, for example, bear walk, kangaroo jump, etc.	Science
Antonyms	Words that describe opposite movements	Language Arts
Area of a shape	Moving inside of and around the perimeter of a shape	Math
Balance	Maintaining a state of equilibrium while remaining stationary or moving	Science
Base of support	Generally, the placement of the feet to increase or decrease stability	Science
Beginning letter sounds	Used in games such as "ccrrsooowwwsss" in Crows and Cranes. Taught by identifying letter sounds or making shapes with their body or a jump rope	Language Arts
Body part identification (anatomical terms)	Touching, leading with or moving a body part when asked; identifying the body parts with the correct anatomical term	Science
Building sequences	Putting together a number of movements in proper sequence to perform a complex skill; performing a number of movements in activities like rhythms	Math
Categorization	Identifying how activities and movements are grouped by similar characteristics such as exercises and skills	Language Arts
Cause and effect	Explaining how one movement or force creates other movements; understanding the effect of applying force to a piece of equipment	Science
Center of an area	Knowing where the center of an area such as circle or rectangle is and being able to move there quickly	Math
Center of gravity	Estimating the point on one's body through which gravitational forces act; knowing how lowering the center of gravity increases stability	Science
Choral response	Responding to questions verbally in a group setting	Music
Choral rhyming	Using chants in activities such as jump rope chants, simple games, or rhythmic activities	Language Arts
Circumference	Learning to move around the perimeter of a circle in clockwise or counterclockwise directions	Math
Coin value and recognition	Knowing the values of different coins and being able to add or subtract their values in a game setting	Math
Components of fitness	Knowing all the components of health-related fitness (See Chapter 12 of *Dynamic Physical Education for Elementary School Children*)	Science
Contrasting terms	Similar to opposites; used to teach different movements such as move slowly-move quickly	Language Arts
Counting	Using counting sequences in activities such as jump rope chants	Math
Counting forward and backward	Used in many activities with an example being "Countdown"	Math

Academic Concept	Definition of Academic Concept	Integration Area
Counting steps (with pedometers)	Learning to use pedometers to count steps; also estimating the number of steps to complete an activity or cover a distance	Math
Cultural awareness	Understanding activities and customs of different cultures, for example, rhythmic activities	Social Studies
CW and CCW	Learning to move clockwise and counterclockwise in games and rhythmic activities	Science
Degrees: 45°, 90°, 180°, 360°	Knowing the meaning of different degrees to stipulate a change of direction; often used in Frisbee golf or orienteering	Math
Diagonal	Slanting between opposite corners of an area	Math
Diameter	A straight line running from one side through the center of to the other side of a circle	Math
Directional cues	Specific words to help students learn directions such as forward, backward, left, right, north, south	Geography
Directions (N/S/E/W)	Learning to identify the direction of movement in a variety of settings, i.e., gymnasium, field, or track	Geography
Dismounts	Getting off a piece of equipment such as balance beams or benches in a stipulated manner	Language Arts
Distance recognition	Estimating how far a projectile has been propelled or the distance between two points	Math
Division	Dividing into equal groups or splitting into smaller groups in games such as Chain Tag	Math
Dodging	Moving to avoid another person or projectile	Language Arts
Estimation	Estimate personal performance such as how fast can I run, how many times can I complete a task in a specified time	Math
Estimation of time	Estimating how long it will take to complete a task	Science
Flower recognition	Being able to identify different types of flowers in games such as Flowers and Wind	Science
Following a checklist	Used often in station teaching where points to follow are listed on the station sign	Language Arts
Following a course or map	Learning to follow a map or sequence of directions to complete an activity such as Challenge Course or Orienteering	Geography
Fractions	Often used in directions such as a ½ turn	Math
Geometric shape recognition	Being able to recognize a number of shapes such as figure 8, rhombus, octagon, hexagon, circle, oval, spiral, star, semi-circle	Math
Gravity (center of)	Understanding how the center of gravity impacts stability; often used in teaching stopping under control or moving on beams or benches	Science
Greater than and less than	Often used to teach students to form groups of "greater than _____ or less than_____"	Math
Grouping	Used in many settings such as grouping students, like movements, skills, or equipment	Math
Health concepts	Teaching students a wide variety of health concepts such as relaxing, substance abuse, nutrition, and weight management	Science
Heart rate calculation	Learning to calculate heart rate using a 10-second count of pulse rate	Math
Height vs. distance	Understanding the relationship of leaping or jumping as high as possible versus jumping or leaping as far as possible	Math
High/medium/low	Being able to demonstrate movements that are performed at different levels	Language Arts
Horizontal and vertical	Moving in different planes and being able to identify such planes by name	Science
In front of/behind/beside	Moving in relationship to an object or another person	Language Arts
Intersecting lines	A set of 2 or more lines that have common points (intersections)	Math
Isometric exercises	Muscular contractions that are performed without movement	Science
Letter recognition	Being able to make or identify a variety of letters; using the body or pieces of equipment to form different letter shapes	Language Arts
Level identification	Identifying the level of different movements that are being performed	Math

Academic Concept	Definition of Academic Concept	Integration Area
Listening skills	Understanding the proper time to listen; being able to translate a verbal concept into a physical movement	Language Arts
Matching colors	Showing success in playing games that require color matching such as Color Tag	Language Arts
Matching shapes	Being able to match or identify a shape	Math
Measurements (yards/feet/inches/miles)	Used in many lessons such as Track and Field	Math
Measuring time with a stopwatch	Used in cross-country running and track and field	Math
Mental math problems	Used in many games and relays to identify players, for example, "all players with the number 2 + 5 are it"	Math
Midpoint	Finding the middle of the body, body part, area, or shape	Math
Missing numbers	Often used in introductory activities such as Magic Number Challenges; students must identify the missing number in a sequence	Math
Momentum	The motion of a projectile or person and its resistance to slowing down	Science
Movement factors	Responding to movement factors such as high, low, zigzag, large, small, squares, triangles, circles	Math
Multiplication	Adding a number to itself a certain number of times; used in a variety of games and scoring	Math
Muscle identification	Know the basic names of large muscle groups in the body	Science
Number recognition	Being able to make or identify a variety of numbers; using the body or pieces of equipment to form different numbers	Math
Number sequence	Performing numbers in different sequences such as, "perform 3 hops, 2 jumps, and 5 skips"	Math
Odds and evens	Used in games where odd- or even-numbered players are identified to move	Math
Offense and defense	Being able to explain when a person or team is on offense or defense	Language Arts
Opposites	See antonyms above	Language Arts
Opposition	Used in throwing skills; when throwing with the right hand, step forward with the left foot and vice versa	Science
Ordinal numbers	Numbers that identify order such as first and second; for example, used in squad leader warm-ups	Math
Over/under/around concepts	Moving in relationship to another student or students; also used to learn to move in relationship to a piece of equipment or apparatus	Language Arts
Parallel lines	Two lines that never meet; used in many games where students are lined up across from another line of students	Math
Patterning	Learning to perform a pattern of movements in a rhythmic manner, i.e., step-together-step-stomp!	Music
Percentages	A proportion of a larger set or group	Math
Perimeter	A boundary that encloses an area; most often used to define an area students can move within	Math
Perpendicular lines	Lines that meet at right angles; used to describe movement such as, "hang with your legs perpendicular to the climbing rope"	Math
Pivot	Keeping one foot fixed and moving around that foot such as a basketball pivot	Language Arts
Prediction	Guessing how many times or how far a physical movement can be performed such as, "How many times can you make the hoop spin?"	Science
Prime numbers	A number not divisible without a remainder	Math
Problem solving	Being able to solve a physical movement, such as, "How many different ways can you move across the floor?"	Math
Quadrants	Usually used to divide the teaching area into 4 equal parts	Math
Radius	A straight line extending from the center of a circle to the edge of the circle	Math

Academic Concept	Definition of Academic Concept	Integration Area
Ratio	A proportional relationship between two different quantities; often used when dividing the class or equipment into parts	Math
Reading instructional signs	Most often used in station teaching to explain tasks to be performed	Language Arts
Recognizing order of sequence	Often used in rhythms, skills, or fitness routines; knowing in what order the activities should be performed	Math
Revolutions	Turning the body, body part, or piece of equipment a certain number of times	Science
Right and left	Being able to identify right and left in relationship to oneself or others	Geography
Rotation	A turning motion related to projectiles or body movement; for example, ball rotation or rotating yourself around a piece of equipment; also used in learning to rotate positions such as in volleyball	Math
Scoring	Knowing how to keep score in a variety of games	Math
Segments	Identifying different parts of a shape such as a circle or rectangle	Math
Sequencing patterns	Performing a series of similar movements; often used in activities such as tossing beanbags or juggling	Language Arts
Short/long side of a rectangle	Knowing which side of the rectangle is the long or short side	Math
Skip counting	Counting while skipping numbers, i.e., 2, 4, 6, 8 or 3, 6, 9, 12	Math
Slow and fast time	Most often used in rope jumping	Music
Small word recognition	Writing words with pieces of equipment such as jump ropes and being able to read the words of others	Language Arts
Sorting skills	Being able to separate equipment and skills by similarities such as red beanbags, yellow-handled ropes	Language Arts
Spatial awareness	Being aware of movements that can be made in space	Science
Speed variations	Knowing all the words that identify speed such as fast, slow, accelerate, and decelerate	Science
Steady beat	Learning to move in a rhythm that is even; often emphasized in European running	Music
Steps per mile (with pedometer)	Being able to calculate how many steps equals a distance of 1 mile (stride length must be measured first)	Math
Subtraction	Deducting one number from another; often used to identify players by number such as all players with the number "6 minus 2"	Math
Syllables	A unit of spoken language; used in games such as Flowers and Wind	Language Arts
Synonyms	A word that means the same as another word	Language Arts
Target heart rate	The pulse rate that needs to be reached to enter the "Training Zone"	Science
Time recognition	Knowing the time of day; for example, used in the game of Midnight	Science
Traffic light recognition	Knowing the colors of traffic lights and what they mean; can be used in game of Red Light–Green Light or to signal students to stop or move cautiously	Social Studies
Trajectory	The path a projectile makes through space; used to teach throwing for distance	Math
Tripod	A base of support using three body parts	Science
Unilateral movements	Movements performed on one side of the body only	Social Studies
Upper/lower	Understanding the relationship of upper and lower with relation to the body	Language Arts
Velocity/accuracy	Understanding how velocity often impacts the accuracy of a skill	Language Arts
Weather terminology	Understanding words that describe weather such as thunderstorm, hurricane, or tornado; used in games such as Aviator	Science
Wide/narrow	A relatively large distance (wide) between two points or relatively small distance (narrow) between two points; most often used in base of support	Language Arts

Appendix D

National Association for Sport & Physical Activity Standards for Physical Education

Physical activity is critical to the development and maintenance of good health. The goal of physical education is to develop physically educated individuals who have the knowledge, skills, and confidence to enjoy a lifetime of healthful physical activity.

A physically educated person:

Standard 1: Demonstrates competency in motor skills and movement patterns needed to perform a variety of physical activities.

Standard 2: Demonstrates understanding of movement concepts, principles, strategies, and tactics as they apply to the learning and performance of physical activities.

Standard 3: Participates regularly in physical activity.

Standard 4: Achieves and maintains a health-enhancing level of physical fitness.

Standard 5: Exhibits responsible personal and social behavior that respects self and others in physical activity settings.

Standard 6: Values physical activity for health, enjoyment, challenge, self-expression, and/or social interaction.

Glossary

Chapter 1

physical education That part of the educational program that contributes, primarily through movement experiences, to the total growth and development of all children.

content standards Statements identifying the content of a model educational program; that is, what knowledge students should possess and how they should demonstrate that knowledge when they exit a developmental level.

physical fitness A set of attributes that people have or achieve relating to their ability to perform physical activity.

Chapter 2

need A drive to do or accomplish something.

perceived competence A feeling of capability related to a skill or group of skills; becomes more specific as students mature.

characteristics Age- and maturity-specific physical, cognitive, and social attributes that influence children's learning.

skeletal age Measurement of level of ossification as compared to a set of standardized X-rays.

aerobic activity Sustained movement performed at a pace for which the body can supply adequate oxygen to meet the demands of the activity.

moderate to vigorous physical activity (MVPA) Bodily movement that results in increased breathing or heart rate; moderate physical activity such as brisk walking or low-impact aerobics burns 3.5 to 7 calories a minute, whereas vigorous activity such as jogging or high-impact aerobics burns more than 7 calories a minute.

locomotor movements Movements performed where the body travels through space.

Chapter 3

mental practice Method of practicing a motor skill by thinking quietly about its performance and related sounds, colors, and other sensations; used in combination with regular practice, not in place of it.

whole method Process of teaching an entire skill or activity as one unbroken movement.

part method Process of breaking down a skill or activity into a series of steps or parts, teaching these parts, and then combining them into the whole skill.

complexity A quality of motor tasks that conveys the relative number of serial skills or components that exist in a given task. The higher the complexity, the greater the number of components.

organization A quality of motor tasks that describes how closely the components are related to each other. The higher the organization, the more closely the components are related.

blocked practice Method of practicing a skill in which all the trials of one skill component are completed before moving on to the next component.

random practice Method of practicing a skill in which the order of multiple task presentations is mixed, with no task practiced exactly the same way twice in succession.

class of movements Group of movements, involving the same body parts and rhythms, that are characteristic of a particular motor task, such as throwing, catching, etc.

force A measure of the mechanical energy (i.e., push or pull) applied to one object or body by another.

torque A twisting or turning effect that force produces when it acts eccentrically (away from the center) with respect to a body's axis of rotation.

lever A bar or other rigid structure that can rotate about a fixed point to overcome a resistance (weight of object) when force is applied.

opposition In sports, skills such as throwing or kicking, taking a step in the direction of the throw with the leg opposing the throwing arm, or moving the arms in the opposite direction of a kick.

Chapter 4

entry level A rough estimation of the skill level for the majority of students in a class.

anticipatory set An activity designed to focus students' attention on an upcoming learning task.

instructional cues Keywords that quickly and efficiently communicate proper technique and performance of skills and movement tasks.

integrating cues Activity cues that combine multiple parts of a skill so that learners focus on the skill as a whole.

closure The closing element of a physical activity session; provides opportunity for stressing and reinforcing skills learned, revisiting performance techniques, and checking cognitive concepts.

negative feedback Information about a movement performance that labels the performance in a negative way (e.g., "That was a lousy throw."), which should be avoided.

corrective feedback Information about a movement performance given with the intention of correcting or solving a problem (such as, "Remember to keep your arms up as you dismount.").

positive feedback Information about a movement performance that praises an aspect performed correctly.

intrinsic feedback Information about a movement performance that is internal, inherent to the performance of the skill, and travels through the senses, such as vision, hearing, touch, and smell.

extrinsic feedback Information about a movement performance that is external and comes from an outside source, such as a teacher, a videotape, or a stopwatch.

knowledge of results Extrinsic feedback given after a skill has been performed, focusing on the outcome or product.

knowledge of performance Extrinsic feedback given after a skill has been performed and focusing on the quality of the skill performance; that is, on the process of how it was performed.

nonverbal behavior A method of delivering a message through the sender's body language and without speaking.

multicultural education Form of education in which students from a variety of backgrounds and experiences come together to share educational equality.

Chapter 5

management Organizing and controlling the affairs of a group, such as a class.

discipline Methods for encouraging adherence to rules and changing behavior that is unacceptable.

positive discipline A discipline style that focuses on reinforcing acceptable behavior rather than punishing unacceptable behavior.

prompts Visual or verbal cues that remind students to exhibit acceptable behavior.

social reinforcers Words of praise, facial expressions and gestures, and physical contact that acknowledge acceptable behavior.

activity reinforcers Enjoyable activities that are used to reward acceptable behavior.

extrinsic reinforcers Tokens such as points, stickers, certificates, or trophies used to reward acceptable behavior.

time-out A behavior management technique that moves students who are misbehaving out of the class setting and places them into a predesignated area so they have time to reconsider their behavior.

criticism Communication that identifies what is wrong or bad about someone or something.

punishment A penalty administered for severe or continued misbehavior, often involving some kind of action required of the student rather than simply removal of positive consequences or a time-out.

peer mediation A process for resolving disputes and conflicts between students with an agreed-upon set of ground rules and a neutral peer acting as moderator in the process.

Chapter 6

least restrictive environment (LRE) The educational setting providing a student with a disability the greatest level of interaction with students who are not disabled, but still enabling the child to receive an appropriate education.

mainstreaming Term commonly used to identify the process of placing students with disabilities in classrooms with nondisabled students.

screening Process by which all children in a school setting are evaluated to determine whether or not they should be referred for a special education assessment.

assessment Thorough evaluation performed by a team of educational experts, using clinical and classroom observation and a variety of tests, to determine a child's unique challenges and make recommendations for special education services.

due process In Constitutional law, the principle that the government must respect the individual's legal rights, e.g., when charging a person with a crime, etc. The Education for all Handicapped Children Act of 1975 mandates that schools adhere to due process in special education assessments, e.g., by notifying parents of their right to appeal decisions, etc.

individualized education program (IEP) Learning program mandated for each child with a disability by the Education for All Handicapped Children Act; based on a multidisciplinary assessment, it must include a statement of special educational and related services to be provided.

Chapter 7

integration Instruction designed to combine two or more concepts from different areas to help students see the interrelatedness of knowledge.

Chapter 8

physical activity Bodily movement that is produced by the contraction of skeletal muscle and that substantially increases energy expenditure.

physical fitness A set of attributes that people have or achieve relating to their ability to perform physical activity.

metabolic equivalent (MET) Ratio assigned to various types of activities that identifies how much it increases an adult's metabolic rate relative to resting metabolic rate.

aerobic activity Physical activity performed at a pace for which the body can supply adequate oxygen to meet the demands of the activity.

exercise A type of physical activity performed especially to maintain fitness.

flexibility Ability to use the body's joints through a full range of motion as a result of having long muscles and elastic connective tissues.

single-standard goal A goal derived from a single standard applied to an entire population, such as all elementary school children. An underlying assumption is that it is possible for one goal to be appropriate for a wide variety of individuals.

baseline and goal-setting technique Approach to goal setting in which individuals identify their baseline measurement (e.g., their average daily number of steps) and use it as a reference point for establishing a personal goal.

Chapter 9

physical fitness A set of attributes that people have or achieve relating to their ability to perform physical activity.

health-related physical fitness State characterized by an ability to engage in moderate to vigorous physical activity with vitality, and without undue fatigue. It includes health-related components, such as cardiovascular fitness and muscular strength.

skill-related physical fitness State characterized by athletic ability and a high level of physical performance. Its components are physical qualities such as agility and speed.

cardiovascular endurance The ability of the heart, blood vessels, and respiratory system to deliver oxygen efficiently throughout the body over an extended period of time.

body composition An individual's proportion of body fat to lean body mass.

agility The ability of the body to change position rapidly and accurately while moving in space.

balance The ability of the body to maintain a state of equilibrium while remaining stationary or moving.

coordination The ability of the body to perform more than one motor task at the same time smoothly and successfully.

power   The ability of the body to transfer energy explosively into force.

speed   The ability of the body to perform movement in a short period of time.

circuit training   Fitness routine in which stretching and strength-training exercises are alternated with aerobic exercises.

Chapter 10

nutrient density   The ratio of nutrients to energy (number of calories) in a food. Nutrient-dense foods provide a high level of essential nutrients for a low number of calories.

point-of-decision prompts   Bulletin boards, signs, and other visual or auditory prompts placed at locations where people make decisions for the purpose of influencing those decisions.

body mass index (BMI)   A number representing the ratio of a person's weight to his or her height.

Chapter 11

ultraviolet (UV) radiation   Type of electromagnetic radiation emitted from the sun with a wavelength just shorter than the shortest band of visible light (perceived by humans as violet).

UV index   Scale developed by the Environmental Protection Agency and the National Weather Service for predicting UV radiation levels and helping people determine appropriate sun-protective behaviors.

Index

Note: Page numbers followed by "f" indicate figures; page numbers followed by "t" indicate tables.

A

Abdominal exercises, 268–270
Abdominal strength challenges, 262
Ability, 108, 112–114
Academic performance
   after-school programs and, 338
   nutrition and, 10–11
   physical activity and, 6
Academics, integrating physical activity and. *See* Integration
Achilles tendon stretch, 266–267
ACSM (American College of Sports Medicine), 41, 233
Active and healthy school (AHS) environment, 8–17
   before- and after-school programs, 12–13
   classroom teacher involvement, 13
   community involvement, 15, 17
   need for, 4–6
   nutrition and healthful eating activities, 10–11
   parental (or legal guardian) involvement, 13–15
   physical activity breaks, 9–10
   quality physical education, 8–9
   sun safety instruction, 11–12
Active and Healthy Schools Program (Pangrazi), 220
"Active or Inactive" (pedometer activity), 232
Active involvement, 93
Active Lifestyle Model School, 232
Activity
   breaks. *See* Physical activity breaks
   bulletin board, 225
   calendars, 14f
   contracts, 7
   days, 15
   reinforcers, 143
   zone, 220f. *See also* Playground
Activity Cards for Nutrition and Sun Safety, 327
ADHD (attention deficit hyperactivity disorder), 190
Administrators, sharing school rules with, 132
Adventure, need for, 33
Aerobic activity, 216f, 217–218, 249–250
   capacity for, 42–45
     high-intensity activity, 42–43
     of overweight children, 43
   defined, 42
   distance running, 43–44
   fitness routines, 274–276
   fitness testing, 44–45
Aerobic (cardiovascular) fitness, 214
Aerobic warm-up, 258
Aerobics movement, 261
Afternoon activity breaks, 9–10
Afterschool Alliance, 341
After-school programs, 336–341
   activities, 7
   for AHS environment, 12–13
   benefits and challenges, 336–337
   developing, 340–341
   financing, 336, 338
   quality assurance, 337–339
   selecting, 339–340
Age
   chronological, 40–41, 253
   skeletal, 41
   See also Developmental level
Aggression, 152–153. *See also* Conflict resolution
Agility, 95, 249f, 251
   exercises, 270–271
   students lacking, 180
AHS environment. *See* Active and healthy school (AHS) environment
Alphabetizing, 199
Alternate leg raises, 275
Altitude, UV radiation and, 313
American Academy of Pediatrics, 46, 261
American Academy of Pediatrics Executive Committee, 43–44
American Cancer Society, 318
American College of Sports Medicine (ACSM), 41, 233
American Community Gardening Association, 346
American Dietetic Association, 303
American Meteorological Society, 314
Angle of release, 73
Animal movements, 203, 264–265
Anticipatory set, 95
Antonyms, integrated instruction in, 197–198
Appalachian Educational Laboratory, 190
Appeasement, conflict resolution through, 153
Approval, need for, 32
Arizona, sun safety mandate in, 11
Arm circles, 268, 275
Arm-shoulder girdle exercises, 267–268
Arm-shoulder girdle strength challenges, 260–262
Arousal, managing level of, 66
Assessment, special education, 167–169
Assistive technology devices, 165
At-risk youth, 108
Attention deficit hyperactivity disorder (ADHD), 190
Auditory impairment, 175f
Autism, 165

B

Balance, 178, 202–203, 249f, 251
Balance tag, 278
Ballistic stretching, 257
Basal cell carcinoma, 317
Baseline and goal-setting technique, 227, 228f
Base of support, 71
Basketball, 95
Batting. *See* Striking
Bear hug, 272f
Before-school programs, 12–13, 61
Behavior
   acceptable, 137–145
     levels of responsibility, 138–140
     prompts in, 141–142
     reinforcement of, 140, 142–144
     shaping of, 144–145
     strategies for, 140–141
   backlash against, 129
   off-task, 151
   physical activity and, 189
   plan for changing, 145f
   responsible, 23–24
   sedentary, 4, 5, 216, 219

Behavioral problems, 127–128. *See also* Discipline; Management; Misbehavior
Bend and twist (exercise), 266
Bending, 263, 272, 275
Birthday celebration policy, 292–293
Blocked practice, 69
Block the Sun, Not the Fun (Sun Safety Alliance), 325
Blood pressure, physical activity and, 6, 233
BMI (body mass index), 5, 250, 299–303, 301f–302f
BMI-for-age, 300, 301f–302f
Body
    awareness of, 202–203
    influence of physical activity on, 201
    levers in, 73
Body circles, 272
Body composition, 249f, 250, 253
Body fat, 253, 299, 300
    motor performance and, 41
Body management skills, 20
Body mass index (BMI). *See* BMI (body mass index)
Body part identification, integration of, 200–201
Body positioning, effective speaking and, 114
Body proportions, growth and, 37–40t
Bone health, vitamin D and, 315, 316
Bones, long, 72–73
Boys and girls clubs, 14
Brain injury, traumatic, 165
Brainstorming, 140, 153, 156
Breakfast, school, 290–291
Breast milk, 315
Bulletin board, activity, 223
Bullying, 152–153, 154
Bumping into students, 154
Business, AHS environment and, 17

C

Calculator for Teens and Children, 300
Calendar
    activity, 14f
    weekly walking, 238
Calisthenics, 261
Calories burned during walking, 234t
Camp Shriver, 180
Camps, summer, 346
Cancer
    skin, 11, 312, 315, 317–318, 320
    vitamin D and, 316
Cardiovascular (aerobic) fitness, 214

Cardiovascular endurance, 249f–250, 274
    challenges, 263–265
    fitness games for, 277
Caring behavior, 139–140
Casa, Douglas (University of Connecticut), 46
Cataracts, 318, 319f
Catching, 74, 77–78, 77f
CDC. *See* Centers for Disease Control and Prevention (CDC)
Celebrations policy, healthful, 292–293
Center of gravity, 71, 179
Center for Science in the Public Interest, 292
Centers for Disease Control and Prevention (CDC), 239, 290, 300, 315, 325, 335, 341–342
Challenge, threat vs., 256
Changing the Scene: Improving the School Nutrition Environment (USDA), 288
Characteristics of children, 34–47, 35t–37t
    aerobic activity, capacity for, 42–45
    defined, 34
    growth patterns, 34–40, 38f, 39f
    heat tolerance, 45–46
    maturation, 41–42
    strength and endurance, 40–41
Charity events, 15
Charles Stewart Mott Foundation, 338
Chasing, 195, 199
Child Care and Development Fund, 338
"Child find" process, 167
Child Nutrition and WIC (Women, Infants and Children) Reauthorization Act (2004), 7–8
Children, characteristics of. *See* Characteristics of children
Choices, self-selected, 141
Choking up, 73
Chores, with pedometer, 344
Chronological age
    fitness test performance and, 253
    muscular strength and, 40–41
    skeletal age and, 41
Circles, creating, 136
Circuit training, 259, 276, 277f
Clapping, 68
Class greeting, 203
Class of movement, 69–70
Class organization, small groups to expedite, 136–137
Class performance, monitoring, 100–101. *See also* Academic performance

Classroom
    activity breaks in, 7
    management skills, 206
    mini-breaks in, 10, 18
    physical activity in, 16–19
Closure, 101–102
Clothes
    for hot-weather activities, 47
    protective, 322
    for walking, 236
Cognition, physical activity and, 189. *See also* Integration
Cognitive development, 35f–36f
Collaboration, group, 191
Color tag, 278
Columbine High School shootings (1999), 154
Commanding, 129
Communication
    aggressive, 126
    assertive, 125–127
    with empathy and understanding, 114–117
        effective listening, 116–117
        effective speaking, 114–116
    of expectations, 128, 130
    of high standards, 128
    passive, 125–126, 127
    of social reinforcers, 143–144
Community involvement
    activities, 9
    in AHS environment, 15–17
    in sun-safety efforts, 321
Competence
    perceived, 33, 50, 54, 83
    physical, 33, 43
Competition, 22, 224
    arousal and, 66
    at intermediate skill level, 50
    mixing recreation and, 224–225
    need for, 32
    self-competition, 113
    students with disabilities in, 176
Complexity of skill, 67
Composure, maintaining, 127
Cones, delineating practice area with, 58–59
Confidentiality of student records, 168
Conflict resolution, 152–156
    peer mediation, 154–156
    in public schools, 157
    teacher-directed, 153–154
Conflict Resolution Education Network, 157

Connecticut Department of
    Education, 293
Conscious Discipline (B.A. Bailey), 127
*Constructive Classroom Rewards: Promoting
    Good Habits while Protecting
    Children's Health* (Center for
    Science in the Public Interest), 292
Content standards for physical education,
    19–25
    motor skills and movement
        patterns, 20–21
    movement concepts, principles,
        and tactics, 21
    physical fitness level, 23
    regular participation in physical
        activity, 21–23
    responsible personal and social
        behavior, 23–24
    valuing physical activity, 24–25
Contracts, activity, 7
Conversation, integrated instruction
    in, 204
Cooperation, 22, 199
    conflict resolution through, 153
    integrated instruction in, 204–205
    need for, 32
Cooperative learning, 109
Coordination, 178, 249f, 251
Corporal punishment, 151
Corrective feedback, 103, 115, 145–147
Counting, skip, 193
County health agencies, 17
Courtesy, integrated instruction in,
    204, 206
Crab alternate-leg extension, 268
Crab kick, 268f, 275
Crab position, 260
Crab Walk, 265
Criticism, 150–151
Cross, 271
Cross-country walking, 237–238
Cross-disciplinary instruction. *See*
    Integration
Cues, 97–98
    for acceptable behavior, 141
    integrating, 10, 99
Culture, 106, 108
    concepts of, 206
    See also Diversity
Curl up, 269f
    with twist, 270f
Curriculum guides, 64
Curtatone, Joseph (Mayor of Somerville,
    MA), 16

D

Dance Dance Revolution (DDR), 190
Dancing, folk, 68
David Thompson Health Resource, 303
Decision making, student participation
    in, 112–113
Deep knee bends (full squats), 258
Degrees, integration of, 193
Dehydration, 46, 317
Demonstration of skill, 98–99
Developmental level, 63, 64, 74
Deviant behavior, options for dealing
    with, 127–128. *See also* Discipline;
    Management
Diabetes
    type 1, 316
    type 2, 233
Dieting, 298. *See also* Nutrition
Differential reinforcement, 144
Direction
    concept of, 73–74
    integrated instruction in, 203, 206
Directional runs, 275
Directions, following, 200
Disabilities, students with. *See* Special
    needs children
Discipline, 145–156
    conflict resolution, 152–156
        peer mediation, 154–156
        in public schools, 157
        teacher-directed, 153–154
    corrective feedback, 103, 115,
        145–147
    criticism, 150–151
    defined, 124
    guidelines for applying consequences,
        149–150
    positive, 138
    punishment, 65–66, 151–152, 259
    removal of positive consequences, 148
    reprimands, 147–148
    time-out, 148–149
    See also Management
Discrimination
    against people with intellectual
        disabilities, 180
    gender, 110–112
Discussion sessions, 109
Disruptive behavior, 102. *See also*
    Discipline; Management
Distance running, 43–44
Diversity
    genetic, 23
    impact on assessment, 168–169

issues involving, 23
    teaching for, 107–110
Documented program, 83–84
Dogs, aggressive, 236
Domination, conflict resolution
    through, 153
Doubling up, 177
Duck walk, 258
Due process procedures, 167–168

E

Eating behaviors, data gathering about,
    295–296
Economos, Christina (Tufts University), 17
Edible Schoolyard, The (school garden
    movement), 291
Education for All Handicapped Children
    Act. *See* Public Law 94–142
    (Education for All Handicapped
    Children Act)
Educators for Social Responsibility, 157
Effective instruction. *See* Instruction,
    effective
Effective listening, 116–117
Effective speaking, 114–116
Ego strength, building, 179
EHA. *See* Public Law 94–142 (Education
    for All Handicapped
    Children Act)
Elbow swing tag, 278
Elephant Walk, 264
Elimination games, 176
Emergency care plan, 65
Emotional maturity, 41
Empathy, in communication, 114–117
Endurance, 40–41, 249f
    cardiovascular, 249–250, 249f, 274
        challenges, 263–265
        fitness games for, 277
    muscular, 250
    students lacking, 177–178
Energy balance equation, 299f
English as a second language (ESL)
    program, 168–169
Entry level, determining, 94–95
Environment
    for after-school programs, 337
    fitness test score and, 252
    learning, 92–93, 103
    least restrictive (LRE), 165–166,
        167, 171
    UV exposure and, 312–313
    See also Active and healthy school
        (AHS) environment

Environmental Protection Agency (EPA), 12, 313, 314, 323
Equalization tactic, 176
Equipment, 59–60, 64
    caring for, 131
    daily check of, 62
    effective use of, 137
    playground, 222–223
    purchasing, 222–223
Errands, with pedometer, 344
ESL (English as a second language) program, 168–169
Estimation, 193, 232
Ethnic minorities, special education assessment and, 169
Ethnicity, 107, 108–110. *See also* Diversity
Even and odd numbers, 195
"Exercise Is Medicine" initiative, 233
Exercise(s)
    abdominal, 257–258, 268–270
    agility, 270–271
    bending, 272
    defined, 218
    flexibility, 216f, 217, 218–219, 266–267
    harmful, 257–258
    strength/muscular development, 216f, 217, 219
    See also Physical fitness; *specific exercises*
Expectations, 92, 128, 130
Extracurricular activities, funding for, 12. *See also* After-school programs; Before-school programs
Extrinsic feedback, 103
Extrinsic reinforcers, 143

F

Facial expressions, as social reinforcers, 142t
Fading, 142
Fairs, physical activity and health, 14–15
Falling, safe, 179
Family involvement, 341–345
    education in health initiatives for children, 341–342
    increasing activity level, 342–343
    pedometer use, 343–345
    See also Parental involvement
FAPE (free appropriate public education), 164–165
Fast stepping, 270
Fat, body, 253, 299, 300
    motor performance and, 41
Fatigue, practice session length and, 68

Fear response, in catching, 77
Feedback, 92, 106–107
    conciseness of, 104–105
    corrective, 103, 115, 145–147
    even distribution of, 106
    extrinsic, 103
    immediate, 105
    to increase responsible behavior, 140
    intrinsic, 103
    negative, 102–103
    nonverbal, 106–107
    positive, 103, 105, 256
    in skill development, 50
    specificity of, 104–105
    value content of, 105f
    written, 100
Finger Wrestling (activity), 202
Fish, vitamin D in, 316
Fitness. *See* Physical fitness
Fitnessgram/Activitygram, 45
Fitness testing, concerns about, 44–45
FIT principle, 22
Flannery, Ann (PE4life), 225
Fleeing, 195, 199
Flexibility, 249f, 250
    exercises for, 216f, 217, 218–219, 266–267
Flexion, forward, 257
Fluid intake, adequate, 45–46, 47
Folk dancing, 68
Follow-through, 72
Food, as rewards, 292
Food choices, healthful, 298. *See also* Nutrition
Force, 72, 202–203
Force arm, 73, 74f
Foreign languages, integration of, 198
Formations, moving students into, 135–137
Forward flexion, 257
Fractions, integration of, 193
Free appropriate public education (FAPE), 164–165
Freeze position, 134f
Freeze signal, 200
Friedman, Lucy (After-School Corporation), 338
Friendship spot, 135
Friendships, in after-school programs, 336f
Full mainstreaming, 166
Full squats (deep knee bends), 258
Funding, for extracurricular activities, 12
Fundraising events, healthful foods in, 293–294
Fun Fridays, 293–294

G

Game(s), 21
    elimination, 176
    to encourage activity, 223
    fitness, 277–278
    introduction of, 221
    low organized, 195, 199
    from other countries, 203
    participating in, 82–84
        early specialization and, 82
        labeling and, 83
        pressure to excel and, 83–84
    strategy in, 52
    teaching, 224
    video, 190
Gardens, community, 346
Gates, Joseph (school principal), 338
Gender, 107, 108
    issues involving, 24
    stereotyping by, 110–112
Gender differences
    in height and weight, 36–37
    in motor performance, 42
    in strength, 41
Genetic diversity, 22
Genetics
    fitness test performance and, 252–253
    growth patterns and, 34
    skill-related fitness and, 250–251
Geographical location, UV radiation and, 313
Geography, integration of, 204–205
Geometry terms, integration of, 193
Gestures, as social reinforcers, 142t
Giving, 72, 78
Goals
    learned helplessness and, 254
    modifying for children with special needs, 177, 178
    setting, 141, 227, 228f, 231
Golf, walking (activity), 238
"Good Nutrition" stickers, 298
Gopher Sport Active and Healthy School Playground Game Card File, 223
Grade, physical fitness activities by, 259–278
    kindergarten through second grade, 259–265
        abdominal strength challenges, 262
        arm-shoulder girdle strength challenges, 260–262
        leg development and cardiovascular endurance challenges, 263–265
        trunk development challenges, 263
    third through sixth grade, 265–278

abdominal exercises, 268–270
arm-shoulder girdle exercises,
    267–268
examples of fitness routines, 273–277
fitness games, 277–278
flexibility exercises, 266–267
leg and agility exercises, 270–271
trunk-twisting and bending
    exercises, 272f
Gravity, center of, 71, 179
Greeting, class, 203
Group activities, playground, 224
Group collaboration, 191
Group response, 100
Group tag, 278
Groups, forming, 135–137
Growth charts, 300, 301f–302f
Growth patterns, 34–40, 38f–39f
"Guess and Share" (activity), 343–344
Guided practice, 100
Guidelines
    need for clear, 130
    for small-group instruction, 136–137
Guidelines for After-School Physical Activity
    and Intramural Sport Programs
    (NASPE), 340–341
Gymnastic activities, 21

H
Hand signals, 99–100
Handicapped children. See Special needs
    children
HDLs (high-density lipoproteins), 233
Health
    after-school programs and, 339
    decline in American, 3
    physical activity and, 6
Health committee, school, 287, 303–305
Health fairs, 14–15
Health-related physical fitness, 248,
    249–250, 249f
Healthy Celebrations: Promoting a Healthy
    School Environment (Connecticut
    Department of Education), 293
Healthy Habits for Healthy Kids: A Nutrition
    and Activity Guide for Parents, 303
Hearings on special education
    assessment, 168
Heart disease, walking and, 233
Heat stress, 315, 317
Heat stroke, 317
Heat tolerance, 45–46
Height
    gender differences in, 36–37

growth chart for boys, 38f
growth chart for girls, 39f
growth velocity curve for, 37f
strength and, 41
Helplessness, learned, 83, 254
Help Your Child Grow Up Healthy and
    Strong (USDE), 303
Heredity. See Genetics
Hidden messages, listening to, 116
High-density lipoproteins (HDLs), 233
History, integration of, 205
Hitting, modifying for children with spe-
    cial needs, 178
Holick, Michael (Boston University
    Medical Center), 316
Holiday celebration policy, 292–293
Homework, health-promoting, 332–335
    benefits of, 334–335
    examples of, 332–334, 333f
    guidelines for assigning, 335
Hopping, 264
Household Goal Setting (activity), 344
"How Many Steps Does It Take?"
    (activity), 232
Hu Jintao (China's
    President), 180
Human Kinetics, 45
Hurdler's stretch, 257
Hydration, adequate, 45–46, 47
Hypothesis testing, pedometers for, 231

I
IAAF (International Athletics
    Association Federation) Medical
    Committee, 44
'I care' language, 131
IDEA (Individuals with Disabilities
    Education Act), 167. See also
    Public Law 94-142 (Education for
    All Handicapped Children Act)
IEP. See Individualized education
    program (IEP)
Inactivity, 216f, 217, 219
Inclusion, progressive, 165–166
Individualized education program (IEP),
    169–172
    content of, 169–170
    example of, 170f–171f
    formulating and implementing,
    171–172
Individuals with Disabilities Education
    Act (IDEA), 167. See also Public
    Law 94-142 (Education for All
    Handicapped Children Act)

Infrared rays, 312
Injured Coyote (animal
    movement), 265
Injury
    managing, 67
    preventing, 62
    See also Safety
Institute for Youth, Education, and
    Families, 338
Instruction, effective, 93–102
    anticipatory sets in, 95
    checking for understanding in,
    99–100
    closure in, 101–102
    efficient delivery, 133–134
    guided practice in, 100
    instructional cues in, 97–98
    mainstreaming and, 174–175
    meaningful skill instruction in, 96
    monitoring class performance in,
    100–101
    skill level determination in, 94–95
    skills demonstration in, 98–99
    stated educational outcome goals in,
    93–94, 95
Instructional area, positioning in, 101
Instructional cues, 97–98
    for acceptable behavior, 141–142
    integrating, 98, 99
Instructional signs, 196f
Integration, 186–209
    cues, 98, 99
    defined, 188
    of language arts, 196–200
    of math, 192–196
    reasons for, 188–189
    of science, 204–203
    of social studies, 203–204
    types of, 189–191
Interdisciplinary instruction. See
    Integration
Intermediate School 236, 338
Intermediate skill level, 49
International Athletics Association
    Federation (IAAF) Medical
    Committee, 44
Interrogating, 129
Interval walk, 237
Intrinsic feedback, 103
Introductory skill level, 49
Involvement, 93, 139
Irresponsible behavior, 138
"I Spy" (activity), 237
I statements, 126–127

J

Jogging trail, 222
Joints, types of levers in, 201, 202f
Juggling, 49, 68, 95
Jump rope exercises, 265
Jumping, 264
Jumping jacks, 270–271, 275–276

K

Kaiser Family Foundation, 5
Kicking, 78–80, 79f
   concepts of motion and direction
      in, 73
   modifying for children with special
      needs, 178, 179f
   points to stress about, 79
   stages of, 79
   teaching tips for, 80
Kids' menu challenge, 346
Kids Sun Fun website, 325
Kidswalk, 239
Knee touch curl up, 269f
Knowledge
   need for, 33
   of performance, 104
   of results, 103–104
"Know Your Community"
   (activity), 237

L

Labeling, 83, 129, 137–138, 147
Language
   person-first, 174
   sign, 175f
Language arts, integration of physical
      activities and, 196–200
   sample activities, 199–200
   tips for, 196–198
   topics for, 198–199
Laws, need for, 206
Leadership, 128
Leadership skills, 136
"Learn about Your Friend" (activity), 237
Learned helplessness, 83, 254
Learning, cooperative, 109
Learning environment, 92–93, 103
Learning zone in playground, 221
Least restrictive environment (LRE),
      165–166, 167, 171
Legal guardians. *See* Parental
      involvement
Leg development challenges, 263–265
Leg exercises, 270–271
Leg extension, crab alternate-, 268

Legislation for special needs children,
      164–167
   federal, 164–165
   least restrictive environment (LRE),
      165–166, 167, 171
   mainstreaming, 166–167, 172–179
Leg raises, 258, 275
Leisure-time physical activity, pedometers
      and, 231
Lesson planning, 64
Leverage, 72–73, 74f
Levers, types of, 201, 202f
Liability for forced participation, 64
Lifestyle activities, 216f, 217, 224
Lifestyle Activity Prescription for
      Children, 213, 214t
Lifestyle, fitness test score and, 252
Light physical activities, 212
Lines, single-file, 136
Lion Walk, 264
Lipid, blood, 6
Lipoproteins, high-density (HDLs), 233
Listening, 200
   effective, 116–117
   refusal to listen, 129
Locomotion, animal, 203
Locomotor movements, 48, 264
Locomotor skills, 20, 195, 199, 200, 206
Long bones, 72–73
Lower leg stretch, 266, 267f
Low-intensity zone in playground, 222
LRE (least restrictive environment),
      165–166, 167, 171
Ludwig, David (Children's Hospital
      Boston), 304
Lunch, school, 290–291
Lunch break, supervision during, 61
Lunch and Learn (David Thompson), 303
Lunchtime activity breaks, 7, 10
Lunge variations, 275

M

Macular degeneration, 318, 319f
Mainstreaming, 166–167, 172–179
   determining support necessary, 172
   integration into activity session,
      179–181
   learning about the child, 173
   modifying activities, 175–179
   for lack of balance and agility, 178
   for lack of coordination, 178
   for lack of strength and endurance,
      177–178
   reflection check, 176

   modifying instruction, 174–175
   normalization and, 166
   teaching tolerance to all students,
      173–174
   types of, 166
Malignant melanoma, 317–318, 318f
Management, 124–161
   class management routines, 130–131
   consequences of noncompliance, 132
   defined, 124
   efficient skills in, 133–137
      equipment use, 137
      groups and formations, 135–137
      instruction delivery, 133–134
      starting and stopping class, 134–135
   proper teaching behaviors, 124–130
      assertive communication style,
         125–127
      behaviors that may cause backlash, 129
      leadership, 128
      personal behavior plan, 127–128
      standards, 128
      understand misbehavior, 128f
   rules for school year, 131–132
   teaching and increasing acceptable
      student behavior, 137–145
      levels of responsibility, 138–140
      prompts in, 141–142
      reinforcement in, 140, 142–144
      shaping in, 144–145f
      strategies for, 140–141
   See also Discipline
Manipulative skills, 20, 200
Marching, 68, 270
Mastery skill level, 50
Matching students, 177
Math, integration of physical activities
      and, 192–196
   sample activities, 194–195
   tips for, 193–194
   topics for, 194
Maturation, 41–42, 253. *See also*
      Developmental level
Mayo Clinic, 261
Meals, serving size of, 4. *See also* Nutrition
Measurement, integration of, 193–194
Mechanical advantage, 73
Mechanical principles, 71–74
Mediation, peer, 154–156
Melanin, 313, 315
Melanocytes, 313
Melanoma, malignant, 317–318, 318f
Mental practice, 67
"Messy Backyard" (game), 193

Metabolic equivalent (MET), 212
Mile run test, 44–45
Milk, 315, 316
Mini-breaks, classroom, 10, 18
Misbehavior
    causes of, 128f
    charting, 148
    corrective feedback for, 146
    defining consequences for, 132
    guidelines for applying consequences
        of, 149–150
    understanding, 128
    See also Discipline; Management
Mitchell, Teri (Safe Kids Upstate), 46
"Mixed-up Walks" (activity), 237
Modeling acceptable behavior, 140, 141
Moderate physical activities, 212,
    213–214
Moderate to vigorous physical activity
    (MVPA), 44
Modified Jumping Jack, 271
Monitoring class performance, 100–101
Moralizing, 129
Morning activity breaks, 9–10
Motion, 72–73
Motivation, arousal and, 66
Motor performance, 40, 41
Motor skills, 20–22f. See also Practice;
    Skill(s)
Movement
    class of, 69–70
    concepts, principles, and tactics, 21
    content standards for patterns of,
        20–21
    need for, 32
"Moving across the State or United
    States" (activity), 232
Moving Family Wall of Fame, 14
Multicultural education, 107–108
Multidisciplinary instruction. See
    Integration
Muscle fitness, 216f, 217, 219
Muscle pain, flexibility and, 250
Muscles, force generated by, 72
Muscular strength and endurance, 249f,
    250
Music
    in circuit training routine, 276
    fitness routine with, 274t
    to time activity segments, 259, 265
MVPA (moderate to vigorous physical
    activity), 44
MyPyramid for Kids, 296
    poster, 296, 297f

N
Name-calling, 154
National AfterSchool Association,
    337–339
National Alliance for Youth Sports, 82
National Association for Sport and
    Physical Education (NASPE), 19,
        212, 214–216, 340–341
    guidelines, 214–216
National Heart, Lung, and Blood
    Institute, 296
National Institute on Out-of-School
    Time, 339
National League of Cities, 338
National Program for Playground Safety
    (NPPS), 62
National Safety Council, 325
National Weather Service, 313, 314, 321
National Women's Law Center, 111
Needs of children
    aerobic activity and, 43
    defined, 32
    fitness testing and, 44–45
    understanding, 31–34
    See also Personal needs of students
Negative feedback, 102–107
Negotiations in special education
    assessment, 168
Networking, 287, 346
Newsletters
    nutrition, 303
    sun-safety, 321
Non-locomotor skills, 20
Nonverbal cues for acceptable behavior,
    141–142
Nonverbal feedback, 106–107
Normalization, 166
Novelty, need for, 33
NPPS (National Program for Playground
    Safety), 62
Number concepts, 195
Nurse, school, 64
Nutrient density, 290
Nutrition, 284–309
    in after-school programs, 339
    in AHS environment, 10–11
    classroom strategies for improving,
        294–305
        age-appropriate weight
            management, 298
        basics of good nutrition, 296–297f
        eating behavior data, 295–296
        healthful food choices, 298
        parental involvement, 298–305

newsletters, 303
schoolwide strategies for improving,
    286–294
    action plan, 288–289
    health committee, 287
    initial research, 288
    policies, 289–294
    reflect, evaluate, and progress, 294
Nutrition quest, 334
Nutritional service programs, 7

O
Obesity, 5–6, 304. See also Overweight
Obesity Education Initiative, 296
Objectives, clarity of, 92
Odd and even numbers, 195
Off-campus walks, 238
Off-task behavior, 151
Olympics, 191
O'Neill, Jim (Sports and Arts in School
    Foundation), 338
Open-ended tasks, 113
Open house, school, 343
Opposition, rule of, 76
Ordering, 129
Organization of skill, 67–68
Ossification, 41
Osteoporosis, 6
Outcome, statement of expected,
    93–94, 95
Overhand throwing, 75–77
Over-learned skill, 66
Overweight, 3–4
    adult obesity and, 5–6
    capacity for aerobic activity and, 43
    increasing incidence of, 4–6
    motor performance and, 41
    walking and, 233–235
Ozone layer, 312
Ozone, UV radiation and, 313

P
PABA-based sunscreen, 319
PACER test, 45
PALA (Presidential Active Lifestyle
    Award), 215, 227, 232
Para-aminobenzoic acid (PABA), 319
Paraphrasing, 116
Parental involvement
    activity calendars, 14f
    activity days, 15
    AHS environment and, 14–17
    in charity events, 15
    continual misbehavior and, 150

in health-promoting homework, 335
improving students' nutrition with, 298–305
  body mass index (BMI), 299–303, 301f–302f
  nutrition newsletters, 303
  school health committee membership, 303–305
in physical activity and health fairs, 14–15
sharing school rules, 132
in special education assessment, 168
in sun-safety efforts, 321
in wellness policy plan, 7
Parents, working, 4
Parks, 346
Partial mainstreaming, 166
Participation, 23
Part method of practice, 67–68
Partner rowing (flexibility exercise), 266f
Partners, finding, 135
Parts of speech, integration of, 197, 199
PE4life program, 225
Pedometer Power (R.P. Pangrazi, A. Beighle, & C.L. Sidman), 231
Pedometers, 13, 226–232
  acquiring, 230
  family activity using, 343–345
  goal setting, 227, 228f, 231
  handling procedures, 230–231
  introducing to students, 230
  placement and accuracy, 228–229
  suggested activities, 231–232
Peer acceptance, 32, 43, 179
Peer-checking methods, 100
Peer coaching and review, 60
Peer mediation, 154–156
Peer teaching, integration of, 198f
Pelvis tilter, 269
Perceived competence, 33
Performance
  knowledge of, 104
  monitoring class, 100–101
  teachers' expectations and, 108
  See also Academic performance
Personal behavior plan, 127–128
Personal behavior, responsible, 21–22
Personal needs of students, 107–114
  gender stereotyping, 110–112
  multicultural education, 107–108
  participation in decision making, 112–113
  personalized instruction, 113–114
Personalized instruction, 113–114

Person-first language, 174
Physical activity
  academic performance and, 6
  in adulthood, 6
  in after-school programs, 336, 339, 340f
  benefits of, 213–214
  health and, 6
  health fairs and, 14–15
  levels of, 212
  physical fitness and, 248, 253–254
  recommendations for, 214–219
    National Association for Sport and Physical Education (NASPE) guidelines, 214–216
    Physical Activity Pyramid, 211, 215, 216–219, 216f, 220
  regular participation in, 21–23
  school environment and, 5
  sports vs., 225
  technical definition of, 216
  types of, 213t
  valuing, 24–25
Physical activity breaks, 7, 9–10
  classroom mini-breaks, 10, 18
  lunchtime, 10
  morning and afternoon, 9–10
Physical Activity for Children: A Statement of Guidelines (Corbin & Pangrazi), 22–23
Physical Activity Pyramid, 23, 211, 215, 216–219, 216f, 220
  active aerobics, 216f, 217–218
  active sports and recreational activities, 216f, 217, 218
  aerobic activities, 216f, 217–218
  flexibility exercises, 216f, 217, 218–219
  rest and inactivity, 216f, 217, 219
  strength/muscular development exercises, 216f, 217, 219
Physical competency, 33, 43
Physical contact as social reinforcers, 142t
Physical development, 35f–36f
Physical education, 4, 8–9
Physical Education Soundtracks, Vol. 1 and Vol. 2 (Human Kinetics), 274
Physical education specialist, 7–8
Physical fitness, 246–283
  activities for children in kindergarten through second grade, 259–265
  abdominal strength challenges, 262
  arm-shoulder girdle strength challenges, 260–262
  leg development and cardiovascular endurance challenges, 263–265

  trunk development challenges, 263
  activities for children in third through sixth grade, 265–278
  abdominal exercises, 268–270
  arm-shoulder girdle exercises, 267–268
  examples of fitness routines, 273–277
  fitness games, 277–278
  flexibility exercises, 266–267
  leg and agility exercises, 270–271
  trunk-twisting and bending exercises, 272f
  challenges, 200
  common questions about, 252–255
  content standards for, 19–25
  defined, 23, 248
  factors influencing, 252–254
  fitness awards effectiveness, 254
  implementing routines, 258–259
  physical activity and, 248, 253–254
  promoting positive attitude toward, 255–258
  training program effectiveness, 252
  types of, 248–251
    health-related physical fitness, 248, 249–250, 249f
    skill-related physical fitness, 248, 249f, 250–251
  See also Exercise(s)
Physical maturity, 41
Physical problems from distance running, 43–44
Physical skills. *See* Sport skills
PL 94-142, 164–165
  due process mandate, 167–168
PL 101-476, 165
Placekicking, 78
Play, safe, 224. *See also* Game(s)
Playground, 220–226
  activities for, 221
  activity bulletin board for, 223
  activity-friendly, 220–223
  equipment in, 222–223
  injuries in, 62
  "news network" to promote activity program, 221
  public, 346
  supervision, 223–225
  walking/jogging trail, 222
  zones in, 220–222
Point of decision prompts, 7, 291–292, 292f
"Poker Walk" (activity), 238
Portion Distortion I and II (PowerPoint presentation), 296

Positive consequences, removal of, 148
Positive discipline, 138
Positive feedback, 103, 105, 256
Positive performance points, accentuating, 115
Positive reinforcement, 145–146, 174, 298
Posture, flexibility and, 250
Poverty, special education assessment and, 169
Power, 249f, 251
Power jumper, 271
Practice, 105
    blocked, 69
    designing effective sessions, 66–70
        arousal level, 66
        length and distribution of sessions, 68–69
        mental practice, 67
        process focus, 67
        random practice techniques, 69
        variable practice experiences, 69–70
        whole vs. part method of practice, 67–68
    guided, 100
    random, 69
Practices, harmful, 257–258
Praise, words of, 142t, 143–144
Preaching, 129
Presidential Active Lifestyle Award (PALA) threshold, 215, 227, 232
President's Council on Physical Fitness and Sports, 215, 227, 232
Pressure to excel in sports and games, 83–84
Principal, continual misbehavior and, 150
Product vs. process of skill performance, 104
Program, documented, 83–84
Progress, monitoring, 92
Progressive inclusion, 165–166
Prompts
    to acceptable behavior, 141–142
    fading of, 142
Protective clothing, 322
Psychological problems, distance running and, 44
Public Law 94-142 (Education for All Handicapped Children Act), 164–165
    due process mandate, 167–168
Public Law 101-476, 165
Public reinforcement, 146
Public School/Middle School 20, 338
Pulling, 202–203

Pull ups, reclining, 267f
Punishment, 151–152
    corporal, 151
    fitness activities as, 259
    physical activity for, 65–66
Punting, 78
Puppy Walk, 264
Pushing, 202–203
Push ups, 197f, 260f–262, 267
    rhythmic, 275
    triceps, 268
Push up tag, 278

Q

Quarter-turn, 271

R

Rabbit Jump, 265
Race/ethnicity, 107, 108–110
Ramspott, Ron (Parkway School District, Chesterfield, MO), 190
Random practice, 69
Range of motion (ROM), 250
Reaches, 275
Reading, integration of, 196
Ready position, 71f
Rebound angle, 74
Recess, 189, 220
    cancellation due to heat, 46
    group activities during, 224
    supervision during, 61–63
    See also Physical activity breaks; Playground
Recipes, healthy, 333–334
Reclining pull ups, 267f
Recreation centers, 17
Recreation, mixing competition and, 224–225
Recreational activities, 216f, 217, 218
Reflection, time for, 140
Reinforcement
    of acceptable behavior, 140, 142–144
    differential, 144
    positive, 145–146, 174, 298
    public, 146
    in skill development, 50
    time-out and, 149
Relational skills, classroom physical activity and, 18
Release, angle of, 73
Reprimands, 147–148
Resistance arm, 73, 74f

Resolving Conflict Creatively (developed by Educators for Social Responsibility), 157
Respect, rules requiring, 131
Response plan, 127
Responses, respecting student's, 115
Responsibility
    levels of, 138–140
    opportunities for, 141
Rest, 216f, 217, 219
Resting metabolism, 212
Results, knowledge of, 103–104
Retention, closure and, 101
Reverse curl, 269
Reverse mainstreaming, 166
Reward, food as, 292
Rhythmic expression, need for, 33
Rhythmic movement, 20
Rhythmic push ups, 275
Rhythmic runs, 275
Rickets, 315f
Risks to Students in Schools (U.S. Office of Technology Assessment), 62
Role model, teachers as, 255
ROM (range of motion), 250
Rope jumping, 264
Routines
    class management, 130–131
    fitness, 273–277
        aerobic, 274–276
        circuit training, 276, 277f
        with music, 274t
        squad leader, 273–274
        student leader, 273t
Rumors, 154
Running
    with arms in various positions, 275
    directional, 275
    distance, 43–44
    in patterns, 264
    in place, 270
    as punishment, 66
    rhythmic, 275
    with variations, 275
Running shoes, 236
Rural setting, 206

S

SAD (seasonal affective disorder), 315
Safe Kids Upstate (advocacy group for children's safety), 46
"Safe Walk to School" (activity), 232

Safety, 61–66
    adequate and appropriate instruction, 63–65
    after-school programs and, 336, 338, 339
    guidelines for school walking program, 236
    in partitioning space, 59
    playground, 62
    proper supervision, 61–63
    rules of, 61
    See also Sun safety
Scavenger hunt, 238
School environment
    active and healthy (AHS), 8–17
        before- and after-school programs for, 12–13
        classroom teacher involvement for, 13
        community involvement for, 15–17
        need for, 4–6
        nutrition and healthful eating activities for, 10–11
        parental (or legal guardian) involvement for, 14–17
        physical activity breaks for, 9–10
        quality physical education for, 8–9
        sun safety instruction for, 11–12
    physical activity and, 5
    wellness mandate and, 7
School garden movement, 291
School health committee, 287, 303–305
"School Steps Contest" (activity), 232
Schwartz, Marlene (Rudd Center for Food Policy and Obesity, Yale University), 304
Science, integration of physical activities and, 200–203
    sample activities, 201–203
    tips for, 200–201
    topics for, 201
Screening, special education, 167, 169
Seal Walk, 264
Season, UV radiation and, 313
Seasonal affective disorder (SAD), 315
Sedentary behavior, 4, 5, 216, 219
Self-competition, 113
Self-control, 138
Self-directed workloads, 256
Self-fulfilling prophecy by early labeling, 83
Self-responsibility, 139, 141f
Sequencing skills, 195
Sexual orientation, 108
Shade, for sun safety, 12, 322
Shade Planning for America's Schools (CDC), 325

Shade structures, 321, 325
Shaming, 129
Shape Up Somerville, 16
Shaping of acceptable behavior, 144–145f
Sharing, 140
Shoulder circles, 275
Shriver, Eunice Kennedy (Camp Shriver), 176
Shriver, Tim (Special Olympics), 176
Side bends, 275
Side flex, 272f
Side jumping jacks, 275
Side leg raises, 275
Sign language, 175f
Signs
    activity zone, 220f
    instructional, 196f
"Simon Says" (activity), 200
Single-file lines, 136
Single-standard goal, 227
Sitting stretch, 266f
Skeletal age, 41
Skeletal maturity, 82, 253
Skill check, 100
Skill-related physical fitness, 248, 249f, 250–251
Skill(s)
    acquisition phase of learning, 69
    class management, 133–137
        equipment use, 137
        groups and formations, 135–137
        instruction delivery, 133–134
        starting and stopping class, 134–135
    complexity of, 67
    demonstration of, 98–99
    determining level of, 94–95
    development of, 47–51
    duration of, 68
    leadership, 136
    motor, 20–22f. *See also* Practice
    organization of, 67–68
    over-learned, 66
    product vs. process of learning, 104
    relational, 18
    social, 9
    substitution of, 178
    See also Sport skills
Skin cancer, 11, 312, 315, 317–318, 318f, 320
Skin color
    UV radiation and, 313, 317
    vitamin D synthesis and, 315
Skin, premature aging of, 318

Skip counting, integration of, 193
SmallStep, 345
SmallStep Kids, 345
SMT (synchronized metronome tapping), 190
Soccer kicking, 78, 79f
Social behavior, responsible, 23–24
Social class, 107, 108
Social development, 35t–37t
Social reinforcers, 142–143, 142t
Social skills, 9
Social studies, integration of physical activities and, 203–206
    sample activities, 205–206
    tips for, 203–204
    topics for, 204–205
Social zone in playground, 222
Somerville, MA, 16
Space for physical activity, 58–65
    equipment considerations, 59–60, 64
    predetermining need for, 58–59
    safe environment, promoting, 61–66
        adequate and appropriate instruction, 63–65
        proper supervision, 61–63
        safety rules, 61
Spacing skills, 195, 203
SPARK-related (Sports, Play, and Active Recreation for Kids) program study, 6
Speaking, effective, 114–116
Special developmental classes, 166
Special education, definition of, 165
Special needs children, 162–185
    individualized education program (IEP), 169–172
        content of, 169–170
        example of, 170f–171f
        formulating and implementing, 171–172
    legislative requirements, 164–167
        federal, 164–165
        least restrictive environment (LRE), 165–166, 167, 171
        mainstreaming, 166–167, 172–179
        screening and assessment, 167–169
Special Olympics, 180
Specialization, in sports and games, 82
Speech parts, integration of, 199, 297
Speech patterns, optimizing, 115
Speed, 249f, 251
Spelling, integration of, 197
SPF (sun protection factor), 318

Sport skills, 21
   fostering development of, 70–82
      catching, 74, 77f–78
      integrating simple mechanical
         principles, 71–74
      kicking, 78–80, 79f
      striking, 72, 80–82
      throwing, 68, 69, 72, 74–77
Sports, 216f, 217, 218
   participating in, 82–84
      early specialization and, 82
      labeling and, 83
      pressure to excel and, 83–84
   physical activity vs., 225
Sports, Play, and Active Recreation for Kids
   (SPARK-related) program study, 6
Squad leader fitness routine, 273–274
Squamous cell carcinoma, 317
Stability, 71–72
Staffing, for after-school programs, 337
Standards. *See* Content standards for
   physical education
Starting/stopping class, 134–135
Static stretching, 257
Steam engine (flexibility exercise), 266
Step-a-Thon, 345
"Step It Up Day," 345
"Steps" competition, 13
Steps, number in school vs. outside of
   school, 332
Stereotyping, gender, 110–112
Stickers, "Good Nutrition," 298
Stoop tag, 277
Stop, look, and listen rule, 131
Strength, 41
   muscular, 250
   students lacking, 177–178
Strength/muscular development
   exercises, 216f, 217, 219
"Strength Training by Children and
   Adolescents" (American Academy
   of Pediatrics), 263
"Strength Training: OK for Kids
   When Done Correctly" (Mayo
   Clinic), 261
Stress, heat, 45–46
Stretch(ing), 218–219, 250
   Achilles tendon, 266–267
   ballistic, 257
   guidelines for, 257
   lower leg, 266, 267f
   sitting, 266f
   static, 257
   trunk strength from, 263

Stride, 271
Striking, 72, 80–82
   concepts of motion and direction in,
      73–74
   follow-through in, 72
   modifying for children with special
      needs, 178
   points to stress about, 81
   stages of, 80
   teaching tips for, 81–82
Student leader fitness routine, 273t
Student records, confidentiality of, 168
Success, need for, 32
Summer camps, 346
Sunblock, 318
Sunburn, 315, 317, 318
Sunglasses, 322
Sun protection factor (SPF), 318
Sun safety, 310–329
   AHS environment and, 11–12
   in summer camps, 346
   sun-safety program implementation,
      320–325
      schoolwide initiatives, 320–321
      sun-safety behaviors for students,
         321–322, 322f
      teaching tools, 323–325
   ultraviolet (UV) radiation, 312–320
      benefits of exposure to, 314–315
      defined, 312
      factors affecting exposure to, 312–313
      risks of exposure to, 315–318
      sunscreens and, 318–320
      UVA, UVB, and UVC bands of, 312
      UV index, 313–314, 314t, 321
Sun Safety Alliance, 325
Sun Safety for Kids website, 325
Sunscreen, 236, 318–320, 321
SunWise Meteorologist Tool Kit, 314
SunWise program, 12, 323–325, 324f, 346
SunWise School Program Guide, 323
SunWise website, 313
Supervision
   of playground activity, 223–225
   recommendations for, 63
Support, base of, 71
Surgeon General, 254
Suspension, in-school, 150
Swaying, 263
Sweating capacity in children, 45
Synchronized metronome tapping
   (SMT), 190
Synonyms, integrated instruction in,
   197–198

T
Tag games, 277–278
Talking, walking and, 345
Tasks, 113, 114
Teacher-directed conflict resolution,
   153–154
Teachers
   characteristics of children and, 35t–37t
   involvement in AHS environment, 13
   modeling physical activity by, 13, 26
Teacher-student relationship, courtesy
   and politeness in, 129
Teams, formation of, 176
Technique, 50
Television, daily average viewing, 5
Temporary Assistance to Needy Families
   program, 338
Tests, 100
Threats/threatening, 129, 146–147, 152
   challenge vs., 256
Three Rivers Study, 6
Throwing, 68, 69, 72, 74–77
   catching and, 77
   concepts of motion and direction,
      73–74
   follow-through, 72
   modifying for children with special
      needs, 178
   overhand, 75–77
   points to stress about, 76
   stages of, 75f–76
   teaching tips, 76–77
   underhand, 75
Time of day, UV radiation and, 312, 322
Time management, 92
Time-out, 148–149
Titanium dioxide, 320
Title IX of Education Amendments of
   1972, 111
Toe-to-toe technique, 135
Tolerance, 23, 32, 173–174
Torque, 72
Tortoise and Hare (running exercise), 270
Tossing, 75. *See also* Throwing
Touching of student, 147
Track and field lessons, 194
Trainability, 252–253
Train tag, 277–278
Transportation
   for after-school programs, 336–337
   evolution of, 206
   for extracurricular activities, 12–13
Traumatic brain injury, 165
Travel concepts, 206

Treadmill (exercise), 271f
Treadmills, 275
Treasure hunt, 238
Trekking (walking) poles, 235
Triceps push up, 268
Trunk development challenges, 263
Trunk-twisting exercises, 272f
21st Century Community Learning
    Centers (21st CCLC), 338
Twisting, 263
Type 1 diabetes, 316
Type 2 diabetes, 233

U

Ultraviolet (UV) radiation, 312–320
    benefits of exposure to, 314–315
    defined, 312
    factors affecting exposure to, 312–313
    risks of exposure to, 315–318
    sunscreens and, 318–320
    UV index, 313–314, 314t, 321
    UVA, UVB, and UVC bands of, 312
Underhand throw, 75
Understanding
    checking for, 99–100
    in communication, 114–117
United States Department of Agriculture
    (USDA), 288, 290, 296
Upright rhythmic movements, 275
Urban setting, 206
U.S. Census Bureau, 336
U.S. Department of Education, 303
U.S. Department of Health and Human
    Services, 345
U.S. Office of Technology Assessment, 62

U.S. Surgeon General, 334–335
UV radiation. *See* Ultraviolet (UV)
    radiation

V

Value content of feedback, 105f
Verbal cues for acceptable behavior, 141
Verbs, teaching, 197
Video game(s), 190
Vigorous physical activities, 212, 213–214
Violence, 152. *See also* Conflict resolution
Vision loss, UV radiation and, 315
Visual aids, 98
Vitamin D, 315, 316, 320

W

Walk to school programs, 239
Walking, 233–239
    benefits of, 233
    calories burned during, 234t
    implementing school walking
        program, 236
    recommendations for, 235–236
    programs, 7
    to school, 345–346
    shoes, 236
    suggested activities, 237–239
    weight management and, 233–235
Walking golf (activity), 238
Walking and talking, 345
Walking trail, 222
Walking (trekking) poles, 235
Warm-up, aerobic, 258
Warnings, 151
Water, drinking, 236

Weather
    intense activity and, 47t
    UV radiation and, 313
Weight
    gender differences in, 36–37
    strength and, 41
Weight management
    aerobic activities and, 250
    age-appropriate, 298
    walking and, 233–235
Weight status and percentiles for
    children, 300t
Wellness policy plan, 7–8
Wellpoint, 303
"When before what" technique, 134
"Whistle Mixer" technique, 136
Whistle signals, 294
White blood cells, UV radiation and, 318
Whole method of practice, 67–68
WIC Reauthorization Act (2004), 7–8
Williams, Natalie (Special Olympics
    athlete), 180
Windmill, 272
Words, action-oriented, 97–98
Workload
    measuring in time, 273
    self-directed, 256

Y

Yin Yin Nwe (UNICEF), 180
YMCA, 14
You statements, 126–127

Z

Zero reject, concept of, 164

Photo Credits

p. 9: James A. Sugar/Corbis/Bettmann   p. 11: Mary Kate Danny/Getty Images, Inc.—Stone Allstock   p. 18: Bob Daemmrich/The Image Works   p. 33: Bob Daemmrich/The Image Works   p. 45: Ron Chapple/Getty Images, Inc.—Taxi   p. 50: Dennis MacDonald/PhotoEdit Inc.   p. 286: Adams Picture Library/t/a apl/Alamy   p. 288: Vince Streano/Corbis   p. 290: Bob Daemmrich/The Image Works   p. 315: Biophoto Associates/Photo Researchers   p. 318: Dr. P. Marazzi/Photo Researchers   p. 319 (top): National Eye Institute   p. 319 (bottom): National Eye Institute   p. 334: Creatas Images/Jupiter Images   p. 335: Mel Yates/Getty Images, Inc.   p. 336: Ariel Skelley/Corbis   p. 339: Bob Daemmrich/The Image Works   p. 341: Digital Vision/Getty Images, Inc.   p. 344 (top): Jaume Gual/AGE Fotostock   p. 344: (bottom): Vanessa Davies/Dorling Kindersley